Praise for *Is It You, Me,*

"Most books on marriage offer insights and help to common marital problems such as the traditional conflicts around sex, money, children, time, and in-laws. They offer credible solutions such as conflict management, improved communication, and problem solving skills.

"This book is different. For some couples these problems are exacerbated by the often unnoticed presence of a particular neural wiring in the brain, called Attention-Deficit/Hyperactivity Disorder, that makes traditional solutions ineffective. This book describes ADHD in detail and with empathy and helps couples with this added challenge find hope and solutions.

"I recommend it highly to all couples whose troubles seem incomprehensible, and for all couples therapists it should be required reading to help them distinguish between ordinary conflict and the roller coaster effect of this syndrome."

—**Harville Hendrix, Ph.D., author of** *Getting the Love You Want:*
    A Guide for Couples **and codeveloper of Imago Relationship Therapy**

"In this lucid, provocative, and authoritative book, Gina Pera lets the reader know, at a visceral level, what it's like to be the partner of an adult with ADHD. Alternately humorous and deadly serious, the book is deeply empathic with the experience of such partners.

"Along the way, Pera provides important information about ADHD's causes and treatments and provides empowerment to those who have for too long been blamed for the relationship issues engendered by ADHD. By showing the reality of ADHD in relation to those who must live with its consequences every day, she provides a message of real hope."

—**Stephen Hinshaw, Ph.D., ADHD research scientist, Professor**
    and Chair, Department of Psychology, University of California,
    Berkeley, and author of *The Mark of Shame: Stigma of Mental*
    Illness and an Agenda for Change

"Insightful, helpful, witty, and very practical. This book can change your life."

—**Daniel G. Amen, M.D., author of** *Healing ADD* **and** *Change Your*
    Brain, Change Your Life

"Wow! What a roller coaster ride. *Is It You, Me, or Adult A.D.D.?* contains information that is just not available anywhere else. This book is sure to become the authoritative guide for couples dealing with ADHD and the baggage that accompanies it. Packed with information, but not over-whelming, it is a unique and valuable resource."

—Patricia O. Quinn, M.D., Cofounder and Director, The National Center for Girls and Women with ADHD, and co-author of *Gender Issues and ADHD: Research, Diagnosis, and Treatment*

"Gina Pera has written a stunning book that should be a 'must-read' for all couples where one or both partners have Attention-Deficit/Hyperactivity Disorder. Combining her own experiences, a thoughtful synthesis of the clinical and research literature, and a creative study of her own design, she has grasped the complex ways in which ADHD affects relationships and has translated her comprehensive expertise into a highly readable and extraor-dinarily helpful guide.

"Her prose is extremely effective, at times funny and at other times poignant, and her ability to capture the subtle dynamics of partnerships affected by ADHD is nothing short of extraordinary.

"What is particularly stunning about her achievement is the way Ms. Pera has captured the intricacy of ADHD, including its far-reaching effects on executive function and emotional regulation. Equally impressive is her talent for framing the issues in comprehensible language, with answers to frequently asked questions, quotes from partners with and without ADHD, and snippets of dialogues that are completely genuine. Best of all, this book offers hope and guidance to the millions of adults whose lives have been challenged by ADHD, by providing clear and useful ideas and a richly elaborated framework for addressing the myriad stresses that ADHD imposes upon intimacy and friendship.

"Kudos and thanks to Ms. Pera! I will make this book required read-ing for all my patients. It is nothing short of a *tour de force*!"

—Anthony L. Rostain, M.D., M.A., Medical Director, University of Pennsylvania Adult ADHD Treatment and Research Program; Professor of Psychiatry and Pediatrics, University of Pennsylvania School of Medicine

"My first response to the publication of Gina's book was 'At last! Something for the significant other!' You hate to use the cliche 'long overdue' but as a physician who treats dozens of patients with ADD and ADHD, there's just been nothing available until now. *Is it You, Me, or Adult A.D.D.?* lives up to all expectations, and I can safely predict it will become as much an industry standard as *Driven to Distraction.* As a father of a son with ADD and husband to a wife with ADD, I can professionally and personally attest to the value of Gina's important new book."

—**David Edelberg, M.D. Medical Director, WholeHealth Chicago, and author of *The Triple Whammy Cure: The Breakthrough Women's Health Program***

"While there is increasing awareness of how common and difficult ADHD can be, there are no resources available to help explain the nature of ADHD to those who live closest to it in adulthood: the spouse. Gina Pera has combined a real feel for the disorder with sound reporting skills and the spice of those who tell the story best: the couples themselves. This is a book based on science, but it captures the art of helping couples cope with and move beyond the challenges that ADHD creates."

—**Margaret D. Weiss, M.D., Ph.D., Director of Research, Division of Child Psychiatry, University of British Columbia and Head, Provincial ADHD Program, British Columbia, Canada**

"Even today, people often surprisingly ask, 'Do you believe in Adult ADHD?' Confirmatory brain neuroscience answers this speculation about Adult ADHD: It's a real problem with real and painful challenges, not a belief system. And nowhere is Adult ADHD more evident and more fully identifiable than in our most important, valued relationships. In any long-term relationship, with increasing exposure over time, ADHD patterns endure unabated. They grind partners into a thin paste.

"The reason it took so long to recognize Adult ADHD is simple: Its expression is cunning and well rationalized. With Gina Pera's help, the subtlety of recognizing and the complexity of intervening in these puzzling ADHD predicaments are refreshingly simplified. Gina translates big questions into useful, practical, and understandable answers. She provides not only a good starting place for the ADHD discussion but also a detailed follow-through for the real recovery process."

—**Charles Parker, D.O., Medical Director, CorePsych, and author of *Deep Recovery***

"For many people, having a spouse or partner with Attention Deficit Disorder and its attendant conditions means dealing with painful, disastrous, and heartbreaking issues—financial catastrophes, verbal and even physical abuse, substance addiction, and others. The spouse often feels overwhelmed, isolated, and desperate while struggling in a swirl of chaos. Most books completely ignore the more serious issues that this condition, when left untreated, can create for couples and families. Even health care providers sometimes have no understanding of it.

"Many people have been in relationships for 20 or 30 years, never knowing why their lives are so different from other couples', loving their partners but living lives of chronic frustration and emotional abandonment.

"As co-moderators for almost 10 years of an online support group, we've seen our members grapple with these painful issues, with nowhere to turn for advice, help, and hope except to each other. We've seen this book emerge from the group's plea for a resource that addresses their needs.

"Gina Pera has completed a monumental undertaking in blending our stories with the latest medical advisories on treating ADHD and its co-existing conditions. Real answers on the painful realities. We expect this book will be the bible for all of us dealing with adult ADHD."

—Elizabeth Weathers and Diane Hartson, Co-moderators, ADD Spouse support group

"As any partner of an adult with ADHD can attest, research clearly shows ADHD's pervasive effects on a person's ability to manage life's many demands. This often leaves the partner to pick up the pieces, despite the ADHD person's seemingly good intentions.

"When an adult has ADHD, his or her romantic partner 'has' it, too. Alternately confused, optimistic, and resentful, the partner rides a roller coaster as he or she tries to understand why the relationship seems so unbalanced. Gina Pera has been there and has authored a guide that offers understanding for the confused, practical strategies for the frustrated, and hope for the despondent.

"This book will be a lifesaver for both partners as they strive to create a more satisfying relationship and a happier, more productive life together."

—Ari Tuckman, Psy.D., M.B.A., author of *Integrative Treatment for Adult ADHD: A Practical, Easy-to-Use Guide for Clinicians*

"For all the couples who are struggling with AD/HD in their relationship, Gina Pera has written a wonderful guide to help you navigate these treacherous marital waters. *Is it You, Me, or Adult A.D.D.?* has the unique distinction of including the perspective of the partner without AD/HD, which has been neglected for far too many years. The book is well researched, reader friendly, and includes insights and perspectives from a Who's Who of professionals in the field. For couples struggling with AD/HD, it's the season's new must-have book and bound to become a classic."

—**Michele Novotni, Ph.D., psychologist, coach, and author of**
   What Does Everyone Else Know that I Don't? **and** *Social Success*

Is It You, Me,
or
Adult A.D.D.?

Stopping the Roller Coaster
When Someone You Love Has
Attention Deficit Disorder

Foreword by
Russell Barkley, Ph.D.

Gina Pera

1201 Alarm Press • San Francisco, California

Is It You, Me, or Adult A.D.D.?
Stopping the Roller Coaster When Someone You Love Has Attention Deficit Disorder

© 2008 Gina Pera

First Edition, Sixth Printing

ISBN: 978-0-9815487-0-8 (paperback ed.)
ISBN: 978-0-9815487-6-0 (PDF ed.)

Published by:

1201
Alarm
Press

2261 Market St., Suite 230
San Francisco, CA 94114-1600
1-888-891-6668

Cover and interior design © TLC Graphics, *www.TLCGraphics.com*
Cover illustration by Susan Tolonen, *www.susantolonen.com*

Publisher's Cataloging-in-Publication

Pera, Gina.
    Is it you, me, or adult A.D.D.? : stopping the roller
coaster when someone you love has attention deficit
disorder / Gina Pera. — 1st ed.
    p. cm.
    Includes bibliographical references and index.
    LCCN 2008903632
    ISBN-13: 978-0-9815487-0-8
    ISBN-10: 0-9815487-0-9
    ISBN-13: 978-0-9815487-6-0
    ISBN-10: 0-9815487-6-8

    1. Attention-deficit disorder in adults—Popular
works. 2. Attention-deficit disorder in adults—
Treatment. 3. Attention-deficit-disordered adults—
Family relationships. 4. Interpersonal relations.
 I. Title.

    RC394.A85P47 2008   616.85'89
                    QBI08-600161

For my parents, Elva Radini Motroni Pera and John Vincent Pera, Jr.

*For all the researchers and clinicians who
shine a light to guide us out of the fog*

Table of Contents

PART ONE

From the Tunnel of Love to the Roller Coaster:
Could *Your* Partner Have ADHD?

PART TWO

Roller Coaster Whiplash and G-Force Confusion:
How Many Plunges Before You Say, "Whoa!"

PART THREE

Your Relationship and the Art of Roller Coaster Maintenance:
Four Success Strategies

Acknowledgments

M y deepest gratitude goes to the multitudes of people who supported this effort to help the public better understand adult ADHD, especially as it affects relationships and families.

I especially appreciate all members past and present of the online groups *ADD Spouse* and *ADHD Partner* for sharing their stories and support with compassion, candor, and comic flair. In particular, the moderators of *ADD Spouse* (Elizabeth Weathers and Diane Hartson) and *ADHD Partner* (Carl, Sharon, Martha, Leslie, Judith, Jane, John, Robin, Emily, Susan, and Ruth) have devoted years of informed, impassioned volunteer service to complete strangers, and the world is more enlightened and joyful for it. To the 162 ADHD Partner Survey respondents, please know that your patient slog through endless questions provided a wealth of knowledge and insights. To you and the 160-plus support-group members who entrusted me with your stories, thank you for adding real life to dry data.

This often-lonely endeavor might have derailed without steady support from the "veterans" (Andrea, Beth, Blinky, Carl, Christopher, Joanna, Leslie, Lisa, Marsha, Martha, Mary, Maurice, Melissa, Sharon, Sky, and Suzanne), my friendly morning coffee-klatch, focus group, editorial staff, and on-call lifeline. To all the draft reviewers (Andrea, Angela, Ava, Beth, Blinky, Brian, Carl, Cheri, Chris A., Christopher, Diane, Elva, Eva, Jane, Jennie, Joanna, John, Judith, Julie, Kathryn, Larry, Leslie, Lisa, Marie, Martha, Mary, Robin, Sarah, Sharon, Sky, Susan, and Terri), your time and insights are valued. Marie and Graceann, thanks especially for your long-time support. Greg H., your lavish software donation gave me a boost at just the right time. Mart, your hand-knit "software" provided comfort both physical and spiritual; your Shawl Ministry does wonderful work. And Carl, your technological mastery rescued my last neuron from self-implosion.

Dozens of roses (and chocolates) are tossed to the Tuesday-night and Wednesday-night meeting regulars. Your courage, insights, perseverance, and humor have touched me deeply, fueled my strength in facing the ADHD naysayers, and lured so many tentative newcomers out of isolation and shame into the light of possibility and ease.

I cannot imagine a more accomplished and compassionate group of professionals generously carving out time to be interviewed and/or review content for this book (credit is theirs, but errors are mine alone). I extend my deep appreciation to Xavier Amador, PhD; Daniel Amen, MD; Linda Anderson, MA; Don Baker, MA; Russell Barkley, PhD; Samuel Barondes, MD; Robert Brooks, PhD; Thomas E. Brown, PhD; Stephen Copps, MD; Daniel J. Cox, PhD; Martha Denckla, MD; William Eddy, LCSW, JD; David Edelberg, MD; Herbert Gravitz, PhD; Thomas Gualtieri, MD; Jonathan Halverstadt, MS; Stephen Hinshaw, PhD; Ronald C. Kessler, PhD; Martin Kutscher, MD; Susan Lasky, MA; Kate Lewis, MSN; Harold Meyer, MS; Lewis Mills, PhD; Kathleen Nadeau, PhD; John Norcross, PhD; Michele Novotni, PhD; Charles Parker, DO; Eleanor Payson, MSW; James Pennebaker, PhD; Anthony Pietropinto, MD; Patricia Quinn, MD; J. Russell Ramsay, PhD; Arthur Robin, PhD; Anthony Rostain, MD, MA; Marc Schwartz, MD; Susan Smalley, PhD; Marlene Snyder, PhD; James Swanson, PhD; Margaret Weiss, MD, PhD; Paul Wender, MD; David B. Wexler, PhD; and Annick Vincent, MD. Thanks to Terry Matlen, MSW, for being a helpful resource to the ADHD community.

On behalf of the millions of people you've helped to step off the roller coaster and onto solid ground, kudos to the far-flung volunteers of CHADD (Children and Adults with Attention-Deficit/Hyperactivity Disorder) as well as its staff, board members, conference presenters, members, and especially the awe-inspiring crew of Northern California CHADD. (For your valued personal support to me, thanks Lew, Judy, Donna, Beverlee, Peggy, Bonnie, and Linda.) You are all on the vanguard, doing critical work to counter harmful misperceptions and to provide facts and hope.

Thanks to this book's publisher, 1201 Alarm Press, for appreciating that the adult ADHD community is vastly underserved; its design firm, TLC Graphics, and especially to Tamara Dever, Monica Thomas, and Erin Stark, for presenting this material so beautifully and being an absolute dream to work with; illustrator Susan Tolonen, for patiently collaborating in creating stunning cover artwork; and publisher's counsel Brad Bunnin, for compassionately recognizing this project's importance.

A book could not wish for more perceptive editors. My deep appreciation goes to Garry Cooper, LCSW, whose creativity and clear thinking helped me to tame the intertwining tentacles of information and whose humor kept my spirits afloat and my fascinating tangents to a minimum (only *after* asking for his help did I learn that Garry, a therapist and columnist whose work I've long admired, is also a writing coach); Janis Dworkis, a reader's best friend, who asked all the right questions and questioned all the assumptions; copy editor Robert Johnson, ELS, a most congenial, patient, and thorough word hawk; Dick Christianson, who provided eagle-eyed polish at the proofing stage; and Carolyn Acheson, for a thorough index. (Any gaffes in this book are no doubt the author's, added in final revisions.) The talented Atlas Cafe writers, Jak, Lyndsey, and Alia, inspired me with their own work and offered astute suggestions for improving mine.

For keeping spirit and body together and relatively on track, I'm eternally grateful to osteopathic physician Melvin Friedman and gatekeeper Amy, rub-goddess Karen Cougar, Master Sung Ho Cha of the San Mateo JungShim Ki Center, and my wise and gifted advisers Patricia Meyer and Frank Don.

I am indebted to my big sisters, Elva Louise, Ann Marie, and Sandra, who have supported and encouraged me for more than 50 years; the rest of my family and friends, for tolerating my long absences punctuated only by obnoxious yammering about a condition most people view skeptically; and especially my friend Eric Poulsen, for 20 years of unerringly on-point creative assessments, resourcefulness, humor, and compassion. Finally, I am grateful to my loving and brilliant husband—my favorite hiking partner and resident visionary—for his unflagging support and for hearing the letters A, D, H, and D more than the Geneva Convention surely allows.

Foreword

Only within the last 15 years has adult Attention-Deficit/Hyperactivity Disorder (ADHD) been recognized as a valid clinical disorder. Yet at least 40 years ago—and possibly a century—the scientific and clinical literature acknowledged its existence. Today, we know ADHD to be more impairing than most other conditions seen in outpatient psychiatric and psychological clinics, including anxiety disorders, dysthymia, and major depression. In short, the scientific evidence is overwhelming for this adult version of a disorder long associated with childhood.

In particular, current research details how ADHD can adversely affect all major life activities, including marriage or cohabiting relationships and the skills intimately involved in maintaining a household and raising a family—including driving an automobile, working a job, managing money, taking care of one's health, and parenting.

Until now, however, no books existed that combined both a scientific understanding of adult ADHD with pragmatic recommendations to guide these adults and their partners in coping, problem-solving, and otherwise addressing the difficulties they face in sharing a life and a home. Gina Pera's book does so with an admirable balance of current scientific information mixed with sage advice and wise, practical strategies based on the current science. There is no better book now that addresses such relationship difficulties and with such sensitivity to the complex issues inherent in them.

Thank you, Gina, for writing such a useful book.

—Russell A. Barkley, Ph.D., Research Professor, Department
   of Psychiatry at SUNY Upstate Medical University, Syracuse,
   New York, and co-author of *ADHD in Adults: What the Science Says*

Introduction

I wish I'd had this book 10 years ago, when the world was metaphorically knocking me upside the head, teaching me to pay attention to that human organ called the brain. Teaching me to view the brain, in fact, as an organ, vital to our every physical and emotional function yet oh so vulnerable.

At the time, my 84-year-old mother was slipping tragically into an Alzheimer's-like stroke dementia—recognizing me as her "great friend" but not her seventh and youngest child. It broke my heart. But if her memory had remained intact, it would have broken *her* heart to see her oldest child and my brother, then age 60, succumbing to brain cancer.

Amidst these family dramas, I met my future husband. Over dinner one evening, this newly minted scientist, fresh from completing his doctoral degree at a neurological institute, sprang this unsettling idea on me: *Everything we think, do, or feel happens due to chemical reactions in the brain.* I shuddered, alarmed at the thought of reducing the seat of the self, the seat of the *soul*, to a chemistry-lab experiment. And he didn't stop there: Given all the vulnerabilities of the brain from conception until death— from genetics, viruses, toxins, and even seemingly minor bumps to the head—it's a wonder that any of us have a working brain, he said.

I surely didn't like the sound of it, but there was no arguing with the evidence: Their brain diseases meant that my own mother's and brother's force-of-nature personalities would peek out only for brief glimpses in the slow march toward their physical death.

My then-boyfriend's birthday gift to me that first year together was *Molecules of Emotion*, written by pharmacologist Candace Pert. She is the scientist whose team discovered endorphins—brain molecules that affect how pain and pleasure are experienced. That book set me on a remarkable path of discovery. Little did I know, though, how much more personal this path would become. For this brilliant, handsome, and sometimes even sweet man, the one with whom I could laugh and talk for hours on such a broad range of interesting subjects, would slowly start driving me to distraction. Literally. Perilously.

How could someone educated and smart enough to decode the human genome habitually miss the freeway exit and tailgate at top speed? Less physically endangering (but still unnerving), how could he "mis-hear" and "mis-remember" so often and so significantly? You'll just have to trust me that our miscommunications lay far beyond any Venus-Mars or human-scientist thing. It was more like Earth-Spacetime Continuum.

Lacking information—namely, that he might have adult Attention-Deficit/Hyperactivity Disorder, or ADHD—my resourceful mind spun plausible theories. Maybe my Southern accent proved sometimes indecipherable to his Yankee ears. Maybe his recent-transplant status in Southern California left him freeway-challenged. Or maybe he was simply a *scientist*, distracted by loftier thoughts as he sped past the exit, forgot an important commitment, or missed a critical cue to show that he cared about me.

Make no mistake: His brain worked brilliantly much of the time. But when it didn't, when some inexplicable glitch snagged the system, the glaring disparity defied credulity. The fact that he typically failed even to perceive any such glitch, confidently insisting that *I* had misspoken or forgotten, gave me even more reason to doubt my perceptions.

I had an inkling about why my mother's strokes and my brother's brain cancer tumor had affected their behavior the way they did. But what could account for the funny feeling that my physically healthy boyfriend's puzzling actions weren't "right" either—not his personality, not his intentionality, but something else entirely. The question nagged at me.

Could his stressful workload be a partial explanation? Possibly. Then, too, it was the dot-com era. Everyone in California was revved up and overcaffeinated, plugging in and tuning out, getting ever more disconnected in their fevered scramble for "connectivity."

After a few years of futile searches through couples therapy and holistic health routes—dietary changes, exercise, meditation classes, yoga, and caffeine-cessation crusades, all of which helped but not nearly enough!— I chanced upon an eye-catching new title at the public library, neuropsychiatrist Daniel Amen's *Change Your Brain, Change Your Life*.

Amen's vivid descriptions of adult ADHD stunned me. When my husband read it, he agreed that ADHD explained a lot about his life. But how could we, a molecular biologist with a sophisticated knowledge of neurochemistry and a well-read journalist who knew a *little* bit about everything, not have already known about adult ADHD? Especially that many adults have the "stealth" version (meaning no physical hyperactivity).

Easy. Because Adult ADHD came on the official radar screen only in the mid-1990s, and not one of the physicians or therapists from whom we'd sought help had read the memo by the time I found Amen's book in 2000.

Newly armed with ADHD awareness, I carefully scrutinized my towering stack of relationship self-help books. So many authors (including psychologists) describe in lurid detail the damaging effect that certain behaviors have on a relationship. Yet, they never introduce the strong possibility that these might be highly treatable ADHD-related traits! Worse, most of these books offer scant advice other than coping, detaching, or leaving. Some books even blame readers' dysfunction for making such bad choices in a mate, and others insist that these troubling mates act willfully and are consciously abusive.

Continuing to read voraciously on the subject, I stumbled upon a new online support group for the partners of adults with ADHD. Assiduously comparing notes, we members learned that we weren't alone, that others' experiences closely mirrored our own in ways never covered in the ADHD books. One thing we learned: If we passively left the solutions to the physicians and therapists who failed to acknowledge or understand ADHD or to our "in denial" ADHD partners, we'd keep looping around the roller coaster until we dropped from nervous exhaustion.

Shortly after assuming leadership of a different online support group, I also began organizing local lectures and support groups for partners, adults, and parents of children with ADHD. To me, the news about adult ADHD was that inspiring, that *revolutionary*. What a rare privilege to see lives expand and long-dormant possibilities unfold before me: All that these people had needed were solid facts, validation, and support.

How appalling then to hear so many horror stories about how our mental health system had failed them, some for decades. It was almost as bad as the barrage of bizarre propaganda attacking ADHD medications and even the diagnosis itself. Neuroscience has bestowed upon us new knowledge to elevate our lives. To my mind, we cannot afford to stay in an 18th-century mindset, promulgated by a blasé healthcare system or anti-psychiatry conspiracy-theorists' twaddle worming its way through the Internet like a virus.

After eight years spent researching, observing, writing, lecturing, and volunteering in this field, I have heard from more than 1,000 partners of adults with ADHD. Hundreds have maintained long-term contact with me, offering in intimate detail their life trajectories—after their ADHD partner developed awareness and new strategies, after the surprise pregnancy, after retirement or a cross-country move, after the roller coaster settled into an enjoyable ride, and sometimes after the divorce.

Common themes cropped up, including this one: When couples learn about ADHD and work together to address problematic symptoms, life can improve dramatically. Even when relationships do not continue, healing takes place and lessons are learned about digging deep into the human capacity for strength, love, compassion, and stretching the mind around new ideas.

As powerful as the support-groups are, we still needed a comprehensive guide that could help new members get up to speed quickly. That's because once they finally hit upon the possible explanation of ADHD, they are often clinging to the end of frayed ropes. And it's tough to piece together a clear path from e-mail posts and several books about ADHD, none of which address the partners' particular concerns or offer step-by-step strategies. With my print journalism background, I seemed the likeliest candidate to gather and synthesize the group's collective wisdom and the best advice from the field's top research and clinical experts.

The way I see it, ADHD awareness is a social justice issue, a question of each person deserving accurate knowledge and access to care that affords us full access to our talents and abilities, much like the revolutionary concept of eyeglasses did in centuries past. The people I've met while volunteering have been generally wealthy enough to afford a computer and educated enough to find a group, and still they suffered and struggled. What about those with fewer resources? Through this book, I hope to reach many more thousands, not with more stigma, misjudgments, or criticism but with compassion, answers, and hope.

I sincerely wish that you find this guide helpful, even life-changing, and that it might inspire you to share your knowledge with others.

Now, to get started, I believe the book will be most helpful if you keep the following points in mind:

Reading roadmap
The book is divided into three sections. *Part One* explains ADHD and the various ways it can manifest, particularly when the diagnosis comes later in life. *Part Two* examines the side effects of living with a partner's unrecognized ADHD, particularly when symptoms are moderate to severe. *Part*

Three focuses on the strategies recommended by leading experts to help you both take charge of ADHD and your life as a couple.

Endnotes are included not because of any academic pretensions on my part but instead to point to the extensive body of published ADHD-related research.

Terminology used in this book

ADHD: The official term is Attention-Deficit/Hyperactivity Disorder (AD/HD). In most cases, for readability, this text omits the slash. The book title also eliminates the *H* because many people mistakenly think that *ADHD* refers only to the subtype that includes hyperactivity. In fact, that's the *least common* subtype in adults.

ADHD partner: The person in the couple who has ADHD. It's best to avoid defining a person by a diagnosis, but this can make text unwieldy, so please accept here the compromise of *ADHD partner*.

Support-group member: The partner of an adult with ADHD who has joined a discussion group to give and receive support and information. Some support-group members have ADHD, along with their partners, and that is why the term *non-ADHD partner* does not fit. (Please note: When you come across a quote from a man referring to his boyfriend or a woman to her girlfriend, it's not a typo. Some support-group members are in same-sex relationships.)

Expect to find many voices in this "support group in a book"

You'll find many quotes, introduced by first name only, within the text, introducing the chapters, and in stand-alone text boxes. These come courtesy of 160-plus support-group members who kindly provided permission to share with you their e-mail posts to the group (with names and identifying details changed). We all hope that this multitude of voices—typically without preamble or in-depth background—simulates the healing power of actual group exchanges for those with no access to such a group.

Consider this a resource foundation, not a quick read

This guide is designed to help you and your ADHD partner at every point along the journey. Take it at your own pace, skip around, and keep it handy for future reference. Please don't think you have to follow all the strategies at once. And if you're feeling particularly stressed and isolated, consider starting with Part Two before trying to understand more about ADHD.

A word about "tips": You'll find plenty in Part Three as well as at this book's companion Web site (ADHDRollerCoaster.com). But until you gain a strong foundation of ADHD awareness, the support-group consensus is, "Don't waste your time and energy with tips."

This is not a global portrait of ADHD

ADHD is a syndrome, meaning that its symptoms are highly variable and range from mild to severe. Consequently, it is inappropriate to make blanket statements—positive, negative, or otherwise—about the estimated 10 to 30 million adults who have ADHD in the United States alone.

At the same time, this book presumes that you came here to cut through the briar patch that is enveloping the good things in your relationship so that you can make it better—and not simply to read other people's praise for their wonderful partners who happen to have ADHD. In part, finding clarity hinges on naming and recognizing the "invisible enemy" that is causing problems for you both. That's why this book details common challenges that ADHD creates and then explains how to start resolving them.

If these pages don't seem to gush with words of love, try reading between the lines. You'll see that many ADHD partners have inspired great loyalty and affection, which strongly manifests in support-group members' perseverance in learning about this condition and encouraging their ADHD partners to learn, too.

The reality is that many adults with ADHD are simply not connecting the dots in their lives. And it requires deep love to coax effective treatment from our mental healthcare system for a partner who is convinced that nothing can improve or, worse, that nothing is wrong, when it obviously is.

Please keep an open mind about medications for ADHD

Full disclosure: I have practiced Yoga for 25 years, know the farmers who grow the organic food consumed at my house, was raised by a mother with Old World wisdom in self-care, and avoid medication until *all* alternatives have been exhausted. I have also read scores of books and scientific papers about ADHD and attended five international conferences to learn from this field's leading authorities. Most important, I have listened with empathy but also critical thought to hundreds of adults with ADHD, their partners, and parents of children with ADHD when they have shared their dramatic before-and-after medication scenarios.

The net result? This book is "pro-medication" and makes no apologies for it. If the message seems stronger than necessary, consider it a clear, unequivocal statement to counter dangerously pervasive myth. Gingerly, and with some justified trepidation, our society is discussing this topic less emotionally and more factually. More physicians are learning to properly treat ADHD, meaning that more people gain benefits without experiencing unnecessary side effects. Soon, I hope, people with ADHD who choose to take medication will feel as little embarrassment about it as most people feel about wearing eyeglasses (itself an historical source of stigma).

Maybe you and your own ADHD partner will get along just fine with ADHD education and awareness and without medication. That's a common story, too. But please consider that, if this skeptic can be convinced that ADHD medications might actually be life-enhancing and *health-promoting*, maybe it's worth keeping an open mind—especially for others who might be grappling with more severe symptoms and would appreciate your acceptance and compassion.

Welcome to readers who have ADHD

When ADHD goes unrecognized for years, it takes a toll on everyone. Many good books more fully examine the emotional issues particular to late-to-diagnosis adults, but only this book (particularly Part II) addresses the impact of untreated ADHD on loved ones.

Still, my efforts to outline effective adult ADHD diagnosis and treatment, which I've found in no other single source, are as much for you as for your partners, parents, siblings, and other loved ones. I hope you find it helpful.

For more information

You'll find more stories, tips, resources, and links at this book's companion Web site: ADHDRollerCoaster.com. I welcome your thoughts and reactions via e-mail (*Gina@ADHDRollerCoaster.com*) or letter sent care of the publisher (1201 Alarm Press, 2261 Market Street, Suite 230, San Francisco, CA 94114).

About the ADHD Partner Survey

After several years as a member and then a moderator of support groups for the partners of adults with ADHD, I'd heard plenty about the "hot spots"—issues with money, household chores, clutter, sex, co-parenting, and video-game addictions. Perhaps, though, the more vocal group members weren't truly representative of the majority in certain problematic areas. Might there even be topics that few knew to connect with ADHD—perhaps a mate's restless-leg syndrome or reckless driving habits? What about subjects that members might be too timid to broach, including verbal or physical abuse? And for those whose partners had tried medication for ADHD, what factors seemed to contribute to its success or failure?

Because the *partner* of an adult with ADHD is often the more reliable historian of the relationship (and often of the ADHD partner's familial, educational, and vocational background), creating a survey to answer those questions seemed a worthwhile pursuit.

To date, this is the largest, most comprehensive survey on this subject. Although not scientific, its methods were rigorous and its findings mirror those of existing ADHD studies, including those that focus on partnership. Moreover, most scientific studies involve people with ADHD who either are already diagnosed or are pursuing treatment (so-called "clinic-referred" patients). The ADHD Partner Survey covers that population, but it also offers a rarer, more intimate glimpse into lives wherein ADHD has gone unrecognized and untreated for decades and firmly remains that way.

We cannot know for sure that those partners who remain unevaluated actually have ADHD, but the chances seem strong, given the respondents' selections from a list of ADHD diagnostic traits. In fact, of the 118 respondents whose partners had sought an evaluation, 92 percent were indeed diagnosed with ADHD. This indicates that support-group members might be rather astute at linking ADHD symptoms with their partners' behaviors. (Several more might have been diagnosed if the person had not abruptly walked out of the appointment or if the professional had better expertise in evaluating for ADHD.)

The survey data presented in this book is limited to a select group: the 111 respondents whose partners have been officially diagnosed with ADHD. Moreover, these respondents knew their ADHD partners *before* medication treatment (79 percent of the 111) or their ADHD partners have never taken medication (21 percent). Why select this sub-group? Because this book addresses the challenges created by *untreated* ADHD and explains treatment strategies. This group could therefore provide a clearer picture of life before and after treatment. (Unless a survey question specifically asked about the effect of medication on behavior, respondents based their answers on their ADHD partners' behavior *before* medication.)

We do not know how data from support-group members (the majority of survey respondents) compares to a control group—that is, people who are *not* in a support group, *not* having trouble in their relationship, or *not* involved with an adult who has ADHD. That might happen in the future, but it will be tricky to identify couples in troubled relationships that aren't, in fact, affected by ADHD; it is too widely missed and misunderstood, even by nationally recognized relationship experts. For now, the data is simply meant to help readers piece together the puzzle of recognizing how ADHD might be affecting their lives.

Survey method: In October and November of 2004, 148 respondents completed the password-protected, 175-question online survey. Another 14 completed the survey in spring 2005, for a total of 162 respondents. Each had many opportunities to include textual responses that clarified or expanded on their selections. Anonymity was assured.

The sheer number of respondents is remarkable, as is the completion rate: only a handful dropped out, typically because of technical problems with their computers or Internet access. Clearly, these respondents were highly motivated to help educate others.

Participants: Participants were limited to individuals whose stories I had followed long enough in the support group to be confident of their legitimacy. The 111 respondents whose answers are reported in this book show the following demographics:

- 86 percent had male partners and 14 percent had female partners.
- Most reported being in heterosexual relationships, with 6 percent being in same-sex relationships.
- Ages ranged from 22 to 75 (with the majority from 36 to 53).
- Most respondents lived in the United States, but 14 percent resided in the United Kingdom, Canada, Australia, New Zealand, or Israel.
- 50 percent were college graduates and 28 percent held postgraduate degrees. (By contrast, only 26 percent of their ADHD partners were college grads, but 29 percent held postgraduate degrees.)
- Of the 71 percent who disclosed annual household income, 50 percent reported earning $91,000 and above, and 20 percent reported earning $50,000 or below.
For more information: Visit ADHDPartner.org

PART ONE

From the Tunnel of Love to the Roller Coaster: Could *Your* Partner Have ADHD?

The Surprising Signs, Symptoms, and Poor Coping Strategies That Might Be Creating the Dizzying, Exhausting, or Just Really Annoying Ups and Downs in Your Relationship

*I was on the verge of filing for divorce when I read about ADHD.
I was amazed that a medical condition might explain
my husband's video-game fixation, his moods,
his absent-mindedness, and our roller-coaster life!*

—JEANETTE

*We just learned that my husband has ADHD. We dated
long-distance for five years, but only after marriage did this
roller coaster of mood swings and miscommunications begin.
I want to exit this ride, but I'd like my husband
to come with me. Is that even possible?*

—SUSAN

*For years, my husband and I blamed each other for all the
confusion, hurt, and miscommunications. Meanwhile, the emotional
and logistical roller coaster kept us both too dizzy to see
straight. The idea of ADHD is the only thing that's
made sense in our lives for a long, long time.*

—ABBY

*Our relationship has been a roller coaster of good times
and bad for 16 years. We have something special so I lived
with the frustrations, but I'm getting too old for this.
I thought she'd learn to stop doing things so impulsively,
but she never does. I love her, but something must change.*

—CHRISTOPHER

*We can have a great conversation, lay out plans,
and the next day he has forgotten it—or has an entirely different
memory! This mental roller coaster is messing with my mind!*

—MARSHA

Introduction

The View from the ADHD Roller Coaster— Both Sides

Monday, 8 PM

The monthly meeting comes to order in the heart of Silicon Valley, a world center of leading-edge technology. Household names such as Google, Yahoo, Apple, YouTube, Netflix, and Hewlett-Packard dot this short stretch of coastal California between San Francisco and San Jose. In attendance this evening are software developers and computer scientists, some from these very companies.

What's on tonight's agenda? The Next Big Thing in high-tech? Not exactly. Not unless you have adult ADHD (Attention-Deficit/Hyperactivity Disorder). In that case, keeping track of your keys can be a very big thing indeed.

Phillip,* 32, a talented software programmer with a beautiful smile and an engaging personality, begins: "Okay, I've been practicing some of the suggestions we talked about last time for keeping track of my keys, and I can't believe how well they're working." No one snickers. No one rolls their eyes. Most people attending this support group for adults with ADHD chuckle and nod in agreement, relieved to hear someone speak openly about an embarrassing problem that they, too, have, or a problem similar to theirs.

Make no mistake: Silicon Valley might be a worldwide magnet for people with ADHD, what with their stereotypical love of the new and novel. But even here, ADHD is not limited to young men who tinker in high-tech,

---

* Not his real name. Descriptions of activities and individuals throughout this book are drawn from composites created from multiple accounts.

3

and its challenges aren't limited to lost keys. The people gathered tonight—male and female, professionals and blue-collar workers, teens and retirees, long-time locals and new immigrants from many different nations—find themselves dogged by a few or many of these other difficulties:

- Losing track of priorities
- Arriving late to events and missing deadlines
- Having trouble initiating tasks and following through to completion
- Being chronically disorganized
- Managing finances poorly
- Losing their temper easily
- Overspending, smoking, video gaming, and other addictions
- Not being "present" in relationships

As you would expect, behaviors like these seldom won them kudos from bosses, coworkers, family members, or even grade-school teachers. As a result, some people have lost jobs, partnerships, houses, large fortunes, and self-worth. Or, at best, they believe (or have been told often enough) they have fallen far short of their potential. Some have been unsuccessfully treated for anxiety or depression for years without knowing that, in fact, untreated ADHD was making them anxious or depressed.

Many of these late-to-diagnosis adults have long suspected that they were a bit "different." When they finally learn about ADHD, most wish they'd learned sooner. Much sooner. It explains a lot about how their unwitting actions generated unpleasant consequences as well as why, just when they started getting traction in life, they'd often slip on that invisible banana peel.

Meanwhile, tonight, as these adults share their triumphs and difficulties, ones that their families and the public frequently fail to understand or accept, you can almost see the lightbulbs flashing on. Apprehensive newcomers relax their jaws. Arms unfold. Possibilities expand as they realize that they are not alone, that other smart people, accomplished people, well-meaning people ride the same roller coaster.

They begin to realize they're not "lazy, stupid, or crazy," as that breakthrough ADHD book title goes. Most important, they learn that practical solutions exist for helping them optimize their abilities. For many, this is the only gathering where they feel truly understood.

But if you stumble on this group while looking for the Toastmasters meeting down the hall, and if you stay a while to listen and watch, you might wonder why these "normal-looking" adults have never picked up certain "mature adult behaviors," like getting organized or getting to bed at a decent hour. You might ask yourself:

- "Didn't their parents teach them?"
- "Don't they realize why these issues are important?
- "Do they just *not care*?"

The short answer: ADHD challenges have little to do with intelligence, caring, the lessons their parents tried to teach, or what they know to be right or wrong. It has more to do with

- having difficulty focusing one's attention *right now,*
- on the most critical task, speaker, or activity, and
- once focus has been achieved, maintaining it instead of yielding to distraction.

As one prominent ADHD expert, psychologist Russell Barkley, says, "The challenge is not knowing what to do. It's in doing what you know." So, instead of calling it an attention-deficit disorder, we could call it an *intention-inhibition disorder*. That's because it's a condition in which the best intentions go awry.

Same Meeting Room, the Following Tuesday, 8 PM

Be careful talking about good intentions to newcomers at *this* week's gathering! It's the same room but a very different crowd. The people gathered here tonight aren't adults with ADHD; they are their partners. And most have *had it* with good intentions. They are also done with being doormat and "dumpee," warden and watchdog, crisis manager and caretaker, and a parent instead of a partner.

Ironically, the two meetings that take place one week apart—one for adults with ADHD and the other for the partners of adults with ADHD—typically show little overlap. That is, one partner or the other in a couple is either "in denial" about ADHD or feels no need to learn about it. It's too bad, because when couples act as a team in learning about ADHD, they tend to speed through the learning curve—with fewer bumps and bruises, too.

The group assembled tonight *has* come seeking knowledge. They also seek clarity and hope that they can somehow stabilize their lives with partners who seem focused on destabilization. Until recently, most did not know that adult ADHD exists, much less that it can affect their lives so profoundly. Or they've suspected ADHD for a long time, but they just can't get their partners to consider the idea or do anything about it.

When they finally hear other people voicing similar threads of befuddlement, the floodgates open. Let's listen in as the new folks introduce themselves:

- *"Communication problems" plague Donna and her husband.* "When we started dating, we had great conversations. Now I can't speak a word before he changes the subject or zones out. I hate the way this makes me feel, like I'm boring or not worth listening to. When I try breaking off the relationship, though, he becomes attentive again, only to backslide two weeks later. He finally told me last week that he has ADHD, but he insists it is an asset. I've read some Web sites that advise us spouses to be more understanding, but that's not helping."

- *Jose's partner has a spending problem.* "On impulse, she bought 20 expensive handbags on sale months ago, planning to sell them online. She's procrastinated and they sit in the spare bedroom, along with the other 'bargains.' I love her, but we can't afford this. If I complain, though, she says I make her feel bad. She's been treated for depression for years, but a friend recently suggested learning about ADHD."

- *Sheila's husband gets distracted while watching their child.* "He left our squirming baby on the changing table when the doorbell rang— and stayed to chat with the mail carrier! Maybe he has ADHD, as our therapist suggests, but is that an excuse? To top it off, he got angry with *me* when I pointed out the risk! But what do I do when I can't trust my husband with our child?"

- *Surrounded by clutter, Lauren feels she's "catching" ADHD.* "Our home is so crammed with my partner's crafts projects that I can hardly move or think! I've read about the association between ADHD and hoarding, and came to learn more."

- *Brenda's fiancé is the love of her life, but his difficulties at work are driving them apart.* "Paperwork takes him twice as long as it does his coworkers, who seem half as smart as him. He loses track of time, works until midnight, and then forgets to phone me. He was diagnosed with ADHD as a kid but says he outgrew it. I don't think so."

- *Does Dan's new girlfriend find him a boring kisser?* "I like her so much, but she keeps showing up late—or not at all—for dates, and later she's super apologetic. And, while we're enjoying a long kiss, she'll get distracted by the least little thing. One time she blurted, 'Forgot to feed Rex!' That's her dog. She says she was recently diagnosed with ADHD, but maybe she's just using that as an excuse and she's really not interested in me."

- **Doreen's teen son says his Dad has ADHD, too.** "Our son won't accept that he has ADHD, but he's failing in school. He also asks why he should take medication if Dad won't. My husband 'copes' with his own ADHD by drinking beer and riding herd on our son. Their constant fighting is driving me nuts."

- **Eric went from being a "catch" to "dropped" in three months flat.** "My new boyfriend wanted to be with me all the time and was over-the-top thoughtful. But when it stopped suddenly, he implied it was my fault, which made no sense. I'm just trying to understand what happened."

- **Jade discovered her husband's credit-card debt after the honeymoon.** "He owes $30,000! At first he said he'd hoped to pay it before I found out. Totally overoptimistic! Then he blamed me for overreacting. I'm feeling some kind of emotional whiplash, from our honeymoon to this. Our pastor suggested looking into ADHD, but is *lying* a trait? He'd told me he was entering the marriage debt-free. I love him, but I'm not sure I can forgive this betrayal."

- **Liz is tired of other people holding her responsible for her husband's failings.** "He's my sweetheart and now we finally know why he does what he does. I'm not angry with him, but I *am* angry with the people, including his family, who blame me for not making him do things they expect of him. They don't believe in ADHD and think it's the woman's role to be a 24/7 executive secretary for her husband."

- **Frank can't compete with his wife's BlackBerry.** "When she learned she might have ADHD, my wife researched it and hyperfocused on getting better organized. She claims her BlackBerry helps her focus on the job. Great, but where's the focus on me? If I take more than 30 seconds to say something, she eyes her 'CrackBerry' for the latest text message. We both work hard, but she *never* turns it off."

As these introductions continue, comments echo all around the room: "Your partner does that, too?" Some people laugh in amazed relief, but others fight back tears. Sure, they're grateful for the long-overdue validation, but reality can hit hard:

- "You mean our problems aren't all my fault—not me being rigid, anal, controlling, demanding, or 'no fun'?"
- "You mean our problems aren't all my partner's fault—not bad temper, selfishness, or apathy?"

- "You mean the invisible enemy we've been battling not only has a name, it has a *solution*?"

Most group members here tonight still love their partners. That's why they've come to this meeting. (Some, though, are straining to remember why they went on that second date, and a few are asking for referrals to good divorce attorneys.)

The confusion crept up on them stealthily, they explain, and most of their partners' behavior grew sharply more problematic with time and new responsibilities. They tackled each particular set of problems as it turned up, and so the roller coaster ride smoothed out, lulling them into the idea that their lives would stay less chaotic for a while. But then the next dip happened and the next and the next. And, so the roller coaster will continue, until they either stagger to the exit sign, succumb to permanent emotional whiplash, or develop awareness about ADHD and get on a new track.

Teresa: "You Aren't Crazy. Things Aren't Right."

Never in a million years would I have thought my husband has ADHD. That's because, like most people, I had a lot of misconceptions about it—that only children have it, that it means you're "hyper," that it's just an excuse for bad behavior, or that adults with advanced degrees or good jobs can't possibly have it. Fortunately, my husband figured it out and sent me to a support group to learn more. That has made all the difference in our life together. In fact, it's kept us together.

We were living where I think a lot of people live right now, dealing with something "a little out of whack." A spending problem. A shoot-off-the-mouth problem. A clutter problem. A motivation problem. A can't-quit-drinking or -smoking problem. Not to mention all the confusing ups and downs of selfishness and generosity, irritability and sweetness, brilliance and boneheadedness. Both parties are just muddling through.

When I now observe friends struggling with similar issues, I suggest they look into ADHD, which is far more common than most people know. They seem encouraged to hear, "No, you aren't crazy. Things aren't right, and they can be better."

From living with my husband's unrecognized ADHD for so long, I can almost spot couples affected by it in a crowd. These people are metaphorically stumbling around blind. We need to focus on educating them.

It's not solely ADHD's symptoms that afflict relationships, though, and double the rate of divorce for adults with ADHD. It's the years of ignorance about the symptoms' existence—and misattributing them to lack of caring, selfishness, and immaturity. Moreover, people who've grown up with undiagnosed ADHD often lug around a lifetime of poor coping strategies. And typically, the same is true for their loved ones. With both of you reacting blindly, your life together might feel like a wild ride indeed.

Could ADHD be contributing to *your* relationship woes? You'll have a good idea if it's "you, me, or adult ADHD" by the end of Part One of this book. Then, if it is ADHD, you'll learn what you both can do about it. As many support-group members have learned, and their stories will illustrate, there's simply no reason to keep struggling or simply coping when you can start creating big, positive changes.

Part One begins with the basics and expands slowly into the complexities, helping you to:

- **Identify ADHD symptoms** and understand why the term *Attention-Deficit/Hyperactivity Disorder* confuses everyone (Chapter 1).
- **Gain a solid overview of ADHD**, including its central challenge of self-regulation (Chapter 2).
- **Distinguish between actual symptoms and poor coping skills** developed over a lifetime's lack of awareness about ADHD (Chapter 3).
- **Recognize common patterns** in the areas of driving, money management, sexual intimacy, and more (Chapters 4, 5, and 6).

Along the way, it's important to remember: *ADHD can manifest itself in many different ways. There is not one way of having ADHD.* You might relate to many, or only a few, of the examples in this section, but if someone you love has ADHD, a clear enough picture should start to emerge.

ADHD Partner Survey Snapshot:
Scatter-brained, Lazy, or ADHD?

Survey question: "Before you learned about ADHD, how did you explain your partner's problematic traits to yourself or others? (Select all that apply. Then add any not listed and/or comment on this subject.)"

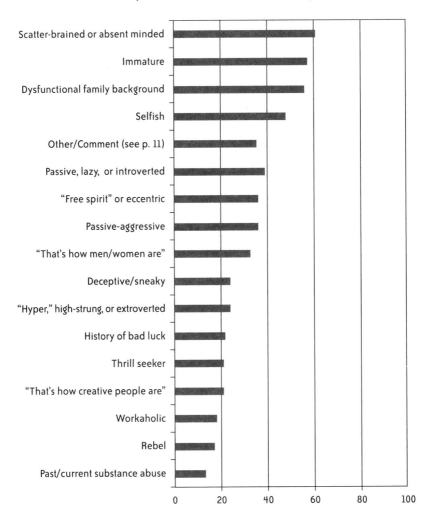

For the question on the opposite page, one in three ADHD Partner Survey respondents selected "other/comment." Many amplified this selection by briefly explaining why they didn't recognize a partner's ADHD symptoms from the very beginning. Here is a sampling:

- I really had no idea why she acted like she did!
- He'd left a miserable marriage and was worried about finances. Then I learned he's always had financial trouble.
- I loved and believed in him but could not understand why he couldn't get his act together.
- Every one of his friends and family had the same phrase: "Well, that's Joe for ya!"
- Low self-esteem; bad school experiences.
- I just thought he was wired this way: very smart but slow and methodical. He could not multitask very well.
- The world revolves around her.
- I figured he never learned consequences because his parents always cleaned up his messes. Now I see he just doesn't learn from consequences!
- My wife changed so drastically after we had two children I simply thought motherhood overwhelmed her.
- Little willpower or discipline.
- Nasty jerk!
- His entire family saw him as being just "out there"—he was the way he was and no one cared to ask any questions. I just thought he had a lot of growing up to do.
- Who knew? It was the '70s!
- I attributed his problems to his father abandoning the family, coming from a different culture, and the economy (lots of people were being laid off at that time).
- I figured that since I couldn't get him to talk much or maintain eye contact, he must be very shy.
- Coming from a dysfunctional family myself, and this being my first serious relationship, I did not have a good frame of reference for comparison.
- I chalked it up to her being a Type A personality.
- I was baffled. Friends and family thought he was lazy but generally a nice guy.
- His IQ is very high—hence the "absentminded professor."
- I thought she might have bipolar disorder because of mood swings and avoiding sleep until she dropped.
- Socially impulsive; hotheaded.
- Commitment-phobe; had emotional baggage.
- I knew "theoretically" about ADHD and had friends with ADHD, but it's quite another thing to live with it full time. So I mistakenly thought a lot more than ADHD was going on.

Red Flags for Adult ADHD

Some adults with ADHD experience only a few of the challenges listed below—and perhaps to a relatively mild degree—while others face a greater number of more significant challenges.

- A lifelong history of difficulty with attention and/or a history of disruptive or impulsive behaviors
- Organizational challenges (time management difficulties, missed appointments, frequent tardiness, unfinished projects)
- Erratic work history (frequent job changes, lack of preparation, missed deadlines, poor reviews)
- Anger control problems (argumentative, overly controlling parenting style, conflicts with coworkers or child's teachers)
- Marital stress (partner complains that he/she does not listen, forgets promises and important events)
- Being over-talkative, interrupting, speaking too loudly
- Parenting problems (difficulty establishing and maintaining household routines, inconsistency in dealing with the children)
- Money management issues (impulsive purchases, failure to pay bills or taxes, bankruptcy)
- Substance use or abuse, especially alcohol, marijuana, or caffeine
- Addictions such as excessive collecting, shopping, sexual avoidance or hypersexuality, overeating, and/or compulsive exercise or gambling
- Frequent accidents on the job or in sports activities
- Problems with driving (speeding tickets, accidents, or excessive caution to compensate for attentional problems)
- Familial factors, such as being the parent or child of a person with ADHD, receiving an ADHD diagnosis in childhood, or being "just like" a relative with ADHD
- Considered successful but showing impairment when compared to their potential; expending more energy than others for the same amount of work
- Over-reliance on coping strategies to compensate for their weaknesses, but still experiencing problems with career or workaholism

Source: Adapted with permission from the Web site of the Canadian ADHD Resource Alliance (CADDRA), CADDRA.ca.

Who Has a Ticket to Ride?
Spotting ADHD's Surprising Signs

Our couples therapist suggested that my husband be tested because, in her experience, every time a client said, "My spouse acts just like a teenager" the "teenager" usually had ADHD. Bingo!

— HEATHER

"We're all married to the same person!" says new online support-group member Sheila. "And somehow this person manages to live in 300 cities at one time—and be both male and female!"

It's easy to see why Sheila and others draw this wry conclusion: Group chatter typically bubbles over when classic ADHD challenges arise, typically with communication, cooperation, money, or organization. Conversation cools, though, when topics diverge into phenomena that ring a bell for only a few members—for example, the garage overflowing with rototiller parts or a mate's "important memorabilia" (if you consider 10-year-old foil ketchup packets memorabilia).

Sure, support-group members are relieved to know they are not dealing with a bigamist, but some become confused by the apparent disparities in reported behaviors and even grow doubtful of the ADHD diagnosis. If your partner is an excellent driver but the group goes on a rant about reckless driving, well, that must mean your partner can't have ADHD, right? Wrong!

Each ADHD roller coaster sports its own particular twists and turns, and we will keep building on that theme throughout this and future chapters. But it's important to first recognize the basic signs that point to this ride.

Toward that end, this chapter answers some common questions and helps you to:

- Know that the official term is *Attention-Deficit/Hyperactivity Disorder* and that it has three subtypes.
- Realize that most adults have *no* physical hyperactivity.
- See how traits involving hyperactivity, impulsivity, and inattention play out in real life.
- Identify ADHD's symptoms, ranked according to reported prevalence in the ADHD Partner Survey.
- Find out how the diagnosis is made and why leading experts consider ADHD grossly *underdiagnosed*.
- Accept that having ADHD does *not* mean a person lacks intelligence, talent, and strengths.

Q: Is It Called ADHD, ADD, or What?

The current official term is *Attention-Deficit/Hyperactivity Disorder (AD/HD)*. Years ago, it was simply Attention Deficit Disorder (ADD). Then it became the very snappy *Attention Deficit Disorder, plus or minus Hyperactivity*.

Unfortunately, the name was established before we really understood the true nature of the condition, because it *seemed* as though a lack of attention and/or surplus of physical restlessness were the problems. That's why, if you ask a room of today's ADHD experts what they think of the current term, they will pepper you with alternate names they consider far more accurate—or at least less misleading. Here's why:

- **There's no attention deficit.** People with ADHD must cope with the central challenge of *directing* their attention and summoning the motivation for doing so.
- **There's often no hyperactivity.** That's why there's a slash mark before "hyperactivity," to indicate that it is not required for the diagnosis. (For readability, this book omits the slash in the acronym *ADHD*.)
- **Moreover, the term creates stigma.** Who wants a "deficit" *or* a "disorder"—much less both?

Will the term ever change significantly to better reflect the condition's true challenges? It's unlikely, given its entrenched history in public policy. But at least we now have three subtypes that more accurately describe the general "flavors" of ADHD, and we might see more in the future as neuroscience continues to refine our understanding of the human brain:

- *ADHD, Predominantly Inattentive Type.* This person has trouble paying attention, getting organized, and ignoring distractions but can have little trouble sitting still. Instead of physical hyperactivity, there's a more "sluggish" tempo, but there can still be less-obvious mental restlessness.

- *ADHD, Predominantly Hyperactive/Impulsive Type.* This person has difficulty sitting still and thinking through consequences before acting but finds it easier to focus than the person with the Inattentive type. This is the *least* common type.
- *ADHD, Combined Type.* This person exhibits both previous sets of traits, including problems with sustaining attention, avoiding distractions, thinking before acting, and sitting still. This is the *most* common type.

The subtype is determined by the number and type of symptoms the individual has, but we'll get to the specifics of diagnosis shortly. To finish answering the question, a simple *ADHD* covers all three types. But if you say *ADD*, most people will know what you mean, and, in fact, that's the term many experienced clinicians still use.

Q: What? You Can Have ADHD Without Hyperactivity?

Yes, and you can even have it without impulsivity, too. So, if you use physical hyperactivity and impulsivity as your litmus test for ADHD, you may mistakenly assume that your "couch potato" partner doesn't have it. (Unfortunately, many healthcare professionals make this mistake.)

Even physically hyperactive children often lose that trait as they mature—or it takes on a subtler adult guise such as restless Web surfing or video gaming. That's just one of the reasons why ADHD was once considered a condition solely of childhood: Clinicians focused on obvious physical hyperactivity, and when that ceased, they thought that ADHD did too. Current research indicates that about 65 to 70 percent of children with ADHD exhibit symptoms into adulthood, including challenges that significantly affect academic, vocational, and social functioning.[1]

Most people get a bit confused trying to understand how the "big three" traits of hyperactivity, impulsivity, and inattention show up in everyday life, so now would be a good time to ask about those.

Q: How Do the "Big 3" Traits Show Up Daily in Life?

As we examine these traits in layperson's terms, illustrated by examples from the support group for the partners of adults with ADHD, it's important to remember: The presence and severity of each trait depends upon the person's ADHD subtype (predominantly inattentive, predominantly hyperactive/impulsive, or a combination).

1. Impulsivity: Can't stop. Can't wait. Can't resist.

If you're impulsive, you have trouble delaying gratification. You don't always think before you act. And you often make important decisions too quickly, based on scanty information or a failure to consider consequences.

People with poor impulse control can find themselves at the mercy of each fleeting thought, event, or TV infomercial. Without further ado, they whip out that credit card, blurt out that blunt remark, or eat *all* but one scrawny slice of that cake you made for your own birthday—*before* you get a chance to blow out the candles. ("Why are you mad?" they'll ask. "I left you some!") In other words, impulsive people have trouble *inhibiting,* or *stopping,* their responses.

They might exhibit behaviors like these:

- Get easily distracted while concentrating or working
- Have difficulty waiting their turn
- Succumb to quick gratification instead of working steadily toward bigger, more-sustaining rewards
- Put their mouth in gear before engaging their mind
- Rush through tasks, making errors in haste
- Yield easily to temptations, such as food, shopping, and sex, even when it will touch off highly negative repercussions
- Fail to change a strategy even after it's been shown ineffective or inappropriate

To illustrate that last point in clear terms, Rory offers an example:

Clint and I had just wormed our puppy. So, every time she poops he sets it on fire so the other dogs don't get worms. This being the dry season, the pasture went up in flames. He tried mowing around it and caught the lawnmower on fire. He tried making a firebreak with his truck and scorched the paint. Meanwhile, I'm lugging five-gallon buckets of water out to the blaze. That's the story of our five-year marriage: He impulsively starts the fires while I haul the water bucket.

Most impulsive acts, however, prove less slapstick and more subtle. Yet they still impart a cumulative effect, especially regarding communication problems.

Example: Trying to get a word in edgewise. Janet grew up with a mother who has ADHD. Then she married a man who has it. "When the three of us are together, I feel like a squirrel attempting to cross a busy freeway," she says. "It's impossible to make my point unless I interrupt and talk louder."

Example: The 10-second "serious discussion." Rachel shares a typical interchange with her impulsive, impatient husband about their youngest child's school situation:

Ray: What is happening with the school thing?
Rachel: I talked to the superintendent and principal and they recommend that we do not hold Johnny back a grade—
Ray: Get to the point!
Rachel: I was.
Ray: So he is getting help, right?
Rachel: Well they have a program that—
Ray: Good. (Walks out of the room.)

If you don't understand what's at play, it's easy to label your partner's impulsivity as being simply rude or uncaring. In fact, impulsivity means that even if your partner knows the right thing to do, he or she can't always do it. Put another way, your partner might have trouble *not* doing the *wrong* thing.

2. Hyperactivity: "On the go" physically or mentally

Children with hyperactivity might literally climb the walls or be little motor mouths or busybodies. By adulthood, individuals might still display excessive or pointless movement as they go about tasks. For most, however, hyperactivity matures into more covert, subtler guises:

- Constantly moving from one unfinished project to the next
- Running unnecessary errands
- Incessantly talking on the phone or channel-surfing
- Frequently doodling, humming, whistling, or making odd noises
- Being a workaholic
- Feeling overwhelmed or overaroused
- Experiencing nervousness or crankiness in situations where getting up and moving around is impractical or impolite

Example: The Hyperactive Home Improver. Recurring themes in the support group involve home-renovation projects. "I've been worried about driving home one day and finding the house torn down just because my husband wanted a new one," Lily says. "He's just always got to be *doing* something to the house, but he seldom finishes it."

Example: The Hyperactive Hostess. Chuck enjoys the dinner parties his wife arranges but wishes she could enjoy them, too. "Instead, she's getting up to clear the dishes before everyone has finished eating. She simply can't sit still long enough to enjoy a leisurely meal."

Example: The (Mentally) Hyperactive Lover. Maybe your ADHD partner *appears* calm, but his or her mind might feel like a neurochemical pinball machine, with ideas and thoughts pinging to and fro. Claire noticed a blank look on her boyfriend's face while they were starting to get amorous, and, when queried, he explained that he was writing computer code in his head. Thus came her first clue that while his *body* seemed relaxed, his hyperactive *brain* was not.

3. Inattention: Low "staying power" in the face of distraction

Faced with less-than-stimulating tasks, the distractible brain faces challenges like these:

- Losing track of their thoughts, daydreaming, "tuning out" on what someone else is saying
- Making careless mistakes, losing track as thoughts drift

Example: Out of Sight, Out of Distractible Mind. Jamie's husband started frying bacon on the stove. Finding zilch stimulation gazing at bacon strips browning, he moseyed over to see the neighbor. Chatting outside for the next 30 minutes, he never noticed the smoke alarms blaring and smoke billowing out his kitchen window. "Instead," Jamie recalls, "I drove home to all that and him outside *still* yakking." The story has become a family heirloom—right up there with the time he started walking around while brushing his teeth one morning and left the sink faucet running all day—but it wasn't so darn funny at the time.

Example: World's Slowest Closet Reorganization. Rosa's husband, Don, finally agreed to excavate his closet. He began by staring at it for a good 10 minutes. Then the phone rang, and he answered it instead of letting the machine get it. Thirty minutes later, Rosa pointed him back to the closet. Don then became distracted by a noise outside. Going to investigate, he entered a protracted conversation with the neighbors about their new outdoor grill. Rosa directed Don back to the task.

Resignedly, he started dragging stuff out of the closet onto the bedroom floor. Wow! The long-lost ski pants! He *had to* immediately check out Sierra snowfall on the Internet. An hour later, hearing Rosa calling for him—oops!—he sped over to a Web site on closet organizers. Ah, this closet business was finally getting interesting: a system to solve his problems forever. Best of all, it involves a trip to the hardware store—aisles of gizmos and gadgets!

Rosa won't be surprised if Don schleps home tools they already own (but are obscured by the weeds grown up around them or the garage clutter enveloping them) but little in the way of closet paraphernalia. And when he gets home, she predicts he will step right over the closet debris to take a nap. All this work has left him *exhausted*, he'll say.

Along with hyperactivity and impulsivity, inattention can challenge social interaction.

Example: Internal distractions sidetrack communications. Connie says to Jack, "Honey, we need to talk about money and how on earth we're going to pay the bills this month." Unbeknownst to her, she'd lost Jack's attention after the word *money,* which had triggered stimulating thoughts in his mind of buying something. Imagine Connie's surprise when Jack responds, "Let's go shopping for a flat-screen TV." When she shrieks, "How can you even suggest that now?" Jack gets defensive: Why is she always so angry? Because, remember, Jack never heard the second part of Connie's sentence, and Connie wasn't privy to Jack's internal primrose-path digression.

Example: External distractions sidetrack communications. "My wife starts all her statements with 'listen,' but I think she is talking to herself," Mike says. "She says her hearing is going, but I think she can't tune out distractions, like the TV or the kids. Meanwhile, I must repeat myself constantly. Just call me Little Sir Echo."

Q: But What Does Adult ADHD "Look Like"?

If adults with ADHD were clones, that would be an easy question to answer. Despite widespread theories, however, they aren't all entrepreneurs or risk-takers or even particularly quick-witted or creative. They are *individuals*, with distinct personalities, talents, and attitudes.

That's why you might not get the big picture if you rely on a single portrait, or even several, of people with ADHD. (Even the subtypes form only very general categories.) More likely, you'll see only caricatures, not people with a complex condition that closely resembles the human condition—writ large. More important, you'll miss the fact that your partner might have it.

You can, however, start to gain a clearer snapshot of ADHD by considering its symptoms, as shown in the chart on p. 21. (Note: You don't need *all* the symptoms to qualify for the diagnosis, just a certain number.)

From this symptom list (adapted from the current official diagnostic criteria), ADHD Partner Survey respondents were asked to select behaviors that their ADHD partners displayed more frequently or strongly than most people their age. (That's because you don't expect a 22-year-old to have the same maturity as a 50-year-old.) Selections are ranked from the most commonly reported to the least.

As you can see, these are the top vote getters:

- *Distractibility*—Being easily diverted from the intended focus of attention
- *Disorganization*—Losing track of time, items, and the order in which tasks should be done
- *Poor sustained attention*—Difficulty initiating and/or finishing tasks
- *Forgetfulness*—"Blanking" on everything from small tasks to important obligations to entire conversations
- *Restlessness*—Feeling "on the go" mentally or physically
- *Poor listening skills*—Hearing only half of what is said or mishearing huge chunks of it

If you don't recognize in this chart your ADHD partner's biggest hot spot (could it be anger, irritability, or spending impulsively?), don't worry; we're just starting to explain how cut-and-dried symptoms come to life and take shape in real people.

As you read the list, also keep in mind that your reaction to each topic probably reflects your own ADHD partner's specific behaviors. So, if you can't imagine why disorganization is such a big deal, then that probably *isn't* one of your partner's problems.

The truth is, depending on its severity, each listed trait can be chronic and cumulative, insidiously creating bigger problems in every aspect of life. Take a minute to imagine how, for example, disorganization can extend its messy tentacles into much more than closets or cars:

- Losing important papers (checks, bills, tax documents)
- Failing to meet work deadlines and consequently losing jobs
- Never making it out the door on time in the morning
- Constantly having to replace costly misplaced items
- Being unable to regularly do laundry, prepare meals, or exercise

These are just a few of the problems that disorganization can cause. Then there are the rest of the behaviors to consider! And, as you've probably learned, they can intertwine and crossbreed in bewildering, shape-shifting combinations.

Next, while the chart on p. 21 indicates the *prevalence* of traits observed by survey respondents; it doesn't indicate how *problematic* each is. For that, consider the chart on page 22.

ADHD Partner Survey Snapshot:
Rating the Traits

Survey question: "Select *all* traits that describe your partner's behavior." (Note: Unless indicated otherwise, all survey data is based on pre-ADHD treatment behaviors.)

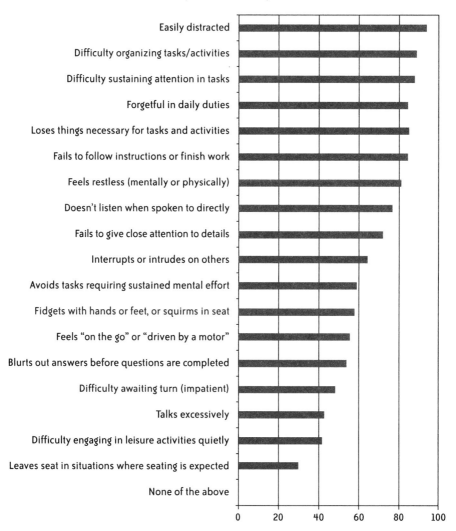

ADHD Partner Survey Snapshot:
Big Problems, Mild Problems, and No Problem

Survey question: "For each item listed below, rate your partner's behavior or ability in this area as being either no problem, a mild problem, or a big problem to your partner or the relationship. (Again, this is prior to any ADHD treatment.)"

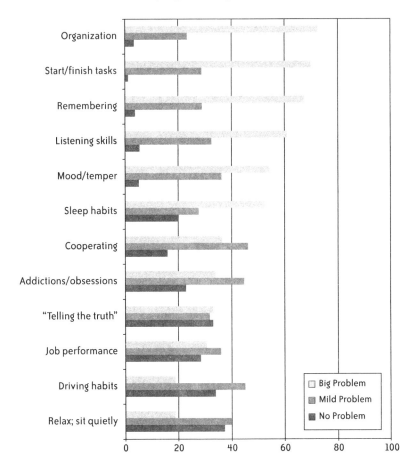

To gain a sense of relative impact, respondents rated common ADHD-related behavioral patterns as a big problem, a mild problem, or really no problem at all for their partner or the relationship. Surprise! Organization again places at the top of the list, but plenty of runners-up give close chase.

Q: With So Many Variables, How is ADHD Diagnosed?

First of all, ADHD is considered a *syndrome*: a condition with multiple symptoms that vary among the individuals who have it. That doesn't make ADHD a "squishy" diagnosis, though. Being a syndrome places it in the same category as dozens, if not hundreds, of other well-recognized medical conditions that range from Reye's Syndrome to Diabetes Type II.

"The brain is extremely complicated, and there are many kinds of ADHD, with hyperactivity or not and with distractibility or not," says psychiatrist Samuel Barondes, director of the Center for Neurobiology and Psychiatry at the University of California, San Francisco, and author of *Mood Genes: Hunting for Origins of Mania and Depression.* "Multiple genes are believed to be involved, as are many different circuits in the brain, but that's true for all the psychiatric diagnoses. Depression, bipolar disorder, and schizophrenia can also exist in a variety of forms and reflect a variety of causative factors," adds Barondes, author of more than 200 original research articles, primarily in the area of psychopharmacology and psychiatric genetics.

Second, just as there is no physical, genetic, or blood test for those disorders—not to mention Alzheimer's or even a simple headache, for that matter—the same is true for ADHD. It all comes down to careful assessment by a trained professional. (Appendix A details this process. It also includes both the current official diagnostic criteria, originally developed to diagnose ADHD in children but never tested in adults, and highly problematic for that reason, as well as proposed new criteria specifically for adults.)

Please keep this in mind: An ADHD diagnosis requires more than a symptom or two. Otherwise, everyone would have ADHD! It requires both a certain number of symptoms and significant *impairment*—for example, in the area of career, money, education, or relationships. Of course this can be subjective, but beware of factors that can actually mask symptoms:

- Family members often protect adults with ADHD from their impairments by bailing them out financially or in other ways.
- The person smokes cigarettes, chews tobacco, or uses other substances—self-medicating habits that can mask symptoms by acting on key brain chemicals.

- The person is clever enough to compensate for any deficits but in fact might be functioning *far below* their capabilities or desires and often feels under enormous, even health-threatening pressure.

What Does It Mean to Self-Medicate?

Self-medicate is a term loosely used to describe a person's attempt to feel better by using certain substances to excess (such as tobacco, alcohol, or marijuana and other legal or illegal substances) or excessively pursuing activities (such as driving recklessly, having sex, or starting conflicts). Although the person might experience some initial relief, the substance or activity tends to exacerbate symptoms and add new complications around addiction.

Q: What About Those ADHD Quizzes I've Seen?

Stephanie tells the support group that her husband scoffs at the idea that he might have ADHD. He enjoys satirizing an ADHD quiz in a magazine, saying, "Do you ever look out a window? Do you ever need to use the restroom? Then you most likely have ADHD!"

Perhaps you've seen such a short test. Did you (or your partner) dismiss the idea that a few questions could provide meaningful information? Guess what? The best ones do.

They're called *screening* quizzes, because they act as a screen just as a net does for fish: They catch only certain size fish, letting the rest slip through. They don't diagnose, but they can indicate whether it's a good idea to pursue a professional evaluation. In fact, if you screen positive after taking the popular World Health Organization screener (page 25), a Harvard Medical School study shows you have a 93 percent chance of actually having ADHD.[2]

Q: I've Heard that ADHD is Overdiagnosed

That's the myth, but you do the math.

One comprehensive survey concluded that about 4.4 percent of the U.S. adult population age 18-44 has ADHD; yet, only 10 percent of that 4.4 percent are being treated for it.[3] As it turns out, that treatment rate is far *less* than that for anxiety, substance use disorders, and mood disorders such as depression and bipolar.[4]

Adult Self-Report Scale-VI.I (ASRS-VI.I) Screener

from WHO Composite International Diagnostic Interview
©World Health Organization

	Date				
Check the box that best describes how you have felt and conducted yourself over the past 6 months. Please give the complete questionnaire to your healthcare professional during your next appointment to discuss the results.	Never	Rarely	Sometimes	Often	Very Often
1. How often do you have trouble wrapping up the final details of a project, once the challenging parts have been done?					
2. How often do you have difficulty getting things in order when you have to do a task that requires organization?					
3. How often do you have problems remembering appointments or obligations?					
4. When you have a task that requires a lot of thought, how often do you avoid or delay getting started?					
5. How often do you fidget or squirm with your hands or feet when you have to sit down for a long time?					
6. How often do you feel overly active and compelled to do things, like you were driven by a motor?					

Add the number of checkmarks that appear in the darkly shaded area. Four (4) or more checkmarks indicate that your symptoms may be consistent with Adult ADHD. It may be beneficial for you to talk with your healthcare provider about an evaluation.

Clearly, ADHD is *underdiagnosed*, say top experts, including that survey's lead researcher, psychologist Ronald C. Kessler, professor in the Department of Health Care Policy at Harvard Medical School and co-director of the World Health Organization's surveys on mental health in 28 countries.

Psychiatrist and ADHD expert Daniel Amen echoes this medical consensus in saying, "The idea that ADHD is a minor psychiatric disorder is dangerous and leads to undertreatment; the consequences of untreated ADHD are highly concerning." Kessler agrees, pointing out the enormous impairment associated with untreated adult ADHD and, furthermore, the *effectiveness* of treatment in reversing this impairment.

The dangers become even more apparent when you consider that 4.4 percent is a very conservative estimate. Many researchers suspect the true adult population with ADHD lies closer to 10 percent—and possibly as high as 16.4 percent.[5] It all depends on how broadly the diagnostic criteria are applied. The bottom line: Anywhere from 9 to 35 million U.S. adults age 18 and older likely suffer some degree of impairment from undetected or untreated ADHD.[6]

If those large numbers surprise you, consider these figures from the National Institute of Mental Health's recent report called *The Numbers Count: Mental Disorders in America:*

- 58 million U.S. adults age 18 and older suffer from a diagnosable mental disorder in any given year.
- 21 million have a mood disorder (major depressive disorder, dysthymic disorder, or bipolar disorder).
- 40 million have an anxiety disorder.
- 15 million have social phobia.
- 4.5 million have Alzheimer's Disease.

As for the parallel myth, that ADHD in children is overdiagnosed, one recent study confirms the general scientific literature in showing that, in fact, the opposite is true.[7] Researchers found that of the 8.7 percent of U.S. children who met the criteria for ADHD, only about half had been diagnosed and one-third were consistently treated with medications.

Unfortunately, children without health insurance and children from poor families (thought to have the highest rates of ADHD) were the least likely to have been treated consistently, thus creating the misperception that ADHD is a white middle-class condition or, worse, a yuppie make-believe disease.

It's also noteworthy that the conditions listed above (and more) commonly co-exist with Adult ADHD. "Strikingly," Kessler says, "epidemiological data show that many adults with ADHD obtain treatment for related emotional problems like depression, anxiety, and substance use disorder, but that their underlying ADHD is generally not recognized or treated."

Given the high prevalence of adult ADHD, he suggests that mental health professionals should always screen for ADHD when they are treating adults with these coexisting conditions.

The idea that ADHD is overdiagnosed is just one of many well-worn myths. Perhaps you've heard a few others:

- "ADHD is for children."
- "ADHD's just an excuse for irresponsibility."
- "The symptoms are basic human behaviors."
- "Modern life makes us all act ADHD'ish."
- "It's a ruse to make pharmaceutical firms rich."
- "ADHD is a controversial condition."
- "ADHD is a minor difference, not a big deal."

If so, feel free to jump ahead to Appendix B for a little myth-busting before continuing.

Q: But How Can My Talented Partner Have a Disorder?

Make no mistake: A person can have ADHD *and* be intelligent and talented and possess abundant stellar qualities. Many adults with ADHD fit that description, including famous scientists, physicians, astronomers, race-car drivers, politicians, professional baseball players, educators, and representatives of virtually every other profession.

In recent years, some authors set out to correct what they saw as ADHD's all-negative image (for example, the often-cited higher-than-average rate of bankruptcies, educational drop-outs, and incarcerations) by extolling what they perceive as ADHD's gifts, such as spontaneity and out-of-the-box thinking.

Leading clinicians and researchers, however, caution against romanticizing some truly troubling traits. Yes, stimulation-seeking behavior and impulsivity often lead to brilliant innovations and incisive decisions. Then again, these qualities also might cause individuals to take too-dangerous risks in many areas of life, hurting themselves and others.

Here's the bottom line. No one-size-fits-all statement can possibly describe ADHD's challenges *or* strengths. It manifests too variably. And remember, it affects *individuals* who have many other aspects to their personalities and life experience.

"People with ADHD have many positive strengths and qualities, but we have got to stop confusing them with what they'd have if they had ADHD or not; their strengths are independent of their ADHD," says one preeminent ADHD expert, psychologist Russell Barkley, research professor in the Department of Psychiatry at the SUNY Upstate Medical University in Syracuse, New York, and co-author of *ADHD in Adults: What the Science Says*.

On the other hand, great gifts do often come with great deficits, it seems, and very few of us have a "normal" brain—that is, a brain in which every part works optimally. As psychiatrist John Ratey, another prominent ADHD expert and an associate professor of psychiatry at Harvard Medical School, writes in *Shadow Syndromes: The Mild Forms of Major Mental Disorders That Sabotage Us:* "It is possible that genius (or simply talent) in one realm develops as a result of deficits (or weaknesses) in another.... All brains possess their relative weaknesses."

Obviously, it's important to keep sight of your ADHD partner's bright qualities, not to mention your own dark ones, but it's even more important to know that ADHD fog can obscure the best of qualities. And that seems hardly fair to anyone.

The truth is, most people aren't geniuses, and our extremes aren't so mutually exclusive. We can take steps to gently adjust the balance of strengths and deficits. Whatever our challenges might be—depression, anxiety, ADHD, or obsessions with reality TV shows—most of us can sharpen our strengths and minimize weaknesses through awareness, lifestyle changes, medication, therapy, or all four. That way, the fog lifts, allowing our gifts to shine. John's story illustrates that point.

Did John's "gifts" elevate him above the mundane world?

Thirty years ago, at age 13, John set his sights on becoming a computer scientist. Despite almost flunking out of high school, he went on to earn his doctorate. It required Herculean effort, though, and tanks of ulcer-inducing coffee, not to mention a tunnel-vision focus that eclipsed a social life and other healthy habits. Sure, John noticed that other students, many less intelligent than he, didn't suffer concentration problems like his. But he thought it was just his nature, something unchangeable.

Upon finally leaving academia's structure for the business environment, John found himself constantly on the outs with managers for missed deadlines, miscommunications, and an uncooperative attitude. "So here is this wonderful, smart guy who has worked so hard to achieve his goal telling himself he's a failure," says his wife, Abby. "And his disappointed anger about it, along with his workaholic tendencies, was wrecking our marriage."

But ADHD? Not one of the therapists, doctors, or executive coaches they saw mentioned it. They opined that John had "personality problems" or was narcissistic, but they offered no lasting remedies.

Meanwhile, Abby was increasingly finding her own ability to think clearly—and her joy in life—diminished. "John's erratic and contradictory behaviors, not to mention our garbled communications, had me in a spin," she remembers. "Was this what it meant to live with a 'gifted' person? If so, could I survive it? Could *he* survive his adrenaline-driven behaviors and lousy lifestyle habits? He definitely seemed on the fast track to a heart attack."

Yes, some observers might have focused on John's high intelligence and viewed his troubling behaviors as the obligatory price for it. His therapist encouraged him to "follow his bliss"—drop out of the rat race and go live in a van. "But that therapist had no clue that living in a van *was not* his bliss!" Abby protests. "John was depressed because he was on probation at work. We were separated at the time and heading toward divorce. I looked John in the eye and said, 'Is that what you *really* want, because if it is, go for it, buddy. Or is it that you see no other options?' He just hung his head and nodded yes to the latter."

A few days before that, Abby had heard a radio show on adult ADHD. It hit home. John's professional ADHD evaluation the next week proved her instincts right. Fortunately, identifying his challenges as being ADHD-related and seeking treatment meant he wasn't forced to abandon the work he loved, which required cooperating and communicating with people, or, as it turns out, his marriage. He could have his computer code and work well with others, too.

Solving "the problem that had no name"

These days, John is *more* innovative, not less, and his career opportunities have expanded. New efficiency, thanks to fewer mistakes on the job, means he has more time (and inclination) to exercise. Plus, he no longer self-medicates with coffee, junk food, and video games, all of which used to send his brain chemicals (and moods) reeling on the wild roller coaster. Later in this book, you'll read about John's perspective on the changes brought by awareness and medication, along with other before-and-after stories. For now, Abby has this to say:

> Most important in my eyes, he's finally *content* and has strong self-esteem instead of obnoxious grandiosity, and I'm glad that we're married, after several hellish years of seriously questioning my sanity for sticking it out.
>
> Prior to learning about ADHD, sometimes he could be incredibly selfish and insensitive. I was realistic enough to know that if I stayed with him without anything changing, my life would quickly keep

going downhill financially, psychologically, and in every other way. I was prepared to get out and save myself.

But, strangely enough, I never felt that the behavior, however hurtful, reflected his true nature. Initially, this perception alarmed me; I worried that I'd grown delusional, seeing things I wanted to see rather than reality. Eventually, though, it just seemed that anyone with heart and intelligence could see that even when he was acting like a Grade-A jerk, something was "off."

We persevered through many non-ADHD-savvy psychiatrists and therapists. It was a nightmare in many ways, but the effort has brought us closer in a way that, say, fun vacations and easy times wouldn't have.

Now I just want to revisit their offices and say, "See! The problem wasn't me being 'controlling' and 'codependent' or his 'difficult personality.' It was ADHD. He *has* changed, and we're happy, so dammit, wake up, do your job, read the literature, and learn about this!"

As for those people who don't believe that ADHD is a valid condition and criticize its diagnosis and treatment, my husband and I can't fathom it. Why on earth would they want to deprive others of this choice to feel better and do better in life? Would they take away someone's eyeglasses and scold him to simply try harder to see? It has to be their fear talking. That's all. Fear of new ideas. And ignorance.

Laying the Track's Foundation
What *Is* ADHD, Anyway?

For too long, I was lost in my husband's fog. I would never have guessed ADHD. Now that we know he has it, it's amazing what a little clarity can do. It feels like being reborn. For both of us.

— JANE

A fter *roller coaster,* the word that people most typically use when telling their story to the support group is *fog.* And for good reason: Living with unrecognized ADHD, in a loved one or in oneself, can feel like being lost in the fog—often on a roller coaster.

"I hope others can be spared from stumbling through the fog like my husband and I did," Edith says. "For our first 25 years together, I thought Joe was lazy or selfish or both." Edith also wondered if she was failing as a wife because she had so little success in motivating Joe to be more cooperative and thoughtful toward her and the children. At times she chalked it up to she and Joe marching to the beat of different drummers. "For years, I went back and forth in confusion, with no idea that adult ADHD existed," she says. "Then he was diagnosed at age 55."

Adults with ADHD also use the fog metaphor, including this woman, who was diagnosed at age 52:

I don't quite know how to describe my life to people who haven't experienced ADHD the way I have. Imagine driving a car in heavy fog. You get tense, because you can't see the edges of the road or what's in front of you. In other words, you often can't see how your actions will result in predictable consequences, which instead seem to come out of nowhere. So you inch along, gripping the wheel, anxious that you're going to crash into something.

That's how my life was for a half century, until I figured out ADHD. Few people other than my family members would have guessed I had ADHD just by looking at me or talking to me. I worked hard to "pass for normal," had earned some impressive college degrees, and had tons of plausible excuses for my goof-ups.

When I started taking the stimulant medication, though, the fog suddenly lifted and the road ahead was clear. I could relax my hold on the wheel and enjoy the drive. I could even appreciate the scenery without worrying that I'd get distracted and run off the road. The things most people take for granted, most people with ADHD struggle over for years until they figure out they have it.

Until now, perhaps you and your ADHD partner have been slogging through serious mental fog, not understanding how your life together got so *confusing*. Even if you have learned about ADHD, maybe you harbor concerns or misconceptions about the validity of the diagnosis or the safety of the medication that help treat it. You are not alone. Everything about ADHD seems to cause confusion, including its name, *until* you get the facts.

This chapter pulls the plug on the fog machine by addressing more of the common questions posed by support-group members, in the process helping you to:

- Understand that ADHD's core challenge is not so much *paying* attention as *controlling* attention.
- Recognize that adults with ADHD seem to require higher-than-average stimulation to release brain chemicals that fuel attention, motivation, and self-control.
- Know that, strictly speaking, ADHD is considered a developmental disorder, involving a slower-to-mature function of the brain.
- Review some statistics reflecting ADHD's highly genetic nature.
- Grasp the central challenge of ADHD: self-regulation.
- Learn that the first-line medical treatment for ADHD is called stimulant medication and that of all medications available for any medical condition, stimulants are among the best-studied.

Q: My Partner Has Lots of Attention—for Some Things!

That's true for most people with ADHD, and that's one big reason why unrecognized ADHD symptoms can cause hurt feelings between partners. "You can pay attention when you *want to*" is the tiresome phrase that has echoed throughout the lives of adults with ADHD. Chalk it up as more unfortunate fallout from the misleading words *Attention Deficit Disorder*. It has nothing to do with attention deficits or even short attention spans.

"ADHD is really not so much a disorder of attention as it is a disorder of self-regulation," says psychologist Russell Barkley, who detailed his theory in 1997 in the landmark book *ADHD and the Nature of Self-Control.*

Recent brain science discoveries have indicated that ADHD affects specific brain areas, including the frontal lobe, the basal ganglia, and the cerebellum. These areas show less activity and less reactivity to stimulation than in people without ADHD symptoms.

What does having "less reactivity to stimulation" mean? And how does it relate to regulating attention? All humans need stimulation. It engages us in life and helps us meet our goals. Our mere *interest* in something—an appealing object, thought, or event and even potential danger or risk—triggers the release of brain chemicals that help arouse and maintain attention until the goal is met.

Given genetic differences in people with ADHD, you might say they sit at one end of the human spectrum, the end that requires higher-than-average stimulation in order to trigger interest and release those chemicals. That's why one psychiatrist calls ADHD *Search for Stimulation Syndrome.* For example, these adults might find themselves doing "stimulating" activities (such as talking on the phone or playing video games) when they should pursue "boring" activities (such as falling sleep and paying bills). In fact, one support-group member jokingly suggests a name much more explicit than ADHD: *If It's Boring, It Ain't Gonna Happen Unless You Make Me Disorder.*

These adults *know* that the "more mature" pursuits are important, but knowledge alone cannot fuel motivation or attention; the payoff is simply neither sufficiently immediate nor rewarding. (In fact, it's the mere *anticipation* of a reward that our brains find most stimulating; in comparison, the actual reward can feel like a letdown.) Moreover, what might feel boring or tedious to you might feel unnerving and undoable to your partner—like physical and mental "static" or even pain.

Once you understand this, it's easy to see why many adults with ADHD flock to highly stimulating activities that offer quick rewards—driving fast, spending money, smoking cigarettes, picking fights, eating junk food, jumping out of airplanes, playing video games, being the life of the party, or even pushing themselves into a workaholic frenzy, to name a few.

These activities produce initial feelings of focus and a paradoxical inner calm, but over time, over-the-top stimulation typically makes everything worse. The challenge: Finding *healthier* ways to get sufficient stimulation and feelings of being rewarded.

In fact, given what you've learned about ADHD and stimulation, it should come as no surprise that the first-line medical treatment for ADHD is called stimulant medication, with brand names such as Ritalin, Concerta, Adderall, and Dexedrine. We'll return to this topic by chapter's end, after you understand more of the basic challenges associated with ADHD.

Kitty— Can You Hear Me Now? It's Not a Guy Thing

I used to get so hurt and angry when my husband "tuned out" during a conversation—or forgot it completely. I felt ignored and unloved, and I let him know it. In turn, he'd get defensive and shut down. A therapist called his behavior passive-aggressive. Friends dismissed it as a "guy thing."

Now that he's been diagnosed with ADHD, I've learned that he truly was trying to listen to me, but he couldn't focus for more than short bursts, unless the subject was very stimulating. (Guess what? "Our credit-card bill was way too high last month" wasn't very stimulating!)

I've learned that most of us don't even have to think about it. When we engage in conversation, we "put the brakes on" everything else and focus on the other person, noticing things like facial expressions and tone of voice. My husband, however, could not tune out the slightest distractions, such as the TV or his internal barrage of thoughts. For him, they were as distracting as a smoke alarm blaring. If the message he was supposed to be hearing was highly stimulating—for example, "Run! Fire!"—he'd hear that all right, but he couldn't focus on boring details of the household budget.

The heck of it is, I had no clue he was like this, and he thought everyone was like this. He was born this way! So, he'd accuse me of being unreasonable, taking too long to get to the point. What a jerk! I'd get hurt. He'd get angry. I'd get indignant. We both felt rejected. Oh, the horrible things we said to each other, things we both regret and luckily have put behind us.

How do I know that he was trying to hit the brakes? Because now he tries and can, thanks to medication. He can even stop whatever he's doing—and listen—without biting my head off. Conversation is not a problem. In fact, it's a joy.

Turns out, it wasn't passive aggression or a "guy thing." It was an ADHD thing. A treatable ADHD thing. And yeah, I know it's hard to believe. I wouldn't have believed it myself.

Q: My Partner Gets the Fun, and I Get the Drudgery?

Unfortunately, this is a common scenario when ADHD remains both undetected and unaddressed. Understanding why these disparities exist marks the first step toward rectifying them.

For example, no one enjoys cleaning out the garage, but most people *without* ADHD can drum up the motivation to complete this tedious task. Why? Perhaps because they remember how annoying it is to search for items in a messy garage or park the car on the street in the wintertime. Moreover, they can integrate information from both the past and future *and* keep it in mind as they temporarily put the brake on fun distractions and bite the boring bullet. Simple, eh? Not quite.

As you will soon learn, people with ADHD can possess challenges in each of those critical areas that most of us take for granted: summoning motivation, thinking of future consequences, remembering past difficulties, "putting on the brakes," and following through on tasks that aren't *immediately* gratifying or stimulating.

What about the consequences they *know* will take place—for example, the utilities being shut off mid-winter for lack of payment or arriving at retirement age without savings? That's where challenges occur in what psychologist Barkley calls *cross-temporal organization*. It might sound like a term from *Star Trek*, but it actually means that people with ADHD tend to view two kinds of time: *Now* and *Not Now*. And if you can't possibly imagine yourself in the time of *Not Now*—where the consequential chickens come home to roost—it might as well be a million years in the future. Something that irrelevant to *Now* simply doesn't kick the attention machine into gear.

Q: My Partner is Consistent—at Being Inconsistent!

Congratulations. Your observation matches that of most ADHD experts. That's why some prefer the term *Variable Attention Syndrome*.

Some people with ADHD might find only a few subjects or activities highly stimulating or rewarding, and they lock on those targets to the exclusion of all else. (This is often referred to as *hyperfocus*, a phenomenon touched upon several times in this book.) Others find so many things interesting that they can't pick out the most relevant. This man, diagnosed with ADHD at age 42, describes what it's like to constantly deal with both challenges:

The way I experience ADHD is like being at a loud party where everyone's talking and the music is blaring, and you're trying to hear what one person is saying but you can't because you're seeing, feeling, and hearing *everything* happening around you—at the exact same time. Then five minutes later, it's like you've finally locked into what that one person is saying, but the focus is so intense you're no longer aware that the rest of the universe exists and so you miss your ride home. Repeat this situation 100 times a day.

Q: So My Partner Can't "Try Harder" to Pay Attention?

Now you're catching on. In fact, trying harder can make things worse.

Here's why. One thing our brains need in order to sustain attention is glucose. Glucose fuels our brain cells, and because they cannot store it they demand a steady supply. Groundbreaking research in 1990 using brain-imaging techniques showed *lower than average* glucose metabolism in the brains of adults who had been hyperactive since childhood.[8] The largest reductions were in brain areas known to be involved in the control of attention and motor activity.

The fun doesn't end there, though. Typically, when we need to concentrate, more glucose flows to our brain. Yet, when a person with ADHD (remember, who already has lower glucose levels) tries harder to concentrate, the brain activity slows even further. Some describe it as "brain freeze."

You will learn more about the neurochemical issues associated with ADHD in Part Three of this book. For now, please try to accept one remarkable idea: People with ADHD typically can't just *decide* to find an activity interesting or to perform *on demand*. Their brain chemistry must cooperate, and no amount of your crying or pleading will help. In fact, it usually makes things worse.

Q: But What is ADHD Exactly? A Disease? A Disorder?

"I have read about ADHD but the explanations seem so technical," says Becky, a support-group member whose boyfriend was diagnosed two years ago. "What is it exactly? A disease, a mental illness, a disability, a chemical imbalance, a psychological condition, or what?"

Technically speaking, experts view ADHD primarily as a *developmental disorder*—that is, a condition that shows up early in life and interrupts or slows normal development of certain physical, emotional, and social skills.

"With ADHD, many parts of the brain are working beautifully, but a slower-to-mature part of the brain isn't working as well," says Martha Denckla, a neurologist and research scientist at Kennedy Krieger Institute. That part of the brain is thought to perform an all-important function: *self-regulation*. It helps us to direct and control our emotions, behaviors, and attention. And while some children with ADHD do seem to catch up with this developmental lag, research shows the majority do not—a riddle researchers have yet to solve.

Whatever you call this brain function, self-control or self-regulation, the ability to conduct ourselves as mature adults depends on it, as the following chapters will illustrate. It's why adults with ADHD have so much trouble with core issues such as inattention, hyperactivity, and impulsivity; they all seem to spring from difficulties with self-control.

By the way, ADHD is really nothing new; researchers say that it has been with us throughout human history. But some contend that as environmental and occupational demands increase, so have the challenges that ADHD poses. In this Digital Age, our health and very survival increasingly depend on our ability to regulate our responses to a dizzying array of technological stimuli, details, and other demands on our attention. (Moreover, substances such as alcohol and tobacco, widely relied upon in previous generations to boost brain chemicals, are increasingly shunned as health risks.)

We can imagine that a similar shift happened with the invention of the printed page; until then, most humans probably never imagined they might one day need to don a pair of reading glasses—which, by the way, became widely available and accepted only hundreds of years later.

Q: Isn't There a Genetic Link with ADHD?

"ADHD runs around in our family," concludes Jenna, age seven, observing that she has ADHD and so do her mother, aunt, and cousins. Jenna might be exactly right, if her family members are hyperactive. But perhaps she meant to say that ADHD runs *in* her family. Jenna's right there, too. Genetics exerts the single largest influence on a person's likelihood of having ADHD, making it almost as strongly heritable as height (which is highly genetic).

Thirty years of research with family and twin studies have clearly demonstrated that ADHD carries a strong genetic component, with estimates at about 76 percent, according to medical geneticist Susan Smalley, cofounder and member of the Center for Neurobehavioral Genetics at

University of California, Los Angeles, and a professor in the school's Department of Psychiatry and Biobehavioral Sciences. That is, if one identical twin has ADHD, then the chance of the co-twin having ADHD is from 70 to 80 percent. With fraternal twins, who share far less genetic material, the rate is half that. And with regular siblings, it's even less, though still higher than in the general population.

"All in the Family" Factoids on ADHD

Consider these points that further illustrate ADHD's genetic connections, from UCLA's Semel Institute for Neuroscience and Human Behavior and its Program on ADHD and Related Conditions:

- When one child in a family has ADHD, a second child will also have it about 20 to 25 percent of the time (compared to 5 percent in the general population).
- About 15 to 40 percent of parents who have children with ADHD are themselves affected with ADHD (compared to 3 to 7 percent in the general population).
- There is an approximate five-fold increase in ADHD among first-degree relatives (who share 50 percent of their genes in common).
- Even among more distant relatives, there is a higher frequency of ADHD compared to the general population.

With overall genetic influence estimated at about 76 percent, the balance of ADHD risk seems linked to difficulties during pregnancy, prenatal exposure to toxins (including tobacco and alcohol), premature delivery, significantly low birth weight, high body lead levels, and postnatal injury to the prefrontal regions of the brain (such as from a car accident, fall, or other blow to the head).

Genes and Environment: A Complex Interplay

Even in these cases that don't *seem* genetically linked, however, we cannot rule out a genetic component in their ADHD. It could be that they are more genetically susceptible to environmental stressors. ("Environment" begins in the womb, with the neurological system forming almost at conception.) As more than one geneticist has explained: "Genes load the gun, but environment pulls the trigger."

Smalley prefers phrasing it more gently: "A genetic predisposition to ADHD means that genes play a role in the development of the underlying biology, but the degree of impairment and problems associated with that particular way of seeing the world [ADHD] can be strongly influenced by environment as well."

The fact is, it's thought that *all* humans carry genes that play a role in ADHD. As Smalley points out, attentiveness and activity are biological domains just like IQ or height, with all of us sitting at different points on the spectrum. Researchers are hard at work teasing out information about the complex interplay of environment and the multiple genes thought to be involved with ADHD.

Q: Maybe My Partner Just Needs to Grow Up

It's true. Adults with ADHD often catch flak for being irresponsible and immature. After all, we commonly associate maturity with establishing and meeting priorities while still managing to pay bills, perhaps earn a living or take care of the house and children, and tend to our own health and relationships. But, in fact, these are a few of the ways in which ADHD's core challenge in self-regulation can, when left untreated, thwart mature behavior.

We'll use a simple, everyday metaphor to explain. Consider three key areas in which a person's poor self-regulation impairs the ability to drive an automobile:

Challenge #1: Stepping on the accelerator

In psychological lingo, this is called *motivation* or *arousal*. People with ADHD often have difficulty getting started on a task. Instead of initiating the first step, they might procrastinate, waiting until the last adrenaline-spiking moment to step on the gas. (Or they never begin, vexed by all the planning and distractions and lacking the motivation to overcome them.) Then, even once they gain forward motion, they might fail to regulate acceleration, which brings us to:

Challenge #2: Putting on the brakes

"My boyfriend just doesn't know how to stop," says one support-group member. "Stop talking. Stop spending. Stop to think of consequences. Stop to think about me for a change."

In fact, many ADHD symptoms reflect an inability to stop, or inhibit, undesirable behavior, as born out by more than 200 studies in the literature. The "mental brakes" just don't grip very tightly. "When you put the brakes on your actions, you're inhibiting, or controlling, behavior," says one leading ADHD authority, private-practice physician Patricia Quinn, author of the classic book for children with ADHD: *Putting on the Brakes: Young People's Guide to Understanding Attention Deficit Hyperactivity Disorder.*

In fact, the "big three" common ADHD traits—inattention, impulsivity, and hyperactivity—each relate to the act of braking. A concise summary comes from pediatric neurologist Martin Kutscher, assistant clinical professor at the New York Medical College and author of *Kids in the Syndrome Mix of ADHD, LD, Asperger's, Tourette's, Bipolar, and More!*:

- *Inattentive*—Unable to put the brakes on distractions
- *Impulsive*—Unable to put the brakes on thoughts
- *Hyperactive*—Unable to put the brakes on *acting upon* distractions or thoughts

Braking plays a pivotal role in self-regulation because "a lot of what we do in life is based upon what we *don't* do," explains Kennedy Krieger Institute's Martha Denckla.

Drivers must also know when to move forward and prepare for doing so, which brings them up against:

Challenge #3: Shifting gears, steering clear, changing routes

Driving from point A to point B efficiently, enjoyably, and safely requires self-regulation. The driver must coordinate a delicate balance of braking and accelerating, turning and going straight, and watching the road and avoiding obstacles while taking in the scenery (not to mention taking rest stops and refueling).

With challenges in self-regulation, your ADHD partner might find it tough to create balance in *any* activity, behavior, or thought, much less coordinate many things at once. What you might witness is a tendency to live at the extreme of any behavior. For example, he or she might be super frugal or super extravagant, super productive or super slothful, the super fun parent or the super disciplinarian.

In fact, if your partner didn't learn about ADHD until well into adulthood, the scene in the rearview mirror might resemble this, from a man diagnosed at age 40:

> I now see how I spent much of my life veering down a highway where only a cliff on one side and a guard rail on the other kept me on the road, bouncing against one to the other and back again. It seems that I was always either overshooting or undershooting, overworking or underworking, overdetailing or underdetailing, and never doing anything consistently right.

Stopping something when they should stop. Starting something when they should start. Not underdoing and not overdoing, but finding the middle ground in being a mature adult. That's the challenge for all humans, but it looms even larger for people with ADHD. The good news: Riding with your partner on the actual road or this road trip called Life needn't feel like being whipped around on an out-of-control roller coaster.

Gordon—My Wife Now Brakes for Car Keys

We used to think my wife had a poor memory, but since she started taking medication for her ADHD, we've learned she has an excellent memory! She just never "braked" to access it or store new data. For example, it's not that she always forgot where she put her cell phone; she simply never stopped to notice where she set it. She hasn't lost her cell phone in months now.

Q: What About Medication for ADHD?

Increasingly, many adults benefit from taking medication to help with ADHD symptoms. To explain stimulant medication's role with a whimsical metaphor, physician Stephen Copps, director of ADD Specialty Healthcare in Macon, Georgia, takes the automobile metaphor a few steps further:

> We've been told that people with ADHD have only two speeds, full throttle and sound asleep. Do you know why that is? It's because the accelerator gets stuck in the on or the off position. There is nothing in between.
>
> Not only does the accelerator get stuck, but also the brakes are faulty, so the person with ADHD has a hard time stopping once they get started. The radio's sensitivity knob is frozen, and so only the loudest signal gets through. You could even say the driver's "zoom lens" is rusty. When you drive, you need to constantly be zooming in and out from the big picture to the smaller detail and back again. The driver with ADHD either sees 40 things at once or over-focuses on only one.
>
> What do we do about this? We squirt a little stimulant on the problem. Stimulants are the WD-40 of ADHD. They lubricate the brakes, and so impulsivity is controlled. They unstick the accelerator; the color *gray* is recognized and compromise is possible. They unfreeze the sensitivity knob; the less interesting but necessary task is attended to, and achievement improves. The rust is removed from the zoom lens; all is seen but only the most important is concentrated upon.

The public receives confusing messages on the safety of stimulant medications. But, when properly prescribed and taken, they are widely considered among the best-studied, safest medications available, and the cornerstone of ADHD treatment.[9] Leading medical authorities are unequivocal about this because the evidence is that clear.

Every medication carries risks, including penicillin and aspirin (which kill a significant number of people annually). But medicating for ADHD is far less risky than *not* treating it, contend leading ADHD experts, including Yale University psychologist Thomas E. Brown, author of *Attention Deficit Disorder: The Unfocused Mind in Children and Adults*. The fact is, untreated ADHD is associated with higher rates of accidental injury, car accidents, overeating, smoking, and illegal substance use—all of which come with life-threatening side effects.

At the same time, "we have to recognize with humility that we are stumbling forward, doing the best we can to be well-informed, conscientious, and helpful to the patient," explains UCSF psychiatrist Samuel Barondes, author of *Molecules and Mental Illness*. He advises caution about taking extreme positions about medication. "There's a lot of subjectivism and trial and error, and one has to walk humbly."

You'll find more information about medication in Part Three of this book. Right now, let's dive a bit deeper into the tell-tale signs and experiences of living with adult ADHD, particularly when no one knows it's there.

Yes, Women and Girls have ADHD, Too

In many people's minds, ADHD refers to little boys with "ants in their pants." That means many non-hyperactive adults fall through the cracks, but it also means that females with ADHD, in particular, remain undiagnosed and misdiagnosed. Or, they lack care providers who understand the unique angle of ADHD treatment for women. Special medical issues include pregnancy and hormonal considerations.

Two leading authorities in this area are psychologist Kathleen Nadeau, author of *Understanding Girls with ADHD*, and physician Patricia Quinn, co-author with Nadeau of *Understanding Women with ADHD* and *Gender Issues and ADHD: Research, Diagnosis, and Treatment*. They cofounded the nonprofit National Center for Girls and Women with ADHD (NCGW) to promote awareness and research (see Resources page at the end of this book).

Deconstructing Your Coaster:
Why Each Is Unique

Understanding what my wife is doing and why is figuring out the unfigurable! It's like getting caught up in a mystery novel where all the threads come together in the end. After 15 years, I'm still not there yet.

— MIKE

There's a whole lot more to understanding ADHD and its broad effects on behavior than reeling off the list of symptoms. "I used to think, what kind of disorderly disorder *is* this?" Grace recalls. "Just when I thought my husband would zig, he'd zag."

She couldn't understand what was ADHD and what was personality or family conditioning—or, for that matter, where ADHD ended and *jerk* began. "It took a few years to piece together the puzzle, but I'm glad we did," she concludes. "Our relationship and our family life is one thousand percent better now."

It's true. Trying to understand ADHD can feel like trying to nail Jell-O to a wall. Even within one person, the traits can appear slippery and shape-shifting over time or in different circumstances. Typically, the first step in "nailing it" comes in understanding that ADHD's core challenge involves difficulties with *self-regulation,* as explained in Chapter 2. That is, adults with ADHD typically have trouble achieving balanced behavior and instead zigzag between one extreme or the other.

Then too, we're discussing *individuals*, each with their own particular family and socioeconomic background, generational references, and education—not to mention subtype and severity of ADHD symptoms and possible "traveling companions" (such as depression, anxiety, or obsessive-compulsive disorder). These factors and more affect how well the person can manage ADHD-related issues, and they form the design features and flourishes of your own particular roller coaster.

"Adults with the diagnosis of ADHD are *not* a homogeneous group," confirms psychologist and ADHD expert Robert Brooks, an assistant clinical professor of psychology in the Department of Psychiatry at Harvard Medical School and former director of McLean Hospital's Department of Psychology. "Their cognitive style, thoughts, and behaviors that led to their being diagnosed with ADHD do not define their entire functioning or existence."

People are complicated, whether they have ADHD or not. You'll never know exactly what makes someone tick, and that keeps life interesting. But when you're ready to begin fostering positive changes in your relationship, Brooks advises that you try to start distinguishing essential ADHD challenges from common "red-herring" attitudes and negative mindsets. In other words, most adults with ADHD have lived for several decades *not knowing* they have ADHD; consequently, they've usually developed some counter-productive coping skills and distorted explanations to explain their challenges.

This chapter dives deeper into the various possible components of ADHD roller coasters, helping you to:
- Appreciate that lasting change begins when both of you acknowledge ADHD and deal with it rather than react like its victims.
- Learn how five "mental modules" of brain function affect everyday actions.
- Recognize three common ADHD-related patterns that can throw your relationship dangerously off track—namely, a poor sense of empathy, a lack of cooperation, and being difficult to please.
- Understand why your partner's poor coping strategies might include controlling, blaming, and avoiding.
- Acknowledge your relationship's strengths—the ones you lost sight of during too many confusing loops around the amusement park.

The Goal: Hope, a Sense of Control, and a Calmer Ride

During his longtime private practice, psychologist Brooks has treated many children and adults with ADHD as well as couples and families affected by it. Some people in this population, he's found, are optimistic and resilient; when facing ADHD-related challenges, they apply effective coping strategies. Others grow pessimistic and retreat into self-defeating behaviors. He wanted to know: What accounts for the difference?

The answer, he determined, was that optimistic, resilient individuals feel a sense of control over their lives. "They were able to acknowledge the condition and cope with it rather than feel like a victim," explains Brooks, a popular national speaker on this topic and coauthor (with psychologist Sam Goldstein) of *The Power of Resilience: Achieving Balance, Confidence, and Personal Strength in Your Life.*

Nurturing hope and resilience seems essential to dealing successfully with ADHD. But first—whether dealing with ADHD in yourself or your partner—you need to grasp, as best you can and as best as the current science can tell us, ADHD's neurological foundation. You also need to develop an appreciation for what Brooks calls the *mindsets* and poor coping skills that can develop when people grow up uneducated about their ADHD symptoms.

Support-group members frequently comment that although their ADHD partners possess self-defeating attitudes, their children with ADHD often don't. They suspect it is because their children are growing up with awareness, understanding, and often medical treatment, whereas their ADHD partners often grew up with uninformed criticism and judgment.

The good news: It's not too late for adults with ADHD to change their mindsets. Simply becoming aware of negative thought processes can help solve or avoid the problems of the past. And as ADHD awareness and

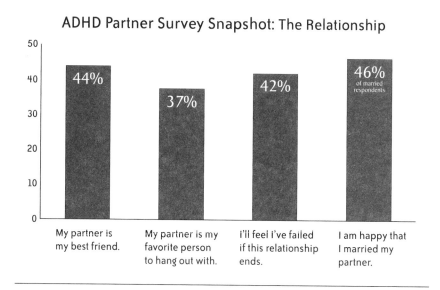

ADHD Partner Survey Snapshot: The Relationship

- 44% — My partner is my best friend.
- 37% — My partner is my favorite person to hang out with.
- 42% — I'll feel I've failed if this relationship ends.
- 46% of married respondents — I am happy that I married my partner.

treatment progresses, helping them to increasingly experience more success in life and their relationships, they begin to think more positively about themselves, the world, and you.

This message hits home for Grace and her husband, Frank. "It took several years of married life to realize that the reason he offered for a particular behavior pattern wasn't typically the *real* reason," she explains. That's not to say that Frank was *lying*; he simply didn't always know why he did the things he did. But that didn't stop him from concocting an explanation—sometimes plausible, if only on the surface, and sometimes illogical, yet always keeping her guessing.

At home, for example, Frank had no qualms about arguing with her and the kids, making his displeasure or opinion known—and loudly. In public, however, he morphed into Caspar Milquetoast, avoiding any hint of confrontation. "Whether it was a dry cleaner ruining an expensive pair of slacks or a car repair gone wrong, Frank would not even try to diplomatically approach the person to work out an agreeable solution," Grace says. "He'd just say it's not worth worrying about."

"The thing is," she continues, "Frank can pinch a penny until Lincoln screams, so I just didn't understand why these things weren't worth his worrying about." On the other hand, Frank had always been content to let Grace handle all the "dirty work" while he did more fun or interesting tasks. In her mind, that seemed the more plausible rationale, and she resented it.

It wasn't until a few years after Frank was diagnosed with ADHD and began treatment that he shared with her the *real* reason why he avoided any risk of conflict with outsiders: "He said he learned long ago that he cannot predict when the effort will turn into a heated disagreement and frankly, he might lose control and clobber somebody. So he just avoided it completely."

This explanation clicked for Grace. Frank's a big guy who could pack a wallop if he wanted to (though he never has) and once he gets angry, he's not so rational. Correction: That's how he *used* to be. These days, he's pretty good-humored. He has more patience with listening to people, and he's more cooperative. Moreover, the old Frank would *never* have taken the time to contemplate about why he did the things he did—much less think about sharing such insights with Grace.

Given Frank's newfound abilities, Grace sensed that maybe it was time to revise his attitudes toward negotiating conflicts. "When I suggested it, he was doubtful at first," she says. "After all, this had been his pattern for 40 years. But I'll be darned, when our crankypants neighbor rang the doorbell recently with yet another new complaint, Frank answered it and calmly handled the guy. When Frank closed the door, he seemed rather surprised with himself, and very pleased."

Caveat: Understanding Doesn't Mean Excusing

"I hear sometimes that people feel they need to excuse or overlook the behaviors of their partners who have ADHD, even though the behaviors make them anxious or angry," says psychologist Robert Brooks. "People who have ADHD should not use a diagnosis as an excuse, because it's up to them to learn more effective ways of dealing with it."

By the same token, Brooks emphasizes that understanding your ADHD partner does not mean accepting or giving in to poor behavior. "Instead, understanding the behaviors is a jumping-off point to learning how to change them."

Coaster Construction: From the Ground Up

If you've been in this relationship a few years, you know well your particular roller coaster's loops, drops, and topsy-turvy tilts. You know at which points to squeeze your eyes shut (and pray) and when to raise your arms and yell, "Whee!" Still, you get surprised. It might help to know a bit about the principles of ADHD roller coaster construction.

But first, consider how humans develop. We begin life with a physical body, including a brain and nervous system that has certain genetically influenced characteristics. Those characteristics affect how we react to the world and, in turn, how the world reacts to us. Back-and-forth the dance continues over the years, perceptions and reactions reinforcing each other and interweaving until an "identity" emerges.

That is to say, ADHD symptoms *begin* in the brain. So, let's consider physical differences in the brain, and the resulting behaviors, as the roller coaster's foundation. It's the base structure from which all the other features emerge. You've learned that the brain-based symptoms of ADHD are variable—consider them the roller coaster's tracks—but so are what comes next: the world's reactions to those behaviors. Sometimes, the overall reaction will be positive. Too often, it's negative, especially when the person with ADHD doesn't know he or she has it or what it really means.

Now that you have an overall idea of roller coaster construction, let's further explore some of its components.

Support and Cross Beams: Five "Mental Modules"

"The ADHD diagnosis explained a lot about my wife's behaviors and helped me take things less personally," Scott confirms. "And while I've read the symptom list and understand the basic problems around self-regulation, it still seems a little abstract. I mean, it's just not enough to explain her sometimes-strange ways of thinking and flat-out poor judgment, all of which create so many ups and downs in our life together."

We used an automobile-driving metaphor in Chapter 2 to quickly explain how ADHD symptoms can challenge self-regulation—activities like getting started, navigating, and braking when appropriate. Now let's expand that idea a bit.

The experts call the self-regulating set of brain capacities *Executive Function (EF)*. In general, EF is the ability to plan, focus, activate, integrate, prioritize, and modulate effort. EF finds its physical home largely in a section of the brain called the *prefrontal cortex* (right behind the forehead).

Researcher and neuropsychiatrist Thomas Gualtieri, medical director of the North Carolina Neuropsychiatry Clinic, describes EF as the capacity to

- formulate goals,
- plan for their execution,
- carry them out effectively,
- change course and improvise in the face of obstacles or failure,
- and do it successfully, in the absence of external direction or structure.

To clarify this concept, consider these metaphors used to describe EF.

Example: A corporate executive. You have a top-notch workforce, a stellar product, and strong market demand. Yet, if the chief executive officer can't keep it all running smoothly over time, then debts accrue, employees lose jobs and pensions, and bankruptcy looms.

Example: An orchestra conductor. This popular example comes from Yale University psychologist and prominent ADHD expert Thomas E. Brown. The conductor's function is to organize, activate, focus, integrate, and direct the musicians, producing well-coordinated music. Lacking a *maestro*, the result is cacophony.

Example: A chef. Neurologist Martha Denckla's metaphor hits close to home. Despite having a well-equipped kitchen, the "disheveled cook" fails to gather all the ingredients in time or in order and forgets to preheat the oven and defrost the frozen roast. Despite the cook's knowledge of terms from *al dente* to *zest,* dinner's going to be late—or indigestible.

Example: A life partner. Strong EF lets you think about what you say before you say it, contemplate and prioritize your values, keep your promises, and select viable alternatives when problems arise instead of thoughtlessly making things worse.

These examples all describe a capacity that forms the very foundation of a mature and well-functioning personality. Moreover, the existence of this capacity is *hard-wired*, Gualtieri emphasizes. That means it's based directly on the brain's prefrontal cortex and its connections throughout the brain. In other words, you don't *learn* this capacity. "The functions can be enhanced by learning and experience, but they are hardwired to begin with," he adds. "And in some people, this hardwiring is not quite so robust as it is in others."

You guessed it. With ADHD, the hardwiring isn't what it could be. To be clear, though, having less-robust EF does *not* mean a person lacks intelligence, ability, or talents (that is, inferior brain parts). Yet, that weaker EF, left unaddressed, can in fact sabotage a person's intelligence, ability, and talent.

All these brain theories are well and good, you might say, but what has it got to do with why your ADHD partner is "in denial" about the need to take out the garbage? And does it explain why you can't get your partner to turn off the TV and come to bed at midnight instead of falling asleep on the sofa, rousing only to jot down the numbers for too-good-to-be-true infomercial products? Stay tuned. We're getting there.

To translate the abstract idea of Executive Function into real-life challenges, we turn to psychologist Russell Barkley. During his 30-year professional career, he has published 12 books, more than 200 scientific articles and book chapters, and seven videos on ADHD and related disorders. He is also the founder and editor of the newsletter *The ADHD Report.*

Barkley breaks out ADHD-related impairments of EF into five "mental modules":

1. Poor ("leaky") working memory
2. Delay in developing an internal voice
3. Difficulty regulating emotion and motivation
4. Challenges in pursuing long-term goals
5. On-again, off-again performance

1. "Leaky" working memory

You ask your partner to go to the grocery store for eggs, bread, milk, bananas, and napkins. He comes back with eggs, bagels, a lawn chair, and 10 pounds of lamb shanks ("on sale!"). He remembered the first item, eggs, and something close to the next item, bread (bagels). After that, though, it's Supermarket Sweep. This is one example of poor *working memory*.

> With strong working memory, our actions stay anchored to the past (where goals are set) and connected to the future (where goals are *met*).

To be clear, *working memory* isn't simply a memory that works. It is our ability to hold information in our minds and use it to guide our actions. With strong working memory, our actions stay anchored to the past (where goals are set) and connected to the future (where goals are *met*).

Poor working memory disconnects cause from effect, impairing the ability to predict and prepare for outcomes. It can also hinder the capacity to do things on time and in proper sequence. For example, Margaret notices that when her boyfriend tells stories, the events are often out of sequence, and the same thing happens with their arguments: "He'll be convinced that he's upset because of something I've just said but he doesn't recall he was upset long before I said whatever it was he claims upset him!"

Finally, studies in young adults have shown that ADHD impairs their ability to sense or gauge the passage of time accurately[10] and thus manage time and organize for upcoming events. Here is an adult example:

You: "Come to bed, honey! It's late."
Your ADHD partner: "Okay, in five minutes."
You (three hours later): "Are you still on that *&%(# computer?"
Your ADHD partner: "Relax! It's only been five *&%(# minutes!"

We also need working memory in subtler ways to organize ourselves—whether packing for a trip or composing an essay—and to know where to start first, figure out what goes next, and remember why the heck this task is so darn important in the first place.

Scott's wife, a fifth-grade teacher with newly diagnosed ADHD, used to open her classroom's cabinets, view with horror the mess therein, and quickly shut them. No organizing system, coach, or tips did the trick.

"She says she didn't know where to begin, that she couldn't see distinct *things*, just *mess*," he says. "Yet, when she takes her stimulant medication, she sees the things and organizes the cabinets easily."

2. Delayed development of the "mind's voice"
Remember Pinocchio and his sidekick Jiminy Cricket, that squeaky little voice of conscience perched on his shoulder? Recall that Jiminy's persistence eventually succeeded in steering Pinocchio in the right direction.

Most of us have a Jiminy Cricket inside us. It pipes up to remind us of events and concepts—from that cake baking in the oven to our love for our partner (even when truly annoying). It reminds us that if we don't go to sleep soon, we're going to snooze through the alarm and run late for work. Delayed development of this internal voice, Barkley explains, creates significant difficulties such as these:
- Following rules and instructions, managing "to-do lists"
- Making plans and following through
- Acting with legal or moral principles in mind: socializing into a culture
- Comprehending complex or "dull" reading, especially when combined with poor working memory
- Contemplating and reflecting

One night, Brenda's boyfriend told her that he's developing *her* voice in his head. As he goes about his day, he "hears" what she'd say, the decisions she might make. "When I realized he wasn't being sarcastic, it freaked me out," she says. "Now I understand that his internal voice just felt weak by comparison."

3. Difficulty regulating emotions and motivation
Most people are surprised to learn that ADHD often confers a degree of neurologically based irritability, moodiness, hypersensitivity, or outright anger.

Consider it impulsivity's cranky cousin: a tendency to become easily frustrated and growl or blow up, but react 10 minutes later with over-the-top excitement to something else. In fact, moods can change so quickly in response to external events that the less-than-savvy clinician often mistakes ADHD for bipolar disorder.

What's more, tempers might fly into action if you don't respond—immediately—with whatever it is your partner wants. Furthermore, your partner might grow easily irritated with *your* shortcomings (the children's, too) even while denying and minimizing his or her own.

Besides emotional moods, there can also be challenges in regulating *motivation*:

- Summoning internal motivation, or willpower, for tasks that hold little immediate or obvious benefit or appeal ("surely that garbage can sit there for a few more days" or "they'll send a few more past-due notices before they cut off our utilities")
- Sustaining effort when no immediate environmental cue tells them how hard and long they should work

As a result, some ADHD partners rely on a mate for motivation, but that is a job easier said than done. It is also fraught with dangers that plague the relationship and might force you into unhealthy habits. As one new support-group member put it, "I am so glad to hear that there are others feeling like they either have to be a martyr or a bitch in order to move their partner to action."

4. Challenges in pursuing long-term goals

No matter how well we plan a goal, roadblocks happen. If we are to persist in meeting the goal, we must act resourcefully and flexibly to identify alternatives. Some individuals with ADHD, however, tend to give up when obstacles appear. Or the opposite: They keep plowing ahead with the original bad idea.

5. On-again, off-again performance

Sometimes the person with ADHD can complete work quickly and correctly; at other times, he or she performs poorly and erratically. That's one reason why many people contend their partner *can't* have an attention-deficit—because sometimes they *can* pay attention. But people with ADHD *typically* show substantial variability over time in their attention, including the quality, quantity, and even speed of their work, Barkley stresses.

As you can see, these five "mental modules" lie at the heart of self-regulation. Barkley emphasizes that it is essential to understand these concepts "because they help us appreciate the greater breadth of ADHD symptoms and the reason for its wide scope of impairments in virtually every major life activity studied to date." In other words, ADHD involves much more than forgetting and, left unaddressed, it can negatively affect relationships, driving safety, financial management, parenting, employment, personal health, and much more.

Three Loose Planks That Derail Relationships

"For the most part, I could live with the forgetting and distractibility," Bob confides. "What did us in was my girlfriend's attitude that compromising with me on anything, however trivial, was tantamount to selling her soul."

To be sure, many ADHD traits can put a whammy on a relationship. Yet, any one of these three common patterns can prove particularly devastating:

- *Insatiability*—Being tough to please and seldom satisfied
- *Rigidity*—Uncooperative; either/or thought patterns
- *Low capacity for or expression of empathy*—Failing to think of others

These qualities guarantee undesirable outcomes and reinforce a pattern of negative mindsets, says Harvard Medical School professor and psychologist Brooks.

1. Insatiability: Being difficult to please

"My ADHD partner really had me going for 10 years, thinking I was a lousy wife," Peg says. "But it turns out he's never satisfied with *anything* in life." That's insatiability for you.

Indeed, many parents of children with ADHD have said to Brooks, "My child is impossible to please." In reaction, they feel they're bad parents. Similarly, support-group members often feel undue responsibility for their partner's unhappiness. It's often hard to avoid when it's in your face so often. In fact, the group's old-timers have a common way of welcoming newcomers: "It's not your fault!"

But accepting the blame for your ADHD partner's unhappiness is an easy trap to fall into, especially if he or she has any of these tendencies:

- Always sees only the negative in any situation
- Has an intense need to be right
- Perceives compromise as giving in
- Has low self-observation and ability to link cause with effect
- Often forgets past favors and accommodations from you

These problematic traits might be obvious to everyone but your partner. Among the couples Brooks sees in therapy, the adults with ADHD often minimize such descriptions of themselves, saying they would feel fine if only other people were more giving and considerate. (Overlooking the fact that other people *have* given—to the point of depletion!)

He calls this feeling of insatiability "inborn, part of the ADHD biology, and not easily quenched, leading to the perception that the world is unfair." Even when pleasure is achieved, it is soon forgotten. Says one woman, who was diagnosed with ADHD and took stimulant medication for the first time at age 60, "I started to feel what I first thought was mania, and then I realized no, wait, this must be happiness I'm feeling."

Jeff—The Magic Phrase: In the Last 10 Minutes

The concept of insatiability [page 53] resonates strongly for me. I was diagnosed only two years ago with primarily inattentive type ADHD, and everything I'm learning is helping me to reframe my entire life. For example, I'm certain my parents loved me and did their best. Yet it's only now that I understand why I didn't *feel* very loved. It just seemed there was not enough love and acceptance and "stuff" in the whole world to make me feel right, but I didn't know why until my diagnosis at age 33.

I recall taking out frustration on my little sister with practical jokes—stimulating for me but traumatizing for her. I wasn't a mean kid. It just felt that any amount of attention she received took something away from me. I had no sense of "sharing" our parents, because there didn't seem to be enough of anything to satisfy me.

Making sense of my childhood perceptions means I better understand my wife's chronic inability to be happy. (She also has ADHD but has only recently begun treatment.) She has such immediately consuming needs but never is satisfied. She shopped us right into bankruptcy—and with my own ADHD untreated at the time, I was slow in seeing reality and taking the initiative to stanch the financial bleeding. Still she whines if she can't buy this or that. And, I'll spend the entire weekend with her, but two days later she'll complain, "You never spend any time with me."

Meanwhile, I've come up with a bit of "self-talk" that helps me cope. When she says something like, "You never buy me anything I want," in my mind I add, "in the last 10 minutes." That puts things into perspective.

---

2. Rigidity, inflexibility, and an inability to compromise

Clare was happy to see her husband finally taking a more active interest in her daughter (his adopted child). But then he immediately became over-involved, telling Clare to butt out of every decision. "He's gone from one extreme to the other," she complains. "In his mind, it's either his child or my child. He doesn't know how to do *our* child, and it seems as frustrating for him as it is for me."

Add this to the lengthy list of paradoxes about ADHD: Someone who is disinterested one minute turns hyperfocused the next, and someone who is impulsive and disorganized one minute turns rigid and inflexible the next!

Actually, impulsivity and rigidity can represent two sides of the same coin, Brooks points out. You could tag the two extremes yet another manifestation of that difficulty in finding the middle path of self-regulation. "The adult who has ADHD knows he or she can be impulsive," he says, "so rigidity might represent an attempt to cope with the rampant disorganization and lack of control in life, a way to try keeping things in order."

An inflexible mindset, however, can leave little room for compromise. For example, your partner might perceive only one solution to a problem: namely, that others should do as he or she wants. When this fails to occur, a meltdown might ensue, followed by your partner's claims of being horribly victimized. Among other irritating effects, this can make for an authoritarian parenting style. (And it spells double trouble if the child also has ADHD and a similarly inflexible nature.)

Moreover, don't bet that your pleas for reason will always register. "With some kids or adults with ADHD, if they make up their mind about something, you're not going to budge them from that position one iota," Brooks adds. "They simply don't want to hear it, and even if they hear it, they immediately dismiss it."

3. Low empathy: "All take and no give"

"My wife seems to have empathy for movie characters, stray animals, or the grocery store clerk," Alex offers. "But when it comes to her husband and teenage daughter, she often acts downright self-centered."

Actually, empathy involves two sets of skills, according to Brooks:

- The ability to take the perspective of another person
- The ability to understand and identify emotions

Yet, for many people with ADHD, the world can seem so chaotic and their focus so erratic, they don't even know what *they* feel, much less what someone else feels. Even if an adult with ADHD possesses both sets of empathic skills listed above, the person's impulsivity or rigidity might obscure seeing the world through another's eyes. "And if a person is lacking in empathy" Brooks adds, "he or she is likely to misread a situation and misunderstand the intentions of others. They often expect others to adapt to them, but they aren't as willing to change themselves." It could be that change seems impossible—and the resulting feeling of powerlessness frustrates them even more.

In general, we can't assume that all humans are capable of "normal" levels of empathy. Empathy is largely a function of the brain, and we all have different capacities. Treating ADHD with medication often enhances the ability to act empathically, but certain coexisting conditions, such as Asperger's Syndrome, complicate the picture.

Yet what about this? Many support-group members report that their ADHD partners *were* very empathetic initially, only to pull an abrupt about-face months into courtship, after marriage, or after the stresses of a mortgage and a baby. If you've wondered what happened to the empathy you thought your partner possessed in spades, Brooks offers possible reasons:

• *The initial behavior wasn't empathy.*

Perhaps you mistook courtship behavior—such as being considerate or buying thoughtful gifts—for empathy. "My husband loves and is very kind to children and animals," Annette says. "So I always thought that meant he had empathy, but now I see that's something else entirely, perhaps even a way for him to feel more in control or competent by comparison."

• *Courtship was "stimulating."*

"Novelty is much more exciting to people with ADHD, so they can remain much more focused during courtship," Brooks says. That is, the excitement can act as a sort of medication that boosts brain function.

• *"The honeymoon's over"—magnified by ADHD.*

Most romantic relationships enjoy a honeymoon period where the couple lavishes each other with consideration and patient understanding. Researchers who study this type of thing say this period lasts from about 12 to 18 months before both parties start letting their hair down. With untreated ADHD involved, the timeframe accelerates.

"In the beginning, the partners who have ADHD also might not feel the same kinds of pressures that occur with time and more obligations," Brooks says. Demands and distractions tend to increase just as stimulating novelty wanes—a crippling one-two punch.

Children with ADHD who have unhappy experiences in school often remain hopeful that *this* new teacher, *this* new school, will be better. As adults, they might think, "Maybe *this* person will be different." Trouble is, until they become aware of how ADHD is undermining their relationships, they might think it's always the other person's fault.

• *Empathy can fail when you disagree with a person.*

"It's easy to act empathically when people agree with you and do what you want," Brooks says. "When you are with a person who has disappointed or angered you, however, it's harder to be empathic."

If your ADHD partner's idea of cooperation means doing it his or her way, you become the source of anger simply for suggesting that your needs or preferences deserve consideration. What's more, as you suffer increasing fallout from your ADHD partner's irresponsibility or thoughtlessness, you might begin to complain or cry about it—definitely "disappointing behavior."

• *Poor coping mechanisms can interfere with empathy.*

Adults with ADHD often *do* notice when their mates are in pain, Brooks explains, yet they seldom know how to deal with it. So they dismiss it or push blame on their mates. It's incredibly easy for the adult with ADHD to hear the message "You're wrong or deficient" and, in response, become rigid, anxious, and often angry.

A Rickety Structure Makes for a Risky Ride

We're reaching the top of the roller coaster now. Are you dizzy yet? Hold on tight, because this vantage point gives us a closer look at how ADHD, when left unrecognized from a young age, creates a more complicated effect—and an unreliable structure for the individual and anyone involved with him or her. Consider the basic trajectory:

1. Society gives negative feedback on brain-based behaviors.
2. The person then develops negative ideas about his or her capabilities.
3. These negative mindsets lead to developing poor coping skills.

1. Behaviors meet world; world gives feedback

The neurological symptoms associated with ADHD—disorganization, insatiability, low frustration tolerance, and more—affect life on every level. "People with ADHD come into the world with these characteristics, which in turn interact with the world," Brooks explains. And remember, they typically lack knowledge about the nature of these characteristics, as do most of the people they encounter. "Throughout life, the individual often received all kinds of feedback, and for characteristics such as rigidity, impulsivity, or low empathy, the feedback probably fell more into the negative than the positive column," he adds.

Consider, too, the backhanded compliments, such as "You have so much potential!" Left unsaid but clearly implied: "Now when are you going to finally live up to it?"

The negative pattern starts early, too. A hyperactive child, for example, will quickly be labeled as bad, careless, and/or willful. A dreamy and inattentive child might be judged intellectually slow or a space cadet.

Teachers or parents might accuse these children of defiantly misbehaving or not trying. Siblings might complain about them, and they might be punished, sometimes severely, for both their actions *and* inaction.

Not surprisingly, many children with ADHD grow discouraged, depressed, resentful, and irritable. They might chastise themselves ("I never do anything right") or others ("Get off my back!"). It's understandable that some finally raise the white flag of *learned helplessness*, the therapeutic lingo for "why even try anymore?" The backlog of shaming incidents eventually looms large for these children as they grow up. It can also lead to a hypersensitivity to criticism that eventually drives away their partners, or leads their partners to nervously walk on eggshells.

After trying an ADHD simulator on the Internet,[11] Cheri better understood what her partner had been facing for decades, before being diagnosed with ADHD. To demonstrate visual distractibility, for example, the text fades in and out. "Predictably," she reports, "I failed, because *who wouldn't?*" Yet, her emotional reactions surprised her. "When the paragraph faded before I could finish it, I was ticked off. And I sort of felt like an idiot even though I've always done really well on standardized testing." If her whole day were like that, every day, Cheri suspects, she would be in a constant state of self-loathing, despair, anxiety, and anger.

The discouraging "report card" the world gives to many people with ADHD is born out in the studies that show higher-than-average risk for these poor outcomes:

- Dropping out of school, not completing college
- Having few or no true friends
- Underperforming at work, leaving jobs quickly
- Engaging in antisocial activities
- Using tobacco or illicit drugs
- Experiencing traffic accidents, money problems, and interpersonal discord

It's *extremely* important to remember that plenty of adults with undiagnosed ADHD defy those statistical odds, but for many others, Brooks warns, the chorus of negative feedback can wield a profoundly demoralizing and isolating effect. In turn, that negativity compounds an individual's interactions with the world, and especially personal relationships.

2. Negative mindsets develop from feedback

If you think that adults with ADHD always are precisely aware of how these negative reactions have affected them, think again. They might be quite unable to verbalize or recognize these negative mindsets they have developed or to realize that they're based on faulty information:

- "I do not have a great deal of control of my life."
- "When I am successful, it is based on luck or chance."
- "I'm less worthy than others."
- "The world is unfair."
- "People seem angry with me."
- "I have little, if anything, to offer the world."
- "I am pessimistic that things will improve."

The last point proves especially critical when the ADHD partner thinks about pursuing treatment. Take Cecilia's husband, for example. After he was diagnosed with ADHD, she says he inflexibly locked onto the impression that going to a support group constitutes ADHD treatment: "From there, he got stuck in another negative thought loop. That is, the ADHD chaos isn't improving and therefore it's pointless to try anything further. He's lost hope, and he hasn't even started treatment yet!" His negative mindset had slipped right into a poor coping strategy, the next layer in the complex picture of ADHD.

3. Poor mindsets lead to poor coping strategies
What's a poor coping strategy? Anything that exacerbates the situation by creating self-defeating and counter-productive behaviors.

"Poor coping strategies don't lead to effective solutions," Brooks insists. "They simply magnify problems." An example: The highly impulsive person who keeps losing jobs and "copes" by blaming a bad economy. A better strategy would be to notice the pattern and think, "Maybe I'm doing something that perpetuates this pattern." Yet, it can be very tempting to fall back on poor coping strategies because they often seem to relieve stress—at first, anyway. "The initial feeling may be relief," he concedes, "but what follows is often regret." Regret at avoiding a challenge or reacting badly to it.

He offers examples of typical poor coping strategies, also called *defense mechanisms*:

- *Avoiding*—It's human nature to avoid a task that you believe will lead to failure. And, if you've had more unsuccessful than successful experiences with the task, why risk another failure? (The trouble is, people with ADHD often forget their successes.)
- *Quitting*—These folks quit at the first whiff of difficulty, sensing failure just ahead.

- *Rationalizing and blaming*—When you offer excuses rather than accept responsibility, you're *rationalizing*. When the excuses go "external," you're *blaming others*. Consider it a way of pushing off one's own feelings of inadequacy.
- *Controlling*—Feeling an overriding lack of control, some people seek to impose control all around them.
- *Being aggressive*—When things don't go their way, some cope by bullying or aggressively striking out at others.
- *Rushing through tasks and activities*—Impulsivity is a key ADHD trait, but it can also be a way to get a boring task "over and done with."

Keep in mind that to you, your ADHD partner's actions and attitudes might scream "poor coping strategy," but your partner might not have a clue. Brooks emphasizes that he's worked with some very bright people who aren't even aware they're getting angry or blaming others. So don't expect your partner to always articulate these things. Keen self-observation isn't an ADHD strong suit. In fact, your partner might go into anger or anxiety too quickly to even notice it.

"For some individuals who have ADHD, it simply becomes a feeling of overwhelming pressure where the overriding thought is, 'My partner wants me to be someone I can't be,'" Brooks offers. With one couple, he asked the man, "What was going through your mind when your wife just spoke?" The client immediately said, "I was angry." When Brooks asked why, the man had to think a very long time before coming up with, "Because she's expecting more from me than I can deliver."

The longer a person lives without self-awareness of ADHD challenges, the more that core symptoms, negative mindsets, and poor coping skills swirl and morph with hydra-like complexity, permeating every area of life. With a diagnosis comes the first hope for change. The adult finally knows what he or she is dealing with and can stop "globalizing" his or her failures or blaming others for them.

"At this point, medication consultation is indicated," Brooks advises, "but new skills need to be developed, too—particularly in problem solving and showing empathy." You will learn how adults can turn around poor coping strategies in Part Three of this book.

Riding the Track of Resiliency and Optimism

Once you understand the lifelong challenges that people with ADHD have struggled with, it's easy to admire the tenacity and perseverance that many show despite these frustrations. Much of the work with ADHD involves redirecting that tenacity toward healthier behaviors.

When Brooks works with individuals who have ADHD and are weighed down by a burdensome mindset and self-defeating behaviors, he focuses on helping them to develop both an optimistic outlook and an adaptive approach to stress management.

He associates a sense of personal control with the attitude that "If changes are to occur in my life, I must take responsibility for these changes and not wait for others to come to my rescue or immediately satisfy my needs." Professionals treating ADHD must provide realistic hope by offering practical strategies for success.

In his popular lectures nationwide, Brooks uses the term "islands of competence" to describe the areas of strength we all possess. We can expand the concept to couples, he says. Just as ADHD partners often suffer from negative mindsets and thus fail to acknowledge their strengths, the relationships in which ADHD has long gone unrecognized can founder from negativity, too. With awareness and optimism, couples can start to rediscover and remind each other of what brought them together in the first place.

Ian and his wife are succeeding in doing exactly that. He'd always known that his wife's actions were not deliberate, but that didn't make life easier for either of them. With new strategies for change, he feels the marriage is finally living up to its early promise:

> My wife "knew better." She always felt badly about so much of what she did, whether it was impulsively lashing out with mean words or not getting her work done. Now I understand that, prior to diagnosis, her entire life must have been like one long slog uphill, carrying "the boulder that had no name." I know exactly what that's like, because when we got married, I ended up slogging along beside her, shouldering that boulder, too.
>
> Finally—I can't believe it—we are having fun again. Yesterday, we drove for three hours round-trip for our son's basketball game. Instead of gritting my teeth through argumentative flare-ups, we had a good time and laughed more than we have in years. If it's possible for us, it's possible for others.

Tip Sheet: Don't Avoid "Prickly" Discussions

Joanna speaks for many others in the support-group when she expresses this frustration: "I've tried so hard, but I cannot find a way to communicate with my husband that won't lead to him getting defensive. If the subject is anything other than praise, he doesn't want to hear it."

If, like Joanna's husband, your ADHD partner is hypersensitive to the merest hint of criticism, maybe you've learned to avoid prickly discussions entirely. Psychologist Robert Brooks cautions against it: "If it's an issue that will cause you to simmer with anger, frustration, or hurt, you need to discuss it. But you want to do it in a way that won't immediately put him or her on the defensive."

Awareness and treatment, as outlined in Part Three of this book, will help. Meanwhile, try practicing these two steps:

- Pick a quiet time, not when you're in the midst of angry conflict. Some support-group members say conversations work best when they are taking a walk or a hike together.
- Introduce the conversation in a way that helps to prevent any automatic escalation; for example, "I really want to talk about this, and it's not to find fault. It's to find solutions. If at any point anything I say feels like a criticism, just let me know."

Financial Loop-the-Loops
"It's Only Money, Honey!"

*Years ago, I saw that my husband would take
us down to living in a refrigerator box if his
spending didn't get under control. It has been
a battle royal ever since.*

— LUCY

"**W**ell, my husband has done it again," Danni explains to the support
group. After saving for months to buy a new car, she was shocked
to see their bank statement had instead been *overdrawn* by $2,000. "He
had promised to be careful, and had been for months, but just when you
think everything is on the level, the roller coaster drops again. Kick me! I
should have known better than to let him keep the ATM card."

While Danni lost her chance for a car, Wendy and her husband risk
losing their house. "He simply acted on impulse and decided to leave his
six figure job without a plan in place," she says. "Now, three months later,
my salary can't cover his extravagant toys—a brand new truck, a motorcycle, a new set of drums, and, well, it's too painful to list the rest."

Wendy says that she initially fell in love with her husband's fortitude,
creativity, drive, and generosity. "Now, when the going gets tough, he
shuts down. Who knew? I feel like we're drowning in debt." Before marriage, she paid off credit cards in full every month. Now, she just sighs
and shakes her head. "I don't know how this all happened. God, I just
don't want to think about it anymore."

By contrast, Danni's husband doesn't spend on the big-ticket items but
still fritters money away on fines, fees, and frivolous items. "He can suck
a bank account dry with ATM withdrawals for fast-food, candy, or gizmos
at the gas station," she says. "I finally had to ask him to turn in the card,
but then he started running a tab at the gas station!"

His procrastination has also cost plenty—getting traffic tickets, failing to take care of them, and paying big penalties. With three young children, two of whom have ADHD, Danni loathed going back to work. "I had no choice, though, because we had to get caught up," she says. "He finally has an appointment to get evaluated for ADHD. Who knows, maybe hell will get a little cooler?"

The Big Picture: Billions and Billions

The same ADHD deficits that create challenges in other areas of life don't typically stop at the buck. Even so, many adults with ADHD manage finances just fine. "My wife is very careful with our money," Joe says. "She would feel nervous if we didn't regularly contribute to savings. She is better with finances than I am!"

Indeed, 21 percent of ADHD Partner Survey respondents with joint finances credit their partner's actions for a "comfortable lifestyle and money in the bank." (And, keep in mind, most respondents had sought a support-group because ADHD was causing problems in their lives.) For the rest, however, ADHD partners score big in these debit columns:

• Debt from compulsive or impulsive spending (55 percent)
• Bad credit rating (39 percent)
• Secret credit cards and debts (27 percent)

Surprisingly to some, a few support-group members describe their ADHD partners as extreme tightwads. Remember, though, that many late-to-diagnosis adults sport some not-so-helpful coping mechanisms. Being extremely frugal might be a habit learned in childhood, or it might represent an extreme attempt to avoid chronic overspending; again, there's that central challenging of finding a reasonable middle ground.

When it comes to the price some couples pay for the symptoms of untreated ADHD, however, spending problems form only the tip of the iceberg. Take Janine and Fred, for example. When Fred's Social Security statement arrived in the day's mail, it hit Janine hard. (Note: Your Social Security statement is a record of the earnings on which you have paid Social Security taxes during your working years and a summary of the estimated accrued lifetime benefits payable to you and your family.) Staring at the numbers, she realized they would be "paying twice" for her husband's work gaps—paying the first time during all the years he earned no money and paying the second time when that income loss is reflected in reduced future benefits.

ADHD Partner Survey Snapshot: Money

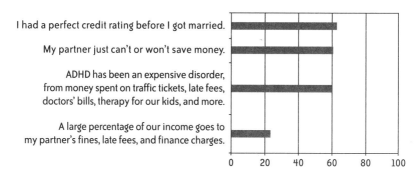

There it was, the gap of nine long years that he spent getting his bachelor's degree, dabbling in different educational paths, and unemployed, while she supported him by working full-time. "It brought back a lot of bad memories," Janine says, "and it made it clear how puny his Social Security payments would be."

Multiply Janine's story by a few million, toss in some variations, and soon you're talking real money—at least $67 billion and maybe up to $116 billion. That's the estimated U.S. workforce productivity loss due to ADHD, according to a 2004 survey[12] conducted by two of psychiatry's most widely cited researchers: psychiatrist Joseph Biederman, professor of psychiatry at Harvard University and head of the adult ADHD program at Massachusetts General Hospital, and psychologist Stephen Faraone, director of medical genetics research and head of child and adolescent psychiatry research at the State University of New York Upstate Medical University.

"ADHD is one of the costliest medical conditions that we have," Biederman told the American Medical Association in a media briefing for the survey. "The impact on quality of life is extraordinarily profound, from marriage to friendship to ability to make a living."

Furthermore, the study shows that adults with ADHD are less likely than non-ADHD control groups to have finished high school or to pursue further education. Higher education means not only higher income but also greater likelihood of steady, full-time employment. Even when matched for educational levels, however, those with ADHD still earn less than those who do not have ADHD; household incomes are about $10,791 lower for those with ADHD who are high school graduates and $4,334 lower for college graduates. Moreover, only 34 percent of subjects with ADHD were employed full-time, versus 59 percent of controls.

But wait. Did these costly calculations include eBay shopping benders? How about that $99 Super Soaker when your child simply wanted a squirt gun? The closetful of items "as seen on TV?" Some people with ADHD find shopping the perfect self-medicating activity; in fact, it's the *prospect* of buying new and exciting things (not so much *having* them) that can release that "reward-system" brain chemical dopamine, the same brain chemical targeted by ADHD neurostimulant medications.

How about lost or ruined tools or clothing constantly being replaced instead of cleaned properly and put away? And, what about the psychological and physical costs (from poor health habits) to the adults with ADHD as well as their stressed-out mates and children, not to mention the years of pricey therapy with clinicians who failed to recognize the symptoms of adult ADHD?

Could it be that the *true* societal costs come closer to $1 trillion or more? "Cha-ching!" support group members say.

How ADHD Symptoms Add Up

In his book *Out of the Fog: Treatment Options and Coping Strategies for Adult Attention Deficit Disorders*, psychologist and ADHD researcher Kevin Murphy, director of the Adult ADHD Clinic at the University of Massachusetts Medical Center, offers these examples of how three common ADHD traits affect finances:

- *Inattention*—Losing track of money, checks, and bills
- *Impulsivity*—Careless spending, overloaded credit cards, impulsive buying
- *Hyperactivity*—Too little time spent planning, too much spent spending

The adults with ADHD studied by researchers Russell Barkley, Kevin Murphy, and Mariellen Fischer showed more financial difficulty than a comparison group in three key areas (as reported in their book *ADHD in Adults: What the Science Says*):

- Deferred gratification (for example, saving and putting away money for retirement)
- Impulse buying
- Meeting financial deadlines (for example, nonpayment of utilities resulting in their termination)

Moreover, marriage or partnership expands the potential for collateral damage; a partner and children depend on the ADHD partner's ability to manage money prudently and cooperatively. In the following examples, support-group members describe the challenges their ADHD partners pose to the household budget:

No brakes on spending

Before they knew about his new wife's ADHD, Steven agreed that she would handle one part of their finances. "Four months later I find 'we've' overspent by $8,000," he says. "I was so angry, but I stayed cool and calmly told her that means we can't remodel the bathroom as planned."

Instead of accepting responsibility, his wife snapped that Steven should have reminded her to track the money. *But he had*, several times, and she had huffily brushed him off. Her proposed fix now? Take the money from his premarital savings. "When I said no, she yelled at me for *judging* her," he recalls. "She wasted $8,000, causing us to scrap our mutually agreed-upon plans, wants to take it out of my savings, and *she's* the one who feels wronged? Sheesh!" They learned about her ADHD a few weeks after that issue came up. But she decided she didn't want to pursue treatment. The couple divorced four months later.

Can't decide? Buy it all!

Rita describes her girlfriend's prioritizing skills as "nonexistent," especially where expenditures are concerned. For example, instead of deciding which home-improvement items to purchase from a list of 20, her partner will burst out with "I don't know what to do!" and then buy them *all*. "Not that our small flat can accommodate these items," Rita points out, "but they'll be joining the others that have been sitting undisturbed in the corner for three years."

"What's yours is mine and what's mine is mine"

Amy worked full-time for 10 years and paid all the household bills. "I had no spending money," she remembers, "but my husband blew his income on whatever he wanted. When I questioned him, that always started a fight. I don't like fighting, so I gave in. That was my mistake, I know. I've learned."

Last year, when her husband said that she could cut down to part-time work, she was grateful for the chance to give more attention to their four-year-old son, who also has ADHD. She had examined the budget and felt confident they could manage. But she made one critical mistake: letting him assume bill-paying duties. "It just didn't seem right for me to say, 'Give me your check, and I'll dole out your allowance,'" she explains.

As a result, the family now finds itself in dire financial straits. Her husband blames it solely on Amy's lost income. He fails to fault his financial mismanagement and propensity to spend on whatever he wants without thinking of the family's needs. With a heavy heart, Amy has decided to return their son to daycare and resume full-time work.

When "no money" means "spend money"
Dave's family lives paycheck to paycheck, and when his wife needs to go to the store or get her hair done, "I give her the debit card and pray for divine intervention." Last week he reminded her that funds were low and to buy only essential groceries. Instead, she spent close to $200 on prime rib, wineglasses, and seldom-used utensils.

"I have no idea what goes on in her head," he admits, "but it's like she is thinking, 'Oh, we're almost out of money, I better stock up while I can.'" When Dave expressed surprise at the purchases, she reacted in "typical victim mode, angry that I don't trust her and instead treat her like a child. But what should I do when she *does* act like a child?"

"I can do it myself!"
More than 60 percent of ADHD survey respondents with joint finances said they assumed responsibility for paying bills because their ADHD partners did it so poorly. Another 26 percent said that either their partners refuse to let them assume bill-paying responsibilities or they are afraid to even suggest it. "My wife thinks I'm demeaning her by offering to do it, and so she rages at me," Jason says. "But she'll procrastinate on paying the electrical bill until it's shut off even though we get very cold winters here in Minnesota and our boys are very young."

Tip Sheet: "Stop Robbing from Peter to Pay Paul"

That phrase summarizes one expert's advice to those dealing with ADHD-related money challenges. "Having ADHD myself, I struggled with my own issues of impulsivity and had to develop limits and guidelines for myself—not an easy task!" says Kate Lewis, a psychotherapist and advanced practice nurse based in St. Charles, Missouri.

When her clients with ADHD repeatedly asked for help in managing their own impulsive financial habits, she began sharing her personal system and workbook, which she calls *Divide and Conquer: My Money, My Self* (available from her Web site MyMoneymyself.com).

Lewis's advice in a nutshell: "Start with facing reality, and that means numbers." From there, she offers step-by-step directions to daily money management. It all seems like standard money-management advice until sharply deviating to meet special ADHD challenges. For example:

- Use an auto-pay system to pay bills—no more late fees.
- Stop the use of handwritten checks and credit cards.
- Maintain two accounts, one for household bills and one for cash.

When using this strategy, the household account is protected; the choices you make with your cash account, for good or ill, will have no effect on whether or not your mortgage and insurance get paid on time. "The cash account won't completely eliminate impulsive spending, but it will help protect you from spending money needed for your routine bills," Lewis suggests. (You can also allocate a limited amount to the cash account each month.) The separation of funds will also give you a chance to think through a purchase rather than acting rashly "in the moment."

Those with compulsive shopping issues might even consider setting up each account at different banks. "This adds another layer of defense to prevent impulsive spending," she explains. "It might also be helpful to prevent direct access to the household account from the compulsive spender."

This strategy's bottom line, Lewis maintains: "You begin to make choices about money that have to do with your values, not your impulses."

Driving While Distracted:
The Roller Coaster Hits the Road

My husband's driving has improved since taking medication. He no longer "punishes" drivers who pass him—by flashing his lights, making rude gestures, and yelling. I'd be so embarrassed, I'd slink down in the seat.

— ELIZABETH

Carol, married 15 years, says her husband is the absolute best driver ever: "At night, Ken notices little animals on the side of the road and has stopped for moose and deer that I never would have seen."

Denise's husband stopped for a moose, too—after he slammed into it at 50 mph. "He says it jumped in front of him," she says, "but God help me, I wonder if Michael could have avoided the collision had he not been playing with the radio, fussing with the cell phone, adjusting the heat— all the things he does while *not* watching where he's going."

Hubby Michael also doesn't connect the dots, for example, between speeding citations and higher insurance premiums. What's more, if he gets one more ticket, he will lose his license and therefore his transportation to work. "But he can't see the 'big picture' in anything," Teresa says.

"White-knuckling it" is how Rory describes the experience of riding with her husband because, as she explains, "It used to be, if I was going to ride with Clint for more than 15 minutes, I took a nerve pill." After a particularly nasty road-rage incident, she put the brakes on riding as his passenger ever again; instead, whenever they rode together, she did the driving. He didn't like it, but she valued her life too much to care. A few months later, she learned about ADHD, and "That explained *a lot.*"

The Big Picture: Your Mileage May Vary

There you have it: Some ADHD partners drive extremely well, some drive less well, and some downright menace our highways. None of these stories, or others shared in the support group, surprise the researchers who've made driving one of the most heavily studied facets of ADHD in teens and adults. They've gathered mounds of data demonstrating that ADHD's driving-related deficits are real, and even life threatening. What's more, they've shown that adults with untreated ADHD often remain unaware of their driving challenges.

Consider the results of one 2005 study by a pioneering researcher in this area, psychologist Russell Barkley, and colleagues.[13] Echoing many other studies, the group diagnosed with ADHD showed these outcomes:

- Had a higher rate of collisions
- Had a higher incidence of speeding tickets
- Had higher total driving citations in their driving history
- Rated themselves lower in the use of safe driving behaviors
- Used fewer safe-driving behaviors in lab simulators

Here's the clincher. Despite their quantifiably poorer performance when compared to a control group, the adults with ADHD in this study thought they did just fine.

Of course, plenty of people with ADHD prove to be excellent drivers, and many dangerous drivers do *not* have ADHD, cautions Daniel J. Cox, a professor of psychiatry at the University of Virginia Health Sciences Center. Author of more than 170 scientific articles, he has extensively researched driving safety and how disorders such as ADHD, alcoholism, Alzheimer's, and diabetes affect it. By and large, though, when it comes to untreated ADHD, the preponderance of evidence suggests critical, even life-threatening, disruption.[14]

To sum it up, research indicates that "a person with untreated ADHD might drive like someone who has had a few drinks," says psychologist and ADHD specialist Angela Tzelepis, an assistant professor and clinician-educator at Wayne State University School of Medicine. What if your ADHD partner also drinks before driving? Alcohol has an even greater detrimental effect overall on drivers with ADHD than on those who don't have ADHD, preliminary study indicates.[15]

Finally, Barkley and colleagues propose that any list of new ADHD diagnostic guidelines include as a common symptom "excessive speeding,"[16] indicating just how severe and ubiquitous this problem is.

Let's look at some other ways in which unaddressed ADHD symptoms can affect driving ability and safety.

When ADHD Symptoms Collide

"Core ADHD deficits pose serious implications for driving safety," says educational consultant Marlene Snyder, author of *ADHD & Driving: A Guide for Parents of Teens with ADHD*. To illustrate how untreated ADHD might hit the road, she offers these examples (fleshed out with nail-biting, dashboard-grabbing anecdotes from the support group):

Inattentive drivers might miss signs and hazards

Rosalie learned 30 years ago to avoid driving with her husband, but recently she has needed him to take her to and from her chemotherapy treatments: "He gawks all around instead of paying attention to his driving. The last time I rode with him, he didn't even notice the train warning right in front of us. Big red lights flashing and the bells clanging 'ding, ding, ding,' but he drives ahead until I yell at him. The black-and-white arm clunked down on the car's hood!"

Impulsive drivers frequently make erratic moves

For Faye, learning about ADHD demystified her husband's behavior behind the wheel: "Oh my God! He is an awful driver. On the street, he'll decide to turn into a fast-food driveway almost after he's passed it. On the freeway, he cuts people off and veers across three lanes because he's lost track of the exit!"

Hyperactive drivers have more erratic reaction times

Julie can relate to this one: "My husband weaves in and out of his lane, unconsciously changing speeds, changing CDs, and even doing text-messaging. The car becomes an extension of his always-restless body, and hazards of the road often escape his notice."

Risk-takers might play dangerous games

Nick swears his boyfriend gets an adrenaline rush from the Empty Fuel-Light Game and that other hair-raising sport called "How fast can I get through the yellow light?" And Jeff, who along with his wife has ADHD, explains that before he started taking medication, his mind felt clear only when he was "pushing the envelope" in his high-performance car. "If I drove slowly, I'd get so bored that I'd actually drive less safely," he explains.

Distractible drivers hunt for that dropped french fry

Laura's biggest fear is that her boyfriend will actually attain his career goal of becoming a truck driver: "His attention is swayed by anything at all, and he almost runs off the road." And could it be that Dave's wife compensates for her distractibility by hyperfocusing on her destination? "She drives like the car is a desktop mouse: point and click. She points the car in the direction she wishes to go and floors the gas pedal. Grocery store or bust!"

Irritable drivers get aggressive

Linda echoes many other group members on this subject: "My husband drives too fast and aggressively. He acts like everyone else on the road is there just to inconvenience him! It scares me to death. I can't figure out how he gets 'road rage' in a sleepy town of 5,000, but he does."

Linda is not alone. One study found what many other support-group members witness: Drivers with ADHD are more likely to report driving anger and aggressive expression through the use of their vehicle than non-ADHD peers.[17]

Then there are the other, less-direct ADHD symptoms to consider. "For example, many people with ADHD lose track of time and are often late," Snyder explains. "Mistakenly, they think they can make up the time by driving faster, which can cause them to lose control of their vehicles." That's certainly true for Denise's husband. "Wherever he is heading, he likes to arrive *quickly*," she says. "Yet, he never wants to leave on time, insisting he will make up time on the road."

In fact, when you stop and think about it, driving is a complex skill that involves coordination of many activities:

- Neuropsychological behaviors such as vigilance, reaction time, and inhibition
- Operational skill, including technically managing the vehicle on the roadway amidst hazards and other drivers
- Strategic thinking, such as applying driving knowledge appropriately and making quick decisions

Perhaps no other area of life (except, as you'll soon learn, sex!) requires such a well-coordinated dance among so many brain functions.

Tip Sheet: The Road Map is Clear

No other life activity affected by adult ADHD has been studied as thoroughly as driving. Consistently, these studies show that stimulant medication is effective in mitigating ADHD driving-related deficits.[18]

You'll learn more about medication treatment later in the book. For now, here is the take-away lesson: *Medication is effective only if it's biologically available at the time they are driving.* Stimulant medications don't "build up" in the system. They take effect quickly, and they wear off within hours—from two to twelve hours, depending on the chosen formulation and the person's unique body chemistry.

"Adults with ADHD need to have medication coverage throughout the day and throughout the week," says ADHD researcher Daniel J. Cox. Unfortunately, too many treatment plans overlook the driving risks before medication has kicked in or after it's worn off. (Think peak commuting hours.) He encourages adults and doctors to recognize the importance of effective medication whenever it is needed, and especially while driving.

Peaks and Valleys:
ADHD in the Bedroom

Who knew so many women were begging their male partners for sex? It must be the world's best-kept secret.

– RORY

"What's the group consensus on ADHD and sex?" new support-group member Jennifer timidly asks. "We're against ADHD and for sex," quips Dave.

Some members joke about their sexual woes, but it's gallows humor. Of course they aren't so much against ADHD as *for* properly treated or even acknowledged ADHD, not to mention being against the devastating impact it can have on a couple's sex life—and a person's self-esteem.

Dave's wife refuses to consider an ADHD evaluation (despite three of her immediate family members being in treatment) or the fact that her sensory sensitivities and distractibility make her more anxious than amorous. The part that really bedevils Dave? They enjoyed a great sex life prior to their marriage, and then the passion went out, "like turning off a light-bulb." Now, he's only half-kidding when he says, "It's death by a thousand nights of silent rejection. It's enough to inspire really bad poetry."

Many of those with male ADHD partners feel the same way. "An amazing number of us go without sex because our spouses never initiate, and we get tired of always being the ones to make something happen," Elena says. "You just lose the energy for it somehow. Then, once you go a long time without intimacy—meaning months and even years—and on top of that your partner causes so much chaos, it's difficult to care for your partner in other ways too."

To be sure, many support-group members *aren't* suffering from sexual starvation. Almost one in five ADHD Partner Survey respondents report having a *great* sex life, including many in long-term partnerships. This seems significant, given that most survey respondents had sought a support group because they were experiencing significant partnership challenges. Moreover, almost half say their partner is a skilled and considerate lover. "Sex is not a problem," says one. "If only everything in our life could be this easy!" Other survey respondents, however, report more deflating scenarios.

For those whose sex lives aren't so sexy or lively (one in three respondents report having sex anywhere from once yearly to never) it might help to know that brain function can affect sexual expression. That's not in itself a solution, but this knowledge can at least relieve psychological pressures, hurt feelings, and blame, and it might pave the way to realistic problem solving.

The Big Picture: Always or Never

When ADHD does create significant sexual problems, it usually falls into two categories: The ADHD partner initiates sex all the time or almost never. Again, it seems, we encounter those pesky ADHD-related challenges in self-regulation and summoning motivation.

In the spirit of times when the support group gets goofy and goes off on a tear to amuse each other and lift the collective mood, let's frame the most commonly troubling scenarios in the context of the animal we typically associate with sex:

- **Energizer Bunnies** self-medicate with sex and want it all the time. For years. Some bunnies *demand* "24/7" sexual access.
- **Power-surge bunnies** hyperfocus so sharply that they zoom to the finish line—yards before you do! Then they hop to the next source of stimulation—the TV, the computer, or revving up the chainsaw or leaf blower (to make some stimulating noise).
- **Generic-battery bunnies** begin in a blaze of glory but taper off to nothing after a few months, weeks, or even days. (The warranty might even expire on the wedding night.) Thereafter, some male motors run only on porno power.
- **"Do me" bunnies** lack an internal power source; they rely on their partners to initiate and then feel victimized and neglected if they don't.
- **Indifferent bunnies** don't "get" sex—or give it (except sometimes early in the relationship, when they tolerate it just to keep up appearances). Maybe they suffer from sensory overload, forget to think about sex, or find the give-and-take of lovemaking tedious and overtaxing.

ADHD Partner Survey Snapshot: Sexual Intimacy

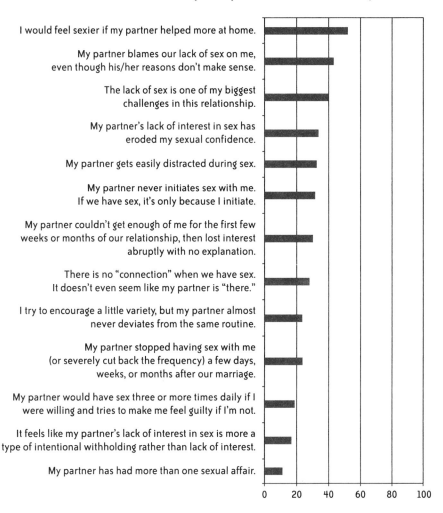

- **Blaming bunnies** lack insight into their own quick-to-lose-interest natures, blaming their mates for their loss of sexual interest.
- **Clueless bunnies** exact a huge toll on their partners' psyches because they don't care about their feelings on any of the above.

It makes sense, for example, that if your ADHD partner can't pay attention long enough to enjoy sex, he or she would not seek it or eagerly greet your advances—*especially* beyond the endorphin-filled days of courtship. At the other extreme, if your partner self-medicates with sex, that's the handy answer to every difficult emotion. Feeling anxiety? Have sex. Feeling angry? Try sex. Feeling at loose ends? Gee, there's always sex.

How ADHD Symptoms Come Together in the Bedroom

New support-group member Carla gingerly wades in with a question: "I was wondering. Since some of you say your partners eat really fast, talk fast, drive fast, I will just come right out and ask, is the sex quick, too?"

Long-time group member Robert complains that his partner's forgetfulness includes forgetting about him and forgetting to have sex with him as well.

And Ellen, a group moderator, says her boyfriend still asks what she likes in bed: "'I feel like telling him, 'Try to remember from one encounter to the next, Bub; we've only been together for three years.' But no, he doesn't have ADHD. That's what he says, anyway. He jokes that he's just Mr. Magoo." Her boyfriend misses the irony in comparing himself to a cartoon character whose nearsightedness always lands him in trouble: Mr. Magoo stubbornly refuses to admit that his vision is the problem.

Margo—So many excuses. So little action.

Everything about our nonexistent sex life was my fault, or so my husband said. Why the sudden change from the days when he couldn't keep his hands off of me? He complained I was too skinny or too fat, even though other men considered me attractive and desirable. I should shave my pubic area, he said, or get a tattoo on my butt or put a mirror on the ceiling or buy some kinky sex toys. (I did all of that and still no dice.) He was thinking about problems at work, he said, or he was tired, but not too tired to play video games or masturbate with online porn.

So many excuses. So little action. Before I realized it, his lack of interest and look of disdain when I gently approached him had brainwashed me, a formerly sexually confident woman. I finally called a former boyfriend and told him the situation, just to get a reality check. "It's not you," he said emphatically. "It's not you."

Here's the bottom line: My husband simply thought that if he didn't feel turned on, it must be my fault. Couldn't be him! Maybe that's why some people with ADHD just keep going from partner to partner; they don't realize they're the ones with a problem.

Then consider that epidemic addiction that seems to hit ADHD-affected relationships harder than average: video games. The 2005 movie *Prime* zeroes in on these libido-killers when the character played by Uma Thurman tells her friend she's getting her boyfriend the video game he wants for his birthday. The friend stops her short: "Do you like having sex? Don't get [that game]."

It bears repeating: ADHD affects *individuals*. "Your mileage may vary," group members remind. That said, it doesn't take a tantric sex guru to conclude that the ingredients of great sex seldom include these common ADHD traits:

- A short attention span
- A high degree of distractibility
- An erratic ability to empathize
- Prickly physical sensitivities
- A need for constant novelty
- Difficulties in cooperating and taking turns

"ADHD symptoms can all work against emotional intimacy," confirms Northern California-based therapist Jonathan Halverstadt, author of *A.D.D. and Romance* and one of the first experts, along with psychiatrist Daniel Amen, to write frankly about the issues of ADHD and intimacy. "In a very basic sense, sex requires concentration, and if you have trouble staying on task in school or at work because of ADHD, you might have trouble staying on task where sex is concerned, too."

Halverstadt will shed more light on this subject shortly. Right now, know that if you feel depressed or angry (or both) about being sexually neglected, you aren't alone. It even hurts doubly when you are unfairly blamed for the problems, because how do you prove it's not true—by having sex outside the relationship?

Some support-group members express jealousy of those whose ADHD partners are hypersexual. Jealousy fades, however, when they contemplate Andrea's reality, for example. "My husband said I had to have sex with him twice daily in order for him to know that I love him," she explains. "But we're married 20 years now. I'm getting tired."

Another common complaint is constantly being awakened from a sound sleep—when they have to be at work early the next morning—because their ADHD partners come to bed late and can't get to sleep without sex. As one member sums it up, "Who wants to feel like little more than someone's sleeping pill?"

Hyperactivity, impulsivity

People with a high degree of hyperactivity or impulsivity might rush to start—either the relationship or sexual engagement—and quickly grow bored. Picture a restless mind, flitting through the day, locking onto targets that offer immediate stimulation, but never alighting long enough on the thoughts and actions that nurture erotic feelings in anticipation of a splendid romantic evening.

Distractibility and inattention

These two traits can generate challenges in getting started, paying attention to details, and maintaining interest through to completion. See where this is going? Or *not* going, as the case may be.

Even when Daniel and his fiancée, who had undiagnosed ADHD at that time, were having sex twice a day, she yawned a lot during sex. "I found it very odd," he remembers. "But worse, she couldn't understand why it would bother me." After a while, her unpredictable responses to Daniel's seductions led to his losing confidence. "We would start something pretty erotic, but she was so easily distracted that boom, she's suddenly talking about getting a haircut. I started getting wary of her out-of-left-field reactions, and that made it increasingly hard to relax into the sensations, as if I had to keep my guard up."

Nick tells the group that his wife subscribes to an e-mail list for women with ADHD, where some list-mates remarked that sex is no different than any other activity: Their minds often wander in the midst of it. She prefers that Nick climax quickly, while she's still paying attention. Nick feels strange about this, because often it leaves her unsatisfied, "yet, she often can't pay attention long enough to even masturbate to orgasm."

Distractibility combined with hyperactivity proved the double-whammy that ended Robbie's marital sex life; her ex-husband simply could not stay in the bed long enough. As she recalls, "He was constantly jumping up to turn off distracting things—the lamp, the clock radio, the heater, and, eventually, *me*! I was *very* turned off!"

Lack of initiation and motivation

"My wife is always willing to have sex with me and seems to always enjoy it," says Alex. "Yet, she *never* initiates. I'm sure this isn't social or gender conditioning. She simply initiates very little in life."

Hypersensitivity to sensory stimulation

After one year of dating, Jessica's boyfriend still had trouble hugging her fully. "He would hold me with one arm while he pushed my other shoulder away with his other hand," she explains. "I interpreted that as him not wanting to be close to me and ultimately that he didn't love me." He said he loved her but, viscerally, his action spoke otherwise.

In fact, Jessica's boyfriend might have had something called *sensory integration disorder*, a condition commonly associated with ADHD and that often responds to the stimulant medication, according to group reports. Also called *tactile defensiveness*, it's thought to be a "filtering" problem within the nervous system, wherein, for example, a partner's delicate touch on their skin essentially presses an alarm button in their brain, triggering anxiety or even anger. (Think of it as being highly ticklish everywhere, not just the typical spots.) As a result, certain types of foreplay feel akin to torture. Of course, because individuals who suffer this have always been that way, they might think it's normal—and wonder why their lovers take pleasure in irritating them so!

Ana—Sometimes It's the Brain, Not the Plumbing!

Standard sex therapy advice has only hurt our relationship. How many books do you find on male sexual dysfunction where it is almost always a plumbing issue or the female partner's fault? And, for the female partners, there is an endless supply of hormonal, psychological, and physical problems.

What about when the man's plumbing is fine but his brain is the issue? You'll never hear about it. When I suggested that to our sex therapist, he thought I was grasping at straws—"delusional," he called it.

Collateral Damage: Too Much Conflict, Calamity

Let's face it. ADHD domestic fall-out can chill the warmest ardor.

"We have no sex life," Greta announces. "I no longer feel like his wife and lover, just the maid—or his mother. Yuck! And if he thinks I'm ready to have 'make-up sex' after one of his hissy fits, he's nuts." The whole thing becomes a vicious cycle; Greta won't get close to her husband because he's a jerk, then he's more of a jerk because he gets no affection.

"He's sometimes less of a jerk after sex," she notes, "but, hey, I'm not a machine, and he never does the right things to elicit that response."

Karen and her partner have less physical intimacy than either would prefer, but it's not for lack of interest or too much conflict. Instead, there's too much distractibility and inattention outside the bedroom. "When Angie's ADHD symptoms give her especially tough problems throughout her work day, she says she simply forgets about sex," Karen reports. "She panics because she is so disorganized, feels 'driven by a motor' until late at night, and is frantically trying to complete her to-do list. By then, her body is simply too exhausted to do anything but drop into bed."

Roberto struggles to clarify how he feels about sex with his wife these days. For many years, it was their area of highest compatibility, but that was before her compulsive spending sent them into bankruptcy, the implications of which still don't register with her. "I can't exactly call sex an unpleasant chore now," he acknowledges, "but the underlying feeling is 'sleeping with the enemy.'"

Executive function in the bedroom

Strangely enough, even many mental-healthcare professionals assume that sex constitutes an "ADHD Free" zone where deficits don't matter, don't even exist, or actually prove a plus. Sex is a "natural" animal urge, right? You don't need to *think* about it.

Yet, we do need to think about how difficulties with that brain capacity called Executive Function (EF), as explained in Chapters 2 and 3, might create difficulties in the boudoir. Generally speaking, EF finds residence in the more highly evolved part of the brain, called the *cerebral cortex*. As such, it acts as a sort of balance against the brain's older, less-evolved parts, namely the limbic system. That's our arousal center, our "animal instincts," controlling our sense of smell and emotions such as fear, aggression, and pleasure.

Left to its own devices, the limbic system is very stimulus-response oriented. There's a noise, and it jumps, so to speak. It doesn't stop to assess the situation first; it just reacts. The EF, however, allows us to pause and consider the wisest course of action, and apparently it's this "response gap" that makes us uniquely human. It also enables us to nurture and deepen a relationship past the time when stimulating novelty fades, and perhaps even makes us a more satisfyingly attentive and receptive lover.

Put another way, the process of human desire, when directed toward another person, involves more than simple reflex action. "It requires the coordination of higher and lower brain centers, emotion and logic, body and spirit," explains New York City psychiatrist Anthony Pietropinto, author of *Beyond The Male Myth* and *Not Tonight, Dear: How to Reawaken Your Sexual Desire*. And this essential coordination of efforts might pose a global challenge for your partner—until ADHD is identified and addressed.

Hyperfocus "presto, change-o": losing the loving feeling

After hanging back in the support group for a few months, John finally ventures forth with a comment: "The fact that my wife hasn't been interested in me sexually since our wedding night—that can be ADHD-related? What a relief! I thought that, too, was my fault."

In general, the term *hyperfocus* used in the context of ADHD refers to being so engrossed in a task or activity that everything else fades into the background, to the point that it ceases to exist. Sometimes, this offers advantages, such as when learning a new skill or solving a complex problem. Many other times, however, it's problematic. For example, the support group occasionally hears about the father with ADHD who has gotten so engrossed in a computer game, he loses track of the toddler encharged to his care.

In the early days of a courtship, however, the ADHD partner might find the stimulation he or she craves by hyperfocusing on a partner, lavishly showering attention and flattery, especially in the bedroom.

"Nothing is more stimulating to many of us, ADHD or not, than a new love," therapist Jonathan Halverstadt confirms. "But many folks with ADHD experience reality through *visceral* feelings—bodily understanding, not logical cognitive processes. Their body tells them what their brain can't." In the case of new love, they can far too easily confuse that surge of brain chemicals and hormones that create euphoria (those "new love feelings") with genuine, sustainable feelings of love for the person.

Remember: Living with untreated ADHD often means a person seldom feels "right" inside—calm, focused. Only stimulation provides that sense of well-being. And the stimulation that springs from a new romance can inspire men and women with ADHD to do the most thoughtful, grand, sweet, and loving things, *because it makes them feel better*. "Of course they also do these things to please their partner, but the biggest reason is to self-medicate their brains," Halverstadt maintains.

When the biochemical tidal-wave ebbs, as it eventually must, passion rolls out with it. Yet, don't expect the adults who experience this phenomenon to always verbalize or even recognize this explanation. All they know is what their body tells them, he warns. They no longer physically *feel* in love; therefore, they must not *be* in love. They simply can't fathom that new-love euphoria does not last forever and that deeper, calmer roots must take hold for courtship to mature into a more sustaining bond.

Left standing on dry ground, and clueless about their self-medicating romantic pattern, some ADHD partners blame the loss of love on the small defects they finally spot in the love interest. Adding insult to injury, they might even complain of being misled or fooled. In an ironic twist, their love interest might feel the same way, because when the novelty fades and the hyperfocus stops on a dime, ADHD symptoms suddenly rush to the fore. Too often, though, their love interest will take such complaints to heart and, in a desperate bid to regain that lost ocean of affection, try to repair those defects. Typically, such efforts are doomed to fail because the perceived defects aren't the problem.

"My husband has been unwilling to explain the lack of our sexual relationship, even to say that he doesn't know why," Amelia offers to illustrate this point. "He simply refuses to acknowledge my feelings of rejection." Initially, her husband said that he couldn't have sex when he felt angry with her. Eventually, she saw that as a red herring: "We had the same problem when we were on good terms. I've learned that it has nothing to do with me and everything to do with his brain chemistry."

If your ADHD partner follows this pattern, he or she might start seeking stimulating brain-fuel elsewhere, breaking up with you or having affairs—either actual or with pornographic images, e-mail exchanges, or in virtual worlds online. For some, the hyperfocus simply shifts to new hobbies or interests. That's what happened with Roxanne, who had wrongly assumed that her macho ex-boyfriend's libido would never flag.

> He's only 28 and one of those rugged big ol' construction guys. But we stopped being intimate after only a few months, and he never would discuss it. He had rushed me hard, wanting to get married within months after meeting, even talking about kids. Then nothing. My friend said that he must be gay, but he's not. He does that with everything—gets very interested and then moves on to the next thing.

Again, the early days of love stimulate *everyone's* biochemistry, ADHD or not. But as those feelings naturally fade, some people make the transition into a more grounded bonding of shared values, interests, and attraction. Others, however, stay "addicted to love" and keep seeking a new supply. If your ADHD partner fits this description, such knowledge won't immediately improve your sex life, but it might help minimize your feelings of hurt and sexual rejection.

Tip Sheet: Off the Coaster, Back Into the Tunnel of Love

When it comes to intimacy, as with any other facet of life, medication can help the person with ADHD be less impulsive, less hyperactive, and less distractible. But contrary to what some ADHD partners assume, it's not simply a matter of popping a pill and making a bee line for the bedroom.

ADHD Partner Survey respondents who reported an improved sex life after their ADHD partners started taking stimulant medication attributed the uptick to a better domestic life in general—co-parenting, employment, driving, managing finances, and the like. In other words, increased good will and cooperation outside the bedroom often translates into better intimacy and vice-versa.

Keep in mind that some medications used for treating ADHD's coexisting conditions may affect sexuality in a negative or positive way. For example, certain SSRI antidepressants may decrease libido or inhibit orgasm—or, they may help prevent early ejaculation. Be sure to talk with your physician; adjustments in the type of SSRI, the time that it's taken, or the dosage typically can make a difference.

More Mystifying Twists and Turns

For years, I didn't truly realize how my wife's ADHD was destroying our relationship. I could deal with absent-mindedness. Only later, though, did I connect ADHD to her tendency to blame and pick fights.

— CARLOS

Support-group members diligently read books and articles about adult ADHD. When baffling behaviors remain unexplained, they turn to each other to compare notes, trying to determine if certain puzzling behavior patterns are "an ADHD thing" or a personality quirk particular to their individual partners. For example:

- "Does your partner complain about clothing textures or labels?"
- "Does stating what you want to your partner constitute starting an argument?"
- "Is the TV volume always turned up extra loud?"
- "Do you ever get time to yourself, or does your partner follow you around all the time?"
- "Do you find that even your most trivial comments are countered?"

Inevitably, they discover similarities in their ADHD partners that aren't mentioned in the official diagnostic criteria or popular press.

"It came as such a relief to hear that others have similar puzzling experiences with their ADHD partners," Jeanette remembers. "I thought I was losing my mind or imagining things." When you're living in a whirlwind of confusing phenomenon—where your partner insists that up is down and green is orange—it's easy to get confused.

The behavior patterns we explore in this chapter are *not* universal, but they are common enough. Your jaw might drop with recognition, or you might say, "But my partner doesn't do *any* of these things." That's because these patterns have a variety of causes; some are associated with brain-based ADHD challenges and others with not-so-effective coping mechanisms, as explained in Chapter 3.

Surprisingly, though, a few patterns spring from unwitting attempts to stimulate an understimulated brain, according to psychiatrist Daniel Amen, an assistant clinical professor of psychiatry at the University of California, Irvine, School of Medicine psychiatrist, and author of many books and audio-video programs about the brain. He is also the founder and medical director of Amen Clinics, Inc. In the second part of this chapter, Amen details common self-medicating behaviors and offers advice for avoiding conflict escalation with someone who seems intent on it.

Even your own ignorance about ADHD can contribute to the problem, as you unknowingly react in ways that make matters worse. Yet, for some of these behaviors, trying to figure out the "whys" behind them is almost as befuddling as living with them! Support-group members just want them to stop, and in large part, these behaviors do tend to disappear with ADHD awareness and treatment.

The findings explored in this chapter are grouped into two parts:

- *Field Notes from the Front Lines:* Quirky patterns reported by support-group members, from "Saturday Morning Fight Syndrome" to the "It's Your Fault Delusion"
- *Conflict as Self-Medication:* Real-life examples that illustrate conflict-provoking behaviors

Whatever their cause, it's important to recognize, understand, and stop reacting to these behaviors before they negatively affect your brain.

Field Notes from the Front Lines

"You mean your ADHD partner does that, too?" goes the refrain. Here are the most commonly observed examples of "does that, too"—presented in no particular order, with no reliable statistics on occurrence, and mostly just for fun. (But in humor lies truth!)

The "Following You Around Like a Puppy" State

Some ADHD partners' presence around the house falls into either of two extreme categories:

- *Prolonged unannounced disappearances*—"The kids call their dad Disappearing Man," says one support-group member. "I think he just loses track of himself or needs to zone out."

- *Sticking to you like a shadow*—Another member calls this the "You're everywhere I want to be" symptom. "Everywhere I turn, he's there, psychologically tugging at me, wanting my attention, as if he'll cease to exist without it."

Given the second situation, chores take three times as long, frustration simmers, and there's no time to catch your breath and regroup. Some report feeling guilty about wanting time away from their partners. Going to work can feel like a vacation.

The "You Have ADHD, Too!" Phenomenon

Adriana is worried. Her guy has turned the tables, saying that *she* has ADHD. The worst part is, she can hardly disagree! She is having trouble focusing at work, and her home office brims with unfinished projects. This scattered state of mind, however, is new for her, a result of living with her boyfriend's untreated ADHD symptoms. At a recent get-together with longtime girlfriends, they remarked that Adriana seems to be in constant motion these days. "It's true," she says. "Since I started living with Michael, I am so anxious I've become a nervous wreck."

The "Criticizing What I Can't Do" Complex

When Rose's husband joined friends for indoor rock-climbing, he returned home grumbling about this "useless activity." Later, Rose learned from the friends that he could not perform the left-right maneuvers with the rope. Then she read that ADHD's potential neurospatial deficits include confusing left and right. "No wonder he was frustrated," she realizes now. That prompted a larger revelation. Her husband has been negative about many activities throughout his life simply because he could not do them.

The "It's Your Fault!" Delusion

If bad outcomes are never your ADHD partner's fault, that leaves only a few other candidates: the boss, the coworkers, and *you*. (And sometimes the traffic cop.) "My guy always oversleeps for work and then is angry that he's overslept," Blaine says. "If I attempt to wake him in time, he blames me for nagging him. But if I don't, he blames me for making him lose his job." If she sets the alarm so that the wake-up comes from a "neutral" source, she ends up resetting and resetting.

The "Nobody Else Has Trouble With Me" Defense

Erin's husband repeated this phrase whenever she voiced a problem with him, and she believed it until talking to his ex-wife. "He's telling me the same things he'd told her when they were married," she says. "Of course, it's never *him* creating problems."

Sometimes, though, it is true that other people don't have any problems with your ADHD partner. But that still doesn't mean that *you're* the fly in the relationship ointment. It could be simply that your partner stays on "best behavior" with everyone else—and flies the freak flag only at home. On the other hand, your partner might not realize (or remember) when others actually do register complaints about his or her behavior. Owing to brain-based difficulties reading social cues and self-observation (and sometimes clouded by overoptimism), your partner might assume the best and ignore the rest.

The "Tossing Almost-Empty Containers" Aversion

Leslie asks a burning question, unsure if this is a Mars-Venus thing or an ADHD thing. "Okay, why does *nothing* get put back where it belongs, *except* when it's empty and should be tossed?" Support-group members immediately recognize this phenomenon as it plays out in their kitchens:

- The cereal box with two lone flakes
- The carton containing three drops of milk
- The Chinese take-out leftovers from the Ming dynasty

Those with female partners quickly dispel the gender connection. As Jeff says, "Every so often, I just pull up the garbage can, hold my nose, and start dumping. I can understand the forgotten leftovers and so on. But when my wife puts something back, knowing it's already bad or empty? *That* I don't get."

Members put their heads together, trying to puzzle out what's happening in their cupboards or refrigerators based on their understanding of ADHD challenges, aiming for comedic relief in the process:

- *Black-and-white thinking*—"Something came from the fridge so something goes back in it."
- *Taxing decision-making*—"If you consume the last bit, an unspoken pact says that you must do something with it—replace it, recycle it, toss it. Too much decision-making for my husband! He leaves a drop so that technically he didn't *finish* it."
- *Poor follow-through*—"Whatever cabinet door or drawer my partner opens stays open until I close it. Similar principle with food. Once it goes into the fridge, it stays until it's eaten."
- *Reminder strategy*—"I think Alan leaves the empty container so that I will know it needs replacing, as a sort of placeholder. He wouldn't

notice or remember if something were missing, so he assumes I can't, either. Of course, I can't tell we're out of something unless he throws away the container!"

- *All of the above, from untreated ADHD*—"My husband stopped doing this when he started taking medication. Before that, though, he conjured up fanciful explanations. My favorite was 'It's too sad,' like he'd become deeply attached to his close friend, the peanut butter jar. I was so desperate to make sense of his eccentricities that I believed him. Yet he's also so sensitive that he hates my pruning the roses. 'Stop hurting them!' he says.

The "Saturday Morning Fight" Syndrome

When Angela married 10 years ago, she jokingly nicknamed her husband *Pazzo di Sabato*—Italian for the "Saturday Nut." A few years later, his behavior wasn't funny in any language. Now that he has been diagnosed with ADHD, Angela's connected the dots: "The workweek provided him with structured routine, and the weekend was the wild card." Indeed, facing unstructured time can send some people with ADHD into a panic. In fact, in one study, youngsters with ADHD reported feeling stressed on the weekends more than 10 times as often as comparison children.[19]

Making transitions is another factor in ADHD challenges—shifting focus from work to home, work to fun, or work to chores. To summon the adrenaline necessary to meet that challenge, some subconsciously pick a fight. The likely neurological underpinnings of "Saturday Morning Fight Syndrome" manifest in other phenomena, too, as you'll learn next.

ADHD Partner Survey Snapshot: Conflict

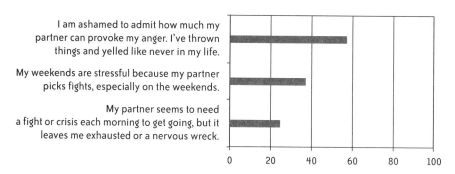

Conflict as "Self-Medication"

For Kimberly, here's the hardest thing to understand about her husband. It doesn't matter how accommodating she is, how hard she tries to avoid doing things that would make him angry; as long as he *wants* to be angry, he will find a reason. Moreover, he wants to get angry a lot, and he will always find a way to make his anger *her* fault. Then when he finally succeeds in provoking her anger and she loses her temper, she'll suffer more accusations from him about *her* anger-management problem. Kimberly ends up feeling ashamed yet defensive because, she says, "Most people have no idea how determined some people with ADHD can be at provoking others."

This apparent desire to be angry, and to provoke an angry response in others, can result from the ADHD partner's biologically based need for stimulation, according to psychiatrist Daniel Amen. "Being mad, upset, angry, negative, or even oppositional immediately stimulates the brain's frontal lobes," he explains. "These behaviors can produce increasing amounts of adrenaline in the body, stimulating not only heart rate, blood pressure, and muscle tension but also brain activity. And many people with ADHD might pick on others to get a rise out of them." As Kimberly puts it: "My husband gets his adrenaline kick. But I just plain feel kicked."

It's hard to believe, isn't it? That fighting can make some people feel calmer, *and* that they would be unaware of that fact. But believe it.

We asked support-group members for personal examples of the following self-medicating patterns that Amen, a brain-imaging specialist, outlines in his book *Healing ADD: The Breakthrough Program That Allows You to See and Heal the Six Types of ADD*. "Until I read about these behaviors," Gail says, "my husband and I—and our therapists—had thought that much more than ADHD was going on here. Learning about this pattern of fighting and stimulation was our lifeline to sanity."

See if you can recognize any of these self-medicating patterns:

"Let's have a problem"

Lucy, who operates a business with her husband, sums it up this way: "Every morning, it's as if he can't start work until he's put his mark on my day, the way a dog marks his territory." He gets energized for focusing on work by negatively obsessing on imaginary business problems until her energy gets ground down to a nub. It took years for Lucy to realize what was happening. By then he'd sabotaged their best business opportunities. Now they struggle to hold on.

"No, no way, never, you can't make me"

Oppositional behavior—for example, disagreeing with whatever the other person says or refusing any request—can also increase adrenaline in the brain of some people with ADHD, Amen says. But again, for the partner, it's extremely draining. Shelby says her ex-husband frequently went into "automatic no mode": "I could ask nicely or blow my stack and it made no difference. The whole point was that he refused to do it—take out the trash, come to dinner, or something more important. I called him Mr. No."

"I say the opposite of what you say"

You could call this a subcategory of oppositionality. Or, you could call it the weather report. That's because even the safest of topics, like the weather, can unleash a storm. "If I just casually mentioned it's hot outside, my husband would insist it's *not* hot outside," Madeleine says. "Then for hours he would attempt to prove me wrong." A friend once commented that Madeleine's husband would argue with a brick wall. "Thank God that this self-medicating behavior went away when he started legitimate medication," she says. "He even has actual conversations now; you know, the back-and-forth kind, instead of delivering monologues."

"My thoughts are more terrible than yours"

More than half of the ADHD Partner Survey respondents agreed with this statement: "Nothing's ever about me. If I had a bad day, my partner had a worse day." For some ADHD partners, hyperfocusing on all the gory details of their bad days can prove vivifying, but it's a real downer for their mates.

In his practice, Amen notes that he's seen many people with ADHD who display expertise in picking out the most negative thoughts possible. Then they focus on them as if they'd have no mental energy to function otherwise (possibly the case!). He's coined the term ANTs for these *automatic negative thoughts* and warns his patients that self-stimulating with negativity is a dangerous and isolating game.

"I say the first thing that comes to mind"

Some people are stunned at what their ADHD partners blurt out in private, in public, at office parties. Trina and her boyfriend of six months were walking down the street when he said, "Wow, that girl's much prettier than you are." When she expressed feeling hurt by his comment, he snapped that she was making a big deal out of nothing. (Trina is starting to think the same of the relationship.) "How can he just say those things to me and think I won't be hurt?" she asks. "What's more, where does he get off, being irritated by *my* hurt feelings?"

Many of Amen's patients with ADHD proudly proclaim they are "brutally honest." That's nothing to brag about, he reminds them, because relationships require tact. This behavior might initially spring from impulsivity, but it then becomes a feel-good habit. "It's as though my boyfriend gets a charge out of the shocked look on people's faces when he blurts out these things," Trina says.

"Let's call it even"

Amen calls this a game of deflection, wherein the individual with ADHD adopts the complaint someone has made about them and hurls it back at that person. This maneuver may not seem overtly self-stimulating; the adrenal kick comes with the challenge of mounting a good defense. As we've all heard, the best defense is a good offense.

Randi experienced this when she told her boyfriend she'd appreciate more help around the house. "You just *think* I don't do anything," he responded, "but I do things that you don't even notice." Asked for specifics, he said that he takes out the garbage and, oh, other things that he can't think of right now. Then he got very worked up about it, dramatically sighing in exasperation, before launching into a lengthy lecture that "It takes two people to run a household, you know." It's amazing, Randi says, "because he really thinks I'll be fooled into believing him if he's insistent enough, and darn it, for too long I *was*."

"I bet I can get you to yell at me or hit me"

Pushed to the brink by their ADHD partners, even formerly mild-mannered people end up screaming, flinging something, or worse. Gwen, who has been there, tries to explain: "When someone is pushing, pushing, pushing you, just dying for a fight, when they won't get out of your face, well, you just have to live with it to understand it." It's as though the adult with ADHD senses a person's most vulnerable issues and works on them until there is an explosion, Amen notes.

Consider ADHD Partner Survey respondents' major reasons for breaking off their relationships: "More fighting than I've ever experienced" and "more fighting than I could stand."

Tip Sheet: Don't Take the Bait!

It used to be that Dave argued with his wife because he thought it would help them work through their conflicts: "Our couples therapist said that fighting is healthy. Finally, however, I learned there is nothing to resolve! I had to face the fact that my wife's brain tends to creates conflict out of thin air."

Remember that many fight-provoking patterns actually involve unconscious attempts to self-medicate—to get calm, to physically feel better. When you "take the bait," you reinforce the pattern of fighting so that your partner can feel "medicated." You also fall vulnerable to your partner saying, "Just look at yourself; you're losing it." Your partner assumes the demeanor of a Zen master, and you're left looking like a babbling nincompoop.

"Real" medication often stops this type of provocation cold, but Amen also advises remembering these points:

- *You needn't be your ADHD partner's "medicine"*

Your anger needn't supply the fuel for his or her frontal lobes, he says. Ongoing conflict is not healthy for either of you. When you don't react to the provocation, the provocateur typically stops trying.

Gwen admits it wasn't easy to wean her husband off his "fix" of punching her buttons. "Twice in two days he tried to get to me and couldn't. I did get hot under the collar and felt like crying, but I didn't so I felt strong." Her new motto is: "I don't have to attend every argument I'm invited to." When she feels the pattern developing, Gwen simply walks out of the room, saying "I love you and I'm not going to fight with you about this."

- *When provoked, delay and cool down*

Don't counterattack. "I know it's really hard, because you feel attacked and belittled," Amen acknowledges. "You're just incensed by the level of injustice, so counterattack is your first reaction. But then you get pounded for the counterattack." So, what could you do instead?

- Take a deep breath.
- If you are very upset, go for a walk. If you choose to invite your partner, say nothing for the first half of the walk. "By then, your partner will be getting more blood flow to the brain and be able to engage in a more reasonable conversation," Amen says.
- Try the "Bathroom Technique." This is where you say, "I really want to hear what you have to say, but I need to go to the bathroom first." Then you bring a big book to read while tempers cool. From behind the door, you can mumble, "My stomach's not feeling well" because it's probably true, Amen points out. When you're upset, your stomach's probably upset, too.

PART TWO

Roller Coaster Whiplash and G-Force Confusion: How many Plunges Before You Say, "Whoa!"

*The Predictable Stress Responses
and Poor Coping Strategies That You Experience
When Your Partner Has ADHD—
But at Least One of You Has No Clue*

*What an emotional roller coaster. Just when I am ready to
pack my bags and move out, she becomes nice again and
promises to change. My friends think I am a door mat or needy.
But frankly I'm so confused and worn out that I believe
her each time she says things will be different. The fact is, she's
very convincing—I think because she sincerely believes it, too.*

—MICHAEL

*After two years of arguing with my new wife about her
saying or doing inconsiderate things, we read an article
about ADHD. After being diagnosed, she tried medication
and life was good! Now, she's decided she doesn't need it,
and it's back to the roller coaster.*

—JACK

*Ack! I feel like I've been living on a roller coaster. I never know
whether my husband will be up or down, loving or critical.
His mood swings often and unpredictably. Before he was diagnosed,
I blamed myself for our unhappiness, because he convinced
me that was true. He's always been good in sales.*

—SUZANNE

*I've been off the roller coaster for six months. With distance,
I see that things really were as bad as I thought, but my boyfriend
had kept talking me out of it. Finally I figured out the connection
to ADHD, and he was diagnosed. But he was opposed to treatment.
Opposed to cooperation. Opposed to me, the sun, the moon,
and the stars. That's why he's my ex-boyfriend.*

—LESLIE

Introduction

The Three Plunges of the ADHD Roller Coaster

For Jeanne, knowledge that her husband had ADHD came two days after their 30th anniversary—and one week after 30 years of poor judgments culminated in one huge disaster. Kenneth had finally managed to create a massive crisis, racking up huge debts on credit cards he'd opened secretly. That compelled her to issue an ultimatum: Get help or get out.

Her entire married life, Jeanne lived with the anxiety of knowing that, even if life went well for a few weeks or even months, the other shoe would always drop; it was just a matter of time before Kenneth managed to create a new problem. "Who but a centipede—and Kenneth—could have as many 'other shoes'," she jokes, calling on the sanity-saving humor common to even the most frazzled support-group members.

As she and Kenneth raised their family, Jeanne developed the habit of personally keeping all the balls in the air, constantly thinking ahead to contingency plans for when Kenneth failed to show up, forgot to keep promises made to the kids (or forgot that he had ever made the promises), lost another job, or lost his temper. Trouble was, Kenneth could toss as many balls as he could drop other shoes, ultimately overwhelming Jeanne's prodigious coping capacity and juggling skills. (As for the shoes, even Imelda Marcos herself couldn't have kept up with them.)

Hanging on Until the Kids Go to College

Allowing herself to look back now, Jeanne says she long felt trapped in a joyless marriage: "It was a never-ending cycle of our battling over what I now see clearly as Kenneth's unrecognized ADHD, and it took an immense toll on the kids and me." As she focused on creating family stability,

Kenneth seemed focused on upending it. She was just hanging on until the children went to college. "I thought it would be the wrong message to send them, to bolt when the going gets rough," she says. "But now I see how we can rationalize anything. We gave new meaning to the phrase *dysfunctional family.*"

Kenneth held 20 sales jobs in 30 years, leaving because he was fired or because he grew bored and sought a get-rich-quick opportunity. "Looking back, he says he always figured that his debts would go away if he made more money," says Jeanne, whose salary supported the family without interruption. "He never saw that his poor spending habits simply got bigger, too." Couples who didn't seem to fight about money left her in awe.

Fathers who were patiently instructive with their children left her feeling guilty. She knew that her husband loved their two sons, but, based on how he treated them, she wasn't sure *they* knew that. Kenneth sprang to best behavior when their sons' friends dropped by the house, becoming the life of the party for hours. But when he was alone with his family, he mostly sulked around in shutdown mode or watched TV—a relief compared to the times when he played the martinet, issuing orders right and left.

Jeanne says that one of the worst parts was keeping their struggles private: "Kenneth is so witty and charming in public, I figured everyone would assume I was being a shrew if I voiced any troubles with this *great guy.*" She hid her emotions for so long she ceased to feel them. "I lost the ability to cry years ago; just no more tears left. Mostly, I felt dead to everything around me."

Seeing Again the Man She Fell in Love With

As it turns out, Jeanne wasn't the only one bearing secret turmoil. In a counseling session soon after being diagnosed, Kenneth mentioned that he felt he had always lived a secret life—covering his mistakes, concocting excuses, pretending to be in control when he was not. He never wanted to *look* as pathetic as he *felt.*

"I know what he means," Jeanne says. "Hiding money from him was another part of my secret life." She was not going to let his fiscal recklessness squander their children's stability. "Still, having a secret account made me feel dishonest, which I am not," she says. But what was the alternative? Kenneth always viewed her efforts to save for the future as depriving *him* now. "Over the years, I let his problems, and my trying to compensate for them, completely erode and distort not only my priorities but my self-perception."

Jeanne and Kenneth had sought marital counseling many times over the years. He had even been treated, unsuccessfully, for depression. The ADHD diagnosis surprised them both. Fortunately, Kenneth is showing strong commitment to treatment. "I'm seeing again the person I fell in love with 30 years ago," Jeanne says, "and we are both working to repair years of damage from 30 years of living in ignorance about ADHD."

Jeanne's is only one of the thousands of "roller coaster stories" told by support-group members of all backgrounds and ages—and dealing with various points on the ADHD spectrum, from "mild" to "hot." Jeanne and Kenneth wrestled with this invisible enemy for 30 years, and that's fairly common. In fact, you'll find three more first-person stories in Appendix C from members who were married for decades before ADHD was even suspected, following commonly reported trajectories from courtship to senior citizenship.

Part One of this book explained ADHD's more challenging aspects to illustrate that your partner probably wasn't *trying* to drive you crazy; it just felt that way. But neither were you imagining things.

No, you can't blame *all* your relationship troubles on ADHD, psychiatrist Daniel Amen advises, "but it's so helpful to understand the challenges particular to your partner's ADHD and know that the behavior is not about you." That said, just as your partner might have developed many poor coping strategies over decades of living with undetected ADHD, you might have developed your own poor coping strategies in reaction to your partner's behaviors, never knowing about ADHD.

That's why Part Two focuses on *you.*

Funny thing about roller coasters: Some thrill you, but others cause whiplash. The anticipation that builds as your little cart clatters up the incline can fill you with glee—or terror. It all depends on what you've learned to expect is coming up next: a graceful, exhilarating drop or an out-of-control plunge. Even post-plunge, you might be reassured to find that the ride soon flattens out and things seem okay for a while. Next thing you know, the uphill tension mounts until the bottom falls out again.

Your own particular ADHD roller coaster ride might mostly radiate humor and affection because your cart never flies off the rails. Perhaps that's because your partner has "ADHD Lite" or good coping skills—or both. Or maybe it's because you both have developed strong ADHD awareness and your partner has sought treatment. But if none of that is true for your situation and your cart *does* occasionally fly off the rails, know that it typically takes more than breezy "tips" to get you back on solid ground.

Our guide to Part Two is Santa Barbara-based psychologist Herbert Gravitz, known for his work in systemic traumatology, specifically the impact of disorders such as alcoholism, bipolar disorder, and ADHD on family members. A Fellow of the American Academy of Experts in Traumatic Stress, he has authored numerous books, including *Trauma and Adversity: Triumph's Crucible* and *Obsessive Compulsive Disorder: New Help for the Family*.

"Any serious illness, addiction, or trauma creates remarkably similar effects for partners and all family members," Gravitz explains. "Physical illness, though, engenders more legitimacy because it's more *real* to outsiders." Your new support-group member friends know full well that the ride is real, and you'll hear from them throughout this section.

He breaks down the effect into roughly three progressive stages of *stress responses,* each stage associated with intensified efforts to cope. We call these stages the Three Plunges of the ADHD roller coaster, and the following three chapters examine each:

- **First Plunge: Explaining the Inexplicable.** Faced with confusing actions and excuses, you try to make sense of it all (Chapter 8).
- **Second Plunge: Managing the Unmanageable.** Your prolonged attempts to cope result in destructive patterns that worsen over time (Chapter 9).
- **Third Plunge: Breaking Down in Illness or Through to Truth.** Your brain and body are telling you it's time to slow the roller coaster—or exit entirely (Chapter 10).

You might find this section validating, or painful, or both. But until you face the reality of how your partner's ADHD has affected *you,* there is a tendency to stay immobilized. The goal is to face reality head on so you can move forward in a positive way.

"Once you acknowledge your suffering, you can confront your central therapeutic issue: taking care of yourself," Gravitz says. "Then you can move beyond victimization and accept responsibility for becoming the person you want to be. You become the architect of a new life."

First Plunge:
Explaining the Inexplicable

I know life throws us curveballs. That I can take. But when your partner is a curveball, it just gets so confusing.

— MELISSA

Juanita knew nothing of adult ADHD or why her second husband changed so suddenly just months after their marriage. They'd dated for two years, and she never saw this behavior—his constant forgetfulness, denial that he forgot anything, and yelling at her children. Her spirits sank as her fears rose for her children's lost feelings of security. "Everyone said that the stepparent relationship takes time and adjustment, so I hung in there, looking for logical explanations and trying to fix it," she says. "I figured he would soon settle down. Instead, he got worse."

When faced with confusing and disorienting behaviors, humans cope by first trying to "explain the inexplicable," filling the gaps however we can, says psychologist and trauma expert Herbert Gravitz. And so we find ourselves on the first major plunge on the ADHD roller coaster, the first set of stress responses and poor coping strategies commonly experienced when dealing with a partner's unrecognized ADHD. You might find yourself:

- Denying and minimizing your initial reaction to dysfunctional behavior, as you try to fit together the puzzle pieces.
- Enabling dysfunctional behavior as you try to compensate for your partner's weaknesses.
- Developing a high tolerance for dysfunctional behavior, also known as "Frog-in-the-Pot Syndrome."
- Ratcheting up efforts to solve problems even as problems grow more complex and insoluble.

- Walking on eggshells, hoping to avoid triggering your partner's anger and irritability.
- Developing a sense of hypervigilance, waiting for the bit of chaos that you are sure looms on the horizon.
- Becoming isolated emotionally and psychologically.

Denying and Minimizing

The human brain is programmed to solve mysteries by fitting the pieces together in a way that seems logical. Lacking solid information about ADHD, however, you're missing a big piece of your relationship puzzle. Initially, many support-group members told themselves the problems weren't so bad, nothing they couldn't handle. "Denial and minimization spring from a mixture of love, fear, anger, and guilt," Gravitz says.

Four more factors can fog clarity and provide fertile ground for your denial and minimization to take root:

1. The stimulation of courtship can fuel "best behavior"

Chapter 6 explained how sexual intimacy can dim as new-relationship novelty fades, but waning stimulation plays out in other ways, too.

"Everyone knows that the honeymoon period fades, but with my wife it was more of a switch turning off," Michael explains. "For two years of dating, things were incredible; she was alive and fun. We married, and, almost overnight, she turned into a different person—snappy, irritable, and often quite mean." He attributed the turnabout to the most obvious variable: the birth control pills that she'd started taking. When she stopped taking the pills, however, the problematic patterns remained. In her eyes, that placed the blame squarely at Michael's feet.

Michael wanted to be fair. *Was* he imagining things? Had *his* behavior changed? Was this simply the natural course, that couples stop being on best behavior? The truth is, Michael was *not* imagining things. In fact, psychologist Arthur Robin, an authority on how ADHD affects couples and families and a professor of psychiatry and behavioral neurosciences at Wayne State University, has written about this phenomenon:[20]

> The honeymoon can end abruptly for couples when a spouse has undiagnosed ADHD. When they settle down and begin building a life together, the spouse with ADHD stops hyperfocusing on the relationship and the romance tends to dissipate. The spouse without ADHD often feels as if the spouse with ADHD has flipped a switch or has two personalities and can't believe the sudden change

when the spouse with ADHD turns off the charm and stops hiding his or her ADHD symptoms.

The forgetfulness, disorganization, and inattention become very apparent, and neither spouse has a context in which to understand these characteristics. They both draw negative conclusions about each other's motives and behaviors. Arguments and disagreements develop and the couple develops negative patterns of communication and ineffective methods of conflict resolution.

Not every ADHD partner behaves this way during courtship—or, for that matter, changes drastically when the relationship matures—but if you've experienced it, you know how confusing it is. Especially if your partner blames the downshift on you for losing your exciting sparkle. Especially if many other destabilizing behaviors are happening at the same time.

2. Good times might continue until a big change happens
The first job. The first baby. A mortgage. The second baby. A sick parent. As adult responsibilities mount, your ADHD partner's ability to cope might max out. If you don't know that, however, you might rationalize that those events can be stressful for everyone and that your partner will eventually adjust.

3. Some red flags can be viewed as benignly charming
Nicole sensed that something was "off" with her future husband, but what? He didn't do anything creepy or crazy. It was more like living in one of those "What's wrong with this picture?" games for children. "You know, you spy a violin in a tree and have to decide if that's strange or wrong," she offers. "But if someone is sitting in the tree, playing that violin? Why, that could be very lovely and imaginative."

Maybe you maturely remind yourself that nobody's perfect. Support-group members whose ADHD partners possess a keen humor or high intelligence figured that a little "oddness" is the trade-off in having an interesting companion.

4. The "Love is all you need" denial and minimization
You tell yourself to forgive and forget, to give 150 percent. Perhaps you suspect that your partner's problems stem from not-so-loving parents. "As things started getting tough with my new wife, I thought the answer was simply to love her, love her, love her," Bruce says. "But the more I accommodated her unreasonable demands, the more out-of-control our lives

became." Unfortunately, love is not enough to treat diabetes or nearsightedness, and it's not enough to treat adult ADHD, either.

5. Your ADHD partner fails to validate your perceptions

"It doesn't help that some people with ADHD are full of denial and minimization," Gravitz points out. Indeed, almost half of the ADHD Partner Survey respondents agreed with the statement, "For too long, I accepted my partner's blame for everything. He/she can be very convincing."

The fact is, your partner truly might not see the problems or, feeling incapable of solving them, shuts down or pushes off the blame. Sometimes, your partner's sheer confidence that inappropriate actions are appropriate means you talk yourself out of your own good sense. James worries about the family's financial future as his wife's spending continues unabated:

> I feel like the Dutch boy and the dike: plugging holes to keep us solvent. But to her, it's a mystery why I seem so obsessed with sticking my finger in that gray wall. It's like she's saying, "Dike? What dike? Water? What water? All I see is you and that boring wall! Why can't we just have fun and let the wall take care of itself?" I know she's wrong, but she tries hard to make me feel like a spoilsport, and she has succeeded way too often. I tell her that I resent always being the adult who says no. Her response? "Well, stop saying no."

Martha—Who Helps the Helper?

My husband of 20 years is one of those "sparkly" people with ADHD, full of energy and creativity. He was diagnosed two years ago, along with my teen son. Now that we all know what's going on, life is better but I still find myself in a quandary. The two of them rely on me for organization and support, but I also have twin sons, 10, who don't have ADHD yet still need parenting, of course.

My husband opened a carpentry business and is doing very well, but because he's so disorganized, I work with him. It sucks every bit of my energy to keep him focused. Then I come home to the kids and try to maintain a peaceful, supportive home—not easy given Dad's unpredictable schedule. I've developed severe hives and have trouble sleeping. I know I need to maintain a sense of myself but how? I'd like to hire someone to help him, but right now, the money isn't there. He overinvested in equipment, and we'll be digging ourselves out from that debt for a while.

Enabling Dysfunctional Behavior

Gravitz sums up this common stress response neatly: "You do all the wrong things for all the right reasons."

> Longer-term goals tend to vanish, along with your peace of mind and ability to feel joy.

Take Michael. He entered marriage and fatherhood as a self-described enlightened male, equally sharing breadwinning and domesticities. "That was a poor strategy, with us not knowing about my wife's ADHD," he admits. He did his share and much more, including being the family's sole financial support after his wife announced her job was boring and quit. Prior to her diagnosis, Michael remembers having an image of being married to a rag doll. As long as he held her up, things were okay. But if he let go even for a second, he says, "It was like looking down and seeing the heap of a rag doll at my feet."

You might start enabling in small ways, perhaps assisting your partner with tasks, fixing mistakes, reminding, and attempting to boost your partner's low self-esteem. Finally it dawns on you. This student never *learns*, and, what's worse, might remain perfectly content (if sometimes resentful) to keep receiving your help. Forever.

Even if you spied red flags initially, you or your partner might have written them off to extenuating circumstances—a recent illness, a car accident, or mistreatment by an ex-employer or ex-partner. An ADHD partner's poor self-awareness and tendency to blame might further fog up the picture. So might this frequently heard promise: "I can improve; I just need to work on it."

Developing "Frog-in-the-Pot Syndrome"

Worn down by her husband's illogical arguments and irritability, Sally started accepting the inappropriate as appropriate and the illogical as logical. If your ADHD partner makes a new art form of defensive denial and blaming, it's easy for you to lose sight of what is truth versus delusion, your failing versus your partner's.

"It was like living in a mental house of mirrors, not knowing which perceptions I could trust," Sally remembers. "When my husband acted really loopy—full of misperceptions and anger over nothing—I began to see it as 'Oh no, he's opening the door to crazy again and he's making me come in after him.'" Would she find her way out again? Or would she eventually lose all clarity about what's reasonable?

Frankly, it's hard to be an equal partner *and* the reality referee. "I love my husband dearly," she says, "but neither he nor I would want to relive those days. His diagnosis and treatment means we're on an entirely better and clearer path."

Prolonged exposure to confusing, arbitrary, and stressful behavior can eventually mar our judgment, Gravitz points out. Group members call it "Frog-in-the-Pot Syndrome." It's said that a frog placed into a pot of boiling water will immediately leap out. But if the water is cool and pleasant when the frog enters it and it *gradually* heats up, the frog won't notice until it's too late, when it's little swollen brain creates paralysis. This fable warns us to pay attention not just to obvious, sudden threats but also to those that appear more gradually.

Like the little frog, your problems might have started subtly and slowly. As the "heat" turned up, perhaps you responded with the previous poor coping strategies, such as trying to explain the inexplicable. That is the froggie equivalent of saying, as the water seems to be getting warmer, "Is it hot in here or is it just me? Maybe I'm getting the flu? I'm sure it will cool down soon if I just stop focusing on it." Yet, until you figure out how ADHD is affecting your partner's interactions with you, you might sit in that hot pot until you are too stewed to move.

Ratcheting Up Your Problem-Solving Efforts

Before marrying in her mid-30s, experience had taught Kristin that most of life's challenges had straightforward solutions. Few problems came completely out of the blue or lay beyond her ability to solve. Then, she says, living with her husband put her in some sort of ADHD tailspin— "trying to figure out what he could possibly be thinking, what impossibly impractical impulsive moves he could be contemplating, so I could head him off at the pass with an individually tailored solution."

She worked feverishly to devise solutions that her husband would accept, understand, and not automatically oppose (or later sabotage). "He's the love of my life and he truly means well, but all this convolution got my head in such a whirl I ended up not thinking straight!" Kristin explains.

Whether it's traffic citations or unpaid bills, messages not relayed or messes covering every horizontal surface in your home, chaos conspires to keep you trapped in putting-out-fires mode. Longer-term goals tend to vanish, along with your peace of mind and ability to feel joy.

Gary's intensified coping efforts paved the way to depression

For three years, Gary's boyfriend insisted he would help more around the apartment *if* Gary told him exactly what to do and reminded him to do it. Yet Gary knew, based on experience, that his partner would vehemently resist such supervision: "Still, I doubted myself, thinking I was being an insensitive jerk because I wouldn't agree to what he insisted was a very reasonable demand. Looking back, that's when I slipped into depression, when I started questioning clear logic."

Holly's partner doesn't know the word "boundaries"

When Holly's new husband asked for her help in the morning finding his cell phone, she did so sweetly, reasoning that marriage and the new apartment must have disoriented him. After a few months, she gently suggested he find it himself. Setting limits, however, proved tricky. That's because when her husband said, "Have you seen my cell phone?" it was not a question. It meant, "Help find it or I will make your next hour living hell."

The stress he created looking for it, yelling and slamming things in frustration, sucked her in, Holly insists. "I paid a price either way, but the immediate price was his anger rippling through the house as I prepared for work—not the ideal way to start a productive day." Instead of standing her ground and remaining clear about individual responsibility, Holly tried to protect herself by stepping onto that slippery slope called *Not Making Things Worse*. Which brings us to the next coping mechanism.

Walking on Eggshells

Even for those people who tiptoe around trying to keep their ADHD partners calm and unprovoked, anger and toxic sniping can still erupt. "My wife's a loving mother in so many ways," Ed begins, "but when she gets in rant-and-rave mode, there's no stopping her. She's gonna blow, and the kids and I are all hostages." His wife will not consider an ADHD evaluation, despite a mother and two sisters who have been diagnosed but whose impairments are far stronger than hers. "I try to look at it like she's defragging her hard drive, but it doesn't make it easier," he says.

Like Ed, Evelyn realized only after joining a support group that her attempts to cope had forced her into a corner, constricting herself as *small* and undemanding as possible to keep the peace. "I grew up with the strong message that women are the peacemakers," she explains, "and if I couldn't make the peace in my own home, it was my fault. I was failing." When her husband went away on a business trip, she and her two teen daughters felt like little prairie dogs that pop out of their holes to bask in the sun. "The house was so calm and pleasant. Then he'd come back, and we'd dart back into our bunkers."

Developing Hypervigilance

Unpleasant surprises lead to fear of more unpleasant surprises. Trudy, casually opening the mail one day, is shocked to learn that her family's auto insurance policy is canceled because her husband forgot to mail the check, despite several reminders. Their daughter, who also has ADHD, is in hysterics because dad's playful roughhousing went too far. Again, incidents like this affect the entire family, so the realistic, protective tendency is to stay extremely vigilant.

Psychiatrist and ADHD expert Daniel Amen explains hypervigilance this way:

> It's like you're in a war. You feel like you're always fighting, always on edge. And you never know when the day is going to turn terrible because you can't predict it: You always have to watch, and that hypervigilance changes your brain. You become more anxious, more worried, more inflexible, and you start to hold yourself more rigidly. And, that only reinforces the partner's criticism. "You're overcontrolling," your partner says. You say, "What else can I be if you won't do anything?"

Staying on guard thus becomes another poor coping strategy, guaranteed to keep constricting one's physical and emotional world. Consider these examples:

Alex scans the horizon, hoping to prevent calamity

His wife insists she doesn't have ADHD. Yet, after 10 years of dealing with her constant and unacknowledged missteps and miscommunications, Alex observes, "I find myself not only treating *her* like a child—making sure she's heard me correctly, double-checking schedules, reminding her of important events—but I've also started doing the same thing with friends and clients who need no such help. I feel like an idiot when I do that, and, furthermore, it's exhausting!"

Rory learned to feel nervous once she felt relaxed

"There's not enough mental stimulation in *relaxed* for my ex-husband, so he always had to be goosing my reality with some calamity or other," Rory says. "I learned that it was better never to relax, because he'd always do something to knock me off my *relaxed* butt." She also learned to dread holidays and vacations. ("Clint could ruin a trip to the mailbox.")

For the first time in her married life, Rory reports not crying on her most recent birthday, and she credits that to her hypervigilance: "When I woke up, my first words after he said 'Happy Birthday' were, 'Don't ruin this one for me!'"

Peg stays on fire watch—and carries an extinguisher

"Imagine giving a child a cigarette lighter and turning him loose in your house," Peg offers. "He lights a fire; you rush to put it out. He lights another one; you put it out. You think you can breathe for a moment, but surprise, he has ignited three more!" The fires represent the messes created by her husband, a physician diagnosed with ADHD but refusing treatment.

The latest blaze is a bankruptcy from mismanaging his medical practice, despite assuring Peg that he was "on top of things." To not step in is to realize you *will* end up fixing an even bigger mess, one that invariably threatens mutual or family welfare, many support-group members insist. And Peg agrees: "That's why people in my situation can become screaming banshees about things other people consider 'little stuff.' Aside from being never-ending, the 'little stuff' forms only the tip of the iceberg."

Lori avoids adding to her partner's low self-esteem

"My sweet husband wanted a bigger bathroom, and, seven years later, there's still a big hole in the wall into the bedroom," Lori says. "Asking him to finish the project creates such a withering reaction about his 'failure' at finishing things, so I just live with it." And until she heard another support-group member mention it, she thought she was imagining a type of chaos energy field enveloping her husband and, by extension, her. "He doesn't mean to break things, but he does. His mom said the same thing about his dad, that he could break something just by being near it."

Becoming Isolated: It's Lonely at the Top

The higher your little coaster cart climbs, the smaller the world below seems. The normal life you once knew shimmers as a dim memory. The longer and rockier your roller coaster ride, the lonelier you become.

"Certainly many people with untreated ADHD suffer," psychologist Herbert Gravitz says. "Yet, what the literature calls the *secondary sufferer*— their partners and other family—they suffer, too, often in parallel ways. Yet, they often suffer alone and in silence."

Ralph—Yoo-hoo, Remember Me Down Here?

It seems that most people with untreated ADHD, including me before my recent diagnosis, are always at the end of their ropes. But here's how it is with my wife, who also has ADHD. She is in the center of her universe, turning every direction but never seeing me and my needs. Why? Because she's standing on my shoulders and never looks down! I think she climbed up there to get a better view and forgot where she was. It seems we can stand there, holding up our untreated ADHD partners the rest of our lives, never being noticed. Or we can drop them on their butts. Or we can just twist their toes so they jump down and say, "What'd you do that for?" At least we'll get noticed.

In fact, the partners of adults with ADHD often resemble an alcoholic's family members, says Gravitz, co-author of the landmark book *Recovery: A Guide for Adult Children of Alcoholics* and a founder of the National Association for Children of Alcoholics. The unpredictability of living "under the influence" of another person's disorder can create a very particular and restricted environment for the partner and children. "What's more, it's often saturated with stress, loss, trauma, and exhaustion, and it's a 24/7 job," he adds. For many, the following factors intensify isolation:

Your ADHD partner has two faces: public and private

To outsiders, Mark's wife is charismatic, vivacious, and smart. She used to be that way with Mark, too. "But after two years of marriage, I seldom see that side when we're alone," he says. "People would never imagine her other side—curt, distant, and lethargic until she gets angry, when she springs to life."

Unless your ADHD partner also behaves problematically with your friends and extended family members, they might suspect you're exaggerating your partner's at-home behavior and therefore offer little validation or support. As Lucy sums it up: "For the most part, my friends don't get it, and when they do, they get tired of it real fast!"

"Outsiders" misperceive you as the problem

Tracey often found herself damned if she did, damned if she didn't, and looking bad either way. If she reminded her husband of something, he'd snap, "Why do you repeat yourself all the time?" Yet, if she *didn't* remind him, he'd blame her for that, too. "Outsiders only saw a wife on her 'charming' husband's butt," Tracey recalls. "Even my family said, 'Why don't you give the poor guy room to breathe?'" In reality, *she* was never allowed to catch her breath. When she asked for a few minutes alone to focus on a task or simply relax, he peppered her with questions and requests. Fortunately, ADHD treatment two years into the marriage resolved such issues, but other couples live with them much longer.

If you have children with ADHD, too, you might suffer doubly from other people's misperceptions and judgments. "Before we realized my son had ADHD, he was kicked out of three nursery schools," Sherry confides. "The teachers implied that his behavior was my fault, which made me feel horribly guilty, on top of feeling I was failing in my marriage." When she attended her first support group for the parents of children with ADHD, she was welcomed with the tongue-in-cheek line, "This is the meeting where all the bad mothers get together."

Your ADHD partner's challenges limit your socializing

Like other adults with ADHD who are vexed by social cues, Brad's wife is friendship-challenged. She expects him to meet those needs, yet he has little free time after earning the money, paying the bills, and performing other household tasks. "If I do get together with friends, she becomes jealous and depressed," he explains, "but she's not interested in many activities or meeting people."

ADHD Partner Survey Snapshot: Feelings of Isolation

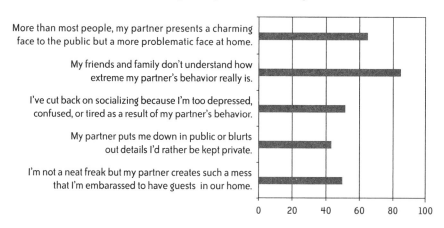

"Couples Troubles" or ADHD?

That ADHD can challenge adult relationships comes as old news to psychiatrist Paul H. Wender. He was among the first to identify and treat ADHD in children (40 years ago) and adults (30 years ago). Today he lectures in psychiatry at Harvard Medical School. Consider this excerpt from his book ADHD: Attention-Deficit Hyperactivity Disorder in Children and Adults *(2000). (Note: Wender uses the pronoun he, but issues cross gender lines.) These examples might represent moderate-to-strong ADHD, but they are commonly reported in support groups.*

The relationship between partners is often strained and "dysfunctional," and we suspect that relationships involving an ADHD partner break up more often than those that do not. Most of the origins of these (relationship) difficulties can readily be seen in the patients' ADHD traits. Their impulsivity, their temper, their failure to listen to their partner, and sometimes a lack of interpersonal sensitivity disturb their interpersonal relationships. These relationships are further stressed if the continuing obstinacy, bossiness, and stubbornness seen in many ADHD children are present.

Communication is difficult. The ADHD person does not attend to the other's conversation. He may tune out and drift off following his own train of thought. Not having listened, he may interrupt his spouse in response to his own thoughts. So the spouse has not been heard and is receiving a reply to a question not asked. Communication breaks down. Many ADHD couples have been treated for communication problems when the communication problem was one symptom of the underlying ADHD problems and not the sole cause of the current ones.

Unpredictable moodiness is difficult to live with. It is tiring to always be walking on eggs. It is likewise tiring to attempt to cheer up the unpredictably sad or try to get the overly enthusiastic partner to look at things realistically. The difficulty of living with a person with a hot temper is not hard to understand. However, the way the ADHD person handles his anger aggravates things. His anger is "a flash in the pan"; after expressing himself he feels fine in five to ten minutes. This is unlike his wife who may feel upset for the remainder of the day.

Disorganization, not planning ahead, can drive the non-ADHD partner wild. If he [the ADHD partner] is the household administrator, she may be repeatedly anxious and upset when bill collectors phone them (because he has forgotten to pay the bills) when credit card limits top out, and when bank accounts have vanished with impulsive buying. The familial disorganization, economic pressures, and job instability can combine to make the partner anxious, depressed, angry, and insecure.

Impulsivity in family decisions—taking or terminating a vacation on the spur of the moment, buying something they had agreed not to, commitments made and commitments broken on a moment's notice—can further aggravate the problem. And the problems may be harder to resolve because the ADHD person is both bossy and stubborn. The spouse cannot expect subtle and accurate perception by the ADHD patient. Like the children with ADHD, many adults with ADHD are socially imperceptive and self-centered. The self-centeredness does not mean they like themselves. It simply means they have not learned how to place themselves in other people's shoes. This lack of awareness by the ADHD patient further torments his spouse because he has a serious difficulty in understanding, empathizing, and recognizing the nature and intensity of her feelings.

The ADHD parent is likely to have difficulty with his children. His personality may make it very difficult for him to parent children who have no problems. Unfortunately, he is very likely to be the parent of children with problems, ADHD problems. His inconsistency, lack of follow-through, unpredictability, and temper may produce behavioral problems even in a child who has no ADHD symptoms.

Very frequently he does have an ADHD child and the interaction between his children and himself may repeat the relationship between his parents and himself as a child. This interaction can lead to a vicious circle, and the increased friction is likely to make all the predictable problems of childhood and adolescence worse.

The normal adolescent often experiences depression, often rebels, often experiments unwisely with sex and drugs. If that adolescent is reprimanded by an ADHD adult whose temper and unpredictability would place him at the low end of the parenting skills chart, severe problems are likely to arise out of ones that might have been temporary.

These parents tend to be dissatisfied with their lives in general. As a result of numerous unsatisfying experiences and defeats, they often have low self-esteem. As one patient who was a baseball fan observed, when your life is characterized by no hits, no runs, and plenty of errors, you do not have a terrific view of yourself.

Reprinted by permission of Oxford University Press, Inc.

Congratulations! Or is it condolences? You made it through the ADHD roller coaster's First Plunge into uncertainty and doubt—a state of losing your sense of direction and wondering why the people strolling far below don't realize that your arm-waving means "Help me!" and *not* "Woo-hoo! I'm having a great time!"

After surviving this first set of stress responses and poor coping strategies, did you realize that you and your partner might be dealing with ADHD and take steps to smooth the ride? Or, did you hunker down in your little coaster cart, determined to try harder to fix things, and not realizing that the next unexpected plunge waits around the bend? If so, you're not alone. Read on.

Second Plunge:
Managing the
Unmanageable

*The children and I are the little people inside
a snow globe—my husband's toy. He shakes
it and finds it amusing, but we're left dizzy
and blinded by a blizzard.*

— JANINE

"**S**ome people are just naturally controlling," Kristen announces to
the group. "But others have controlling thrust upon them; those
others are us!"

After 10 years with her husband, she has exacting standards for just
about everything from laundry to dinner. It is not her nature to be so
rigid, but it's developed in response to her husband's utter inability to
function without rock-solid structure. Oh, and please don't tell her to let
him learn from his consequences. He doesn't. Indeed, learning from mistakes is a key ADHD challenge. In Kristen's case, "letting the poop hit the
fan so he'll learn a lesson means only that, pardon me, the poop will
splatter throughout the house, including on me and the children."

As the stress continues to permeate the relationship—with ADHD still
unacknowledged, undiagnosed, unaddressed—Kristen and many others
respond in progressively unhealthy ways. Some people avoid facing the
painful feelings of grief lying just beneath the surface. Instead, they renew
their attempts, against all logic and experience, to "manage the unmanageable," says psychologist Herbert Gravitz, our guide to the stress responses
common to the partners of adults with unaddressed ADHD symptoms.

"ADHD's core characteristics such as impulsivity and distractibility
can profoundly affect couples and the family," says psychologist and
ADHD expert Arthur Robin. "Without knowing what they're up against,
the partners can get so mired in an endless pattern of chaos and nega-

tivity that they cannot objectively sit back, examine the situation, and make changes."

Prolonged attempts to fix the unfixable can eventually deepen into destructive patterns that further ensnare the relationship or the entire family structure, Gravitz cautions. You don't always see it when you're in the middle of it, of course, but such misguided attempts only guarantee a continuing, pervasive sense of loss. So, as you start feeling the seat dropping from under you on this Second Plunge of the ADHD roller coaster, you may put a death-grip on that safety bar and find yourself:

> Prolonged attempts to fix the unfixable can eventually deepen into destructive patterns that further ensnare the relationship or the entire family structure.

- Becoming more preoccupied with your ADHD partner, neglecting your own feelings and needs as you continue to try to prevent and control damage.
- Feeling guilty that you cannot control the chaos, even while enduring criticism that "You're so controlling."
- Freezing your feelings, a typical reaction to living in a chaos-driven atmosphere where your feelings are not allowed.
- Accepting too much of the blame for relationship troubles.
- Giving up clear paradigms of "bad behavior" as you grapple with new scientific explanations.
- Grieving for lost potential and dreams.
- Giving way to fatigue and exhaustion.

You needn't experience *all* of these feelings to recognize this stage of the roller coaster ride and the stress responses that go with it—just enough to feel out of control. Let's now examine these stress responses one by one.

Becoming Preoccupied with the ADHD Partner

Now that she's one year out of the relationship, Tina wonders why she put up with her fiancé's increasingly poor behavior. "I just got sucked into damage control, with minor things at first but increasingly major things."

Tina describes Jake as a very bright guy, but his habit of staying up late and missing class the next morning wasn't getting him closer to the college degree he'd pursued for seven years. "He'd set his alarm for 5:00 A.M. and hit the snooze alarm every 15 minutes for two hours," she recalls. "I'd lose sleep and he'd never get up!" Moreover, he'd get mad at himself and irritable for days when he'd miss an important exam.

Organizing comes easily to her, so she offered assistance to avoid these debilitating down spirals. She called Jake away from the computer and into bed at an agreed-upon time. Then, she helped complete assignments he'd put off until the last minute. But, like a game of Whack-a-Mole, Jake always popped up with *new* problems, such as when he abruptly quit his part-time job with nary a thought toward paying his share of the rent. "By the end," Tina remembers, "my life revolved around constantly worrying that Jake wasn't doing what he agreed to do, with real consequences for both of us. *My* goals? *My* dreams? *My* desires? They were getting lost in his chaos."

With deep affection for each other, the couple had envisioned marriage and children. Friends said that fatherhood would make Jake grow up, but she was doubtful. When Jake's mother finally told her he'd had ADHD as a child, Tina tried to talk with him about it, to encourage him to seek treatment again. He adamantly refused. With great sadness, she walked away.

Feeling Failure for Not Controlling the Chaos

Despite your best attempts to compensate for your ADHD partner's challenges—perhaps to the point of your utter depletion—confusion reigns. In fact, your partner might criticize you for not doing *more* to help or, the opposite, for being a control freak. Surprise! You might get slammed with both accusations at once.

"In trying to control the uncontrollable, loved ones can feel helpless, impotent, and frustrated, all of which can lead to a pervasive sense of failure and sadness," psychologist Gravitz says. It can also make you look like a certified nut job. Renee paints the picture:

> I can act the miracle worker, fixing nine of my husband's messes in a row with patient aplomb and gentle pleas for avoiding such messes in the future, only to be ignored. Come the tenth mess, I finally hit the roof, flinging an old chipped coffee mug at the floor. Shocked, my husband metaphorically hits speed-dial for the Funny Farm. That's because only extreme behavior gets his attention, and he doesn't remember the other nine messes! The night I found myself hurling a small end table, I knew he'd pushed me to an edge I didn't know I had.

Support-group members are relieved to know they aren't the only ones to "lose it" occasionally. Hidden shame over lost tempers only isolates them further, feeding the idea that they are the ones with the problem.

Comic Relief: How Many ADHD Partners Does It Take to Change a Lightbulb?

Even support-group members who are feeling the most whipped-around on the coaster can take this old joke and run with it. Seeking to lighten the group's mood a bit, they entertain each other with their ADHD partners' imagined (but sometimes too true) responses.

Original:

Q. "How many kids with ADHD does it take to change a lightbulb?"

A: "Let's go ride bikes!"

Revised for ADHD partners:

- "None! If I wait long enough, someone else will do it."
- "Why don't we just move to a new place?"
- "What lightbulb?"
- "You used the light last, so you change it."
- "Great! Let's go buy some cool candles!"
- "Speaking of lightbulbs, we could go off the grid if I built a solar windmill out of those old Chevy parts and dryer lint I've been collecting in the garage. Hey, where'd I put those old gutters?"
- "Lightbulbs! Lightbulbs! Lightbulbs! You're obsessed with lightbulbs!"
- "Honeeeeeeeey! Where are the new lightbulbs? What shelf? I don't see them. Whaddya mean, they've been in the same spot for 20 years? Nobody told me that. When did you tell me that?"
- "Light is overrated."
- "Okay, I'll change the lightbulb but you have to bring the ladder and the fresh bulb—and remove the fixture cover."
- "I'm going to."
- "Well, the answer is simple: We won't use that room."
- "Why don't we have any self-changing lightbulbs?"
- "Ohhhh, something shiny!"
- "My back hurts; you can change the bulb after you rub my back."
- "*You* might think we need light in the kitchen, but *I'm* not so sure."
- "Why spend good money on a new lightbulb? Why don't I just take that one apart and fix it? Put it there. I'll get to it later."
- "Looks like I need to go to Home Depot. Be back soon!" (Comes home five hours later with six bags of eight different colors of bulbs, minus the return receipt, and says, "Hey, honey, you can change that bulb now.")
- "Do you like my new sweater?"

Freezing Your Feelings, Risking Addiction

Does it ever seem like you're losing touch with your feelings? Perhaps that's because when you do try to express your pain and hurt to your ADHD partner, you get one of these reactions:

- Your partner is too impatient and defensive to tolerate even three minutes of really listening to you.
- Your comments are misunderstood and flung back at you in distortion, such as "You're too sensitive," or "No one can please you," or "You are the perfect one who never makes mistakes."
- Your partner greets your attempt with such dejection that you feel flattened by guilt, like you've just kicked a puppy.

In other words, your feelings—maybe your opinions, too—are simply not allowed.

New support-group member Ellen thanks the group for attentively listening to her: "My husband had convinced me that I take too long to get to the point, but now I see that he grows impatient with *everyone* after two or three sentences." Typically, her efforts to find conversational topics that don't upset her husband or try his patience fall flat.

Like Ellen, many other new members initially avoid expressing an opinion in the group, afraid that someone will jump on them—and they scurry to apologize at the first hint of disagreement or possible misinterpretation. It takes them a while to learn that the group is consistently civil, courteous, and compassionate. They've simply lived too long in an intense, chaos-driven atmosphere, one in which they've lost their voice.

Some admit they've stepped up the drinking—or shopping or working. Some have affairs. Separation from your feelings can fuel addictions, Gravitz warns. Moreover, your addiction can then become a smokescreen, something an ADHD partner can point to as the relationship's *real* problem.

During the fifth winter of her marriage, Holly realized she was sipping one too many glasses of wine each evening, and it scared her. How had she come to this? A therapist helped her realize she had lost all contact with her feelings. ("My ex-husband could rant, rave, and slam doors, but when I expressed my feelings in soft, calm words, he'd blow up!") He'd also irrationally accuse her of "putting conditions" on agreements, perhaps because his black-and-white brain processing just didn't allow for give-and-take. Though she'd never had such problems in other relationships, she was much more isolated now, working from home in a city they'd moved to for her husband's job.

Over time, Holly lost all sense of herself as reasonable and fair. "He distorted and misconstrued everything, always trying to make the illogical logical and the unfair fair," she says. "My B.S. detector and defenses had to be on duty 24/7 because he wasn't living in the same reality. As a result, my feelings were locked up tighter than a drum. Even to me."

Holly's feelings started resurfacing—and her confusion clearing—when she realized that Charlie employed the same tactics at work. "He was supposedly managing a company, but when the owner came to town, he said to Charlie, 'Why, you haven't even gotten to step one!' Charlie shot back with 'Well, what have *you* done to make sure that I know how to get there!'" With that, Holly saw how he confidently turned around the blame with everyone.

Accepting Too Much of the Blame

Perhaps you conclude that you're in this problematic relationship "for a reason"—for example, your dysfunctional patterns set in childhood. It's true that examining lifelong patterns can help break a self-destructive cycle of poor choices, but not if the examination becomes an exercise in distorting the evidence to blame yourself.

A surprisingly insidious danger lurks with your accepting unfair blame. It might make you feel empowered, because now you feel you can *do something* about it—change the way *you* do things, *your* tone of voice, *your* expectations—all without your partner having to accept the idea of ADHD or change a thing. That's much easier, right? Not exactly.

"I still go back and forth. Is it me? Is it him?" Ebony says. "In the end, it's easier to blame myself, because then the issue seems resolved and family life can go on." When she tries explaining to her husband how he shares responsibility for their problems, he tells her she's wrong and they argue, leading to her exhaustion.

Accepting blame and avoiding arguments might seem like a good short-term strategy, but it typically obscures reality and the chance to find true, lasting solutions. Remember, too: The possibility exists that you *did*, in fact, choose a good partner for yourself and, with ADHD awareness and maybe treatment, that choice will be validated.

Giving Up Clear Paradigms About "Bad Behavior"

Discoveries in brain science have shed light on "personality traits" previously thought unchangeable—for example, self-absorption, difficulty reading social cues, and low empathy. We now know that these and other common ADHD characteristics sometime spring from brain biology and can improve greatly with treatment. That's the good news.

Here's the troubling news. You now understand that your partner's behaviors have a physical basis, and that knowledge fosters your compassion and empathy. But what if your partner lacks that knowledge and, in fact, remains deeply in denial? And what if, even as your empathy for your ADHD partner increases, your partner's brain-based deficits in empathy, remorse, or self-observation remain unchanged? Consider these examples of how support-group members grapple with this rock-and-a-hard-place position:

Andre asks, "Do I divorce or keep trying to reach her?"

"My wife refuses to consider that she might have ADHD, which I believe she clearly does. Our therapist suggests that my wife is incurably narcissistic. So, do I ask for a divorce, putting my own survival first, or do I keep figuring out how to encourage her to seek treatment? If I leave, is that like leaving a physically ill spouse?"

Anna wonders how to be kind to her boyfriend—and herself

"He started the day again with one of his adrenaline-inducing stunts, unwittingly trying to make me angry. Already tired, I did react in anger but felt guilty the rest of the morning. I called him and apologized, because I know that until he seeks treatment, he doesn't truly understand what he's doing and how it affects me. But that means my apology confirms in his mind that I'm the one totally in the wrong. Back. Forth. I don't know how to be compassionate to both of us at the same time."

Rose tries to discern "not caring" vs. ADHD symptoms

"My husband ruined too many holidays for me, through inaction or opposition to people being happy because he was always unhappy. One Christmas, deciding to forgo trauma (but ostensibly for budget reasons), I asked that we skip the gift-giving. Still, he presented me with a lovely little sculpture of two figures seated on a bench—the embodiment of the warm companionship we often share on our many hikes while resting on a bench. The box, however, was flimsy and, during the time it was stored in his closet, the woman's head had broken off.

"I'd often struggled to know if he *really* loved me, because his ADHD-related actions often betrayed his words. Staring at the decapitated figure, I thought of that comedian who says, 'Here's yer sign.' That woman who'd lost her head was *me*. Too many years of living with him had sucked my brain clean out. And he'd taken as little care with that statue as with our marriage or my feelings.

"How much is ADHD? How much is not caring? For years, I painfully vacillated. Fortunately, five years into ADHD treatment and awareness, I have no doubts because his actions increasingly support his words."

Grieving for Lost Potential and Dreams

Madeleine was well into this second drop on the ADHD roller coaster before she snapped to her senses. "For a long time," she says, "I fought facing how drastically my husband changed after we had children because we'd had five great years before that." She did not want to lose him, even though he disappeared years ago, and—because he refused to accept his role in their problems—might never reappear. Finally, she had to accept that when he was out of town on business, her life was more peaceful and her children calmer. His irritability and short fuse simply had created an intolerably oppressive atmosphere in their home.

It was only when she faced the loss of her dreams that Madeleine could set her sights clearly on a better life for herself and her two sons, both of whom were eventually diagnosed with ADHD. When her husband saw how much happier the trio seemed during the marital separation she initiated (the oldest child even stopped wetting his bed), he finally stopped blaming Madeleine for their tumult and agreed to seek help.

A cooling-off period sounds like a great idea to Chuck. Unfortunately, he fears the consequences of floating the idea past his wife, who cannot see the negative impact of her ADHD-related behaviors on him or their young child. "She would immediately change the locks, accuse me of having an affair, call a high-priced attorney, and divorce me, and I might never see my son again," he maintains. "I have stuck it out only because I adore my boy and know that a judge would never believe how emotionally destructive my publicly charming wife can be. Still, the grief hits me every day. This isn't how I thought our family life would be."

Giving Way to Fatigue and Exhaustion

Constant worry, preoccupation, crisis management, and depression can drain a person dry. Lynn knows that so well, she considers herself a poster girl of the ADHD roller coaster rider. She felt the first major drop when her new husband changed drastically after marriage—including a 180-degree turn from ardent lover to sexually uninterested (except with himself). It left her emotionally wounded and confused. "Some people said a man needs time to adjust to marriage," she recalls, "or they advised us to have a child, which we did, but neither was the issue." Lynn's husband simply couldn't sustain the courtship hyperfocus and, so, stopped it completely. He just didn't know how to do "in between."

Their therapist diagnosed Lynn's husband with Borderline Personality Disorder (BPD). After months of torturously unproductive couples therapy, Lynn happened across an article on ADHD and was stunned to find that its symptoms almost duplicated those of BPD. In fact, ADHD is commonly misdiagnosed as BPD, but the two can co-occur. (According to the MedlinePlus Medical Library, BPD "is characterized by impulsive actions, mood instability, and chaotic relationships.... Other symptoms include frequent displays of inappropriate anger, feelings of emptiness and boredom, and impulsiveness with money, substance abuse, sexual relationships, binge eating, or shoplifting.")

Lynn's glimpse of clarity quickly fogged over, however, as other pressing problems mounted, including revelation of the premarital losses that his business had incurred. She learned about the debt when she'd agreed to help with the books, on top of working her full-time job. "Next time I get married, if there is a next time, I will first ask to view a man's credit report and tax records," she vows. "Maybe a brain scan, too!"

Once she saw the extent of the mess—clients who were owed work and were threatening to sue, employee withholding-taxes not accounted for, and more—she jumped into doing damage control. Meanwhile, she was carrying their first child. After the baby's birth, her husband became even *less* responsible, not more. Both mother and baby stayed stressed, neither sleeping well. "On top of everything else, I was failing my daughter, which made me so sad," she says.

Environmental stressors can change the brain in harmful ways at any time of life, she knew, but especially during early childhood. Given the high occurrence of ADHD in her husband's family, she knew her baby might be even more vulnerable, especially after her stressful pregnancy. This only ratcheted up her anxiety.

Finally, Lynn's parents brought her and her child home to live with them for a few months. "While I was in the middle of it all with my husband, as the daily churn kept worsening, I just couldn't get my bearings," Lynn explains. "Getting away for a while helped me get some rest and develop some clarity about exactly what I was up against and how best to proceed. That's when I had a chance to learn more about ADHD."

"Can't You just Relax and Enjoy the Ride?"

Support-group members' complaints to their ADHD partners about roller coaster whiplash or nausea are often met with comments like this: "Why are you so opposed to *fun*?"

Beware: If being pro-fun means staying locked in denial and continuing to suffer whiplash, it's a deal with the devil. Consider some common scenarios along these lines:

Your ADHD partner complains, "You're too negative"

Some ADHD partners seem to purposefully exploit their mates' natural aversion to being called negative in order to get what they want—a new TV, no responsibility for chores, another poorly conceived self-employment scheme. Others wield the "You're so negative" weapon unconsciously; they truly can't fathom why you're saying "no." Possible explanations:

- Their poor ability to empathize keeps them from understanding that *your* desires really could be different from *theirs*.
- They have "hyperfocused" on a target—there's no turning back!
- They freak at the sheerest whiff of "criticism," having difficulty integrating the good with the bad and seeing the big picture.

Jim's wife complains that he is negative about her ideas for starting a business. "We're already in debt from her spending, she has no business experience, and she is lousy at following through on anything," Jim explains. "I *can't afford* to be positive about her business ideas." But that doesn't stop Jim from feeling guilty.

The way Molly's husband sees it, he is the optimistic bouquet of shiny helium balloons, and she is the negative bag of dull rocks that keeps it from touching the sky. Does anyone ever say, "Yippee, the little bag of rocks is here!"? Molly asks. "My husband has forced me to take so many negative positions just to keep us afloat that it's changed my entire self-image *and* public image." She was never a bag-of-rocks person before marriage, and how can she soar when she must always play the heavy?

Bill finds the analogy apt. The balloons don't foresee their untethered fate because they seldom think of consequences. So not only do they fail to appreciate the rocks' effort, they also castigate the rocks for holding them back! "Most 'rocks' I've met in the support group would be happier living their desires instead of tethering balloons," he jokes. "But, hey, that's what they're stuck with, especially if children are involved, so that's what they do."

In fact, one member reports that, after 12 years, her bullying-with-optimism, balloon-bouquet of a husband felt more like a millstone around her neck. Now that she's divorced, her bag-of-rocks persona has disappeared! Friends and family say they are so happy to have back the optimistic, fun-loving person they once knew.

Oh, but wait. What if, from a young age, you *have* been a tad negative, pessimistic, or rigid? Maybe it's your personality—or a lifelong low-grade depression. And *might* that explain your attraction to a partner who was so "spontaneous" and carefree about consequences? (Even so, you probably had no idea that said spontaneity wasn't a considered choice but a biological imperative.) Whatever the cause, if you've always been overly cautious, you might be extra vulnerable to charges of negativity even when you're simply being realistic.

"ADHD-positive" spin shames you out of your perceptions

It's the rare article or TV news spot about adult ADHD that fails to close on a glib note, implying that having an ADHD partner simply presents an opportunity to "enjoy differences." As a longtime support-group member, Beth deplores stories that gloss over the problems of ADHD "as if it is just an annoyance, like you wanted someone with blue eyes but your guy comes with green, so learn to love green!" Ultimately, she maintains, these stories do everyone an injustice. "They aren't fully truthful and offer no helpful strategies for both parties in the couple living with real difficulties."

Even some professionals downplay potential problems

It's surprising to learn that some mental-health professionals who claim ADHD expertise minimize these problems as a simple case of opposites attracting: a happy-go-lucky, creative ADHD partner pairs with a dull and dutiful mate. Hence they point to the opportunity to loosen up and enjoy life. For some relationships, that might well be true. But such professionals miss one critical fact: These "bags of rocks" might have had to evolve in response to an ADHD partner's out-of-control behavior.

In sum, "being negative" is sometimes the most life-affirming thing you can do in a troubled ADHD partnership. Sure, it is important to look on the bright side—but not at the cost of living in a destructive fantasy. "When the negative in your relationship far outweighs the positive," psychologist Gravitz advises, "the most positive and life-affirming thing you can do is step out of the fog and onto the path of healing."

So you, along with your new support-group peers, survived Second Plunge of the ADHD roller coaster. At the end, were you high-tailing it to the exit sign, hell-bent for peace and predictability? Or, still not understanding the true nature of your ride and determined to be "positive," did you convince yourself that the worst was behind you? If you're like many others, the next thing you felt was air rushing out of your lungs as you lost altitude once again. Um, that would be the Third Plunge, the third set of ADHD roller coaster stress responses.

The good news? You're not likely to get caught off-guard again now that you know what to expect and what to avoid. Knowledge is power. So let's examine this final plunge and then move into solid strategies for setting your teetering little coaster-cart back on track.

Third Plunge:
Breaking Down in Illness— Or Through to Truth

I'm tired physically, emotionally, and spiritually, in ways only others in our situation can understand.

— STUART

"**M**y boyfriend just hurts me and moves on, then hurts me and moves on, and if he is moving on, he thinks I should be, too," Tiffany explains. "He just doesn't get it, that you can poke somebody emotionally only so many times before a giant bruise sets in, and then the person stays tensed up, just waiting for the next poke."

Within this common stress reaction lies a paradox, notes psychologist Herbert Gravitz, introducing this third and final plunge of the ADHD roller coaster: "On the one hand, those traumatized can't get away from the trauma, and on the other hand they can't get near it. They are overwhelmed and obsessed with it, yet they work hard to avoid it, numb themselves to it, or hide it."

As the poor coping strategies detailed in the previous chapters continue unabated and losses intensify, tension and anxiety can start feeling like a mind-numbing fever. Remember: You don't "graduate" after each plunge. Until you realize what is happening, the ride may run endlessly, around and around, down and down.

Moreover, if your ADHD partner's behaviors grow more challenging over time, as often happens, your stress responses might intensify as well, ultimately resulting in your physical or mental illness. At that point, more confusion might envelop you, even pointing to you as the "identified patient," an apparent burden to your long-suffering ADHD partner. Appearances can be deceiving.

If you find yourself developing a *parallel disorder*—physical or emotional—consider yourself well into the Third Plunge. Here's the tricky part: You might not realize just how anxious you've become until you enjoy a getaway from everyone and everything. You might even mistakenly attribute your stress-induced aches, pains, and fitful sleep to other factors, like your own creeping age.

In this way, on this third big drop of the ADHD roller coaster, you risk:

- Developing physical reactions to stress, such as fibromyalgia, gastrointestinal disorders, migraines, and "brain fog."
- Succumbing to depression and anxiety, forgetting what joy feels like—or that it's possible.
- Down-spiraling into low self-esteem, losing confidence that you can possibly turn this situation around.

In the end, your physical or emotional breakdown offers a tremendous breakthrough—to truth and to new resolve in taking care of yourself.

Physical Symptoms: What's Your Weak Link?

"How could I not have known about adult ADHD before?" Chicago physician David Edelberg remembers asking himself after attending a lecture on it in the late 1990s. Immediately he saw a potential connection between his female patients' chronic-illness symptoms and their male partners' possibly undiagnosed ADHD.

"Now, when my female patients talk about their life stresses, and I get enough clues about the husband, I'll ask if he has ever been tested for Adult ADHD," explains Edelberg, cofounder of Whole Health Chicago, a clinic that offers integrative medicine. (Generally speaking, this is a blending of conventional medicine in several disciplines, such as internal medicine and psychology, along with modalities such as acupuncture and nutrition.)

Men living with an ADHD partner's problematic behavior suffer stress, too, but some experts think that women are more biologically vulnerable to stress-induced maladies. "That's because women lose the brain chemical serotonin much more quickly than men do, and replace it more slowly," he explains.

The more stress you have, the more your serotonin buffer is depleted, with some people having particular genetic vulnerabilities. At some point, this deficit, pitted against more stress, will result in physical illnesses. Because men are less serotonin-vulnerable, they have a larger defense threshold against serotonin-related illnesses such as fibromyalgia, gastrointestinal tract irritations, and migraines. On the other hand, when men suffer from severe stress, they tend to get heart attacks and ulcers or languish in depression, according to Edelberg.

According to one small but important study,[21] men married to women with ADHD reported being more distressed than the female subjects with male ADHD partners. The impact of ADHD symptoms on marital relationships may differ for male and female spouses, the authors suggest, with women being more tolerant than men about compensating for their ADHD partners' shortcomings. Then again, the women with ADHD in this study reported the highest rate of difficulties with their own parents, and hence may have been especially difficult for their husbands to live with.

It is not evident which finding might account for the fact that almost 60 percent of men in their study had left their ADHD spouses, whereas only 10 percent of female spouses had left. At any rate, it should be noted

Melissa—To Sleep, Perchance to Stay Asleep

When we were first married, I was always tired. I thought it was the aftermath of wedding planning and working full-time in a demanding job. Then, I started getting sick a lot. Finally, I realized it wasn't just my husband's constant forgetfulness that was zapping my energy, but his temper and his sleep habits, too.

He'd stay up late, fiddling on the computer. Then, he'd come in and throw the lights on. I'd try to go back to sleep. The next day, I'd sweetly ask him to please try not awakening me. He never remembered! As my health and sanity deteriorated from stress and sleep loss, so did our marriage. Finally, I said, "You have to make a decision—either you give me sleep or give me a divorce." He chose divorce! And I just lost it.

We decided to go for therapy, where we were told to make a list of our needs and wants. Number two on my list was sleep. The therapist said that I must have a sleep disorder! When my husband's ADHD was finally diagnosed, everything made sense. Four years later, with treatment, he understands cause and effect. That is, if he deprives me of sleep, I will not be kind the next day.

It's hard to believe, but he used to take it personally if I snapped at him for waking me up! He thought it meant I didn't love him. That was a real eye-opener, learning how easily he gives up if criticized, for anything, how black-and-white his thinking can be. To make matters worse, he also felt powerless to change the situation, which is why he chose divorce. We've come a long way. He's developed more empathy, and I've learned to give constant reinforcement of the good and positive things he does. If not for these changes, I would definitely be divorced—or really, really sick.

that men who join an online support group typically show a strong sense of dedication to their female ADHD partners—and many report being deeply depressed for years before finding the group. Most, however, did not know how depressed they'd become until taking antidepressants and finally feeling "the fog lift."

"My physical health has worsened"

We all have a physical "weak link" that gives way under prolonged stress. Sixty percent of ADHD Partner Survey respondents said that their physical health had worsened due to their partner's behavior. Of those reporting poor health effects, here's how it breaks down:

- Digestive-tract problems—Crohn's disease, irritable bowel syndrome, ulcer, and similar (25 percent)
- Migraines or tension headaches (36 percent)
- Sleep loss, mostly related to ADHD partners' erratic or noisy sleep habits, sleep apnea, or restless legs syndrome (49 percent)
- Chronic fatigue syndrome or fibromyalgia (19 percent)

> "If you're living with a person who exhibits problematic ADHD behavior, then really you're having a low-level stress response all the time—and frequently a high-level response."

Moreover, of those who reported adverse health consequences *and* are now separated or divorced from their ADHD partner, half reported their condition as much improved or in complete recovery.

It's not "all in your head"

When a person expects to be physically or emotionally attacked on a daily basis and feels little sense of control, the adrenal gland switch stays on, notes Edelberg, author of *The Triple Whammy Cure: The Breakthrough Women's Health Program for Feeling Good Again in 3 Weeks*. Chronically high cortisol and adrenaline secretion can cause these problems among others:

- "Adrenal exhaustion" (fatigue, a weakened immune system, low blood pressure)
- "Brain fog" (excessive cortisol is toxic to brain cells)
- Weakened thyroid (fatigue, cold intolerance, weight gain despite calorie restriction)
- Fear responses (cold hands and feet, palpitations, chronic anxiety, tightness in the throat, insomnia, irritable bowel syndrome)

ADHD Partner Survey Snapshot: A Person Could Get Sick!

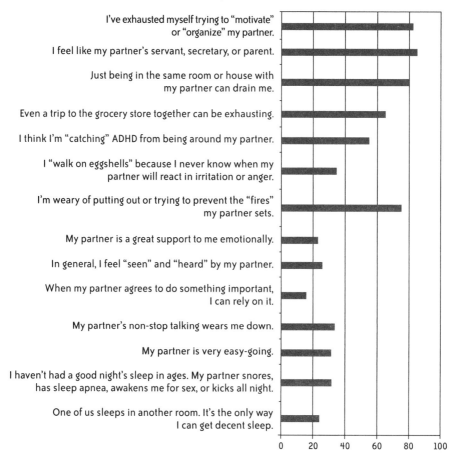

"If you're living with a person who exhibits problematic ADHD behavior, then really you're having a low-level stress response all the time—and frequently a high-level response," Edelberg says. "If you go to a doctor because you're feeling lousy with one of these stress-induced disorders, the doctor will look at tests and say 'Everything is normal.' You ask, 'Why am I feeling so crummy, then?' and the answer is that you're having a physiological response to stress. Your symptoms are legitimate." Understanding this stress response should help you realize you're not "going crazy."

Emotional Fallout: Who Has a Disorder Now?

Heather long struggled with depression during her marriage. Then, when seeking a therapist's help for her daughter, recently diagnosed with ADHD, Heather said that, funny enough, her husband seemed to meet ADHD criteria, too. "After learning more, the therapist suggested I think about easing off my antidepressant and instead encourage him to be evaluated," she says.

Reports of depression, anxiety, and panic disorders constantly crop up in the support group, including among many with no such history prior to the relationship. In fact, the ADHD marital study referenced above showed that spouses of adults with ADHD show no more lifetime or current psychiatric disorders than spouses of adults who don't have ADHD. They do, however, report more *psychological distress* and less marital satisfaction.

The chart on the opposite page shows at what point in life ADHD Partner Survey respondents report *significantly* experiencing various mental health issues:

- During the relationship *only*
- Never in my life
- Before *and* during the relationship
- Before only

Responses indicate that some did enter the relationship with preexisting challenges such as anxiety and depression, but the majority experienced those problems only *during* the relationship.

Perhaps the wrong patient is being treated

"When one person has ADHD, everyone in relationship to that person is affected by it," explains psychiatrist Daniel Amen. "That's why, when you treat ADHD, you treat *families*." For example, when parents ask Amen to treat their child's anxiety or ADHD, he asks about the mother and father, "because parental ADHD can induce anxiety in the children, from making them late all the time to creating other chaos in the household."

The parent who is causing the child's anxiety should also be treated, he maintains, and the same goes for the ADHD partners whose unaddressed symptoms create harmful stress in the family.

Consider the infamous condition "ADHD by Osmosis"

Support-group members use this nickname for one set of symptoms. Stuart finds it pretty ironic that the stress he lives with from his wife's behavior leads him to make the same kind of screw-ups that she makes. He can barely organize his day after he gets his wife and two children

ADHD Partner Survey Snapshot: Respondents' Mental Health

Survey question: "For each condition, indicate if you experienced it to a significant degree before the relationship, during the relationship, or both. If you've never significantly experienced the condition, select 'never significantly'."

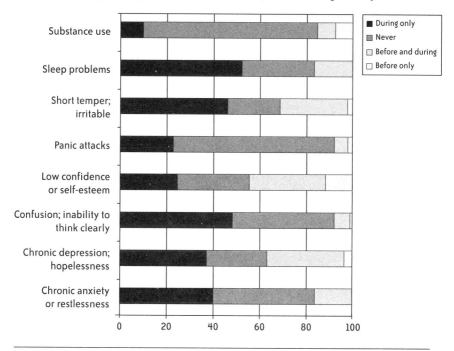

with ADHD on track—and then *back* on track. "Before marriage, I was organized and on the ball," he says. "Now my wife is telling me I need an ADHD evaluation. Does anybody else think ADHD's contagious?"

Low Confidence: Preexisting or New Issue?

If you didn't have low self-esteem going into a relationship where you soon feel neither seen nor heard—but often blamed and criticized—it's easy to develop it. The picture is mixed, though, as far as which comes first: low self-esteem or an esteem-killing relationship. As usual, the ADHD Partner Survey shows that experiences aren't universal. For example:

- 42 percent agreed with this statement: "My partner has helped me to expand my skills and confidence."
- 26 percent report feeling low confidence or self-esteem *only during* the relationship, not before.

Dawn— Feeling Like a Rock in a Tumbler

Tim and I were best friends for 10 years before we dated. That's why I wasn't pre-pared for what happened.

During the friendship years, we'd have Sunday brunches, traded keys to each other's places, and would meet at our favorite club to sing and play guitar. We sup-ported each other in our dating adventures. And when I was a wreck after my long-time boyfriend and I broke up, there was Tim, my best friend. Months later, our relationship turned romantic, and because we had long been friends, things intensified quickly. I moved in with Tim.

A year later, he said, "If I ask you to marry me, will you say yes?" He made it sound like just a formality, that any day now he'd be popping the question in his grand-gesture style—by hiring a skywriter or a carload of clowns. It was clear: He wanted to be a married man and he wanted to marry me. I'm repeating this like a mantra to remind myself that I wasn't irrational or immature; I was deceived. Well, okay, there was some knight-in-shining-armor stuff there. I felt great joy. I felt cher-ished, that our love was something sacred. But is that so unusual to feel when you become engaged?

Well, he didn't propose. Six months later, I finally brought it up, knowing that if he hadn't by then, something must be terribly wrong. "I had no way of knowing you were thinking this!" he bellowed—as if this idea came out of the blue. He had cre-ated this imminent-marriage thing, not me. Never me. Looking back, I see that's when the "ADHD hyperfocus" phase had worn off. He'd "won" me, and I never again felt seen and heard by him.

I was dumbstruck. When I tried explaining it to my friends, they said that I must be misunderstanding; he's such a great guy! So I distanced myself from them. It was just too awful. I couldn't explain it. I had been so sure about my friendship with Tim, and if I could be wrong about that, then I could be wrong about absolutely anything. Meanwhile, I got very sick physically from the stress of living with his erratic behavior.

Before I learned he had ADHD and probably Oppositional Defiant Disorder, though, I didn't understand why he had changed so dramatically. No matter what I tried in the way of self-improvement, I felt invisible. Our "conversations" consist-ed of me asking questions and him staring at the wall. At the worst times, I would chant out loud, "I exist! I said something, and I exist!"

Does it help now to know that ADHD might account for why he'd simply stopped being "stimulated" by the pursuit of me? No, the damage is too deep. Lacking this knowledge, though, I felt like I was losing my mind. If I shared a significant memory, he forgot it. If I organized files, he "tornadoed" them. I arranged furniture; he criticized it. I expressed hurt; he repeated the action. I supported his ideas; he argued with me. I made a joke; he argued with me. I cried; he argued with me. I crawled into a fetal position; he argued with me. Finally, it hit me: I could never make things "right" again.

It took me a while to catch my breath and realize this, because his energy came at me like a juggernaut, inexorable, and I was crushed beneath it, over and over again. My illness didn't help. I was so tired. To think, this man was my friend for 10 years. I knew him. But a whole new side of him had emerged within two years of living together. It's easy to make judgments, presuming you'd never be such a fool. And maybe you wouldn't. But unless you've lived with a loved one's gradually revealed, disordered, inexplicable behavior, it's hard to understand the insidious way in which it can grind you down.

Given more intimate time to observe how he acted in mundane situations, what I saw surprised me. He viewed social interactions as an imbalance of power wherein he had to remain in control. He refused to be subordinate, especially at work but even on the road. A car in front of him on the freeway was an affront to his dignity; he had to pass that car immediately, flipping them off. If someone stated an opinion and he didn't oppose it, it was as though his identity would dissolve. How could he have hidden this ridiculously oppositional behavior from me for so long?

Before I knew it, my sense of priorities had became as skewed as his were. Causal relationships ceased to run along a meaningful track. I questioned my own logic, my own perceptions. He reduced everything into black-and-white. Therefore, his perception of me was flat, plastic. He mirrored a grotesque, diminished version of me. I felt like a rock in a tumbler, bashed up against his unyielding obstinacy, until all my interesting bits wore off. I was shriveling from loneliness, even in the same room with him. That sense of bleakness was unendurable and drove me to do insane things. I screamed. I threw china. I hated myself. I hated him.

I left two years ago, but it took a while to stop walking on eggshells. I'm single and loving it. My sense of humor has returned. I didn't even know it was gone until I found myself making jokes again, having a light heart. My concentration is much better, too. Funny how different the roller coaster looks from way-the-hell across the amusement park—not nearly so exciting and actually a bit threatening—in the placid shade of the lemonade stand awning.

Besides all the other twists and turns on the ADHD roller coaster that can corrode a healthy sense of self, here are a few more factors:

Receiving no positive feedback anywhere

As a stay-at-home mom with three children, all three of whom have ADHD (and one with bipolar disorder as well), Linda dreams about getting away from home for a few hours a week or even finding a part-time job—any-place to get some positive interaction and pull her self-esteem out of the basement. "My mind is mush, my energy level is nonexistent, and my self-esteem so low even a fast-food joint wouldn't hire me," she says.

Her heart sinks when, despite her best efforts to get everyone medically stabilized, her daughter laments, "We live in a half-broken home." The children beg her not to leave them in the home alone with their dad or each other. "If I'm not there to referee," she explains, "all hell breaks loose and I deal with the fallout for days," Linda used to find comfort in her church, but her pastor's advice to let her husband reassume the family's leadership left her stunned and dejected, as if their problems were her fault. "But I learned long ago that my husband controlling the finances spelled ruin for this family," she says.

Learning to feel unworthy of attention or love

After three years together, Vince's wife still didn't remember what he likes and doesn't like, and she acted like she lived alone—making plans, chang-ing plans, and ignoring plans as though no one but her will be affected. Gradually, Vince started feeling invisible even to himself. "I became so con-vinced that if she was treating me this way, I must be a bad husband," he admits, "so bad that, even if I left the marriage, I'd never find someone else."

It also took Lanelle some time to accept her family's sad situation. She and the children will always be her husband's last choice, what he does when he can't find something else to do. "He likes us, I think, but we are just not as stimulating as his latest hobby or helping a neighbor with some project while our own projects gather dust," she says.

For years, Lanelle confused her husband's dependence on her—and need for the structure she provided (because he demanded it)—with his love for her. The more she comes out of the fog, though, the more she envi-sions a lobster, with its skeletal system on the outside "because this is how my husband sees me, and I've come to treat myself, as his exoskeleton, an extension of him that serves his needs but has no needs of my own. Oh, damn. I never wanted to be someone's exoskeleton."

Seeing yourself reflected in a murky "mirror"

"A lot of how we feel about ourselves comes from the feedback of loved ones," Dave figures, "but if your feedback is coming from a fun-house mirror, it's going to be distorted." As much as he can logically explain why his wife's mirror is warped in places, "It still friggin' hurts, every single time, to have my wife misread the situation or my intentions so totally." When she blames him unfairly, it's hard for him to fight the idea that he did something wrong because in her eyes he did. "She is the mirror I face every single day."

The Role of "Gaps" and "Skips" or How Mel's Wife Started Noticing Him

Maybe you've noticed this phenomenon. Your ADHD partner's attention wanders during conversations or events, leaving a Swiss-cheese sort of comprehension or recall. But we humans possess a penchant for trying to make sense of the world around us. So, even though your partner has missed key words or details, he or she unconsciously fills them in, often inaccurately.

Shortly after his wife, Patty, was diagnosed, Mel had an epiphany. Patty's tendency to "skip" (his term for when her attention wandered) meant she had developed huge inconsistencies in her worldview. She had even "filled in the gaps" about him, based on what she expected to see or hear. "She was living her own pieced-together narrative, apart from what really happened, who I am, or what I said," Mel observes. "I never knew why, but I knew she never really saw me."

Mel suspects Patty's scattershot approach to interpreting the world also affected her own sense of self. Experts point to Executive Function as the very brain capacity that fosters a sense of self. Maybe that's why she focused on external things, as a sort of anchor. "She didn't have a job, she *was* her job, her house, her car, her clothes, whatever," he explains. "She always seemed to need more, bigger, better, perhaps so she could feel more, bigger, better than she felt inside."

With Patty in ADHD treatment for several years now, Mel notices that she has fewer gaps or skips. And she seems to be developing a more accurate view of how the world works and a stronger sense of herself. "She's less self-conscious, less worried about looking 'cool,'" he says. "She focuses more on how she feels and what works for her." What's more, she's starting to see Mel more as an individual, no longer as an extension of her. "Before, she always assumed that her preferences were mine and was ticked off if I disagreed." When she presented him with a gift, it was usually something she wanted or thought he should have. "Now, she chooses with my preferences in mind," Mel says. "It's never been about the materiality, though; it's about what a thoughtful gift conveys, that your partner knows you."

Finally: Breaking Through to Truth

Can there truly be any good news about reaching physical or emotional breakdown, on this third and final drop on the roller coaster? Psychologist Herbert Gravitz says yes, because he views breakdown as "the normal state to be in before breaking through to truth, the state where people are until they can make sense of their pain."

For some, disembarking from this dangerous ride remains the sole solution. Short of leaving your ADHD partner, how do you and your family not only make sense of your pain but also seek healing? "There is not one way out," he advises. "You need multiple routes."

Chapter 11 contains a sampling of ADHD roller coaster exit strategies offered by mental-health professionals and support-group members. Above all, healing involves expanding your world, which typically has become very small, restricted, and encapsulated in a narrow view. It demands giving yourself permission, focus, and attention to improve your life.

What's that? This might work for others, you say, but there's little hope that your life can improve? Not so fast.

When Kelly first joined the support group, she was a young mother with few financial resources, home-schooling her three children and feeling isolated and depressed. Now she is working on her master's degree in counseling part-time and enjoying it immensely. Despite her husband receiving an ADHD diagnosis and being recommended for medical treatment, he stays locked in denial. For the time being, she's made her peace with that, even as she continues to try to reach him:

> What I've gained in working through my own situation is a sympathy toward people who feel trapped and see no way out, just like I used to feel. There is *always* a way out. Many women especially have been conditioned to be dependent, and they find it even harder to see a way out. Add exhaustion and the condition becomes ripe for depression. I hope one day, as a counselor, to be able to help women and men out of those feelings of powerlessness so they can be free in body, mind, and spirit. If it was possible for me, it's possible for anyone.

PART THREE
Your Relationship and the Art of Roller Coaster Maintenance

Success Strategies for Stopping the
ADHD Roller Coaster and Standing on Solid Ground—
or at Least Installing Airbags and Shock Absorbers
(So You Can, You Know, Enjoy the Ride)

Every positive thing I've accomplished in my relationship with my ADHD partner has been from a position of strength and a willingness to establish clear guidelines for creating stability and happiness for ourselves. Any weakness from me just made my partner feel more out of control—and act it, too.

—MARGARET

I'm lucky in that my wife was willing to make changes, including seeking treatment. Her mother had severe ADHD, and she doesn't want that for herself, our children, and me. But until I made it clear that history was repeating itself and offered help in finding solutions, she simply wasn't noticing—or didn't feel she could change anything.

—STUART

My husband has every right to live life the way he wants, without ADHD treatment. But he must accept the consequences of that choice because I also have a right to live my life instead of always cleaning up his messes.

—SHARON

Being in these relationships has forced many of us to find our strength. Steel wrapped in soft cotton is what I had to become to turn my relationship around—strong enough to demand what I need, gentle enough to be appreciative of my boyfriend's efforts, and patient as we started to see progress. If you weren't certain of what really matters to you in life before this relationship, it will ensure that you find out.

—SUSANNA

Introduction

Four Success
Strategies

At this point, maybe you're lifting the safety bar, determined to climb off that ADHD roller coaster and tear out of the amusement park altogether. You're reeling from mental whiplash and feeling that if the wacky stuff doesn't stop—right now—your last neuron will short-circuit. Support-group members feel your pain.

It's probably best to acknowledge right now that some relationships affected adversely by ADHD are impossible to salvage. Many support-group members who did depart (typically after years of trying to reach their partners and agonizing over the decision) now report they're doing just fine. Their only regret? Not putting the brakes on the calamity sooner.

But if you are looking for ways to make your relationship work, there's good news: Solutions exist and miracles *do* happen.

Whatever your path from here—and it can be a very rewarding path of growth and discovery—you now have solid information about ADHD and validation for your perceptions. Those two factors alone mean you possess your first *realistic* opportunity to turn your life around.

Because, for most people, awareness goes only so far, Part Three of this book fleshes out comprehensive solutions:

- **Success Strategy 1: Taking Care of Yourself** and accepting that long-term changes might depend on helping your ADHD partner pursue treatment (Chapters 11–12).

- **Success Strategy 2: Dealing with Denial** by learning that its basis can be informational, psychological, and biological (Chapters 13–16).

- **Success Strategy 3: Finding Effective Therapy** by understanding that ADHD requires a special focus (Chapters 17-19).

- **Success Strategy 4**: **Understanding Medication's Role** by learning how the brain affects behavior and how medication can mitigate ADHD symptoms (Chapters 20–22).

Finally, Chapter 23 explains how to implement all that you've learned into practical strategies designed to cool your relationship's "hot spots."

INTRODUCTION

The Amusement Park's Emergency Room

You don't know what the future holds for your ADHD partner. He might change, or he might not. But your journey begins and ends with you.

— SARAH

S ometimes it's hard to know which comes first: taking care of yourself or helping your partner reduce the ADHD-related behaviors that ratchet up your need for self-care. That's why this Success Strategy offers a two-pronged action plan:

- Taking care of yourself right now—solid suggestions from support-group members and professionals who "get it." (Chapter 11)
- Solving ADHD's "double whammy"—understanding why, if long-term change is to take place, your ADHD partner might need your help in recognizing the symptoms and in taking steps to relieve them. (Chapter 12)

IN HER OWN WORDS: ONE SUPPORT-GROUP MEMBER'S STORY

Abigail: We Have So Much to be Grateful For

Abigail provided this update to the group two years after joining. Three years later she confirmed that their happiness continues. In her own words, she explains how she and her husband achieved success:

Life is so much better these days. A few months after my husband was diagnosed with ADHD and started treatment, I went to a new doctor for a checkup and told him about my struggle with migraines and how they are getting worse and how I was crying for no reason. He prescribed a low dose of antidepressant, and I can't believe the difference it has made in my life. I can finally focus again on what I want and be less obsessed with what "isn't"—after so many years of being ground down.

My husband is doing extremely well. He has been substance free for 15 months and loves it. I can once again trust him. What a relief. When I finally stopped being so down over my life, it was a real turning point in our lives together. Admittedly, he had been a real jerk for 10 years and it had taken a toll on me, but once he got properly treated for ADHD, he simply couldn't handle feeling responsible for me feeling so down all the time. So, I'd attribute our success to many factors:

- Finding out about ADHD
- Helping my husband find competent help, stick with the medications, and quit all other substances
- Both of us working through the changes
- My getting the help that my own brain needed

Now that his ADHD's intensity has ratcheted down a few notches, it's possible to work around his remaining symptoms instead of being engulfed by them. That means I can more easily move forward in my individual goals, being less focused on making his life better in order to make our family's life better. He takes better care of himself now, and his former bad habits no longer spill over on our children and me.

Yes, he still is one goofy guy. He takes forever to pack for a trip, spends too much at the home-supply store, gets overfocused on things, and well guess what, he still has ADHD. But he is managing. I love him for being the goofy, great guy that he is. Yes, I still need to curb some of his spending. Frankly, though, he is doing so much better in our business that we finally have money to spend. He can be a real grump at night, after the medication wears off, but I know that come morning he will be himself again. In other words, the patterns are more predictable now and understandable. Furthermore, we have learned to deal with it and accept it. For example, if he takes too long getting ready to go somewhere, I leave without him and there are no hard feelings! Now that the deal-breaking behavior is behind us, it is mostly about acceptance and compassion.

I'm just so happy to be feeling better and that my kids are doing better, too. My daughter, who is a senior in college, is actually going this week for an ADHD evaluation. This is a huge step for her. My youngest son, 12, has been taking medication for two years and the difference is unreal. He is a wonderful person; he has amazing goals that I now know he can meet. He turned into a straight A student, lost the math disability, loves school, and is already starting to choose the expensive college we can send him to (he hated school before and insisted he was never going to college). With both my children, I know that seeing the changes in their father impressed them a great deal. I can't imagine getting them on track while his previous chaos continued.

We have so much to be thankful for, and I thank everyone here for helping my family to gain this new life together. Just this morning, my husband and I were talking about some of the what-ifs, and we are so thankful we stayed together and weathered the storm. So many times I wondered, "Why me?" But I have learned that it isn't all about me! Life has funny twists and turns, and there are many lessons to be learned, but they can't be learned with an unhealthy brain.

I know life holds more challenges, but I feel more prepared to meet them. And, in a funny way, I'm glad for the time spent going through all of the "stuff." It has made me view life in an entirely different way than I used to, and I also view the people around me differently and with a whole lot more compassion and understanding. Thanks for all your help and caring.

CHAPTER
ELEVEN

Strategies for *Right Now*

*In trying to be the one person in my partner's
life who didn't make him feel like a failure, I
internalized too much stress and became very
sick. Only after taking care of myself could I
think about helping him pursue treatment.*

— BRENDA

No matter your situation, you can take immediate steps to begin
reducing your stress, even before you think about approaching the
subject of ADHD with your partner.

For starters, taking care of yourself means deciding that bad behavior
is unacceptable, whether or not your partner ever learns about ADHD or
pursues treatment. Taking care of yourself also means reconnecting with
activities and people that bring you pleasure and learning how to detach
from the chaos.

Fortunately, the trauma staff here at the amusement park is very experienced. Among other recommendations, your new support-group
friends (along with some savvy professionals) will advise you to find support, set boundaries, and spend some time thinking about what you want
in life. So, take a deep breath, pour yourself a cup of tea, sit back, and
reap their wisdom in the following strategies:

Get information
For group members like Rose, getting clear about reality—exactly what
she was up against and what it was doing to her—means she's walking in
the sunshine again. "No more dark alleys and abysses of confusion and

despair," she vows. "At first, facing facts was scary but not half as scary as facing a future with more chaos." Learning solid facts about ADHD helped Rose to feel compassion for both herself and her husband, to know exactly what they were up against, and to plan the next step.

"Invisible is invincible," proclaims psychologist and trauma expert Herbert Gravitz. "You want to put a name to whatever you're dealing with." Namely, understand that a brain condition (a highly treatable one) is affecting the person you love and you as well, along with any children in your household.

Do not tolerate physical or emotional abuse

It's not surprising that brain-based challenges in controlling mood, impulsivity, and frustration lead some ADHD partners to lash out verbally or even physically. ADHD Survey respondents reported the following:

- Their partner has been verbally abusive to them (37 percent).
- Their partner has been *both* verbally and physical abusive (25 percent).
- They experienced *neither* behavior (35 percent).

If you feel physically, emotionally, or financially threatened or intimidated, get help at once. The National Domestic Violence Hotline can offer information and point you to resources in your area. Access their Web site at NDVH.org or call their hotline at 800-799-SAFE (800-787-3224, for the hearing-impaired). If your partner has access to your computer and can track your online activity, please consider phoning instead.

A word of caution: Many counselors specializing in family violence take a strictly psychological perspective, viewing abusive behavior as stemming from a demand for power and control; many do not acknowledge that untreated brain disorders can also play a critical role in poor self-control or empathy. The point is *not* to excuse or tolerate abusive behaviors but to explain the context in which they sometimes arise. It is painful enough to bear the brunt of the behaviors; the implication that they are always volitional, however, can compound everyone's trauma and postpone healing and finding real solutions.

"Put on your own oxygen mask first"

The group's experienced members like to repeat this flight-attendant's command to passengers. Why? Because before you can to help anyone else, you need to take care of yourself. And the more you do that, the more you feel in control of your life, the more you can back off from "monitoring" your ADHD partner. That often helps your partner's anxiety level, too.

For starters, this might mean giving up your impersonation of a carnival sideshow contortionist ("Bombo the Amazing Rubber Man!"), twisting yourself all around to catch every curve ball your partner throws.

From there, the possibilities expand. Consider a small sampling of suggestions from the group:

- **Find your strength; decide that *you* must elevate your life**

Janet: "My life started changing for the better when I came out of the trance I'd fallen into so gradually I didn't even know what had happened. After struggling to keep my family on track for 20 years, I finally accepted that I'm the lead dog in charge of getting the pack in line. I had to decide—finally—what I wanted out of life and stake my claim. No more confusion. No more being whipped around by my husband's impulsive moves. No more waiting for him to get his act together. I firmly staked my claim on a better life.

"What surprised me was that my husband responds to strength, not dependence. All those years I spent waiting, even pleading, for him to be the 'leader' of this family—that just led us all astray. I had put all the balls in his court, and he couldn't manage them, which just made us all more stressed.

"As it turns out, my husband was simply 'scared stuck.' He didn't know how to solve his problems. Finally, one day, I just said, 'Honey, I love you and I know you love our family, so we need to do something. I made an appointment for next week with a good ADHD professional, and we'll go talk to her together. You'll see; it will be easier than you think.' And it was. But it was my confidence in the outcome that turned the corner for us. As a result, I've found a strength and confidence I never knew I had."

- **Maintain close networks of friends**

Tammy: "The reason I've stayed married for five years *and* kept my sanity is because I have a close circle of friends that does not include my husband. For one thing, he tends to be a 'friend stealer,' and he'll really turn on the charm, leaving me in the shadows. For another, it can be a poor strategy to keep all your emotional eggs in one basket. It's too much pressure to put on either of you."

- **Develop a self-care list**

Gloria: "My motto now is 'Pay Myself First'—financially, emotionally, physically, and spiritually. If I wait for my husband to think of my needs, I'll wait a long time. Financially, I allot myself a weekly savings that goes in a private account, and I control all the finances. Emotionally, I don't wait for my husband to decide if he'll cooperate in or sabotage my week-

ADHD Partner Survey Snapshot: Finding Their Strength

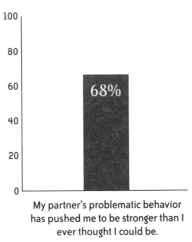

My partner's problematic behavior
has pushed me to be stronger than I
ever thought I could be.

end fun. I make plans and might invite him to come along. If he does, fine. If not, fine. Physically, I drag my happy butt to the gym and hike outdoors. Spiritually, I pray when I awake and before I sleep. I read books with a spiritual focus. I tell my Higher Power everything. This is the one place I am heard."

- **Take a break; get some time away from your partner**

Maurice: "Even if all you can manage is a weekend away to the calm house of a friend or relative and must barter for child-care, it might be just the thing to detach from the chaos and plan the next step."

- **Create a list of things to do during "freak-out" moments**

Leigh: "In the heat of the moment—after being subjected to another of my husband's anger fits, for example—I used to just cry in exhaustion or hide in bed, trying to make myself so small I'd disappear. My brain could do no more. I finally developed a list of activities that make me feel better immediately and keep it handy. When things start to erupt, I pick one and do it."

- **Lighten up**

Elaine: "You know the movie *Night of the Living Dead*? When the zombies smell a 'fresh' human, they go after them yelling 'Brains, I want more brains.' I play this in my head when my husband does his crazy-making stuff, trying to come after my brains! It makes me laugh, and my shoulders relax a bit."

• **Find areas of freedom and expansion**

Rose: "I found that reading *The Artist's Way* and joining a local group based on the book's lessons reconnected me with a vital life force that too many years of stress had beaten out of me. The author talks about removing creative blocks from your life. Getting my husband to realize he had ADHD and helping him to do something about his problems removed my biggest creative block imaginable: his unending negativity and constantly interrupting whatever I'm doing."

Develop and maintain personal limits

For example, you might need to take charge of the finances using the system suggested in Chapter 4. The group suggests other ways to maintain boundaries:

• **Ask yourself, whom exactly will this disaster affect?**

Jason: "How I react to the consequences of my ADHD partner's poor choices depends on if it is a problem only for her or me as well. Either way, I try to protect myself and not shield her from consequences. When it is only *her* problem, I commiserate, give my opinion if asked, and might help if she asks me to do something specific. But I will not do more even if I could solve the problem quickly. I hate to be like this, but until she decides to do something about her chaos-producing behaviors, it's the only way to stay sane."

• **Get good sleep,** *no matter what*

Does your partner's night-owl habit, untreated restless legs syndrome, or sleep apnea interfere with your sleep? (All three conditions, by the way, are increasingly thought to be linked with ADHD and the brain chemical dopamine, and they often respond to ADHD medication treatment.) Group members who've drawn the line at sleep deprivation, even if *someone* has to sleep on the sofa, highly recommend it. In fact, your health depends on it.

• **Consider seeking a higher power, however you define it**

Rose: "What helped me form the strongest boundary was connecting with my Higher Power. When trying to erect boundaries out of helplessness or anger, they'd collapse easily. But knowing that I'm part of something larger, a divine spirit for good, helped me to be strong internally without fighting or being angry. A book that helped tremendously is Marianne Williamson's *A Return to Love,* based on the *Course in Miracles.*

If you find terms like "God" problematic, substitute what works for you, such as *good orderly direction*. This book also helped me to understand the false ego and, in my husband's case, reach around all those defenses to his authentic self. Without this piece *and* medication, all the medication in the world couldn't have brought the changes we've enjoyed."

Brush up on your communication skills

Conversations can go kerflooey when one partner has ADHD deficits in listening and attending, and you'll learn all about that in the chapters ahead. But, for now, consider that most of us can improve our ability to communicate clearly.

"Many people need to learn the framework for talking," says Eleanor Payson, a Michigan therapist who specializes in adult ADHD. "In modern culture, in general, we've lost our compass for this, and some need to learn the basic rules for listening to someone else and talking to be heard." Payson recommends a book called *Difficult Conversations: How to Discuss What Matters Most,* by Douglas Stone, Bruce Patton, and Sheila Heen.

Learn to recognize a mate's narcissistic tendencies

If you're dealing with a narcissistic person who has ADHD, don't count on your endless compassion being seen as a virtue. "The narcissistic person thinks empathy is just being weak, insincere, and sickly, and it can lead to exploitive behavior that leaves you devastated," cautions Payson, author of *The Wizard of Oz and Other Narcissists: Coping with the One-Way Relationship in Work, Love, and Family.*

ADHD proves most problematic when it coexists with an inability to self-reflect and empathize. "Behaviors such as not being able to feel empathy for others or apologize are on the continuum of narcissism," Payson explains, "and narcissistic people can be remarkably capable of manipulation and defocusing the issue away from what it really is." For example, say your partner makes a mistake or forgets something. "The less narcissistic that person is, the more willing he or she is to admit the mistake," she continues. "The more narcissistic person, however, will feel less remorse or guilt and be less likely to admit to the mistake."

(By the way, plenty of people with ADHD are *not* narcissistic, and plenty of people without ADHD *are*, including some partners of adults with ADHD.)

The narcissistic person might often appear charming in public, not to mention always in control and confident, yet at home Dr. Jekyll devolves into Mr. or Ms. Hyde. Of course, this Hyde character doesn't see this behavior as problematic. Moreover, the narcissistic person's talent in projecting their own problems onto a partner can prove so powerful that the partner capitulates in accepting responsibility for the relationship's troubles. As Payson points out, even mental health professionals can miss the signs when conducting individual or couples therapy.

Get "trained instead of blamed"

Stop accepting unfair blame and learn new skills. Get trained in conflict negotiation, communications techniques, and boundary setting. Some therapists specialize in these areas, and groups such as the National Alliance for the Mentally Ill (NAMI.org) teach family members related strategies in dealing with various mental-health conditions.

The better trained you are, the less likely you'll get sucked into a poor reaction. For example, prior to her husband's diagnosis, Julia's biggest problem was his temper, flying off the handle over the smallest things and often blaming her for the outbursts. "Now that I know it's the ADHD talking, I just let him sound off," Julia says. "Then I'll say calmly, 'You're just stressing again. It's not worth getting upset about.'" He settles down and life goes on. "Before, I would react with anger to his anger and we'd wind up with a wildfire," she recalls. "Now it's like blowing out a match." Yes, she hopes that soon he will agree to pursue treatment, because managing his symptoms in this way cannot be her lifetime job. Meanwhile, the household is more peaceful, less adversarial.

Find Meaning in Your Experience

Information, support, and empowering skills are necessary, but they won't take you across the finish line. A hallmark of psychologist Herbert Gravitz's therapeutic approach for three decades has been his inclusion of spirituality and even mythology. With that in mind, he encourages those who've too long ridden on the ADHD roller coaster to embark on a hero's journey and "elevate your small story to something that is universal."

Instead of asking "Why me?" ask, "What am I supposed to accomplish from this experience?" Maybe it's taking the pain that you've experienced and using it to open other people's eyes. "In that way," he suggests, "you move from being an invisible survivor to a visible healer—to yourself, your family, and your community."

Write it out—online and in a personal journal

Pouring out your pain and confusion onto a computer screen can bring you out of isolation and even improve your health, according to University of Texas psychologist James W. Pennebaker. His studies were the first to demonstrate the benefits from writing about trauma, including improved immune function and lower blood pressure and heart rate. "Just setting apart 10 or 20 minutes a day for three or four days to explore your deepest thoughts and feelings can be quite useful," says Pennebaker, author of *Writing to Heal: A Guided Journal for Recovering from Trauma and Emotional Upheaval*.

Find Support; Reclaim Your Voice

"I remember receiving e-mails from the group while at work with tears in my eyes, hoping no one saw me," Marianne says. "It was hard to believe that strangers cared so much about me." After 15 years of therapy, she was also astonished at how much more helpful the group was. They described the exact behaviors in their partners that she saw in hers. That long-sought validation calmed her nerves, allowing her thinking to sharpen.

Marianne says her husband would not accept the idea of ADHD treatment for him and their son, insisting he acted the same way as a child and turned out okay: "But no, he *didn't* turn out okay. He has real problems; he just doesn't see them. I let him talk me out of what was best for our child, and the group helped me regain confidence. Now my child is getting the help he needs, and so am I."

Longtime group member Sharon sums up the group's value this way:

Pre-Internet, many of us stayed stuck for years, thinking we were the only ones. Now, anyone with computer access can connect on their own schedule to a vast community with a common experience and informed collective knowledge—*free*, without worrying about finding babysitters. It speeds our healing tremendously. And, along the way, it even bridges the gaps between people of distinctly different economic, educational, religious, cultural, and political backgrounds—people who thought they'd never on earth have anything in common with each other and then become intimate friends.

A warning to those with "snoopy" partners: Password-protect any e-mail account or computer files. And, to protect your and your partner's privacy, consider using a pseudonym online.

Give up passively hoping that your ADHD partner will change

"People do not change without consequences to their actions," insists Kate Lewis, a psychotherapist, advanced practice nurse, and adult ADHD specialist in St. Charles, Missouri. "Thinking about their actions doesn't change anything, and people with ADHD can think something to death and do nothing." Change comes with action, and the best catalyst for action is consequences. What about adults who know that they have

---

Mostly, sharing stories with others who "get it" lightens your load. "People need to be given permission to have their own life, and they need to have their pain validated," confirms psychologist Herbert Gravitz. Your support-group peers will remind you to take care of yourself, do things that bring you joy, and know that no matter how many times your ADHD partner blames you unfairly, "It's not your fault."

"You know, these people aren't just griping," Renee says. "They're committed to their partners, and they share their progress and setbacks until life becomes easier." Expect some venting, too, though, she warns. "No matter how well we understand and support our partners, until we start seeing progress, it can take its toll. So why should we be expected to be more than human?"

Chris points out that it's better to blow off steam with outsiders than one's ADHD partner or family members: "My boyfriend can't listen because it sinks his self-esteem even lower, and if my friends hear too much negative without the positive, they form a lasting bad impression of him."

A few newcomers, desperate for quick tips to turn around challenging situations, bristle at the "negative" (that is, realistic) advice offered. The hard reality is, you can exhaust yourself doing all the accommodating. When ADHD is involved, standard relationship advice typically falls flat.

Then, too, some group members are dealing with "ADHD Lite" and mistakenly assume that others are simply whiners. Support-group members benefit best when they remember that ADHD comes in many shapes and sizes and that the goal is sharing information, support, and compassion.

For more information, visit ADHDRollerCoaster.com.

ADHD and that it's creating pain for their loved ones and still they do nothing about it? "That's unacceptable behavior," she says. "They need to learn about it and do everything they can to change the behavior and give comfort to the people they love." (You'll learn more about getting through denial in the next success strategy.)

Solving ADHD's Double Whammy

I've learned a lot about ADHD, but it's still hard to grasp how my wife and I can perceive "reality" so differently. We face the same external forces, but either she doesn't see them or she misses their importance.

— RANDY

When Brian's girlfriend decided to be evaluated for ADHD, she made an appointment with the only therapist on her insurance plan who was accepting new patients. Unfortunately, that therapist knew little about ADHD, and his girlfriend gave up on ever getting an evaluation. "She gives up easily with most obstacles," Brian says. "For a long time, I didn't push for a competent evaluation because I didn't like the idea of acting like Big Daddy."

To Brian, intervening just didn't seem healthy. Then again, his girlfriend's problematic ADHD symptoms presented fertile ground for a bumper crop of unhealthy reactions on his part. Finally, he realized it wasn't a question of her learning to be a more responsible adult or him being a dominating male if he stepped in to help. "If she suffered a knock to the head that resulted in cognitive impairment similar to that of ADHD, I wouldn't expect her to go it alone, would I?" Once he clarified this in his mind, he could think about collaborating in finding a more qualified professional.

Wait a minute. This success strategy is called "Taking Care of Yourself," isn't it? It's not called "Here's How You Can Do *Even More* for Your ADHD

Partner," is it? That's correct. Yet, as Brian and many other support-group members have found, sometimes the best way to take care of themselves—and their children—is to actively help their ADHD partners find the help that they need and deserve.

This chapter explains two key points to remember in this regard:
- Your partner's ADHD symptoms can obscure the ability to perceive his or her challenges.
- Your ADHD partner might need your help initiating an evaluation and guiding treatment, and that's not "codependence."

The Two Biggest Obstacles to Success

So what about *your* ADHD partner? Is he or she "in denial" about behaviors that you perceive as obvious ADHD symptoms or dragging heels over making that appointment? Or are *you* in denial that your partner truly has a medical condition that causes honest-to-goodness impairment? Join the club. Denial: It's the biggest single challenge tackled in the support group, sufficiently complex and important to merit a success strategy all its own.

But here's the second-biggest challenge: understanding the difference between denial and the fact that ADHD can create deficits in the ability to initiate solutions, follow through with plans, and focus on priorities. Says one new support-group member, "My husband read an article about ADHD in relationships and said, 'Wow, this is us' but then he'd forgotten all about it by the next day!"

And this is ADHD's Double Whammy: The very brain deficits that cause problematic behaviors can inhibit your ADHD partner's ability to perceive them and, furthermore, to seek, select, and follow through on viable solutions. If change is going to happen, *you* might need to help your partner see his or her behaviors in a new light and encourage an evaluation. Then, if the ADHD diagnosis is made, your help might also be needed to inform treatment decisions, at least in the beginning.

Some support-group members initially balk at this advice, but their reasoning isn't always logical. For example, they bitterly complain that they are tired of their ADHD partners acting like children, leaving them to pick up the mess, do all the reminding, all the prodding. Yet, when it comes to helping their partners pursue an ADHD evaluation and then treatment—in other words, gaining the tools to finally start *acting* more like more mature adults—they might say, "Oh, that's too much like parenting."

Jazmin had a similar resistance when she entered the psychologist's office exhausted by propping up her husband of six years, only recently diagnosed with ADHD. She bristled when the psychologist suggested that she needed to help just a little more. Then the psychologist explained that her husband's unaddressed ADHD symptoms (procrastination, distractibility, and so forth) meant he was unlikely to successfully follow through on the psychologist's recommendations. Jazmin agreed to try. She found a psychiatrist qualified to treat ADHD, made the appointment, and went with her husband to the doctor. With that help, her husband was finally able to start on the path to success.

The psychologist in Jazmin's case was ADHD expert Michele Novotni, coauthor of *Adult ADHD: A Reader-Friendly Guide to Identifying, Understanding, and Treating Adult Attention Deficit/Hyperactivity Disorder*, and she admits that asking Jazmin to intervene sounds like unorthodox advice. After all, aren't adults supposed to be responsible for themselves? "I know it isn't *supposed* to be this way with couples," Novotni concedes, "but this is often necessary in order for the individual with ADHD to get the help that's needed." This type of support, she emphasizes, should *not* be confused with codependent caretaking.

To be clear, accepting that your partner's ADHD-related deficits might impede treatment does *not* absolve him or her of responsibility. "It's very important that the ADHD partner actively participate in the treatment process," Novotni urges. "Over time, the ADHD partner will be able to assume more responsibility for his or her own treatment. That, however, should be a *goal* in treatment, not a *demand for beginning it.*"

Why Professionals Need Your Feedback

In recent years, it's gotten easier to find therapists and physicians qualified to evaluate and treat ADHD, yet it still takes some detective work. That's another reason for you to get involved: to help your ADHD partner assess the professional's thoroughness and competence during office visits. Two heads are better than one.

Genevieve learned this lesson the hard way. She had worked patiently for months to encourage her husband to talk to a professional about his chronic "monologuing" in social situations, forgetting important details about important clients, and one fender bender too many. Because his brother was recently diagnosed with ADHD and their two children have it as well, she thought he seemed a good candidate for an evaluation, too. So she was understandably flattened by the doctor's assessment of her husband: "Well, you probably have ADHD, but if you made it this far in life, you don't need medication now."

The physician had not conducted a full evaluation—more of a quick eyeballing with questions like, "How're you doing?" And he did not ask for the perspective of a spouse or other loved one, which most ADHD experts recommend. As a result, this doctor had no clue about her husband's actual impairments—the ones he doesn't remember, never notices, or didn't think relevant to tell the physician—or about the fact that he heavily self-medicates with the nicotine in chewing tobacco.

(By the way, "chaw" contains 28 carcinogens and is a known cause of human cancer, according to the Centers for Disease Control. Unfortunately, chewing tobacco and cigarettes hold a special appeal for many people with ADHD because nicotine can create the calming focus they otherwise find elusive. In fact, more than a few people with ADHD, like Genevieve's husband, are self-medicating through habits that pose significant risks to their health, cognitive functioning, and legal status—like alcohol abuse, addictive sexual issues, using marijuana or other illegal substances, and

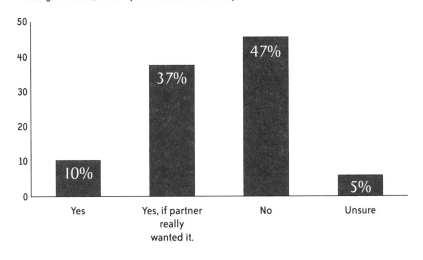

ADHD Partner Survey Snapshot: Going It Alone?

Survey question: "Do you feel your partner has the skills and ability to seek ADHD evaluation and treatment on his or her own, without help from you or a close friend? (This would require an ability to initiate sometimes-complex tasks and reliably follow through on them, fill out questionnaires accurately, remember instructions, and the like.)"

adrenaline-boosting behaviors like driving recklessly. Even sugar and caffeine can adversely affect brain function. For those reasons, it's especially desirable to find a professional who can view such activities holistically, in the context of ADHD.)

Have you, like many others, encountered a professional who cites career success as a litmus test for the absence of ADHD? That is another indication that you might want to keep shopping for someone with better ADHD expertise.

The support group clamors with stories of ADHD partners who manage to "hyperfocus" on their work but experience significant problems in their domestic life, social relationships, driving, and financial management. Still, too many physicians mistakenly perceive a patient's employment, advanced degrees, or even marriage as proof that the individual could not possibly have ADHD or that medication is unnecessary. Yet even among those ADHD partners who seem to enjoy career success, it's often just a matter of time before a critical judgment error finally unravels their success.

Now, do you remain skeptical that your help is really needed? Maybe you're right in perceiving your partner as fully capable of going it alone. ADHD is a spectrum condition, after all, with many points on the spectrum.

Just in case you're undecided, we'll let two sets of experts (support-group members and leading ADHD experts), tell you in their own words why they consider third-party feedback critical to the evaluation and treatment process. (The evaluation process is outlined in Appendix A.)

Support-Group Members Speak Out

Whoa! I looked at my husband's partially completed ADHD evaluation form. It asks if he can concentrate when he reads. He wrote, "yes." But he can't even finish one short newspaper article! What if he answers all the questions inaccurately and I'm not there to set the record straight? From what I hear in the support group, some doctors and therapists are easily fooled. Yet I know if this doctor says, "No, you don't have ADHD," my husband will say, "Case closed!" Then what do I do?

—Leslie

My boyfriend doggedly tried to find help for years but he didn't know he had ADHD, and the doctors never asked the right questions and never asked for input from family or friends. Consequently, they had him on antidepressants, antianxiety pills, and you name it—plus therapy—none of it working and some of it making things worse. I finally figured out he might have ADHD, but his HMO had no ADHD specialists, and my boyfriend didn't have the mental stamina to battle with them. Plus he lacked the judgment to know if a physician was well qualified. If I hadn't gotten involved, I'm sure my boyfriend would have given up or done something tragically desperate. He was at that point.

—Dana

My husband came home from the evaluation saying that, according to the psychiatrist, he had a very mild form of ADHD. He said, "The doctor thinks I'm doing so well in life that I don't need medication, but if I felt it would help with work, I could try it." With the group's support, I worked up the courage to ask the doctor about this, because my husband has some significant problems, including being very irritable with the kids and being a computer addict. The doctor said he'd actually advised my husband to also take the medication at home, to help with family life. So, it's a good thing I asked. I think my husband just couldn't admit anything was "wrong" with him.

—Kristen

After two years of so-called ADHD treatment, my wife casually mentioned how she feels like crap most of the time—"fuzzy," disorganized, and unmotivated—until she visits her physician. Then the excitement of having the doc's focused attention perks her up and she feels good. As a result, she's been telling him that she's doing great! That means her entire treatment has been based on how she felt while she was in the doctor's office, with the facts of yesterday lost in the mist of time. No wonder treatment hasn't helped!

—Hank

Part of the reason my boyfriend didn't get better for so long, despite his wanting to, is that he was too embarrassed to talk honestly to the doctor about whether the medication was helping and how his life was really going. He always just said, "Things are fine." So now either his brother or I go with him. He says he's relieved to have our help articulating his challenges and his progress because, on his own, he gets "brain freeze" when he walks in the office door.

—Tammy

Group experience says your involvement is very important. Your partner might not be able to accurately describe or recall the problems experienced or the impact of medication on behavior—or remember the physician's or therapist's instructions. If your partner is highly defensive, explain that you want to go so that you can learn how to be more patient and understanding. It might sound manipulative, but when you're dealing with a person in denial of his or her challenges, that's often what it takes to help them to a point of clarity.

—Susanna

Leading ADHD Experts Weigh In

Most psychiatric patients will come in and say there are changes. The person with ADHD doesn't complain of any changes at all. They have been like that all their lives. They aren't often objective. When they hear others describe their behavior, they feel it is someone else being discussed. One handles that clinically by not being accusatory. Yet, it's essential, when possible, to talk with the partner. I find it mandatory for an evaluation of a patient's status. Besides defining the problem, which the patient might not recognize, the partner is also able to recognize changes as the treatment progresses. It's essential to have that information.

—Paul Wender, M.D., pioneer in the diagnosis and treatment of pediatric and adult ADHD, in a 2007 interview with the author

What is one of the cardinal symptoms of ADHD? Failing to pay attention to both outer and internal phenomena. Psychologist and ADHD researcher Russell Barkley has followed up on the children with ADHD from a study he conducted in the late 1980s. These subjects are now in their early twenties. How many of them still have ADHD? It depends on whom you ask. If you ask those young adults, it's 5 percent. If you ask their parents, it's 50 percent. Moreover, if you loosen the diagnostic criteria to measure the adult manifestations of ADHD, as opposed to those of children, it is nearly 70 percent. The moral of the story: Even for the diagnosis, much less for the treatment plan, you need another person's corroboration.

—Stephen Hinshaw, Ph.D., ADHD research investigator, Professor and Chair of the Psychology Department at the University of California, Berkeley, in a 2007 interview with the author

Many adults with ADHD may have a limited awareness of how ADHD-related behaviors cause problems for them and have an impact on others. In the case of couples, it is to their advantage for the clinician to interview them together when reviewing the ADHD symptoms. This procedure also helps the non-ADHD partner develop an accurate understanding and an empathetic attitude concerning the impact of ADHD symptoms on the relationship, setting the stage for improving the relationship after the diagnostic process has been completed.

—**"Diagnosis of AD/HD in Adults" from the National Resource Center on ADHD**

Part of the reason why adult psychiatrists have not previously identified ADHD in adults may be that, unlike their child counterparts, most adult assessments focus on the patient rather than other informants. This means that the psychiatrist only has access to information about family complaints or employer frustration to the extent that the patient is aware of those perspectives.

With ADHD, insight is variable.... By comparing the reports from two different informants, the clinician has access to multiple informants and a sense of the compatibility of the patient's report with that of others for the full range of comorbid diagnoses. For example, the clinician may observe that the patient does not identify difficulties such as lying, defiance, or poor social skills, but these are major areas of concern for his or her spouse. On the other hand, both patient and informant may show good agreement on report of ADHD symptoms. This feedback is in itself helpful to the patient.

—**Margaret D. Weiss, M.D., Ph.D., and Jacqueline R. Weiss, M.D., "A Guide to the Treatment of Adults With ADHD,"** *The Journal of Clinical Psychiatry* **2004;65**

INTRODUCTION

"Roller Coaster? What Roller Coaster? You're Imagining Things!"

Many of our partners refuse to consider ADHD. They just blame their troubles on someone else.

— LESLIE

David's wife acknowledges that she has ADHD but fails to see how her behaviors adversely affect the kids and him, so she does nothing about it. "She read that changing her diet can help her symptoms, but she keeps forgetting what that diet is supposed to be," he says.

Merrie's husband refuses to consider the possibility that he and ADHD have anything in common. But to Merrie, his lifelong symptoms read like a textbook case. He is a smart man whose chronic misjudgments on the job and at home make his life—and his family's lives—unnecessarily hard and frustrating. "If an evaluation and treatment could make your life happier, why wouldn't you try it?" she asks. "It makes no sense to me."

Collette's fiancé also insists that he doesn't have ADHD, three decades of classic symptoms to the contrary. "I am not your enemy and I am not telling you this to be mean," she says to him. "I'm trying to help you." Collette suspects he feels threatened. When he was a child, teachers labeled him everything from class clown to underperformer, and worse. As a teacher herself, she works with students who have ADHD. "What if our own kids have troubles in school?" she asks him. "Are you saying that we won't get them help?" Sighing deeply, he replies that he *knows* his future kids will have the same troubles he's had, but he just doesn't want to talk about it now (translation: *never*).

To be sure, legions of adults with undiagnosed ADHD leap on the opportunity to have an ADHD evaluation once the idea is presented to them. They're bone tired of puzzling over why they struggle more than others who seem no smarter—and often less smart. "My wife was incredibly open to the idea and relieved to finally understand her multiple frustrations," Joe says.

Others, however, obliviously sail on, missing the connection between their dysfunctional behavior and dysfunctional work situations, relationships, and finances. They blame a bad economy, a pointy-haired boss, disharmonious feng shui, or a "high-maintenance" partner. Echoing other leading ADHD authorities, psychiatrists and researchers Margaret Weiss, Lily Hechtman, and Gabrielle Weiss offer this observation in their book *ADHD in Adulthood: A Guide to Current Theory, Diagnosis, and Treatment*:

> Individuals with ADHD are unaware of the behaviors that provoke negative reactions in others. They are aware, however, that others hover around them nagging. The connection between their behavior and this nagging response remains opaque. The white noise of nagging becomes an ever-more-distant hum, which the patients tune out; meanwhile, their families turn up the volume, becoming even more angry and controlling.

Of course many people with ADHD fall in the vast middle. They acknowledge they're not "living up to their potential," but they don't relish hearing that anything is *wrong* with their brain. (When it's put that way, who would?) They want to believe, for example, that the right organizational system will solve their problems. And that might be true, but often only until the novelty wears off.

The four chapters devoted to this success strategy on denial explain:

- **The psychological reasons** why your partner might refuse to acknowledge problematic behaviors or do anything about them (Chapter 13).
- **The biological reasons** that might prevent your partner from recognizing the problematic behaviors (Chapter 14).
- **New ways to break though denial** (Chapter 15).
- **More solutions and strategies**—because you can't have too many tools in your dealing-with-denial toolbox (Chapter 16).

Ann to Jerome: "Yearn for the Vast and Endless Sea"

At first, Ann had trouble convincing her husband, Jerome, that he might have ADHD, despite telltale signs at home and at work. Yet her options appeared constrained. What was she supposed to do? Divorce him? Drag him in for an evaluation against his will? Clearly, this situation called for less-draconian measures.

"After I joined the support group and learned more about ADHD, I gained some clarity," Ann remembers. "I soon realized that someone had to break the trauma cycle and start creating another reality. That 'someone' seemed to be me." That's because Jerome remained locked in his attitude that "This is how I've always been, and it's not going to change." As a chemical engineer, he understood chemical reactions, including those in the brain, far better than she did. But did that special knowledge sharpen his ability to perceive his own behavior and understand its effect on Ann or others? Not a chance.

Even more strangely, he scoffed at the idea that a medication could change anything, even though he had once worked at a pharmaceutical company, personally helping to develop a very effective treatment for a brain condition. He wasn't exactly thrilled with the way he was—just resigned to being that way. "It was hard to fathom how illogical this logical engineer could be," she says.

One day after a particularly upsetting interaction, she took a deep breath and then a long walk. Out in the fresh air, a quote came to mind, from a book she'd read years ago by Antoine de Saint-Exupery, the French poet and author of a classic book called *The Little Prince*:

> If you want to build a ship, don't drum up the men to gather wood, divide the work, and give orders. Instead, teach them to yearn for the vast and endless sea.

Increasingly, the support group was validating her perceptions of what was going wrong at home—perceptions her husband had long denied. That buoyed the courage of her convictions. They also encouraged Ann to try detaching mentally a bit from the chaos and Jerome's pessimistic mindset, not to mention letting up on her rather desperate attempts to change that mindset. She stopped pushing him to read books about ADHD and stopped listing the problems it was causing him, her, and them. She stopped the ultimatums, too. Who has ever *yearned* for an ulti-matum? Who has ever *yearned* to be told they have a disorder?

Instead, Ann started using her imagination, setting aside a few minutes each day to envision a life together of joy and harmony—the "vast and endless sea" worth yearning for. It took some imagination, too, because at the moment their little sea felt quite storm-tossed. And she couldn't pragmatically plot their course because she'd run fresh out of pragmatic strategies. Simply holding this vision, however, lifted her spirits. And the stories of hope she heard in the group convinced her that reaching this destination wasn't a siren call but an attainable reality.

Soon after that, amazing things started happening. She started sleep-ing better and feeling less stressed. In turn, Jerome grew calmer, too, and less defensive. One day, he nonchalantly flipped through a book on ADHD. The next evening, at a dinner party, friends mentioned their relief at finally finding a skilled psychiatrist to help their child with ADHD. Jerome asked for the physician's name and, as it turns out, they worked in the same office building. He stopped in the next day to meet the psychiatrist and judged him "smart enough" to trust. Once diag-nosed, Jerome agreed to try medication, which made a huge difference in his life and their life together. Coincidences? Maybe. But Ann has a different perspective:

> It all started with my becoming very mentally clear about a new des-tination on the horizon. I had to change course first, before our little ship crashed on the rocks, and hold out the vision for my husband, a vision of how life could be. I couldn't wait for him to change course, because he'd long stopped believing in the possibility. In fact, as he confided to me much later, he was simply waiting for this little rat to jump ship.

It took a couple of years for Ann to stop clutching her life preserver, ready to bail at the next wave of backsliding, afraid of heading back into the tempest. And it required much compassion on both their parts. But for Ann and Jerome, it's now smooth sailing, with the occasional squall just to keep life interesting.

CHAPTER
THIRTEEN

Psychological Denial:
The FEAR Factor

My partner couldn't imagine that adding one more hassle (that is, treatment) would ease her stress, but it has. She also expected to fail, as with previous attempts to fix her problems. That was her biggest fear, because treatment seemed our last hope.

— Greta

Yonu can lead a horse to water, but you can't make it drink, the old adage goes. "That's true," says psychologist Herbert Gravitz, "but you can make the horse thirsty." As an expert in understanding disorders that typically involve denial, such as alcoholism, Gravitz says that one of the best ways to make the person thirsty is to first know why the person is refusing treatment.

Many people with as-yet-undiagnosed ADHD will respond positively to the idea of seeking an evaluation and treatment if approached in a straight-forward, loving way with accurate, nonjudgmental information. When people respond negatively, however, it is often because their information is inaccurate, and that creates fear. Make that F. E.A.R., as Gravitz defines it:

False   Evidence   Appearing   Real

For 10 years, David stumbled along with his wife and her three young children from a previous marriage before they realized that she and her children probably all had ADHD. "No one knew about ADHD then, so it took a few years for me to peel back the layers," he recalls. "Beneath the anger, shutdown, and impulsivity, the overarching emotion I saw in my family was fear—fear of being somehow 'not like' everyone else." The way he saw it, that fear and defensiveness, magnified by years of accumulated hurts and resentments, dominated their worldview.

Imagine then, he says, the kind of confidence, strength, and "brain processing energy" it takes to get yourself into treatment, research the options, deal with insurance, and "bare one's soul against a lifetime of self-defenses erected haphazardly because no more logical alternative (that is, an ADHD diagnosis) existed."

So that you can both start stepping out of the fog of denial and into clarity, this chapter focuses on helping you to:

- Discover and empathize with the misperceptions and fears that could be contributing to your partner's refusal to consider an evaluation or, once diagnosed, to consider treatment.
- Examine your own misperceptions and fearful reasons for denying that your partner has ADHD.

Whatever the source of the psychological denial, you need to understand and acknowledge it before you can both move beyond it.

"False Evidence" Contributing to Denial

Given all the misinformation floating around about ADHD, it's no wonder the public is confused. This confusion might be preventing your partner from "connecting the dots" of ADHD to his or her own life. Consider these five common examples of "False Evidence Appearing Real":

1. Many people don't connect ADHD to their challenges

The misunderstanding often grows from the unfortunate name, *Attention-Deficit/Hyperactivity Disorder*, as explained in Chapter 1. Most people with ADHD will protest that they have no attention deficit if interested in what they're doing. Many will also point out that everybody forgets things or runs late sometimes. And they're right on both counts.

All ADHD symptoms do represent "normal" human behaviors; it's the *degree* to which the behaviors are present—and impairing the quality of life—that makes a diagnosis. People who deny ADHD for these reasons might need gentle direction in linking their problems to ADHD symptoms, *drawing their attention* to the connection.

2. Many people don't realize that ADHD "has many faces"

ADHD's widely ranging symptoms and levels of severity confuse those who seek neat categories. For example, if they attend an adult ADHD support group to learn more and encounter a few highly impaired attendees, they might conclude, "Those people are bad off. If they have ADHD, I most certainly *don't* have it."

3. Lifelong rationalizations can obscure reality

David warns to watch for the plausible-sounding "cover" excuses that some ADHD partners offer to explain their actions. For example, he would ask his wife why she consistently stayed up half the night on the computer even though she always had a hard time waking up the next morning. She would say, "I *like* to stay up that late" or "My entire family stayed up late." It never occurred to her to say, "I have no idea why I can't make myself turn off the computer and go to bed at a decent hour" or "Maybe my entire family has ADHD, too."

The truth is, David's wife really *didn't* like staying up late. It made her feel perpetually tired and fuzzyheaded. It seemed normal simply because she'd always done it and doing otherwise seemed impossible. The lesson here: Stay alert to the possibility that behind the offered reason lurks the real reason. In mature adults, behavior follows beliefs, not vice-versa.

Countless other smokescreens come to mind. People who are top performers at work or have a string of graduate degrees can assume that their achievements rule out ADHD. "But I *can't* have ADHD. I make a lot of money!" they protest. Or, "But I am a well loved pastor who has a special relationship with God!"

Yes, maybe they are earning buckets of money—but they also might not be paying their bills.

Yes, they're successful at work—but maybe they pour every ounce of focus into it, leaving little or nothing for the rest of life.

Yes, the congregation loves that pastor—but he shows a darker side of his personality to his family, during the rare hours he spends with them.

4. Some people with ADHD play the blame game

Has your ADHD partner suggested that *you* are causing his or her problems? Or, the opposite, does your partner blame himself or herself for anything that goes wrong, and your attempts to reassure are simply wasted effort? In either case, you're certainly not alone.

In his book *Is He Depressed or What? What to Do When the Man You Love Is Irritable, Moody, and Withdrawn*, San Diego-based psychologist David B. Wexler provides a personal example. He describes how, when he was laid up with back pain, his wife did nursing duty. He was often in a bad mood, "snapping at her and getting irritable when she didn't take care of things just the way I wanted her to."

Chronic pain, and feeling depressed about it, had changed his personality, but he failed to see it at the time. "I felt bad, didn't like it, and didn't know what to call it," he writes. "So I looked around and found someone whose fault it might have been. Hers."

Clearly, disorders such as depression and ADHD can cloud judgment and lead to erroneous perceptions. The fact that the two conditions often coexist only compounds distorted perspectives.

5. "I'm just being a man (or woman)!"

Remember, ADHD symptoms can be viewed as exaggerations of the human condition. Therefore, given that male and female brains do differ in key ways (as a spate of recent books on the subject explain), might not ADHD exaggerate perceived gender differences, too? For example, your male ADHD partner might hyperfocus on football or your female ADHD partner on shopping or chatting, two stereotypical gender preoccupations that could obscure the underlying disorder, the core explanation for the obsessive hyperfocus.

As you can see with the above examples, denial doesn't necessarily come from stubbornness. Misperceptions and misinformation can play a big role, too. Consider now some other examples of "False Evidence Appearing Real"—namely, life-long insecurities and actual fears, often compounded by the lifelong trauma and confusion of living with undetected ADHD.

Your Partner's Possible Fears

Have you complained about your partner's inability to empathize with you or the children? Chapter 3 offered possible reasons for that. But now, shall we turn the tables and explore *your* empathy quotient?

First, let's get our terms straight. Being empathic does *not* mean enabling, rescuing, or feeling sympathy for your ADHD partner. Neither is it suffering stoically or relegating your need for reciprocity to the trashcan. (ADHD is highly treatable, remember? No medals are awarded for suffering through its more challenging aspects.) Being empathic means putting yourself in your partner's shoes, feeling what your partner feels.

For now, it doesn't matter if your partner's fears about an ADHD diagnosis are rational or fact-based. Remember: We're talking about False Evidence Appearing Real, mixed in with some valid emotional fears. At this point, your goal is to understand *why* your partner remains stuck in denial. Only when you understand *that* can you begin to help ease your partner out of it.

For example, perhaps your ADHD partner is like Paul, diagnosed with ADHD at age 32. After reading one prominent psychiatrist's book on ADHD, he wished someone would take away that doctor's medical license. Was it because the information was incorrect or because Paul disagreed? Just the opposite. He was enraged at the mere *idea of* ADHD, specifically that he might have it. "Accepting that I was a loser was a hell of a lot easier than knowing what I could have been if this had been detected years ago," Paul says. "But after some reflection I'm thankful for the man's hard work and ingenuity." Look past anger and you often find trepidation.

Rebecca—"Talking Things Through" Never Worked

As I was filing divorce papers, my mother-in-law said, "If only we could talk things through, if only you could help him get control of his spending problem, his business management problems, his temper." Sheesh. Nothing I've said the last three weeks has gotten through about how untreated ADHD prevents any of this from being accomplished.

Frankly, I'm dead tired from trying to help my husband. We've "talked things through" for 15 years, and it's never made a bit of difference. It seems like many other people in the support group have gone through the stage where we think that if we just explain one more time, in a different way, maybe this time our partner and our partner's family members will understand—and cooperate. And it never happens, because the problem has nothing to do with how we explain it or approach it.

Why do people want to run from the truth? Why is it better to call it anything but ADHD? If it looks like ADHD, talks like ADHD, acts like ADHD, causes all the same problems as ADHD, why not assume that maybe, possibly, perhaps, I dunno...it might just be ADHD!

Now put yourself in your partner's shoes and consider these other possible fears:

Fear of opening the door to self-doubt
After years of Billie hearing messages such as "You're lazy," she's put up a guard against hearing any more criticism. And that's what talking about ADHD feels like: criticism.

Fear of facing the fact that your child also has ADHD
Lin sees her son repeating her own childhood challenges. She can't bear the thought of anything being "wrong" with him, especially a condition that he probably inherited from her. So she channels her misplaced guilt into being a "helicopter parent"—hovering over her son—and blaming the school for his failings.

Fear of being labeled with a "kids' disorder"
Franco struggled all his life to deny his critics. Accepting a diagnosis now means conceding defeat. Besides, no one is going to label *him*, especially with a little kid's disorder. He's six feet tall, weighs 220 pounds, and rides a Harley. Franco fails to realize he's long been labeled with far worse: *jerk* and *irresponsible*, to name two.

Fear of yielding to anyone's control
It's almost as if Brent exists only by opposing any outside force. He won't even take aspirin for a pounding headache. To tell the truth, though, he's sure that if people knew how hard it is for him to maintain control, they'd judge him as weak or crazy. He's sure not going to let some quack with medication mess with that slim margin of control.

Fear of losing an identity
Sean's Mr. Entertainer act has always earned him a free pass. That's when he feels most alive: when he's getting attention for what his girlfriend calls his "symptoms." If he has ADHD and treatment changes his personality, he might cease to be the jokester. Then who will he be?

Fear of trusting science
Jody's never been much of a student or a reader. He listens to one AM radio station because he loves the arguing, the anger, and the simple stances on complex issues. It keeps his attention as he makes the rounds on his job. As for these darn books on ADHD his partner keeps shoving at him, Jody dozes off after three paragraphs. Besides, his family has never believed in "shrinks," and he's not going to start now.

Fear of one's partner "winning"

To Kate, a successful salesperson who's never been keen on teamwork, life is a win-lose game and Kate wants to win. If she gives her partner what he wants, by agreeing to an ADHD evaluation, she loses. She becomes one down. She'll never hear the end of it and never be right on anything ever again. No thanks!

Fear of being "just like (family member)"

Chances are good that someone in Anna Marie's genetic family—a parent, grandparent, Uncle Tony—also has ADHD. If she idealizes that family member as the "fun" one, she might take any comparisons to herself as a compliment, not as a sign that she has a problem. But what if Uncle Tony never could hold a job or divorced three times? She is nothing like him!

Fear of the "crazy" stigma or of being seen as "weak"

People who take medicine for their brain are crazy, announces Ravi, and he is *not* crazy. Sure, he had some career challenges but he's an immigrant, torn between two cultures and working in a competitive field. Meanwhile, his wife calls her family back home, crying about him staying up late every night playing online games. Now he's on probation at work. Ravi's solution? A more powerful personal digital assistant. Oh, and he plans to meditate. He forgets that he's made this exact plan many times before.

Fear of having to be more responsible—and failing

Lu is a real "live wire" who says that if one more person tells her to grow up and be more responsible, she will *spit*. If she agrees to get evaluated, she's sure that her husband will expect more from her than she can deliver. Lu cannot imagine that so-called *treatment* would make a particle of difference in her ability to "get things done." Dream on!

Fear of being told, "You don't have ADHD; you're just stupid"

Sean's worst fear, confirmed. Better never to be evaluated at all.

Fear of becoming like the very people you disdain

Sean's second worst fear. See, he's never really liked "normal" people, with all their boring rigidity—sitting down like anal robots every month to pay their little bills. Why would he want to be like them, especially when it's so easy to manipulate them to do things for him? You won't catch *him* becoming servile because he's *gifted*. He's also bad-boy charming, never at a loss for women falling over themselves to take care of him. If one gets demanding, he just bugs out to the next in line.

Perhaps one or two examples ring familiar? (If it's Sean, let's hope you left him behind!) If you had never thought about these possible fears, you now have a better understanding of what's going on beneath that facade of stubbornness. But what about you? What kind of misinformation and fear could be fueling your own refusal to face facts?

Your Possible Fears and Misconceptions

Attend a support group for adults with ADHD and you'll hear this common complaint: "I wish my partner would learn about ADHD and believe that it's real instead of thinking I'm using it as one more excuse."

That's just one example. Perhaps one or more of these scenarios will hit home:

You fear giving up the larger-than-life romance

In courtship, did your partner sweep you off your feet in grand ADHD hyperfocus style? Do you keep hoping that those days will return as you frantically try to do what your partner says will make that happen ("Act like you used to," "Quit nagging," and so forth)? The truth is, it might be out of your control because it's a question of your partner's brain chemistry. You might also find it painful to contemplate how your own poor self-esteem, or perhaps your own narcissistic tendencies, lapped up all that flattering attention, blinding you to a situation that was "too good to be true."

You fear being unfair, judgmental, or intolerant

Tracey is the first to admit that she has her faults, too. And when her new husband insisted that they simply had different "communication styles" (referring to his hyper-talkativeness), she conceded the point. Then his "style" resulted in a job demotion. "Looking back, I realize how much garbage I accepted in trying to be tolerant of his perspective, in trying to take equal responsibility," Tracey says. "Now, even he's relieved that the medication has slowed his 'motor mouth.' He finally told me that he'd secretly tried to control it all his life but never could."

You fear betraying your partner

"All families have their secrets, but when a family is dealing with someone who has troubling behavior, there is a pact of silence," notes psychologist and ADHD expert Stephen Hinshaw, professor and chair of the Psychology

Department at the University of California, Berkeley. Shame, stigma, and a sense of character failure enshroud honest discussion.

"Sixty years ago, you didn't say someone died of cancer, and 20 years ago, it was AIDS," says Hinshaw, author of a trilogy on societal attitudes toward mental illness that includes *The Mark of Shame: Stigma of Mental Illness and an Agenda for Change*. "The more people can talk about these things, the less it becomes taboo. ADHD is a treatable condition, but treatment isn't going to happen unless there's some openness."

You fear accepting "the ADHD excuse"

ADHD is not an excuse but a reason. A diagnosis doesn't mean that you start accepting bad behavior; it means that you can finally look forward to it *diminishing*.

You fear knowing that your partner has a lifetime disorder

After Jeff found the support group, the truth about his family life finally started to sink in: "I was dealing with a seriously wacky situation." As soon as he started applying logic, though, it could only point to one place: the place he was trying not to look, the place that said his wife had a chronic brain disorder. "It was easier to suspend logic and take the blame she dished out rather than accept that." He'd spent years hunting for some kind of "positive" solution—meaning low-conflict and not damaging to his wife's ego or self-esteem. "Eventually, I had to recalibrate my definition of positive more in the direction of what would help her and our child," he says. "The fact was, my wife's brain wasn't working as well as it could. Life started improving in our home only when I accepted that and moved forward."

You fear that your higher-functioning mate won't need you

Although a few ADHD experts mention this factor, it almost never comes up in support-group discussion. Most people say they never sought a dependent partner. In fact, some express hope that their ADHD partner *will* become higher functioning so they can feel less guilt at breaking things off.

Still, threatening the status quo can be unsettling. "After 20 years, I was so used to my husband being the way he was," Jamie says. Now that he has started medication, however, he's stopped following her around the house, feels much more peaceful, and acts much less needy. "It's pretty weird," she concedes, "and the next several months will require huge adjustments, but the changes are definitely a blessing." Indeed, most group members happily prefer navigating these transitions instead of living with an ADHD partner's untreated symptoms.

You fear taking on even more responsibility

"Not only did I resent the previous 17 years that undetected ADHD stole from me and us, but I became downright hostile when I learned that naming the problem didn't solve it," Gloria says. Instead, she saw more of her life being sucked away if she had to "get educated and become an expert, because the docs and therapists we saw sure as heck had no clue." (Don't worry, she adds, "I'm not feeling that way now that treatment is making a huge difference, but that was an initial fear.")

You fear bucking family members who have ADHD

With a husband and two children who have ADHD and Asperger's Syndrome (AS), Louise says, "When I stop buying into their ADHD/AS-driven chaotic 'family rules' and worldview and instead I bring in outside opinions, my family gets very upset with me." She's the only one who sees how their mindsets and actions make everyone's lives so hard; they think it's just the way they are and see no reason to change. The fact that it's Louise's "worldview" that keeps everyone housed, fed, and clothed doesn't alter their opinion.

You fear that treatment will bring unsettling insights

Charlene suspects that treatment will prove a mixed blessing for her husband, at least initially. "Dale will start seeing things that will hurt, like past losses and even current distorted relationships, primarily the one with his father, who I suspect also has ADHD," she says. Dale claims he has a great father, but that's not the way Charlene sees it.

Dale's father has cultivated a reputation as a pillar of the community, but his demeanor at home is more disturbing. "His father is very dogmatic, black-and-white, and confident he knows everything, even if he doesn't," Charlene explains. "And he always puts down his wife's and children's opinions." No matter how correct Dale's facts, his dad will contradict him and seem to take pleasure in it. Dale capitulates because his father is a school principal and Dale never finished college; he feels guilty that he let his dad down.

Even though the transition might be rocky, Charlene is confident that her husband will come out stronger. "Helping him to be the higher-functioning person I know he can be is worth the risk," she concludes.

You fear "Playing God"

We all want to respect an individual's right to be accepted for who he or she is. And it's ill-advised to try molding a person into our idea of the perfect mate. There is a difference, however, between accepting people and letting them wallow so deeply in their dysfunction that they never have a chance to discover who they truly are beneath the weight of their symptoms.

Denial Protects No One; It Hurts Everyone

In the next two chapters, psychologist Xavier Amador, a leading authority in the effects of mental illness on the patient's ability to self-observe accurately, serves as our guide to the less widely understood aspects of denial, particularly its biological basis.

In the foreword to the first edition of Amador's book *I'm Not Sick, I Don't Need Help!*, Anna-Lisa Johansson writes of her mother, who suffered from severe mental illness:

> The people who loved my mother claimed that they respected her freedom and her control over her life.... All she needed was a few weeks of medication to stabilize her condition and give her a chance at a better life, but no one wanted to impose their will on her.... It was easier to hope that if she were left alone she would calm down and somehow magically get better.

Johansson's mother did not magically get better; she threw herself in front of a train. To be sure, ADHD is not considered as severe as, say, schizophrenia. Yet it can still be highly impairing, even more so than depression or anxiety, experts say. In fact, it is associated with a higher-than-average rate of substance abuse, traffic accidents, and, yes, suicide.

"There is a balance," Johansson concludes, "between the fear of facing the betrayal that you anticipate from your loved one and the regret that can last a lifetime if you do not act on your instincts."

Psychologist M. Scott Peck addressed this dilemma in his long-best-selling book *The Road Less Traveled*. "Failing to confront when the nurture of spiritual growth requires it represents a failure to love equal to thoughtless criticism and deprivation of care," he wrote. Confronting is love taking action, he continues, naming two ways of confronting or criticizing another human being: "With instinctive and spontaneous certainty that one is right, or with a belief that one is probably right arrived at through scrupulous self-doubting and self-examination." The first way springs from arrogance, the second from humility.

CHAPTER
FOURTEEN

Biological Denial:
Not Unwilling to See —Just Unable

Like ADHD, diabetes is "invisible." The diabetic person may not look or feel sick but might still drive off the road when having low blood sugar. People with ADHD might drive off the road because they're distracted.

— Rose

"I would leave if not for the children," Anna says. "My husband has ADHD, knows it, and does nothing about it. I tried to help him help himself, but it simply doesn't bother him enough to fix it. It only bothers me." The result? She wants nothing to do with him romantically and doesn't miss him while visiting her sister for the weekend. She's sure he senses her detachment, but he pretends nothing's wrong. "Yes, I feel sorry for him, but my anger and hurt have finally become the stronger emotions," she says. "He is overly sensitive, easily angered, constantly forgetful, self-centered, and undependable, and he's only gotten worse over time."

As a society, we've largely taken our cue from the psychoanalytic model and toss about the term *denial* with clinical confidence. It's common to hear someone described as being "in denial." And it's often said with smug superiority, implying that the problem is as plain as the nose on the denier's face—if only the denier would face what's in the mirror.

185

Yet, what if steam has fogged the mirror? What if the mirror, along with the person's car keys, has been misplaced? What if it's a distorted fun-house mirror or car's side-view mirror, in which "objects may be closer than they appear"?

In other words, denial sometimes springs not as much from a *refusal* to see—a willful action—as an *inability* to accurately perceive what sits before us.

With the help of the foremost international expert on denial in mental illness, clinical psychologist Xavier Amador, you'll soon be savvier on this subject than many mental-healthcare providers. That's because the revolutionary discoveries outlined in this chapter haven't yet, unfortunately, filtered down throughout the medical and therapeutic communities.

Amador is currently an adjunct professor in clinical psychology at Columbia University and former director of research, education, and practice at the National Alliance for the Mentally Ill (NAMI). He has published more than 100 peer-reviewed scientific papers and five books, and he served as a forensic expert in famous court cases, including those of Theodore Kaczynski, the Elizabeth Smart kidnapping, and Zacarias Moussaoui (the "20th hijacker" from September 11, 2001).

In this chapter, you will learn:

- The technical term for denial, or low insight: *anosognosia* (easier to understand than to pronounce).
- How a family member's denial launched Amador's efforts to focus more research on the phenomenon.
- The brain-based reasons that your ADHD partner might not "see" the problems that appear abundantly clear to others.

The Technical Word for Denial: Anosognosia

People with ADHD might not only deny they have it, they might also deny the presence of its symptoms. Here's the buzzword: *anosognosia* (pronounced ah-no'-sohg-*no'*-zee-ah). It's from the Greek words for disease (*nosos*) and knowledge (*gnosis*), and it literally means "to not know a disease." That is, people with anosognosia fail to realize they have a disease or disorder. Some kink or quirk in their brain wiring actually inhibits accurate self-observation, also called *insight*.

For decades, neurologists used the term anosognosia to describe patients with brain tumors, Alzheimer's disease, or dementia—so-called brain pathologies. Thanks in large part to research by Amador and colleagues, we now know that low insight is highly associated with ADHD, bipolar disorder, substance-use disorder, and other conditions that affect the brain's frontal lobes.

Back in the 1980s, though, as a young psychologist just beginning to study low insight in schizophrenia and bipolar disorder, he found only 10 related studies. In 1990, he called the scientific community's attention to this fact by publishing a pivotal paper with three colleagues. Today, more than 200 studies have focused on insight and mental illness, with Amador contributing 80 peer-reviewed papers on the subject.

The first step in resolving most problems is getting people to realize there is a problem, he explains. You do that with your partner's denial just as Amador did with the study of denial: by *drawing your partner's attention to the problem.*

A Family Member's "Denial" Launches Research

How did Amador come to understand the urgent need for this research? From personal experience, as is often the case with medical and psychological research. He had learned first-hand about the effects of low insight from his brother's schizophrenia.

It may be difficult to believe, but until very recently, even people with schizophrenia were thought to suffer from psychological, or defensive, denial, instead of a brain-based condition that diminished their capacity to accurately observe their behaviors or environment. Before Amador came to understand this, though, he took it personally when his brother refused to take his medications. In fact, after his brother's third hospitalization, Amador found his Haldol in the trashcan.

To Amador, the older brother whom he had admired, who taught him to throw a baseball and ride a bicycle, was acting stubbornly and selfishly. By refusing to acknowledge his behavior, he was hurting himself, his entire family, and everyone who came in contact with him. How could he stop taking his medication when he knew exactly what would happen? Or *did* he know?

When Amador examined the scientific literature, he found that the mental health field had for decades relied primarily on psychoanalytic theories, not brain science, to explain denial. Fear of stigma created the denial, the theories maintained. Yet these theories had never actually been studied, simply accepted. That started changing when two of Amador's doctoral students based their thesis on research in this area. Their findings, confirmed in the 20 years since, included two key points:

- *Fear of stigma never entered the equation.* The degree to which patients viewed their symptoms as potentially stigmatizing had little effect on how much insight they had into their illness.
- *Patients simply did not perceive their symptoms.* "Everyone gets defensive occasionally and some of us are more denial-prone than others," Amador explains. The same holds true for people with serious mental illness. "Everyday defensiveness, however, is not responsible for the gross deficits in insight that are so common in these patients," he says. They honestly do not perceive the symptoms.

These studies focused on schizophrenia, not ADHD. Yet, we can safely infer that any psychiatric disorder that involves frontal lobe dysfunction, including bipolar disorder and ADHD, is vulnerable to anosognosia. (The frontal lobe, among other functions, integrates information.) In his years of clinical experience, Amador has also observed the same low insight in eating and substance-use disorders. As with ADHD, we can also consider anosognosia a "spectrum" disorder, with varying degrees of severity.

Your ADHD Partner Might Not "See" the Problems

This point is critical: What appears obvious to you or other observers might remain invisible or distorted to some people with ADHD. Until you accept this possibility, you risk becoming even more angry or hurt at your ADHD partner's "refusal" to acknowledge the obvious. Moreover, you risk being seen, in your partner's eyes, as unreasonable and unsympathetic—perhaps, in fact, as the enemy.

To illustrate, let's focus on six common ADHD traits:

1. Poor self-observation

After dating for six months, Pat asked her boyfriend, "Why do you lose your keys all the time?" He shot back, "Everybody loses their keys. You lose your keys, too." But whereas Pat might misplace her keys once a month, he lost his five times a week. He never noticed that, with him, it was a quantitative issue.

2. Difficulty linking cause and effect over time

ADHD partners who don't make the "connection" between spending too much on eBay now and facing unmanageable debt five months from now won't be able to conceive that *they* dented the family budget. Instead, they might blame the latest purchase *someone else* in the family made, even if baby needed a new pair of shoes.

Group members often report a partner's inability to grasp the severity of a situation, remaining unduly optimistic in the face of calamity. The irony is that these members were initially drawn to their partner's "confidence" and "optimism," not understanding those qualities often rested on a house of cards and a poor ability to predict adverse consequences.

3. Poor working memory, distractibility

Mark can't understand how his wife can deny her dysfunctional actions. Their boys, age 7 and 9, must constantly remind her of promises she's made. "I never said that," she'll often respond to them. The children are becoming understandably frustrated and even distrustful of their mother.

4. Confusing what you meant to do with what you did

Mark's wife also didn't remember setting her keys in the freezer when she came home frazzled on a hot day wanting some ice. Her mind might have been elsewhere, perhaps worried about what to make for supper or meeting that deadline at work. But even when she accidentally finds her lost keys in the freezer 24 hours later, she can't believe she left them there because, well, that's too darn weird.

Amador shares a remarkable clinical experience that explains how we don't just *see* what is happening; our brain also *interprets* what we see. After suffering a stroke, a patient's frontal lobe condition left him unaware of his impaired ability to write. Asked by Amador to sketch a clock, the patient carefully did so and, upon questioning, pronounced himself pleased with the results. Then Amador drew the patient's attention to the numbers, which were, in fact, all jumbled outside of the circular clockface. Seeing this, the patient became agitated, pushed the paper away, and said, "That's not my drawing!"

"The truly striking part is that at first he perceived the clock looking as it should," Amador says. "But when I pointed to it and asked if the numbers were inside or outside the circle, he agreed they were outside." Growing more frustrated and angry at the disparity between what the patient *thought* he'd done and what the doctor showed he'd *actually* done, the patient said to Amador, "You've tricked me somehow."

Sound familiar? When confronted with the evidence of something that's broken or gone awry, has your ADHD partner ever denied any involvement whatsoever or even pinned the blame on *you*? Has your partner ever told "lies" so blatant they insult your intelligence? (You'd laugh if you weren't so appalled.) Sure, it could be that these folks are protecting their hide, or pride; many people with late-diagnosed ADHD have learned to throw off constant blame out of self-protection. On the other hand, it's entirely possible that protests of innocence are sincere, even if based in misperception.

This concept hit Isabel one day with a sharp thud. Actually, the thud was her husband's elbow landing in her belly. Isabel and Terry had been married for two years, with Terry in treatment for ADHD for the previous two months. They'd been talking in bed on Saturday morning when Terry, illustrating a point with a gesture, lost track of his arm's location in space. "He's a big guy and not that physically coordinated in the morning before his stimulant medication kicks in," Isabel says. The odd thing was, when Isabel reacted with an "Ow!" and curled up in instinctual protection, Terry growled that she was exaggerating.

Before Isabel learned about the neurospatial challenges that sometimes accompany ADHD, and that a person might lack awareness of these challenges, she would have felt hurt by his carelessness. And when he didn't contritely apologize for causing her pain, she might have accused Terry of denying, of minimizing, of lacking empathy. How could he fail to realize that such an action would physically hurt or startle her? On top of that, the incident symbolized so much in their married life: Isabel feeling relaxed and vulnerable only to receive a metaphorical blow to the gut from Terry's latest bit of impulsive or thoughtless action.

For Terry, however, *his* experience (an accidental minor arm movement with never an intent to harm) didn't match *her* experience (of pain and hurt feelings). So, he concluded she was in a bad mood and "touchy." It probably didn't help that he also harbored a lifelong defensiveness about always doing the wrong thing.

5. Wearing deficits like a badge of honor

Giselle spent the first weeks of her new relationship walking behind her boyfriend, partly because he walked so fast but also to stabilize the elderly people and children left teetering in his wake. "I was aghast and asked him why he never learned manners," she remembers. Her boyfriend dismissively said he was a very important person, on his way to making $50 million in high-tech stock options, and didn't have time for slow losers.

In Giselle's mind, though, this explanation didn't truly fit his personality. Only much later did she learn how impatience and poor neurospatial skills inspired her boyfriend's Klingon-like march. Politely moving through a crowd required more modulated finesse that he could muster, so he hunkered down, barreled through, and developed a rationale.

Beverly—Society Denies Dark Side of "Success"

My husband, who has ADHD but refuses treatment, is a former marketing executive for a major software firm. By most people's standards, he was successful for a long time. From my perspective, I see a dangerous mistake in confusing career success like his with life success.

When people hold up executives like he used to be as "ADHD Success Stories," I want to ask them, "Don't you realize that money and power are the biggest self-medicating stimulants possible? Almost as big as porn!" And, people like my husband justify their workaholism by saying they do it for their families, whom they never see. Is this the kind of model to hold up for my son, who also has ADHD?

Besides, the more money my husband made, the more he blew. And frankly, being around our children bored him silly or agitated him, and they knew it. It wasn't their fault; they're good kids. But they didn't understand their father's problem, because their father refused to accept that he had a problem. They did know, though, that he tried to buy their affection with high-priced electronic gizmos.

People like my husband don't always hold onto their "success." Their constant need for more, more, more—never thinking of consequences for their risk-taking—can also prove their undoing, and they take many people, even entire companies, down with them. Truly, haven't we seen enough of that narcissistic behavior in the business and political arenas to stop glorifying people like this?

For 17 years, my husband cleverly got himself transferred every two years, just as his problems started to surface to his coworkers and bosses. Because he's a great salesman, he maintained a terrific image—until he was recently fired. He was getting too old and tired to keep relocating around the globe, and his past was catching up with him.

I didn't know this until recently, but his ex-colleagues had the same problem I did: Whenever any of us tried to point out my husband's problems, his expertise in "spin" just made us look bad, not him. At last, he can't keep blaming everybody else. It's not my problem, because I've filed for divorce, but it's tough on my kids. They want to like their father and he does such jerky things.

Recently, I attended an ADHD adult discussion group where a father with ADHD showed up after a full day at work with his two children; he couldn't find a sitter and his wife had to work late. The children sat quietly, reading books, while he participated in the meeting. How about holding up guys like this as ADHD poster people—people who face their challenges and focus on living balanced lives? That would be a welcome change.

6. A tendency to develop stories that make sense (lies?)

"People will come up with illogical and even bizarre explanations for symptoms and life circumstances stemming from their illness," Amador says. Further confusing their loved ones, pockets of awareness and unawareness often coexist.

The psychiatric lingo for this process is *confabulation*. And until you understand what's happening, it's easy to confuse it with lying. For example, if you've known anyone with early-stage dementia, you've probably seen confabulation in action. For example, an elderly lady with dementia parks her car and forgets where she parked it. Because she's never forgotten such a thing in her life, she's certain the car's been stolen.

Why is this? Because only part of what we perceive comes directly through our senses—what we see, hear, and so on. The rest comes from our brain and how it interprets our perceptions and processes sensory signals. "Our brains are built to create order, and even help construct our perceptions," Amador says. For example, his stroke patient certainly believed that he could draw a simple clock, and that belief superseded the physical evidence when it was shown to him. When perception didn't fit reality, the only explanation was trickery.

With Terry and Isabel, Terry perceived only what he meant to do (make a gesture), not what he actually did (swat his wife). And this is common to a number of disorders: The person gets angry when they are accused of making a mistake, because they don't see themselves as having made the mistake. Similarly, many "communication" problems happen because the ADHD partner has in mind what he or she *expects* to hear—and that becomes, in fact, what *is* heard.

If you and your partner have such different perceptions of reality, you might end up arguing about just who has the problem. When you corner your partner about "your problem," the only thing left for him or her is to say, "*You* have a problem, not *me*."

These days, both Terry and Isabel understand this concept. They can talk about such incidents, which rarely happen now, without tossing angry accusations back and forth. In fact, they can even joke about it. Moreover, her leap of understanding how his brain is "wired" enables him to trust her more and act less defensively. In the end, she's less reactive to his mistakes and he's quicker to say, "I'm sorry. Did I hurt you?"

We'll explore the neurochemical underpinnings of sensory perceptions further in Chapter 20, as it relates to medication, but for now it's enough to understand that this truly can contribute to your ADHD partner's denial.

Now that you understand *anosognosia*, the brain-based denial of illness, what do you do with this knowledge? You start putting it into practice with the guidelines Amador offers in Chapter 15.

Consider making this your mantra: "The organ that's causing so many problems for my ADHD partner is the same organ that my partner is using to evaluate these problems."

CHAPTER FIFTEEN

New Ways to Broach "The Conversation"

This is one of the most painful things a mate can say: "I will not change. If you don't like it, leave." What we want to hear is, "I love you and I am willing to work with you to make things better."

– BETH

Congratulations. You now understand the two critical components of denial: psychological and biological. Newly aware and grounded in this critical knowledge, you can start implementing practical strategies toward reaching through, around, over, or under your ADHD partner's denial.

This chapter explores the heart of these methods by explaining how to:
- Integrate all you've learned by practicing the denial-dissolving strategy called LEAP (Listen, Empathize, Agree, and Partnership), developed by psychologist Xavier Amador, a leader in the study of mental illness and denial.
- Communicate your concerns without triggering your partner's defenses.

"It's not about *who* is to blame," reminds Amador. "It's about *what* is to blame. It's not you and it's not your partner; it's the symptoms." Keeping this in mind can ease frustration and increase your ability to build trust with your "in-denial" ADHD partner.

LEAP into a Denial-Dissolving Strategy

After 20 years spent learning to reach patients reluctant to accept treatment, and studying the scientific evidence, psychologist Xavier Amador developed a four-step plan to change potentially adversarial relationships into alliances. It's called LEAP: Listen; Empathize; find areas of Agreement; and form a Partnership to achieve mutual goals.

Here, he has adapted his four-part strategy to help you reach your ADHD partner. Using this method, which incorporates the other ideas in this success strategy for dealing with denial, you stop focusing on diagnoses and start zeroing in on problematic behaviors and joint solutions. "Common ground always exists even between the most extreme opposition positions," Amador stresses, "and it starts with making observations together."

LISTEN—*Turn off your critical filter as you listen to what your partner feels, wants, and believes in*

"But my partner feels, wants, and believes in unlimited spending and little accountability! You want me to listen to *that*?" you might say. Okay, chill. At this point, you're only gathering information. "When you listen without reacting or contradicting, you avoid creating controversy and building up defenses," he explains. "You want to turn down the heat and keep defenses low, so negotiation can occur."

As you listen, clarify what you've heard: "Let me make sure I understand what you're saying. You're saying you don't feel we should discuss purchases together, that it makes you feel like a child. You think I worry too much about money, and the financial future will take care of itself. Is that right?"

As Amador explains, "Listening also involves identifying the cognitive deficits—that is, problems with memory, impulsivity, focusing thoughts—that create barriers not only between you and your partner but also between your partner and effective treatment."

EMPATHIZE—*If you want your ADHD partner to consider your point of view, first consider your partner's*

Empathizing is *not* the same as agreeing the belief is true. Instead, your empathy as you listen allows your partner to be more receptive to your opinions and concerns.

For example, if your partner expresses entitlement to blaze a credit-card trail, ask, "So how does it make you feel when you 'win' that item on eBay?" It's asking about a person's feelings, not interpreting them. (And it's important to be genuinely curious without oozing veiled criticism or "laying a trap.") Maybe your partner says, "When I buy something new, I feel calm, like my life is okay. It helps me deal with stress." And maybe you say, "If I were you, I'd feel the same way." (Note: You're *not* saying it's how *you* would feel or how someone *should* feel.)

It's quite possible that your ADHD partner never noticed these self-medicating feelings associated with stress and spending money. Notice that you're now having a conversation about your partner's problem dealing with tension instead of fighting about money or a disorder. Conversations like this pave the way to talking about an ADHD evaluation or taking medication the doctor has recommended, Amador maintains.

Oh, but maybe your ADHD partner says, "What problem? We have a credit card and I'm going to use it!" You respond, "Well, the budget can only go so far and then we're broke. I'll cut back where I can, but what else can you do, or what else can *we* do, to deal with it?"

AGREE—*Find common ground and stake it out*

This third step involves acknowledging that your partner has personal choice and responsibility for his or her decisions. During this step, you are the calm, neutral observer pointing out the various positive and negative consequences of decisions your loved one has made. (Tip: Bite your tongue before saying, "See, if you were taking medication, you wouldn't have bought those salvaged church-organ pipes that filled up the garage!")

Instead, you ask questions, such as "So what happened when you tried to cut back on the spending? How did that work and how did you feel?" You are helping your partner to be a detective in his or her own life, Amador says. You're looking for an opportunity to link a solution to the stated problem that your partner now agrees he or she has. Your partner has trouble with paperwork, and it's jeopardizing his or her job? You say, "I hear these medications help people stay focused."

PARTNERSHIP—*Collaborate on mutual goals*

Amador calls this last step the most satisfying. Now you're on the same team against a common opponent, such as the messy house, the scary driving, this spending-tension-release thing. You've stopped the war over "You're sick" and "No, I'm not"—which amounts to name-calling. Instead, you're listening, working with your partner to find new ways to view the problem, and learning about how he or she feels. Eventually, you're going to link the problems you two are now discussing to ADHD evaluation or treatment.

Five Guidelines to Remember About Dealing with Denial

Keep these five points in mind as you talk with your partner about the ADHD-related issues that are affecting your relationship:

1. Brain deficits can be easier to fix than "personality"

"Many people confuse denial or stubbornness about accepting a disorder—or even symptoms of the disorder—as being part of the person's personality, something that can't change," Amador says. If you see your ADHD partner's denial as a negative personality trait rather than a symptom, you risk remaining stuck.

Sarah apparently understood the difference between symptoms and personality when she only half-jokingly said to her husband, "Look, I think that you act this way because you have ADHD, and it's treatable. The alternative is that you're an insensitive twit, and that's not treatable. If I were you, I'd get real invested in convincing me that you have ADHD."

Our culture harbors widespread resistance to the idea that some negative behavioral patterns can be brain-related symptoms, not ingrained personality flaws. That's a dangerous myth, Amador insists. "Medication is the cornerstone of ADHD treatment, and you can also retrain the brain, the same way we work with stroke patients every day to retrain their brains."

2. Avoid getting stuck in the gift-or-difference debate

In recent years, some have touted ADHD as a gift, not a disorder. In fact, some book authors who themselves have ADHD seem to truly believe they are *superior* to people who don't have ADHD.

Perhaps viewing ADHD as a gift does make the diagnosis more acceptable for some, and it reminds us to view a person's challenges in a more balanced context. That's important. Yet, could this ADHD-is-a-gift strategy possibly be reinforcing some individuals' denial and increasing their self-centeredness as well? It's widely thought that an impaired sense of empathy lies at the heart of narcissistic behavior. So, when such people already lean toward narcissism and are then led to believe that they are *more* gifted than everyone else—and that their biggest problem is a hypercritical world that doesn't appreciate their positive qualities—well, it doesn't always lead to a realistic perspective. Or happy relationships.

For decades, romantic notions about schizophrenia being a gift flourished, too. "It caused a lot of tragedy and missed opportunities," Amador says. Ultimately, when a behavior is causing real problems, focusing on whether it is a gift, a difference, or a disorder remains beside the point—a seductive distraction ensured to keep both of you stuck.

In some ways, the *Diagnostic and Statistical Manual* (DSM), used to diagnose psychiatric disorders, is arbitrary, he argues. "There are enough true disorders to convince me we need certain guidelines but there are conditions in the DSM that I consider truly differences, perhaps part of our evolution as humans and perhaps leading us to more complex capacities as a society."

Think of that third X-Men movie, where the government decides that these super-heroes whose powers come from genetic mutations require an antidote, a cure. Are their amazing abilities disease or difference? Ultimately, that's not the issue. "The issue is how we can all live together and function as a society," he concludes.

3. What really matters are these three questions

To get to the heart of the issue, you only have to ask yourself:

- Is the behavior creating distress for the person?
- Is it disabling them in the important spheres of function—relationships, work, and ability to manage basic needs?
- Is it creating havoc for their loved ones?

If you answer "yes" to any question, who cares whether it's a disability, a disorder, a difference, or a gift? "If this difference in the way you think and pay attention to the world around you is creating something negative for you, then do something about it," Amador advises.

4. Lose the labels (including ADHD)

Guess what? You don't have to call it a disorder or anything else to treat the problems. Usually, mental-health professionals preach facing your issues and calling something what it is, but there are exceptions. And for your partner, ADHD might be one.

Another exception might be depression. It's usually harder to spot in men than women. Instead of becoming sad or weepy, men are more prone to the symptoms of irritability and impatience (in addition to that which is common with ADHD), according to psychologist David B. Wexler, author of *Is He Depressed or What?*

In the early stages of depression, he says, men are also more likely to cope by drinking alcohol, thus obscuring the issue. And the last thing some men will accept is that they are depressed because they consider depression "unmanly," connoting helplessness and failure. "It often works better to approach men with the feedback that they seem stressed or burned out or not themselves lately," he advises. "And, rather than pushing them to go into psychotherapy, it is often an easier sell to encourage them to get some 'training' or 'consulting.'"

Whether it's ADHD, depression, or both, it's okay *not* to call it by its official name, as long as you start addressing the challenges. (Keep in mind that the physician treating ADHD with medication will require that diagnosis and most likely the insurance company will, too, but that doesn't mean you and your ADHD partner have to use the term.)

5. Think in terms of "turning down the volume"

Accept that, in some cases, you're just going to lose that argument about whether or not your partner has ADHD. "It's time to unlock horns, stop arguing about disorders and diagnosis, and start talking about something else," Amador recommends.

Many people who are unwilling to be "medicated for a disorder" will agree to "take a little something" for better focus or less anger. (Witness the explosion in "smart" drinks that tout brain-boosting properties. Do they attract buyers by pointing to the buyers' flaws and shortcomings? No, they promote the positive things the drink can do for them.)

Try framing the discussion not in terms of deficits but in terms of increased functioning. You might suggest that a little medication might help your ADHD partner to "turn up the signal on noticing details" or "turn down the signal on interrupting."

If the person you're trying to help doesn't realize he or she is overspending, driving like a bat out of hell, or creating a visual cacophony of clutter—or see why it matters—how do you broach that subject? The simple process outlined next can help.

Expressing Feelings Without Triggering Defenses

Practicing the following three steps will improve your ability to communicate your feelings clearly and without sounding accusatory.

1. Point out the problem and how it makes you feel

For example, say, "When you drive fast, I feel really nervous. Maybe it's my problem but it really makes me sick to my stomach." In this way, you've left your partner to think about how to solve the problem. You're not saying *how* to solve the problem or, more important, that he or she *is* the problem.

The same holds true if your partner is often irritable. You don't say, "I read that people with low impulse-control yell at their children, so go get an ADHD evaluation and some medication." You say, "It really hurts me when you do this. It worries me about how it affects the children and their relationship with you. Do you see the fear on their faces when you start in on them?"

The point is to engage your ADHD partner in adopting a view of their problematic behaviors. *To bring their attention to it.* But what if your partner says, "You're the one with the problem!" Embrace that, Amador says. "Say, 'Maybe I am too sensitive and I'll work on it, but in the meantime, I need you to work on helping me.'"

(Don't get your knickers in a twist just yet about making this admission; keep reading to the third point.)

2. Use "I" statements

Even if you're crystal clear that anyone would consider your ADHD partner's driving erratic, it's important to start by saying, "I feel scared when you change lanes that fast."

Using what's called an "I" statement is very different than saying "What are you trying to do, kill us?" Typically, "I" statements evoke less of a defensive reaction. If your partner still gets defensive, try "Maybe I'm overreacting, but I still feel scared and must do something about it. Either we drive separately or I'll have to get out of the car when that happens."

The trick, Amador points out, is feeling solid about your position even as you acknowledge you could be wrong. Remember: You're not saying your *partner* must do anything; you're saying what *you* must do to allay your fears. Then do it.

3. Get help in learning to validate your perceptions

Some support-group members have learned to doubt their perceptions and judgment after living many years with an ADHD partner's obfuscations such as "I'm fine the way I am; you're just too sensitive/picky/controlling/fill-in-the-blank!" How do you know when you really are being normal and reasonable and when you're trying to impose your personal *judgment* of what's normal and reasonable? "There's your judgment and there's your feelings," Amador points out, "and if you stick with your *feelings*, you're on more solid ground."

If you're seeing a therapist who is familiar with ADHD symptoms, you should be receiving help in anchoring your perceptions. In Ellie's case, joining a support group validated her experience and strengthened her ability to hold her ground when her husband tried to talk her out of it. "His spending a big chunk of money impulsively when we'd agreed to watch the budget was *not* reasonable. And I imagined the whole online gang, standing behind me and supporting me not to back down. Feeling that support eliminated my need to argue the points with him, and that helped us both immensely."

Being clear in your own mind that your concerns are valid gives you mental leeway in saying to your partner "Maybe it's just me, but…." (That is, you can say, "Maybe it's just me" without risking that you'll start to believe it really *is* just you.) The more you learn about ADHD and how it manifests, the more clarity you'll gain. "You've got to be rock-solid in your knowledge while realizing that your understanding won't always be perfect," Amador explains. "When you're at that point, you're going to be nearly invulnerable to blame or feeling guilty for your perceptions."

The guidelines offered in this chapter should provide a strong foundation as you consider which of the solutions and strategies outlined in the next chapter might work best for your situation.

More Strategies and Solutions

One expert says, "No one wants something pushed at them, so try patience and subtle hints. Leave books lying about." Ha! If I'd glued a book to my boyfriend's thighs, do you think he'd have read it? It makes my skin crawl when someone not living with the dag-blasted daily disasters tells us to be patient. We invented patient! That's probably how we ended up in this predicament.

— Diane

Okay, you understand denial's causes, and you've learned about creating dialogue and drawing attention to problematic issues without triggering defenses. As you consider each of the pointers offered below, do a "gut check" to see which ones resonate for you.

Most of all, remember that change starts with you. Being very clear in your own mind that you must elevate your life. That's the first step.

Get over your denial first

If you skipped straight to this section on denial, that's fine. But now, it's time to return to Part One and learn all you can about ADHD.

When you stop attaching motive to ADHD symptoms and start lessening your emotional reactions, you'll know you've cleared the fog of denial. That means your ADHD partner will have a better chance of following suit. Consider it short-term pain for long-term gain. Pay a little more now with your time or continue paying heavily if nothing changes.

Never say never (until you've explored the options)

Repeatedly, members enter the support group bemoaning the certain fact that their partners would *never* consider an evaluation and treatment. Yet, a few weeks or months later, most nonchalantly announce, "Well, my partner and I are going in for an evaluation next week." Breaking out of isolation and communicating with others has a way of subtly breaking down barriers that you *knew* were impenetrable.

One longtime group member puts it this way: "Story after story here shows that it's only when you really get straight in your own head as to what you will and will not put up with and draw those boundaries *very clearly* that your ADHD partner will start to take you seriously."

Examine your own attitude toward ADHD

"My boyfriend has ADHD, but he just won't admit it," says one new group member. A-hem, ADHD is not a crime. Asking for admissions or confessions is neither logical nor compassionate. Moreover, if you mistakenly view ADHD as a shameful scourge or catastrophe, your partner will detect that. Especially avoid saying your partner "is" ADHD. If your partner had high blood pressure, would you say he *is* hypertension? There's a lot more to a person than his or her ADHD.

"Speak to the fear, not the person"

Fears and worries are normal and must be addressed. But psychologist Herbert Gravitz advises to "speak to the fear, not to the person refusing treatment or medication." For example, if the person fears being evaluated for ADHD—as many do—because it means he or she is crazy or out of fear of medication, speak to that fear:

- "You are not crazy; you have a common, highly treatable condition."
- "If the doctor decides medication is advised, we'll work carefully to avoid or minimize side effects."
- "You will be more creative, not less; more free, not less."
- "Your true self will be more able to act as you wish, not as your misfiring neurons dictate."
- "The medication won't control you, it will *give* you control."

Sometimes substance abuse can make a person especially unreachable. That might need to be addressed before the ADHD, yet it's also true that treating the ADHD can often help mitigate addictions. Overall, the course of treatment will depend on the individual, the nature of the addictions, and the treating physician's philosophy.

204

Instead of criticism and belittlement, try humor

"The way to change other minds is with affection, and not anger," as the Dalai Lama has been quoted.

Michelle's husband has been resistant because he feels it is a blow to his ego to have a "brain disease," as he puts it. So, to bring his attention to his problematic behavior, she employs amusing verbal cues. For instance, she'll say, "Sir, you need to calm down," which is a code line from a TV show he enjoyed, *Airplane*. "They use this line when the airline customer is having a fit," she says, "so I began using it when he was over-reacting about something trivial. He gets the reference immediately. He can even laugh about it sometimes." Increasingly, Michelle's husband recognizes his irritability.

Forgive yourselves for not detecting ADHD sooner

If you, like countless others, didn't know that ADHD was challenging your relationship, you might have frequently reacted angrily or critically, even accusing your ADHD partner of doing hurtful things on purpose. Forgive yourself, and maybe ask your partner's forgiveness as well.

Don't necessarily expect reciprocal words of remorse, though, until awareness or medication starts lifting your partner's ADHD fog. Until then, he or she might even initially seize upon your confession as proof that everything really is your fault!

Give it some time as you keep nudging toward awareness, Lori says. When she and her husband talk about the "bad old days" before diagnosis and treatment, she'll say to him, "Poor you! You didn't know what you were doing wrong or why you were doing it and why I was yelling so much." To which her husband playfully responds, "Poor you! You didn't know why I was doing these irritating things, and neither did I! All I knew was that you were criticizing me all the time and I wanted you to shut your trap." "Poor us!" they say, only half laughing, and put the past behind them.

Leave reading material around the home

When Louise tried to discuss ADHD with her husband, a college professor, he asked if she had a Ph.D. in the subject. When she showed him books about ADHD for professionals that described him to a *T*, the tide began to turn. At her house, Kim stopped leaving ADHD-themed books in the bathroom, hoping to spark her boyfriend's interest. "They got buried under auto magazines," she says. Now, she leaves short articles, drawing funny faces in the margins. Those he reads.

Remember: Some ADHD partners don't "get" subtle

Have you been trying the long-suffering-martyr approach, thinking your partner must *surely* notice your misery? That could be a very poor strategy. After all, a common ADHD deficit is not picking up on social cues, and that includes facial expressions, sighs, "cold shoulders," and garden-variety huffiness.

Instead, be direct. Communicate in a way that gets the person's attention, advises Jonathan Halverstadt, a therapist specializing in ADHD: "You want to tell your partner, 'This is serious. This is a problem, and I really don't want it to get to the point where I have to leave.'"

State your complaints as simply and clearly as possible, and make sure that, as you do so, your partner is not distracted by other things (TV, the kids, atoms colliding). If what you're doing isn't working, stop doing it and try something unexpected. "Whatever you do," Halverstadt says, "it needs to come from a place of care and concern, not just about yourself but about the relationship and your partner."

Know that self-interest might be the big incentive—at first

When Lily tried to talk to her ADHD partner about how his behavior was affecting *her*, it had little impact. She got his attention only when she pointed out how his untreated ADHD was affecting his work and his golf game.

Look for "empathy moments"

Experts say that even people with low insight into their own disorder can be quite astute in picking it out in others. That proved true when Christine's husband found himself assigned to a new boss.

Ted came home ranting that his boss has ADHD. "You should hear how he goes on, like it's all news to me!" Christine says. "He complained about how distracted the guy was, how he picked up the phone mid-conversation, didn't pay attention, and so Ted has to repeat himself a million times. It made him want to pull out his hair and run off screaming, he said."

In response, Christine deadpanned, "Imagine that" and smiled sweetly at her husband before adding, "How great you've finally experienced my life first-hand." Ted backtracked, saying the boss wasn't a *bad* guy; he was just really annoying. "That's what I say about you, too," Christine replied. Ted finally got it.

Don't confuse procrastination with denial

Remember: ADHD deficits can include failure to initiate and problems with procrastinating, prioritizing, and following through.

Emphasize access, not defects

Identify an analogy that speaks to your ADHD partner. For example, computer geeks who continually optimize their machines might respond to the idea that their brain, too, deserves the best support possible to function optimally.

When Lorraine talked to her husband about access, however, she meant it on a very personal level: "I tried to explain to him that I know the person I married is in there and I'd love to see him more often."

Take an online interactive test

The self-test at the Amen Clinic Web site (AmenClinic.com) has helped many ADHD partners to see themselves in the questions asked. If your partner won't take it, take it yourself and answer as if you were your partner. It's no substitute for a professional evaluation, but it might help corroborate your hunch that ADHD is a strong possibility.

Concede that you don't have a perfect brain, either

No one has a perfectly functioning, balanced brain—not even you! And certainly there are no perfect relationships. But the goal isn't perfection; it's making the life you have as good as it can be.

Be prepared to counter excuses, delaying tactics

What if your partner says he or she will "try harder"? When San Diego-based psychotherapist Lew Mills, who specializes in treating ADHD, hears a patient say they are just going to try harder rather than confront the diagnosis, he asks, "Has it ever occurred to you to try harder before?" Of course it has. Then he asks if that strategy worked. "They will tie themselves in a knot for few minutes about how they didn't try hard enough at trying harder, but this time they will try really hard to try harder at trying harder. Then they grin and get it."

Attend an Adult ADHD support group

Hearing other adults voice similar-sounding experiences can prove extremely liberating for you both. You might even find yourselves laughing together at stories that sound so close to your own—a true impasse breaker. (Tip: Go solo first to the group, just to gain a sense of how good a "fit" it will be for your partner.)

Consider the "head injury" approach

Many people (especially men, it seems) understand and accept physical injury more than they accept clinical terms such as ADHD and depression. Recently, Brad started realizing that maybe not only his wife but he also had ADHD, so he pursued an evaluation.

"When I was recounting my history of head injuries for the doc, everything from football to motocross, I actually felt proud about the things I wasn't afraid to try," he recalls. Of course he'd rather not have incurred the lumps, but Brad gladly admits the possibility of brain injury, and he thinks that most other men would, too. "There is no weakness involved and sometimes there is pride, however ridiculous it sounds."

Give your partner time to adjust to the idea
Claire-Ellen followed a drip, drip, drip method. She always told her husband when she left for her ADHD partner support group. She reminded him, when he was getting stressed, that it is part of his ADHD. "I tried to make the topic sort of ho-hum, not something to freak out about but something to just keep thinking about," she says. She kept it light, funny, and conversational, patiently wearing down his idea that ADHD is new, scary, and definitely nothing to do with him.

"Be the change you want to see in the world" —Gandhi
Who would you turn to for a valid perspective: someone who is crying and feeling victimized or someone who is enjoying life? Sometimes the most powerful way to reach your partner is to stop focusing on him or her and start taking better care of yourself. In an episode of the radio show *Prairie Home Companion*, host Garrison Keillor tells a story about a Lake Wobegon woman who is starting to get in shape, eat better, and style her hair more fashionably. "Her husband notices that his wife is making some changes," Keillor says, "and he doesn't want to be one of them."

Protect the children
Cynthia faced an awful dilemma: leave the man she hoped to grow old with or continue watching powerlessly as he occasionally inflicted his temper on their children. Most recently, he had slapped their eldest son, 10, leaving a telltale mark on his cheek. Someone at school reported it to Child Protective Services (CPS).

Cynthia adores her husband of 14 years but he has long refused ADHD treatment, contending that his doctorate degree means he can't have a brain disorder. Philip had gotten physical before, but Cynthia rationalized that their three young boys are a handful—two of them so hyperactive she jokes that they have "ADH-H-H-H-D." Besides, he is a good father in so many respects. The CPS report, however, forced her hand; she immediately made a doctor's appointment for her husband. Whatever happens now, she has come out of the fog and faced facts. She is accepting responsibility for making changes in her family's life.

Know That Even Experts Can't Always Reach a Loved One

For some people, no matter what you do, denial remains impenetrable. It's not your fault.

Years ago, top ADHD expert Russell Barkley learned that his fraternal twin brother, Ron, had ADHD, but even he could not convince Ron to seek treatment. Finally, in 2006, Ron, 56, failed to negotiate a bend in the road and, not wearing a seatbelt, died at the scene. That Russell Barkley has contributed significantly to the research detailing ADHD-related impairments to driving safety only adds irony to this tragic course of events.

As he wrote in the October 2006 edition of his newsletter, *The ADHD Report*:

You can provide information on risk all you want to an adult with ADHD. You can even arrange inducements and mild coercions in an effort to get your suggestions adopted. But at the end of the day, it is entirely the adult's choice whether to adopt or ignore that advice. And we all know there is not a damn thing you can do about it if they opt to continue in their self-destructive ways.

Finally, Barkley realized that his good intentions were only enlarging the wedge between them. So, he adopted a supporting role, helping his brother when his actions created dire consequences (such as near homelessness, legal actions, and medical care). This approach isn't enabling bad behavior, he clarifies, "It is facing and accepting the reality of having a persistently disabled family member…. It is the only important role left to play if you wish to stay involved in your loved one's life."

Of course, the situation is different when the person with ADHD is a partner, not a sibling, parent, or child. The factors that determine your continued involvement in the person's life, including shared custody or a deep friendship, become very personal. It's up to each individual to navigate as safely as possible.

When all else fails, consider the "nuclear option"

"It is said that active alcoholics don't have relationships; they only take hostages," says psychologist and recovery expert Herbert Gravitz. "The same can be said of other disorders. It can be impossible to deal with someone who has ADHD or OCD and refuses treatment." Staying in a toxic relationship is harmful to your health and often simply enables your partner to remain dysfunctional.

After years of trying to get through to her husband, Lisa finally resorted to an attitude of "I don't really need to be in this marriage, I'm OK without you." That proved the turning point.

"Sometimes, the only thing that will cause people to enter treatment is giving them a deal they can't refuse," Gravitz maintains. To continue receiving your support, your ADHD partner must get help. Even if such requests seem hard, tough, or even cruel to you, it might be the only choice.

What if the "nuclear option" would destroy you and perhaps your children, too? It's very easy to tell someone to leave a bad situation, but life has a way of complicating matters. Shared finances and parenthood (and predictable difficulties with shared custody) are just two reasons that prevent many group members from issuing ultimatums.

What if you feel overwhelming guilt at leaving?

It can be devastating, but it's life; sometimes your very best efforts fail. "One of the most difficult roadblocks to some individuals' recovery is their inability to leave their loved ones to their own fate," Gravitz says.

Interestingly, some support-group members found that after separation, their ADHD partners suddenly "woke up" and became higher functioning. "As long as I was around, my husband seemed to feel he could just turn off his brain when he wasn't at work," Rose says. Cooperation was never his strong suit, the result being that either she was "in charge" or he was; he didn't know how to do middle ground. Living solo, all responsibility fell to him, and so he managed.

Sometimes it boils down to self-preservation. Consider that Wanda's is only one of *many* stories that have ended this way:

> I left my husband about a year ago after 10 years of marriage, and nothing but good has come of it! My career took off, as I no longer had to worry about crises at home. My finances improved, as nobody was spending money like there was no tomorrow. My energy has skyrocketed. I sleep so soundly. I am sorry I waited so long. It was hard to make the decision, but once I did, life fell into place almost magically.
>
> It finally become clear that if he wouldn't cooperate in dealing with his ADHD, I needn't be further damaged by his poor choices. That would be my number one message to others: If your partner is not prepared to address the issues that are wrecking your life, don't be afraid to set a timeline and leave."

INTRODUCTION

Calling in a Consultant to Help Retrofit Your Ride

For ten years, my husband's therapist focused on his low self-esteem and my being "controlling." Mine focused on my reactions to my husband's addictions. Finally, working with a therapist who understands ADHD and referred us to a psychiatrist for medication, we are seeing positive changes.

— REBECCA

B arely eight months into her new marriage, Jen sought individual coun-seling. "I thought it was me, not my husband, who was acting weird," she says with a laugh. It's the not-so-funny inside joke in the support groups: You can become so confused and blamed by your ADHD partner so often that you assume responsibility for your relationship's woes.

Fortunately, the clinic happened to pair Jen with an ADHD-savvy therapist. When she offered details about their marital problems, the therapist said, "Get your husband in here." The next visit, her husband saw the staff psychiatrist, who indeed diagnosed ADHD. And that has made all the difference in their marriage.

That's the good news. As more therapists learn to identify ADHD and understand its proper treatment, Jen's experience grows more common. Support-group members are extremely grateful to these professionals for recognizing ADHD in their partners and guiding them off the roller coaster—or at least helping them see the behavior for what it is: ADHD symptoms, not intentionally hurtful actions. They also express thanks to professionals who knew little about ADHD yet skillfully helped their clients regain their boundaries and lives.

Now for the *bad* news. Many therapists remain in the brain-science dark ages; they fail to recognize ADHD both in its obvious and subtler manifestations. And this ignorance can hurt you.

Psychiatrists Edward Hallowell and John Ratey, in their book *Driven to Distraction: Recognizing and Coping with Attention Deficit Disorder from Childhood Through Adulthood,* caution that the ADHD diagnosis is often overlooked in distressed couples because the problems ADHD can create seem little different from those most couples face. Indeed, to the untrained eye, ADHD symptoms do resemble human behaviors, albeit in more extreme form. Other factors fog the issues, too. That's why it is critical, if you suspect ADHD, to seek a *trained* eye.

This success strategy for finding effective therapy will help you to:

- **Realize that not all therapists are qualified to recognize or treat ADHD** and that seeking their help can make a bad situation worse (Chapter 17).
- **Understand the special orientation that therapy for ADHD requires** (Chapter 18).
- **Learn how and when to choose a therapist**—for yourself, for your ADHD partner, or in couple's counseling (Chapter 19).

ONE SUPPORT-GROUP MEMBER'S STORY

Bette: Here Comes the (Confused) Bride

With their wedding day approaching, Bette and her fiancé, Alan, agreed to seek couples counseling. Since meeting at the accounting firm where they both worked, the couple had enjoyed a "blissful" year of dating. Then Alan proposed. A few months later, they moved in together to save money for the wedding, and everything went downhill.

While they were dating, Alan surprised Bette with elaborately planned outings. They had wonderful conversations. Suddenly, though, Alan's planning abilities were missing in action, and rather than talking with Bette, he'd come home from work and stare at the computer monitor. "I now saw a man with really horrible organizational skills, using a Palm Pilot to remember everything, but only if he *remembered* to use it, which was rare," she says. The abrupt U-turn came as a bewildering shift, far beyond the normal relaxation of best behavior that occurs well into courtship.

Trying to Read Mixed Messages

Maybe Alan had grown bored? Or was he signaling cold feet about the marriage? How could that be, though, when he insisted on tending to every aspect of the wedding planning, down to the choice of bridesmaids' gifts. "Whatever the topic, he'd get a thought into his head and couldn't hear what anyone else was saying," Bette remembers. "He had no patience for compromise." In fact, Alan's previously unseen temper flared up in force.

Although Bette's friends and family dismissed Alan's behaviors as mere premarital jitters, she sensed something more troubling at play, but what? Was *she* acting differently? Expecting too much of Alan? Was it just a "guy thing?"

The truth is that Bette had no idea what a singular effort Alan had put into that courtship—and how impossible it would be to maintain over time. Because they worked in different departments at the office, she also didn't know that Alan had a long history of missing deadlines and clashing with coworkers. He'd always told her that the job was going well. And as it turned out, Alan wasn't lying about that. He was just completely misreading the social cues.

For his part, Alan had no clue why their relationship had hit the rocks. All he knew was that they were fighting a lot. That's why they consulted a mental health professional. "That's always the first thing people suggest, isn't it?" Bette asks. Yet, instead of clarifying the confusion, the particular psychologist they saw compounded it.

A Common Therapeutic Error: Confusing Result with Cause

"I was so confused at how Alan seemed to be changing from Dr. Jekyll to Mr. Hyde," Bette says. "I would often break down and cry during the sessions, to the point that the therapist concluded *I* was the problem." Like many therapists who don't recognize neurocognitive disorders like ADHD, this psychologist confused *result* with *cause*. Mistaking Bette's agitated and depressed state as the *cause* of Alan's behaviors, the therapist failed to perceive it as the *result*.

Furthermore, the therapist implied that Bette was putting too much blame on Alan, and that she needed to change, too. "Yet, the therapist never mentioned ADHD or how treatment might help Alan change," Bette says. Putting the responsibility to change on Bette, however, was like trying to caulk the bathtub while the water pipe's busted and gushing. Besides that, she says:

> When you're running around being a mother to your partner, wondering why you have to repeat yourself a billion times, getting blamed for everything, and getting sleep-deprived because of his weird sleep habits, plus having a high-stress job, how could you fix yourself without first finding out about your partner's ADHD? I didn't even know "myself" anymore. My personality was changing.

Amazingly, the Marriage Survived

As it turns out, the therapist actually had long suspected that Alan had ADHD, but she chose not to mention that possibility to them until *after* the couple's honeymoon.

Luckily, the couple's deep affection endured as they ricocheted through several mental-health professionals before finding appropriate help. Four years later, they've come a long way. Alan has settled into a good medication routine and is happy with the results at home and at work. Bette sees that she'd mistaken his apathetic behavior as disinterest, when in reality he was dejected at letting her down—and felt powerless to fix things.

As content as they are now, Bette still deeply regrets that their engagement, wedding, and early union could have been so much sweeter had they known about ADHD. "If only she'd told us earlier, we could have forgone all that trauma," Bette says. "We trusted that therapist, and our trust was misplaced."

CHAPTER
SEVENTEEN

Why the Wrong Therapy is Worse Than No Therapy

My fantasy is to put all the couples counselors who blamed us and didn't "get it" on a 14-day cruise with our ADHD partners. No days in the harbor—just out to sea.

— MARY

L ike our couple in the previous pages, Bette and Alan, many support-group members initially had faith in therapy—maybe even blind faith. In fact, as a nation, we've largely come to view therapists as our mental health "gatekeepers": the first line of defense when emotional or interpersonal difficulties arise. We expect that if we lay out the problem, therapy will help name it and address it, based on these assumptions:

- We trust that therapists are trained to detect a broad range of brain conditions, certainly something as common as ADHD.
- We trust that they can distinguish between clients who will benefit from standard "talk" therapy alone and those who might require medication and/or specialized therapies.
- We trust they can help us sort out the mess, because sometimes we're *so* very tired and confused—and if they can't help us, they'll say so instead of wasting our time and money.

Such trust is well placed when we've chosen a therapist carefully, but trust is dangerously misplaced when we haven't been careful enough. To aid your success in finding helpful therapy, this chapter explores common pitfalls to avoid. You will learn that:

- Graduate schools do not routinely train therapists to detect or treat ADHD, and some clinicians actually possess a bias against it as a valid medical diagnosis.
- Pursuing the wrong type of therapy can postpone or eliminate the chance for progress.
- Many therapists mistakenly assume that your "codependence" is the problem.
- Traditional couples counseling assumes that both partners play an equal role in relationship problems, a dangerous misperception when ADHD goes unrecognized.
- Family-court professionals who do not understand ADHD can exacerbate a difficult separation or divorce.

Some "Gatekeepers" Lack ADHD Keys

An effective gatekeeper respects the wisdom of using the right key for each lock. Some locks *do* yield to a skeleton key (in this analogy, standard talk therapy), but neurocognitive disorders such as ADHD usually require unique keys. Do responsible gatekeepers jam whichever keys they possess into a lock, trying to make it fit? No, that only makes it harder for the correct key, once it's identified, to work. These two primary factors explain why some therapists lack ADHD keys:

Few graduate schools offer courses in adult ADHD

More than half of the ADHD Partner Survey respondents expressed surprise to learn that training in detecting adult ADHD symptoms is not a licensing requirement for therapists. But it's true.

Clinicians typically aren't exposed to the topic until after their training has ended and they encounter ADHD patients, says psychologist and ADHD specialist J. Russell Ramsay, an assistant professor of psychology in psychiatry at the University of Pennsylvania School of Medicine. "ADHD might be covered in developmental or childhood psychology classes," he adds, "but in terms of adult development, to my understanding it's not a component of most programs."

They have an anti-science attitude—or old information

For some clinicians, emotions are paramount. "How dare anyone reduce complex human emotions to chemical reactions in the brain!" they protest, even though knowledgeable ADHD experts don't actually do that. They reject or minimize recent breakthroughs in brain science, perhaps having scant academic background for understanding them, not knowing how to integrate brain-science breakthroughs to their traditional approaches, or simply being unwilling to invest the time and effort.

For therapists willing to expend the effort, however, they can learn about effective therapy for ADHD by attending conferences and enrolling in seminars.

Why the Wrong Key Is Worse Than No Key

It might sound hard to believe, but when ADHD is in the picture, the wrong therapy can be worse than no therapy. One long-time support group member echoes the group consensus: "At best, therapy that fails to acknowledge ADHD is a waste of time and money. At worst, it is destructive and can exacerbate everybody's problems."

First-hand experience taught Glenna that lesson. One couples therapist asked her, "Don't you deserve better than this (her relationship with her ADHD partner)?" Glenna's response: "I felt like throwing a book at her! I adore my husband! We are both committed to our marriage, and I am not going to leave him. We are going to keep looking until we find help."

After finally learning of his ADHD a year ago, after 20 years of marriage, pieces fell into place for Glenna's family. Their difficulties ratcheted up when her husband had retired as a professional athlete and found a not-so-stimulating transition into "civilian" life difficult. They came to therapy willing to learn about ADHD and move forward. "That meant finding a therapist who could help us, not move us to divorce or vilify my husband," Glenna says.

Therapy that fails to identify or acknowledge the brain-based symptoms of ADHD might create adverse consequences:

- Postpone helpful treatment and drain already scarce resources such as time, money, and good will
- Lead you to think that your ADHD partner *won't* change problematic behaviors (rather than *can't* or *doesn't know how*)
- Reinforce your ADHD partner's perpetual feelings of frustration for being the butt of blame for involuntary or unintentional actions
- Exacerbate your ADHD partner's feelings of helplessness, triggering defense mechanisms such as anger, denial, and blame on both parts
- *Encourage* your servitude

If that last point sounds strange, consider Susan's experience. When Susan interviewed a prospective therapist, the woman disclosed that she herself and her son have "raging" ADHD. "She said she prays her son will marry an anal-compulsive woman who will be his secretary for the rest of his life," Susan recalls. "This therapist's theory was that people with ADHD are more *special* than the rest of us and that each needed a satellite 'do-er' to help them achieve their potential. Nice life for the do-er, right?"

When the Wrong Therapy Key Blames You

More commonly, your attempts to corral a careening ADHD partner— your so-called codependent or contol-freak ways—will stand out as the core issue. That typically puts the cart before the horse, of course; or, as one support-group member puts it: "Codependence my a**! It's survival mode." But here's the thing about codependence. Most therapists don't recognize or understand ADHD, but they *all* know about codependence; so that too often becomes the problem they focus on, whether it's the core issue or not. (See "Decoding Codependence" in on pages 220-21.)

Another misperception commonly made by non-ADHD-savvy therapists: You are *allowing* your ADHD partner to invade your personal boundaries, the limits that mature adults set to protect themselves from being engulfed by another's endless needs or invasive actions and maintain a good sense of own self-worth. Many therapists, seeing obvious trampling of limits—such as the ADHD partner's overspending, breaking promises, and lack of cooperation—conclude that the partner passively *allows* this to happen, presumably out of a victim mentality possibly springing from family-of-origin dysfunction.

That might indeed be true for some, and in need of addressing, but too many clinicians miss an important point: Many ADHD partners' poor impulse-control and disorganization stymie their ability to respect others' limits (or even their own). In turn, that challenges their mates' ability to maintain boundaries. Moreover, as discussed in Part Two of this book, these behaviors don't always evidence themselves in the beginning, before children and mortgages (or simply novelty-dulling time) enter the picture.

Ellen's therapist firmly told her she needed to start setting emotional boundaries with her husband, explaining that, "Good fences make good neighbors." But what if your neighbor keeps climbing over your fence, despite posted warning signs? What if your neighbor backs a Hummer into it? What if, despite written contracts and Claymore mines, your neighbor refuses or simply can't, until his or her ADHD is treated, quit futzing with your fence? Then what?

Ellen says she never had weak boundaries before, at age 38, she married her husband, and she gets very specific for outsiders who conclude, "Well, you must have sought this kind of partner or you just enjoy being a victim. You could always *leave*, can't you?"

> Let's say I establish a firm boundary that I will not tolerate being yelled at. My husband acknowledges my boundary and signs a document to that effect. Then, he *still* loses it and yells. He has an impulse disorder, folks, one that involves irritability. What then? How much do I turn my family's life upside down in order to enforce this boundary? Sure, I can leave the room or leave the house. And yeah, that might get the point across to most people, but not with Mark. He lives in the now and doesn't learn from his mistakes. He may have truly wanted to *not* yell, but lack of impulse-control got the better of him. Again.

Ellen is working hard to help her husband see how untreated ADHD affects him and his family, and she'd like to find a counselor to help her do so. *That* might actually be helpful. Meanwhile, she finds staying married with murky boundaries more reasonable than breaking up her family and *still* dealing with her husband's untreated ADHD through shared parenting post-divorce.

(Continued on page 222)

Marilyn—ADHD in the Family

I had asked my 10-year-old son's ADHD-specialist psychologist for the name of an ADHD marriage counselor. When I gave him the specifics, he said, "Why don't you divorce him?" Geesh! And this is a guy who claims to have ADHD himself! I needed help, not a divorce.

Finally, he referred me to a woman in the same clinic. I asked her for strategies in handling an all-ADHD household. After three meetings, she told me she didn't know much about ADHD, but I should give her a call when I'm ready to talk about myself, implying that I'm avoiding the "real" issue. But the real issue is the stress from my family. She was my fifth therapist, by the way.

It's a pain in the butt going from doctor to doctor—one for the kids, one for my husband—on top of a full-time job, the kids, and everything else. I'm sick of therapists needing several sessions to decide they can't help me. It's exhausting! It has only cost us money and time and reinforced my husband's opinion that therapy is useless. I feel doomed to plug along until I drop dead from exhaustion.

Decoding "Codependence"

The term *codependence* gets batted about a lot in the support group, and in therapists' offices. Yet its usage seems elastic, applied equally to those who swirl around helplessly in their ADHD partners' chaos and those who vigilantly strive to maintain personal boundaries.

How then do the professionals define the term? Here's an excerpt of one explanation from the online Chicago Health Library of the University of Illinois Medical Center, written by physician Michael Johnson.[22]

There is no common agreement about how to define codependency. It is used in many different ways to describe many different experiences. The idea of codependency was first formed by therapists working with people dependent on alcohol or drugs and their families. These therapists noticed that...their partners seemed unable to remove themselves from the problems of their impaired loved ones. They were bound to them by their determination to change or protect them.... It is unclear whether codependency is an illness or a normal response to being in a relationship with a substance-dependent person. A codependent person may show some of the following behaviors: has a high energy level, has low self-esteem, has very good organizational skills, is competent at a wide variety of tasks and is able to learn new ones quickly, is loyal and willing to put the needs of others before his or her own, never asks, "What's in this for me?", and tends to overachieve. The best way to prevent codependency is to recognize and treat a drug or alcohol addiction as soon as possible.

ADHD is not the same as an addiction, but its fallout can be eerily similar. And, no doubt support-group members would prefer codependence prevention, but they'll settle for relief. For some, that occurs only when they receive support and get educated about ADHD. Of course, some do report lifelong issues with codependency, perhaps growing up with an alcoholic parent, but consider these results from the ADHD Partner Survey:

- *"Living with my partner's untreated ADHD forced me into codependency before I knew what was happening"* (54 percent). That is, their partners' unpredictable actions often kept them on high alert, trying to do damage control, or passively accepting bad behavior because they'd become so confused or worn down.

- *"I am not naturally 'codependent.' Living with my partner's untreated ADHD symptoms forced me into a codependent mindset. As I understand more about the impact of ADHD in our relationship, I'm coming out of 'codependency'"* (63 percent).

As a pioneer in the field of recovery for adult children of alcoholics, psychologist Herbert Gravitz bristles at the trend toward pathologizing people as codependent solely because they are trying to help a family member with a mental illness. "Codependence has gotten such a bad name," he argues, "and helping others has gotten a bad name, especially with some prominent groups that sprang up around the codependent concept. They made caring a dirty word and a god of independence."

Rose, for example, found that the best way to cure her so-called codependency wasn't reading books about it or talking about it in meetings. It was to find help for her ADHD partner. Soon after Rose and her husband learned that he had ADHD (but still weren't sure what that actually meant), they sought couples therapy. Here's her account of the visit:

> This psychologist said to me, "Are you codependent with your husband?" He said it accusingly and conspiratorially, as if it were my dark sick secret at the core of our marital distress. As if my desire to rein in my out-of-control husband, especially his horrible health habits and spending our joint funds, was simply a twisted need stemming from my childhood and not common sense! I was so tired, I let that knucklehead psychologist make me feel ashamed for being "codependent."
>
> Looking back, I suspect that man possessed so little empathy he didn't know what it feels like to watch someone you love self-destruct—and wanting to help but not knowing how to help without hurting yourself. (I also wonder if his wife had the same problems with his spending habits and he was trying to convince her that she was codependent!) The point is, we needed professional guidance, but he knew nothing about ADHD treatment.
>
> I realize that some people might have too much empathy for their own good, just as others have too little, and perhaps my life would have been much easier if my brain had weaker "empathy circuits." But my life would also be less rich, especially in the ability to connect with others. And the fact remains: What helped me wasn't being given a useless "codependent" label. What helped me *and* my husband was finding real answers and real solutions.

(Continued from page 219)

Wrong Keys in Couples Therapy (Define *Tango*)

We've all heard the axiom, "It takes two to tango." As it happens, most couples therapists are trained in what you might call a "tango" perspective. It's the idea that both partners are equally responsible for their relationship problems, and furthermore, if one person in the couple starts acting differently, the other person will, too.

Randi takes issue with the tango theory, however, and so do many other support-group members. When speaking of her three-year relationship with her now ex-boyfriend, diagnosed with ADHD after their breakup, she riffs on the dance analogy:

> A tango? Ha! The way I look at it, I was just standing there, and my boyfriend was break-dancing. Make that break-*neck* dancing. Every once in a while, he would lose control and his leg or arm would come flying at me, and I would have to dive out of the way. I don't call that dancing a tango.

The tricky part of the tango philosophy is that it's sometimes true. For example, when your ADHD partner starts developing awareness and pursuing treatment, you can, in turn, start backing off on the hypervigilance.

Could failure to detect ADHD correlate to couples therapy's poor track record?

"Remember, it's not a marriage; it's a counseling session that can last a lifetime," Dave jokes.

For couples seeking relationship therapy without knowing that a third party sits in the session—namely, that at least one person in the couple has ADHD—that statement can prove all too true. Consider these nuggets from those ADHD Partner Survey respondents who had pursued therapy (93 percent of total respondents):

- Half agreed with this statement: "Seeing counselors who didn't detect my partner's ADHD meant we spent years seeing little or no progress. We had no idea what we were dealing with."
- More than 60 percent had seen two or more couples therapists.

The problem is, therapists too often miss your partner's ADHD. Instead, they advise you to back off and give your partner room to step up to the plate. But in fact, your nagging most likely isn't the core problem; the problem is that your ADHD partner's deficits in initiation and follow-through almost *demand* nagging. Consider these analogous situations:

- If the ADHD partner collects too many traffic tickets, should the police department be held accountable for being too controlling?
- If the ADHD partner can't curb impulse spending, should eBay or Amazon be deemed *enabling* or *codependent*?
- If the ADHD partner doesn't follow through on reasonable, clearly established work tasks, should the boss be taken to task for poor communications skills?

Ridiculous, right? Yet, that is essentially the perspective of many couples therapists, even some who proclaim ADHD expertise.

The essential trouble with tango therapy lies in assuming that each person possesses a sense of reciprocity, of give-and-take, and that each person can change behaviors at will. Yet, when an untreated neurocognitive disorder is involved—one that tends to *inhibit* cooperation and reciprocity—the dance floor is not level. Instead, it's rolling and heaving as in an earthquake; neither partner can gain solid footing, much less do a tango.

- Only 15 percent said that couples therapy helped "very much," and 38 percent said it helped only a little or briefly. As one respondent commented: "When the therapist held my then-undiagnosed ADHD partner accountable for his inaction, we had progress. As soon as the therapy ended, it was all backslide to previous behavior." This is not surprising; it's well known that people with ADHD respond to immediate rewards or restrictions. Difficulty internalizing those guidelines, however, thwarts sustained solo efforts.
- A whopping 41 percent said couples therapy either was no help at all *or made matters worse*.

Studies are hard to parse on this complicated subject, but couples therapy seems to fare little better in the general population. It stands to reason, though, that persons with untreated ADHD are overrepresented in couples therapy. Therefore, when standard methods don't help, it makes sense to question if therapists have missed key neurocognitive issues.

Anthony—Talking About Trauma Never Helped

We've found that many of my wife's long-standing mental and emotional traumas magically clear up when the medication is right. When not taking medication or not taking it as directed, she has an infinite capacity for sharing her misery with anyone who will listen, including counselors, but no healing takes place. She's always ready to simply rehash the same things repeatedly, with the same volume of tears each time. For years!

With the right medication, though, she's suddenly over all the trauma. And no, she's not drugged into a stupor. She acts normal, more normal than she's ever acted off medication. Yet, if she skips her medication for a while, she's ready to "talk through it" all over again, ad nauseum. And there's always a therapist willing to indulge her.

When the Wrong Key Fails to Fit Family Court

If ineffective therapy can jeopardize a marriage, it can create disaster in a separation or divorce. In fact, some support-group members report remaining in deeply troubled relationships solely because sharing custody with an unpredictable parent will put their children at risk. Men especially worry that the courts will favor the mother without question and might even revoke the father's rights entirely if the skewed perspective of the mother is taken at face value.

During Amber's marital separation, when her twin boys were seven years old, her husband took them swimming at a nearby river, something that she had done frequently. "When I took them, though, I was in the water, too, and stayed within arms' reach," she explains. "When he took them, the kids were in the river and he was on the bank chatting up a storm with a friend, his back to the kids and paying no attention to them."

By the time the friend noticed that one boy was going under, a stranger jumped in to save the child. "Had it not been for those attentive bystanders, things could have turned out very differently," she maintains. "Of course, my husband minimized his actions because 'nothing bad happened.' I knew a judge would think I was being a vindictive woman if I tried to deprive my charming husband of his parental rights." Amber's story is not unique and such fears can be well founded for these three reasons, among others:

1. Too often the wrong partner is blamed

Mental health professionals often exacerbate troubles by blaming the partners of adults with ADHD for having "inappropriate anxiety" or exaggerating the ADHD parent's behavior and its effect on the family.

"Couples therapists will often say that both partners need to learn new behaviors in order for both to get better," says therapist and attorney William Eddy, senior family mediator at the National Conflict Resolution Center in San Diego, California. "In many cases, this is true. Yet in my 30-year career, I've found that many family or marital conflicts *are* driven by one person's mental health problem and that it is unfair and unhelpful to blame the other person for some or all of the problems."

In fact, blaming the other person makes things worse, because the source of the problem remains unaddressed, says Eddy, author of *Splitting: Protecting Yourself While Divorcing a Borderline or Narcissist.*

Not too long ago, he points out, parents were often blamed for creating schizophrenia in their children by giving "mixed messages" or "double binds." "After decades of blaming parents, however, scientists discovered that schizophrenia was primarily a genetic brain disorder that could be significantly helped with medications," Eddy points out. "We don't blame parents any more."

2. Many people with mental illness confuse outside observers

What's more, it's common for people with mental illness to behave in ways that obscure their true dysfunction. "They might be strong blamers, which is part of their disorder," he explains, "and unwary professionals may get caught up in the blaming and miss the disorder."

For example, parent A has a disorder that causes distortions of information and perception. Parent A blames Parent B for family problems when in fact Parent B is the reasonable parent. Unless therapists resist tendencies to see the cause of all problems as relational, they can easily miss neurological disorders. "It is vitally important to accurately diagnose these conditions before attempting to assist a family," Eddy says.

Most critically, family court professionals need to understand how neurocognitive disorders, if left unaddressed, can affect life after separation. As with Amber's case above, a parent's inattention, disorganization, poor driving habits, or other safety issues tied to an untreated disorder can expose a child to risk, especially when the other parent is not around to be on guard.

3. Even "successful people" can have dangerous disorders

Most people have difficulty understanding how prominent professors, top executives, or other outwardly successful people can possess brain impairments that threaten their children's safety. Moreover, some dismiss ADHD as a benign, even humorous, condition. Yet, when this professor or executive loses the car or house keys or runs out of gas on the highway in freezing weather and the kids' jackets have been forgotten, it poses a life-threatening impact. Besides safety concerns, children might also be subject to irritability and mood issues associated with untreated ADHD; and a parent might also fail to remember a child's medication regimen, not to mention regulate homework completion and bedtime hours.

Now that you know about therapeutic approaches worth avoiding, let's learn about the special focus that effective treatment for adult ADHD requires.

CHAPTER
EIGHTEEN

Therapy That Works for ADHD

Therapy is helpful when the therapist can see ADHD for what it is—and knows how to help.
— BRENDA

"It's not just that my partner has ADHD; it's all this other emotional baggage, too," goes the common refrain in the support group. One member's boyfriend avoids problems for months only to leap into a quick fix at the eleventh hour, with predictably poor results. Another member confides that his wife beats herself up so thoroughly for perceived failures that she can't see all the things that she does well.

The potential list of negative mindsets and poor coping skills expands in endless variation, as explored in Chapter 3. In other words, it's not solely behaviors such as forgetting and "tuning out" that create problems. Rather, that burden is compounded by poor habits and distorted attitudes developed over a lifetime in reaction to unrecognized ADHD.

Frequently, so-called baggage resolves with ADHD awareness and medical treatment. Even previously identified "core therapeutic issues" disappear (or at least diminish significantly) because they were, in fact, treatable ADHD symptoms. "ADHD is fundamentally a chemical problem," Yale University psychologist Thomas E. Brown, a leading ADHD expert, says emphatically. "Unless the problematic chemistry is changed, other interventions are not likely to be very effective."

Yet, more than half of the ADHD Partner Survey respondents who reported dissatisfaction with their mate's medication treatment cited this reason: "Partner has a lifetime of engrained behavior patterns that he or she is not willing to consider changing." As you'll learn in the next success strategy, on medication, it's highly possible that the culprit is unsatisfactory medical care. But could it also be that the ADHD partners don't know *how* to change these habits—or even doubt that change is possible? Absolutely.

The bottom line: Finding effective therapy for someone with ADHD means finding a therapist who can both distinguish emotional baggage from ADHD traits (like impulsivity and distractibility) *and* address the emotional baggage *caused* by a lifetime of unacknowledged ADHD. Then it takes it one step further, by helping the client to develop new strategies for handling life's practical details.

"Many times, the years of depression or worrying resolve once a person with ADHD is able to sustain focus and attention," says Pennsylvania-based psychologist and coach Michele Novotni, author of two books about ADHD and former president and CEO of the Attention Deficit Disorder Association (ADDA).

For example, consider Nancy. Prior to seeing Novotni as a client, Nancy had been treated for more than 15 years with antidepressants and traditional therapy without much impact. Her once-promising career drifted aimlessly. Nancy's depression lifted only when she was finally diagnosed with ADHD and treated with a combination of medication and counseling directed toward active, practical problem-solving, including getting and staying organized. For the first time in her life, Novotni says, "Nancy has hope that she is not doomed to a lifetime of trying but never succeeding."

Adults with relatively mild cases of ADHD sometimes respond well to medication alone. Other adults, however, find that even optimal medication takes them only so far, and some would rather try therapy before medication. Whatever the situation, this chapter describes the unique approach that ADHD therapy requires and helps you to understand:

- *Changing trends in overall therapy*—Traditional "talk therapy" has largely given way to a model that focuses less on the past and more on solutions and strategies.
- *The ABCs of Cognitive-Behavioral Therapy (CBT)*—Whereas traditional talk therapy focuses on feelings, CBT focuses on the thoughts that create feelings and works to adjust those thoughts.

- *CBT for ADHD*—New models for ADHD psychotherapy adapt CBT models to accommodate inherent neurocognitive challenges.

New Knowledge Calls for New Therapy Models

Married 15 years, Melinda and Ralph made several failed forays into couples therapy before they finally realized Ralph had ADHD. "Each new attempt was always so hard for Ralph," she explains. "He had to recount with each new therapist not only his own lifelong difficulties but also the disappointment he had with his dad, who definitely had ADHD but was never diagnosed and was quite unforgiving of his children's mistakes." Ralph took an emotional beating each and every session. And because the therapist offered no strategies other than letting Ralph ramble on about the past, therapy only reinforced Ralph's belief that nothing could ever change for the better.

Unfortunately, this scenario echoes frequently throughout the support groups, and here's a key reason. For most of the last century, therapists largely subscribed to the idea that to live more healthfully in the present, we must understand the past, especially past trauma, by talking about it. In fact, this approach became so ubiquitous, it's what most of us think about when we hear the word *therapy*.

Over the last 20 years, however, a radical shift has taken place: Therapy no longer requires rehashing the past. In fact, it's sometimes seen as counterproductive. And blaming the parents for the adult child's problems is now a discredited model.

Plenty of therapists still operate solely on the old rehash-the-past model, but positive results happen more quickly with the newer model of cognitive-behavioral therapy, its advocates say. "CBT was the first form of psychotherapy to actually measure progress, as a part of the treatment," explains ADHD expert and psychologist J. Russell Ramsay, coauthor (with psychiatrist Anthony Rostain) of *Cognitive Behavioral Therapy for Adult ADHD: An Integrative Psychosocial and Medical Approach.* CBT is still considered "talk therapy," but the talk coming from the therapist is more focused, active, and directed at problem-solving.

First, let's go back and learn a little more about the traditional therapeutic approach, sometimes called *psychodynamic* or *insight-oriented therapy*. Primarily, it tends to view a person's problematic behaviors as mostly springing from childhood attempts to adapt to dysfunction. The theory goes that once you become aware of these unconscious behaviors that cause you pain, you can replace them with more effective ones. Some people find this kind of therapy helpful, some don't, and some are left scratching their heads, wondering how this is supposed to help them function better in the real world, day to day. Unfortunately, many learn to blame their parents for their continuing unhappiness and stay very stuck.

In fact, some consider old-school talk therapy's tendency to ruminate on the past a particularly *unhelpful* strategy. Clinical psychologist John Norcross, professor of psychology at the University of Scranton and editor of the *Journal of Clinical Psychology: In Session*, has spent much of his career tracking trends in psychotherapy. He considers looking to the past for answers problematic for several reasons:

- It leads to highlighting problems rather than seeking solutions.
- You return to things that cannot be changed rather than progressing to things that can.

The Best Antidote for Poor Self-Esteem? Success!

When ADHD is involved, therapy that tries to boost poor self-esteem simply by talking about it tends to go nowhere slowly.

Success breeds confidence, just as failure breeds lack of confidence, maintains psychologist and prominent ADHD expert Kathleen Nadeau, director of the Chesapeake ADHD Center in Silver Spring, Maryland. ADHD therapy requires a clinician who is "aware that ADHD is a neurobiological condition and uses concrete, practical methods to treat it."

Feelings are important, but therapy that stops there is a dead end. "Traditional therapists might find neurocognitive psychotherapy (the term she uses to describe her therapy model for ADHD) alien," concedes Nadeau, "But with ADHD, it's the practical matters that create so much emotional baggage." In other words, you can't separate clients' daily living problems from their psychological distress. Psychological issues are addressed "but in an integrated fashion, moving back and forth between the practical and the emotional, between the present and the past, and between ADHD and related or coexisting disorders."

Feelings are followed up with a "what to do about it" approach. Instead of being overwhelmed by an invisible enemy, clients take charge of their

- Even if past events contribute to the genesis or maintenance of the current problem, there's little evidence that reviewing those problems directly helps people progress.

For now, consider just two of Norcross's points explaining how traditional talk therapy might prove especially counterproductive when neurocognitive disorders such as ADHD are involved:

1. Perceptions and recollections of childhood can be distorted

People with neurocognitive dysfunction often prove unreliable historians, as explained in Chapter 12. Therefore, it makes even less sense to focus on historical events as though they have caused the present problems.

"When we look back, we need to consider reciprocity—the interaction between a child's behavior and the caretaker's behavior," Norcross explains.

(Continued on page 234)

ADHD and begin to see some special skills they possess. The person moves from asking "What's wrong with me?" to asking "What are my strengths and weaknesses?"

Nadeau advises therapists to learn about ADHD and how it has affected the person, and then to implement a three-point strategy:

1. Improve cognitive functions

The best tool currently available for improving cognitive function is medication, but the therapist should also help identify poor existing health habits that impair cognition (such as stress, insufficient sleep, or exercise) and help to implement new habits.

2. Develop practical strategies

Medication can help immensely, but challenges remain, and some people want to try alternative routes. Either way, the person needs concrete strategies, such as timers and calendars. "Many therapists relegate this critical aspect of treatment to a coach or organizer," Nadeau says, "but formulating and consistently using compensatory strategies constitutes the heart of learning to take charge of ADHD."

3. Create environmental changes

Therapist and client identify challenges at home and work. Drawing in a work supervisor and significant other helps to educate everyone and round out feedback on the efficacy of strategies.

In Session: Less "Support," More "Direction"

"We wasted so much money and effort with counselors who hadn't a clue about ADHD, and our marriage suffered terribly," says Suzanne. "I'd advise others to learn about ADHD first and then seek professionals who 'get it.'"

When ADHD is involved, it's critical that many traditional therapeutic guidelines be reassessed and refashioned. For example, therapists talk of creating an *alliance* with the client. Among therapists who try to treat ADHD without really understanding it, a common mistake made toward that end is being overly supportive of the client.

Psychiatrist Marc Schwartz, director of the Adult Attention Deficit Center in New Haven, Connecticut, advises that when it comes to ADHD, establishing an alliance partially relies on two factors:

- The therapist understands ADHD's neurocognitive underpinnings.
- The therapist knows how to deal with "treatment-disruptive" ADHD symptoms, including missing appointments, going off on tangents, and losing interest in therapy.

In fact, experienced clinicians treating ADHD know to take steps that traditional therapists have been trained to view as overstepping therapeutic boundaries or being too "active." For example, psychologist Michele Novotni asks her assistant to contact clients and remind them of upcoming appointments, sometimes even up to two or three times that day. At the session's end, Novotni provides clients with a copy of the notes to help them remember the items discussed and strategies developed.

ADHD experts agree that, after diagnosis, education is the first step in any treatment plan. "The person should first be educated about the disorder's causes, symptoms, course, and treatment," Schwartz explains. "Next, appropriate medication should be discussed."

If the client responds positively to medication, many treatment-disruptive symptoms can be reduced or eliminated. Medication, of course, should be well-monitored and third-party feedback should be solicited. "ADHD clients often cannot accurately self-monitor the dysfunctions caused by their deficits," says Schwartz, echoing the point emphasized in Chapter 12.

Good therapy for ADHD requires special strategic management. Schwartz offers guidelines for therapists to help clients find and maintain focus:

Keep sessions organized

If the client cannot organize the topics to be discussed, the therapist can solicit the topics from the client at the beginning of the session and collaborate to prioritize them and allocate discussion time.

Actively pursue important topics

Given that ADHD clients can be forgetful, the therapist should bring up topics mutually agreed upon as important. The therapist should "check in" to make sure the client understands why the therapist's comments are relevant.

Limit clients' circumstantial talk

Traditional therapists might value letting the client "talk it out." For the ADHD client who habitually talks excessively or wanders off topic, this strategy simply wastes time. Schwartz recommends that the therapist tactfully let the client know that, in fact, talking at length without getting to the point that the client really wants to talk about is a common ADHD symptom.

Help the client listen

Most traditional therapists are taken aback at a client who interrupts and doesn't listen. Once the therapist understands this behavior sometimes goes hand-in-glove with ADHD, the therapist can get over the idea that it's rebellious and calmly help the client to focus.

Deal with lateness and absences

The therapist should assure the client that lateness is unsurprising behavior when ADHD is concerned. Yet, it's important to recognize that it is a symptom amenable to various behavioral techniques. The therapist should also maintain a clear policy for such matters.

Reduce the frequency of absences

The therapist might help develop strategies that aid forgetful clients. These include making standard weekly appointments (same day, same time), phoning with a reminder the day before, and asking the client to write down the time before leaving the office.

Pace sessions

A planned agenda with sufficient time scheduled to talk about each agenda topic ensures that important matters are addressed adequately. Letting the client know when 10 or 15 minutes are left in the session can set the tone for wrapping up the session on time.

(Continued from page 231)

The newer therapeutic model understands the relationship as an interpersonal dance, in which one person's movements elicit a complementary movement from someone else. For example, some children with untreated ADHD can punch the buttons of even the most patient parent, making that parent seem short-tempered to outsiders—and in the adult child's one-sided memory. Similarly, even the best-behaved child can drive some parents with untreated ADHD to distraction. The bottom line: Each person's perspective represents only one part of the story.

2. We need explanations, including scientific ones

For thousands of years, humans have looked to events outside themselves as a way to make sense of their lives. "Every patient needs a rationale, a personal narrative to make sense of their disorder and its origins," Norcross says. "What changes with each generation, as knowledge progresses, is the paradigm used to explain disorder and the type of treatment offered. Today's paradigm is informed by breakthroughs in brain science. Who knows what the next one will be?"

Today, it's important to expand one's narrative of personal history to include genetics, medical conditions, and events such as blows to the head, but only as one thread in the narrative. "To the extent that such a rationale is useful or even necessary, you want to spend some time on it," Norcross advises. "But treatment that spends hours ruminating on the original cause—whether it's family dysfunction or genetics—is not usually helpful."

Here's the clear consensus among prominent ADHD specialists: Psychodynamic or insight-oriented therapy proves an especially poor fit for ADHD.

That doesn't mean we should underestimate the help that many people with ADHD have received from traditional talk therapy. Some gifted therapists find ways to help patients, no matter what their orientation, Ramsay is quick to emphasize. "But overall," he adds, "any approach not adapted to account for the effects of ADHD will miss very important components of what brings these patients to treatment, and so it decreases the likelihood therapy will be effective."

As a psychologist specializing in ADHD, Novotni also views psychodynamic therapy's *nondirective* approach as ineffective for this neurocognitive condition. Because the therapist simply mirrors the client's statements instead of directing the session, psychodynamic therapy is likely to go nowhere fast. Yet occasionally, so-called insight-oriented therapy might be necessary and critical, she concedes: "Many times core beliefs are resistant to cognitive behavior therapy alone and require the deeper understanding provided by a more psychodynamic approach. A therapist needs to be skilled enough to use more than one treatment modality with ADHD clients."

When CBT is adapted to address ADHD's unique symptoms and challenges, it's widely considered the most useful overall approach. Thus far, eight published studies have examined the benefits of psychosocial treatments, primarily CBT (those addressing both psychological and social behaviors) for adult ADHD.[23] More study is necessary, but these eight studies represent the best evidence so far concerning which type of therapy helps ADHD, and that evidence points to CBT. The research shows that the combination of CBT and medication management is associated with significant improvements in ADHD symptoms, mood/anxiety, and overall functioning.

Let's now briefly explore the principles of cognitive-behavioral therapy that focus on ADHD.

The ABCs of CBT—Cognitive-Behavioral Therapy

CBT is based on the idea that each of us has underlying assumptions, or "scripts," that run our life. Even though we're usually not even aware of these assumptions, they still guide our behavior and emotions. Once we do start examining our scripts, we often find parts that are completely irrational—not to mention counterproductive. At that point, we can consciously choose to revise the script.

Traditional talk therapy focuses on feelings. CBT focuses on the thoughts that create those feelings, and it works to adjust those thoughts in a way that changes behavior and creates a more productive outcome.

Essentially, CBT combines two types of therapy:

- **Cognitive therapy** explores how certain thinking patterns create errors in perception. When you have *cognitive distortions*, you see a distorted picture of what's happening in your life. That distorted picture makes you feel anxious, depressed, or angry at situations for no apparent good reason.
- **Behavior therapy** examines how certain situations might trigger your habitual reactions (for example fear, self-defeat, anger, avoidance). It also teaches you how to calm your mind and body and change your responses and behaviors so that you can feel better, think more clearly, and make better decisions.

As you learn more about this approach, it's helpful to keep in mind these three basic principles:

1. CBT Focuses on Four Steps: Event, Thought, Feeling, Action

To illustrate the importance of cognitive distortions in our lives, Ramsay provides an example he offers to his students at the University of Pennsylvania School of Medicine, where he is an assistant professor of psychology in psychiatry.

Early one morning, a roaming canine leaves a "gift" on the doorsteps of three neighboring houses. At the first house, a highly anxious person comes out, accidentally steps in it, and tells himself, "Oh no, I'm covered in germs. I'm going to catch a disease!" He runs off to douse himself in antiseptic gel. At the next house, a depressed person comes out, also stepping in the gift. She tells herself, "I knew I shouldn't have tried to go outside today because something bad was going to happen." She goes back to bed. At the third house, an optimist come out, steps in it, and says, "It's a good thing I wore my shoes this morning." He continues with his plans for the day.

The point of this story is *not* the power of positive thinking, Ramsay stresses. The point is that each person developed a different interpretation of the *same event* (the doggie deposit). In turn, each person's thought (what they told themselves about the event) determined how they felt and the next action they took. Again, the sequence is event, thought, feeling, action.

Simply by viewing the event differently, those neighbors could have changed their emotional reaction and subsequent action. The tricky part: Because we speed so quickly through event, thought, feeling, and action, we typically aren't even aware of the thoughts that enter our minds automatically—or that better, alternative thoughts might exist. *Until we start questioning.*

2. CBT often works with medication, not instead of it

Some types of psychodynamic therapy shun or minimize the role of medication, but CBT is often paired with medication for most psychiatric disorders (depression and anxiety, for example), and none more so than ADHD. "CBT picks up where medication leaves off," Ramsay notes.

3. CBT is not about "positive thinking"

It's hard to overemphasize this point, especially when it comes to ADHD. Living with undiagnosed ADHD into adulthood may predispose some people to develop negative and erroneous interpretations and beliefs about themselves, others, and the world. Therefore, it's useful for people with ADHD to understand how they came to adopt these distorted beliefs. "Negative thinking is the effect, not the cause," Ramsay insists. That's why positive thinking alone won't turn it around.

Now that you understand the principles behind CBT, let's look at how it is adapted to create effective ADHD therapy, including addressing distorted beliefs.

CBT's Special Focus on ADHD—Three Core Steps

Several clinician-researchers in the U.S. are developing and testing CBT models designed to help therapists adapt their practice to meet the unique needs of clients with ADHD. These researchers include the University of Pennsylvania's Ramsay and psychiatrist Anthony Rostain, psychologist Steven Safren at Harvard University, and a few others, most of whom are affiliated with university medical schools. Essentially, their strategies recommend a three-step process:

1. Identify core beliefs and automatic thoughts—for instance, "I never do anything right."
2. Reassess compensatory strategies—all the good and bad coping skills.
3. Create awareness of self-defeating thoughts and poor strategies and implement more effective ones.

Step 1: Identify Core Beliefs and Automatic Thoughts

"Most individuals referred to our ADHD clinic share a negative core belief system based on chronic and recurrent frustration related to having ADHD," Ramsay explains. They tend to describe themselves with terms like *failure*, *defective*, *socially undesirable*, and *incompetent*.

These core beliefs and automatic thoughts (such as "I always screw up" or "I'm a failure") can start early in life and seem to fuse with the individual's developing personality, as explained in Chapter 3. For one of Ramsay's clients, ADHD symptoms had become so intertwined with his self-identity that he said, "I don't know whether I *have* ADHD or I *am* ADHD."

These unquestioned beliefs mean your ADHD partner might have tendencies to do the following:

Exhibit "learned helplessness"—what's the use?

The core belief is, "Nothing I do is ever going to work, so it is a waste of time and effort to try anymore." Individuals will walk away from a job or a relationship rather than trying to salvage it. Partners, children, and friends left behind are doubly hurt, because it seems like those people simply don't care.

Personalize setbacks—"It's all my fault"

Rick assumes that everything that goes wrong in his life is his fault. Upon seeing his car's flat tire, Rick tells himself, "I must be an incompetent car owner." Individuals with this belief tend to react emotionally, not logically, to any challenge. (And sometimes your ADHD partner might feel self-blame to such an uncomfortable degree that he or she reflexively shifts the blame to others.)

Do comparative thinking—better/worse than other people

"We all do this to some degree," Ramsay concedes. "We compare, say, our physical shape to someone who goes to the gym five days a week. But with ADHD, it's almost as if they compare their brains' executive functions."

For example, Bob gets his reports done early and Larry is always late. Instead of trying to find a strategy to help him finish his work earlier, Larry tells himself he is inferior to Bob. "That's how the thoughts start contaminating effective coping," Ramsay adds. "Even though people with ADHD might need to approach things differently, they interpret 'different' as being 'less than' and resist making the accommodation."

Think in all-or-nothing, black-and-white terms

Support-group members often report that their ADHD partners think in black-and-white terms, such as "your way or my way but never *our* way." Perfectionism also can fall under this heading with attitudes such as "If it is not perfect, it is horrible."

Make "should" statements with unrealistic standards

Mari constantly loses her keys, but her attitude is, "I'm an adult and I *should* be able to find my keys." That keeps her from seeking solutions such as hammering a nail into the wall and hanging her keys there when she gets home.

Mind reading: misinterpreting another's actions or words

This is the most common distortion afflicting couples, Ramsay observes. A person with ADHD tells herself she knows what her partner is thinking about her. For example: "She's a screw-up for forgetting to turn on the oven after putting the food in it." Maybe you do this type of unhelpful mind reading, too. For example: "My ADHD partner didn't care enough about me to even turn on the oven!"

Overgeneralize—always/never statements

Bill's wife had to work late preparing for an important meeting the next day. Bill, who has ADHD, promised to pick up the suit she needed in the morning, but he did not write it on his to-do list and forgot about it until his wife came home. His first thought ("Oops, I screwed up.") was not wholly inaccurate. Yet subsequent thoughts ("I'm a lousy husband.... I never do anything right.") were very much out of proportion to Bill's error, thus dampening his confidence to come up with a repair strategy.

But What About My ADHD Partner's Overoptimism?

If you're wondering why your partner, instead of having the I-fail-at-everything-I-do attitude, typically exudes overoptimism about a scheme or project's likelihood of success, psychologist J. Russell Ramsay posits an explanation.

"Somebody who has anxiety sometimes overinterprets the existence of threat or danger and may feel overwhelmed," he explains. "Some individuals with ADHD, on the other hand, may underinterpret potential problems and may end up being underwhelmed—or overly optimistic—and so they may miss important warning signs of potential trouble."

Again, it sometimes comes down to that finding-the-middle-ground challenge of ADHD.

Step 2: Reassess "Compensatory Strategies"

Adults who have ADHD often protest, "Oh, I took medication as a kid, but as an adult I've learned to *compensate*." For those with minimal impairment, that might well be true. The trouble is, many individuals have developed *not-so-effective* compensatory strategies, or coping skills. In fact, these strategies might prove unsustainable over time.

Indeed, poor compensatory strategies often prove problematic in their own right. Until marriage, Jeanette's husband had always coped with his disorganization and poor sense of time by strictly structuring his day. This worked for him personally, and Jeanette was able to accommodate him—until they had a family. Then, try as he might, he could not make their young children follow his exacting plans. His strategy simply proved too inflexible; he needed to find some middle ground between rigid planning and no planning.

Of all the poor compensatory strategies Ramsay encounters with clients who have ADHD, two are the most common: avoidance and procrastination.

Avoidance: often lurking under "coping" strategies

Elaine doesn't know she has ADHD. When she finds herself running late for a business meeting—again—the automatic thoughts pepper her consciousness. "They'll be angry" and "I'm going to get fired." Her anxiety skyrockets. Instead of continuing straight to the meeting, she delays her arrival further by stopping at the grocery store to buy lavish snacks. "They can't be too mad at me when they see I've brought these," she tells herself, proud of her resourcefulness.

The trouble with Elaine's strategy? Rather than directly addressing her terminally tardy behavior, she avoids facing it. Moreover, she's reinforcing her core beliefs. Her coworkers *weren't* happy. They didn't want snacks; they wanted an on-time meeting. What's worse, her credit-card debt is only growing bigger, creating more brain-zapping stress.

Procrastination: "self-medicating" in the act itself

Procrastination is often an unconscious compensatory strategy. Those who procrastinate put off a necessary task because they think it will be unpleasant, disregard the benefit as being too far in the future to be important, or assume they will perform the task inadequately. Procrastination also seduces with two sweet spots:

- Postponing the task provides *immediate* relief ("I'll pay the bills after I watch this show.").
- Putting the task off for so long ensures that it eventually must be done in a big hurry, with the resulting intensity that can create a self-medicating adrenaline rush.

Viewed through the lens of untreated ADHD, the duties associated with adult life—paperwork, bills, emptying the garbage—can get magnified into huge stresses. Rather than tolerating the mild to moderate feelings of discomfort that come from doing what's difficult or tedious, the person with ADHD gains short-term relief by avoiding and procrastinating. If and when the person returns to the task later, it's probably a more complicated mess. (Imagine late fees, interest rates compounding, not enough money to cover the mounting bills, and very smelly garbage.) Ah, but they've already learned that avoidance makes them feel better, so they shove the bills back in the drawer.

At the same time, avoidance makes the problems harder to solve, further reinforcing their sense of inadequacy and confidence in tackling future challenges. "I knew I couldn't do it." In reality, Ramsay contends, they just procrastinated too much and didn't have a fair opportunity to see how well they could have done if they'd tried different compensatory strategies from the beginning.

Step 3: Create Awareness, Develop New Strategies

In very simplified form, here are eight key principles helpful in guiding therapists practicing CBT for ADHD, according to Ramsay (note that a few principles overlap with the treatment provided by some prescribing physicians, including psychoeducation and monitoring symptoms):

1. Obtain diagnosis and assess readiness for change
An accurate diagnosis provides the first opportunity for reframing difficulties and reexamining negative beliefs through a more accurate lens. Some people leap on the diagnosis, eager to seek treatment and change; others harbor doubts about their ability to change. ("It's never worked before.")

2. Provide psychoeducation
This involves clarifying misconceptions about treatment and ADHD's neurobiological nature. Clients are advised to read popular books, explore reputable online resources, and attend support groups. They are reminded, though, that while therapy will be personalized to their unique circumstance, these other resources will be more general. Because clients spend more time with their therapist than with a prescribing physician, therapy is also a logical place to examine their attitudes toward medication to inform their decision.

3. Define treatment goals and revisit them over time
The therapist and client work together to identify goals for therapy. Setting those objectives allows the therapist and the client to measure and record progress. People with ADHD often lose interest in long-term goals or forget how far they've come, discounting therapy's effectiveness or their own successes. Defining and revisiting treatment goals proves especially valuable as treatment progresses.

4. Adopt an active, not a passive role
"Therapists who work with adults with ADHD cannot afford to act passively," Ramsay emphasizes. They must work to keep sessions focused on the agenda and changing dysfunctional patterns.

5. Keep an eye on the big picture
Each person has a unique mix of issues that affects his or her particular belief systems, such as mood or anxiety problems, life history, and rela-

tionship or parenting issues. Understanding these multiple factors helps the therapist identify each client's automatic reactions and develop individualized strategies for facing challenges.

6. Establish a therapeutic alliance, explore grief reactions

Although an accurate diagnosis might bring relief, it can also bring a sense of regret. The first step in forming an alliance often comes when the therapist understands the client's need to talk through past frustrations, and they both attempt to put the puzzle pieces of the past into place. While taking care not to become stuck in the past, understanding it in light of ADHD helps many individuals accept their current struggles with more accurate, less self-blaming explanations.

7. Implement behavioral interventions ("experiments")

Developing new skills and overcoming entrenched maladaptive beliefs takes practice. Giving clients structured tasks to work on between sessions accelerates therapy and provides opportunities to succeed during the week. Instead of using the term *homework*, the therapist might call it an *experiment*. This takes pressure off the client, lessens the likelihood of viewing the process in win-or-lose terms, and avoids awakening childhood struggles with parents over schoolwork.

8. Implement cognitive interventions

Cognitive behavior therapists help clients question and expand their knee-jerk thoughts and erroneous beliefs. For example:
- "What is the evidence that the thought is true in this situation?"
- "Is there any evidence that it is *not* completely true?"
- "If a friend had that thought, what would you say to him or her?"
  Clients thus learn to discover a wider array of coping options.

CBT for ADHD in Action: Examples

Even some therapists mistakenly assume that CBT is done by the manual or "by the numbers." In practice, however, the therapy can be dynamic and creative. Ramsay provides a few examples to give you the flavor of CBT in action:

Retraining patterns of avoidance

Sean, a college student, always procrastinates on writing term papers. Last time, he waited until the day before deadline, hoping to write the entire 10-page paper in six hours. Then he put it off, one hour at a time. First he watched the sports report, then he ate lunch, and finally, he took a nap. Before he knew it, he'd run out of time. Why did he keep putting it off? Because each time he thought about getting started, he told himself, "This is going to be overwhelming."

Ramsay decided to help Sean learn to stick with a troublesome task for a minimal time to help him change from a lifetime of avoidant behavior to proactive behavior. He asked Sean, "Could you work on the task for at least 10 minutes before deciding it is overwhelming?" Sean said that he could, and actually ended up being able to work much longer.

This and a few other simple exercises helped Sean realize how unrealistic—in fact, a setup for failure—his current strategy had been. "We don't even do *enjoyable* tasks for six hours," Ramsay notes. "How could Sean expect to spend that much time writing a paper?"

Breaking down difficulties into manageable pieces

Let's say a client is procrastinating or avoiding something and doesn't understand why. Instead of focusing on the client's childhood history, the CBT therapist helps examine their thought patterns.

For example, the therapist will ask Sean to notice, as he starts to think about writing the paper, "What thoughts are stopping you?" What, *specifically*, are you having trouble with? By at least trying to do the task and asking that question when feeling the resistance, the individual might recognize he or she is having trouble organizing thoughts, for example. "At that point, we're getting more specific about the barriers, which often yields hints about helpful coping tools," Ramsay says.

Honing skills in communication and impulse-control

Even the process of working with the therapist provides opportunities for learning new skills in acknowledging and handling frustrations constructively rather than "blowing up" in disagreements. It also reminds patients that it is acceptable to admit mistakes, request help, and advocate responsibly and effectively for their own needs.

In this chapter, leading ADHD experts described the components of effective therapy for ADHD. This foundation of knowledge will help you to be a smart mental healthcare consumer as you consider the next chapter's therapeutic solutions and strategies.

CHAPTER
NINETEEN

More Solutions and Strategies

If you are working with a therapist who doesn't understand ADHD, you are doomed.

— FRANK

Wouldn't it be nice if therapists could all be miracle workers? As much as we'd like that, successful therapy depends upon everyone involved. If you and your ADHD partner do your homework ahead of time, you can play a major role in ensuring that success. The tips that follow should help.

Know the meaning of the term therapist

Surprisingly, in many states, a person can use the titles *psychotherapist*, *psychoanalyst*, or *counselor* without possessing any particular degree, training, or license. Consequently, titles alone mean nothing. First consider a person's education, training, licensing, and, in some cases, special certification.

Here are the general categories of mental health professionals:

- *Psychiatrists* (M.D.) are medical doctors trained in the diagnosis and treatment of mental and emotional disorders. Because they are physicians, they can prescribe medications (although in a few states psychologists can prescribe in a limited fashion).
- *Psychologists* (Ph.D. or Psy.D.) have doctoral degrees in psychology.

- *Social workers* (ACSW, LCSW, MSW, or CSW) have a master's degree in social work.
- *A marriage and family therapist* (MFT) has a master's degree in that specialty.

Licensing requirements vary and are available at your state's or province's Web page.

Seek ADHD expertise

In general, cutting-edge treatments are found at university teaching hospitals, so that is a good place to start. Independent ADHD specialty clinics offer comprehensive treatment as well.

As a consumer, you have a right to ask these questions of the therapist to whom you might entrust your resources and intimate lives:

- What is your familiarity with ADHD?
- How many clients with ADHD do you treat, or what is the percentage of your practice?
- Which books have you read or whose workshops have you attended? (If possible, look for a clinician familiar with the work of psychologists Russell Barkley, Thomas E. Brown, Kathleen Nadeau, Michele Novotni, J. Russell Ramsay, Arthur Robin, and Steven Safren, among other experts quoted in this book.)
- What is your approach to treating adults with ADHD (or couples)?
- Do you have a working relationship with a physician who prescribes medication for ADHD?
- Do you solicit feedback from your ADHD clients' partner or a third party? If so, why and how?
- What do you commonly see as the ADHD issues that affect partnership?

If the clinician can't answer these questions compassionately or to your satisfaction, you might want to keep interviewing. Also, try to check out the therapist's reputation by attending local support-group meetings.

Know that medication management is not therapy

Many managed-care insurance programs restrict coverage to psychiatrists' services prescribing medication only, not providing psychotherapy. So, if your ADHD partner sees the psychiatrist for 15 minutes each month, understand that those visits are for medication management, not therapy. Experts recommend *multimodal* treatment, meaning medication *plus* therapeutic behavioral strategies.

Choose the right type of therapist for the situation

The order in which you pursue therapy—yours, your ADHD partner's, or as a couple—will depend on many factors, with specific pointers offered on pages 248-49. As for the clinician's skills, here are some basic guidelines:

- *For your individual therapy*—Support-group members typically report that the therapist's ADHD knowledge ranks as less important than an understanding of what it's like to live with a partner's brain dysfunction and knowing how to help you manage stress, establish and maintain boundaries, and take care of yourself. ADHD savvy is important to the extent that the therapist avoids misattributing your partner's ADHD symptoms to a conscious motive, thereby further obscuring your clarity and maximizing your pain.

- *For your ADHD partner*—Consider seeking a cognitive-behavioral therapist *with knowledge of ADHD*, as discussed in the previous chapter. "A traditional CBT therapist who is not versed in ADHD symptoms may become too focused on trying to correct distorted thoughts without appreciating the very real difficulties these individuals have handling the complex demands of adult life," warns psychologist J. Russell Ramsay, associate director of the University of Pennsylvania's Adult ADHD Treatment and Research Center.

- *For couples counseling*—Like many other noted ADHD experts, psychologists Michele Novotni and Kathleen Nadeau recommend finding a clinician familiar with both ADHD and Imago Relationship Therapy. This approach trains people to communicate and slow down enough to understand the partner's point of view. "Imago therapy offers the structure of the dialogue, which a person with ADHD needs because they'll just run off into tangents," explains Eleanor Payson, a Michigan-based therapist who specializes in ADHD in couples. "Also, it makes things fair in a behavioral way and helps develop empathy." Whichever therapeutic style you choose, look for someone trained in treating ADHD in couples, advises ADHD expert and psychologist Arthur Robin, a clinician and professor at Wayne State University's School of Medicine.

- *For the family*—Sometimes two or more family members have ADHD, and it can help to work with one therapist. Robin recommends an initial interview before committing. Usually, you'll have to pay for it, but it's very important for each person to be comfortable with the therapist.

(Continued on page 250)

Therapy—"Yours, Mine, or Ours?"

What *kind* of therapy should you choose—individual or couples or both—and in what order? That depends on many factors, including the extent of difficulties and whether your partner has already been diagnosed and begun treatment. Experts offer a few general guidelines:

Initially, sharing a therapist is seldom a good idea

"Each partner might be in a different place, and it's difficult to meet both partners' needs simultaneously," says psychologist Michele Novotni. For example, you might be exhausted, overwhelmed, and frustrated by the needs of your ADHD partner. And your ADHD partner might feel beaten down and frustrated with you, too. Initially, each of you might benefit from individual therapy. At the same time, psychoeducation about ADHD is critical for both partners. Later, combined couples therapy with a therapist skilled in ADHD often adds an important component.

The path taken by Jackie and Paul worked well for them; it's also one that Novotni recommends. When Paul was first diagnosed with ADHD, he pressed Jackie to enter marriage counseling immediately. "I refused because we each had too many individual issues to deal with first," Jackie recalls. "Paul had low self-awareness, and I had years of resentment."

For a year, each pursued individual therapy while Paul also worked to establish an effective medication regimen. This independent effort resolved many marital issues. Jackie also benefited greatly from reading several books on ADHD and joining a support group. One thing was certain, she says, "I was not going to waste my time on couples counseling until his symptoms improved. We had done that for years, and it was a complete waste of time and money."

Therapy for you can help with self-care, boundaries

"Therapy helped me to reestablish boundaries and take care of myself," said 61 percent of the ADHD Partner Survey respondents who'd sought individual therapy. Almost half said it "helped *very* much." Only 6 percent found it "of no help at all or made matters worse."

As Glenna remarks, "Individual therapy was very helpful for me, because it helped me recognize and accept my feelings, to get rooted in reality again after living so many years with my husband's 'spin' on things." Couples therapy *prior* to his diagnosis proved less helpful, however, because he was "extremely defensive and simply not willing to look inside himself."

For Amanda, now a single mother of three who works full-time, it took several attempts to find a psychologist who truly understands what it is like to deal with someone who has severe ADHD symptoms, but the search was worth it. Even after her divorce, the therapy proved critical to dealing with shared custody. "I receive a lot of support and ideas for coping skills," she says.

For Penni, couples therapy before her own therapy or before her husband's ADHD diagnosis did little more than frustrate her: "It took the entire hour for my husband to 'get' one basic concept—because he kept opposing it—and I just had to sit there waiting for him to understand it."

Finding her own therapist made a huge difference in her life; she regained her sense of self and started back on the road to sanity. "If you're hesitant about therapy for yourself," Penni offers, "don't feel you have to have some big agenda; just taking care of yourself and getting in touch with the real you is enough."

Then again, after too many disappointments in therapy or simply having neither the time nor money for it, many share Elise's view: "What helps me most is talking with others who walk in the same shoes, and I get that from the support group."

Therapy with untreated ADHD can prove futile

Bob admits he had little idea of what his wife talked about for years in therapy before her ADHD diagnosis. "She simply claimed to be bored by therapy, which is probably why she went through five therapists in one year," he says. Apparently, they had all left the agenda up to her, and she couldn't understand what she was supposed to talk about. Highly frustrated, she quit going to the fourth therapist two weeks after the ADHD diagnosis. "Three months after she started with the fifth therapist, we were separated."

If your partner refuses to acknowledge the problems unaddressed ADHD symptoms might be causing, couples therapy might be worth considering over your ADHD partner's individual therapy for one reason alone: The therapist has a greater chance of hearing the full story.

"My partner's lack of honesty—or shall we say inaccurate self-observation—with therapists has been a tremendous problem," Gordon explains. "They all believed her characterization of events and just encouraged her misperceptions, which only made her work life and our family life worse. Couples therapy has been a little better because I can provide some checks and balances."

(Continued from page 247)

Make sure your input is considered important

"If the ADHD partner's relationship is part of the area of impairment—and it is almost 100 percent of the time—the therapist must not take an individualistic view," Robin advises.

Ask if the therapist will help monitor medication

Therapists can also prove invaluable in monitoring medication treatment. Northern California therapist and ADHD specialist Jonathan Halverstadt uses a standard form to track medication each visit. For example, he'll ask what time the dosage was taken, when it seemed to wear off, and if it is helping with concentration or temper.

"As someone doing a lot of case management, I need this information so I can pass it along to the physician," he notes. "The client is seeing me weekly, not monthly, as with the physician. Plus, my fee is much lower." When he conducts workshops for therapists, he emphasizes building a bridge to the medical profession. "This isn't taught in graduate school. Therapists have to learn it elsewhere."

Point your therapist toward helpful information

A good therapist should be open to learning more. Psychiatrist and ADHD specialist Marc Schwartz offers an article called "For Your Therapist" from his Web site (HealthCalls.com) that highlights ADHD's special considerations. You can also refer your therapist to these clinician guides:

- *Attention-Deficit Hyperactivity Disorder: A Handbook for Diagnosis and Treatment.* Russell A. Barkley. (Guilford Press, 2005)
- *Attention-Deficit Hyperactivity Disorder: A Clinical Workbook.* Russell A. Barkley and Kevin A. Murphy. (Guilford Press, 2005)
- *Clinician's Guide to Adult ADHD: Assessment and intervention.* Sam Goldstein and Anne Teeter Ellison, Eds. (Academic Press, 2002)
- *Cognitive Behavioral Therapy for Adult ADHD: An Integrative Psychosocial and Medical Approach.* J. Russell Ramsay and Anthony L. Rostain. (Routledge, 2007)
- *Integrative Treatment for Adult ADHD: A Practical, Easy-to-Use Guide for Clinicians.* Ari Tuckman (New Harbinger, 2008)
- *A Comprehensive Guide to Attention Deficit Disorder in Adults: Research, Diagnosis, and Treatment.* Kathleen Nadeau. (Brunner/Mazel, 1995)
- *Mastering Your Adult ADHD: A Cognitive-Behavioral Treatment Program.* Steven A. Safren, Carol A. Perlman, Susan Sprich, and Michael W. Otto. (Oxford University Press, 2005)

Know whether you need a therapist or an ADHD coach

As both a cognitive behavioral therapist and ADHD coach in private practice, Michele Novotni finds much overlap between CBT and coaching. "Coaching is focused on client goals and developing effective strategies, structures, and supports to manage ADHD," she explains, "whereas CBT addresses these issues but also focuses on the thought process and feelings."

Coaching offers an opportunity for more frequent contact, even daily in some cases, and that can mean more accountability. "Because it builds on clients' strengths, it can be a very effective approach for many people with ADHD who are emotionally stable," she adds.

Strict coaching approaches, however, often prove too narrowly focused on specific compensatory strategies for ADHD, thereby overlooking important cognitive and emotional issues that play an important role in individuals' well being. The best approach for you and your ADHD partner—the right mix of therapy and/or coaching—depends on your particular challenges.

As with therapists, you'll have to do some searching to find an ADHD coach with the right skills for you. (By the way, geography poses no limitation; most coaches are trained to work by telephone.) Linda Anderson, president of the Attention Deficit Disorder Association (ADDA) and an ADHD coach, suggests a few questions to ask during the interview:

- Are you a certified coach? Do you have an ACC, PCC, or MCC from the International Coach Federation?
- What is your training in ADHD coaching? How long and with whom did you train? Do you have certification? (More information can be found at the Web site for the Institute of the Advancement of Coaching: ADHDCoachInstitute.org.)
- How long have you been a coach? Do you specialize in a certain area (for example, running a household or a business)?
- What is your philosophy or style?
- How would we work together? What would a session look like?
- What are your fees?

"In the end," Anderson notes, "you will also base your decision on *fit*—whether or not you feel this coach is a good match for you."

Consider a couples workshop or group therapy

Even some former couples therapists say that, in general, couples do better to take marriage education courses instead of pursuing therapy together. These workshops focus on the practical matters of getting along with a partner. Novotni advises that ADHD couples' workshops are best when they include psychoeducation regarding ADHD and its impact on relationships as well as effective strategies to manage it. "In addition, couples realize that they are not alone," she explains. "It can be very healing for them to hear and share their frustrations and strategies in this type of environment."

Don Baker, a licensed mental health counselor in Seattle specializing in ADHD, has offered such couples' groups for years. Typically, four couples meet two hours weekly for three months, but a few couples have come for several years. "They find that just showing up together—making the commitment and following through—helps them to maintain traction," he says.

In workshops such as these, one of the main topics is the common parent-child dynamic that often develops when one partner has untreated ADHD. "The partner without ADHD plays parent by assuming organizational and financial responsibilities, and the ADHD partner often plays the child or victim," Baker observes. In this way, couples who've been together for many years can develop some "pretty nasty" relationship patterns and thus harbor huge amounts of anger and resentment. "By participating in the group, long-established roles begin to shift," he says.

An open attitude helps

Support-group member Nadine offers these parting words of advice:

> If you're going to couples counseling with the idea that the only problem is your partner's ADHD, you won't get anywhere. I knew I had to go into couples therapy fully prepared to admit my own problematic behaviors. Sure, they might pale in comparison to how my husband acted before medication treatment. But it's got to feel like a team effort, with both people doing their part, or it will fail.

INTRODUCTION

Tightening the Brakes on the Roller Coaster

Medication eliminated all the stuff that wasn't my husband, freeing him to be his best. He isn't really the controlling, cranky, hypercritical, anxious, depressed, and disorganized person who wore his face for so long.

— GLENNA

No doubt about it: Where ADHD symptoms are concerned, medication can bring astounding changes. Changes of such magnitude that in prior centuries witnesses would have relegated them to the realm of magic—or witchcraft. Changes so astonishing that even some modern mental-health professionals dismiss the reports as delusional. Changes that manifest so quickly they challenge bedrock belief that only *buckling down* (or years of therapy) creates behavioral improvement.

Lest you get the wrong idea, the changes aren't *creepy*, as if from a science-fiction novel where everyone acts with eerily perfect logic and equanimity.

Consider the brief examples on the following page, outtakes from the ADHD Partner Survey. Dramatic outcomes like these abound. (You'll find full details in the three first-person accounts that begin on page 255.)

An overwhelming body of research documents the effectiveness of stimulant medications in treating ADHD.[24] That said, if you think that your ADHD partner will enjoy substantive changes by simply taking a pill, that *is* delusional.

As you've probably learned by now, any ride on the ADHD roller coaster can shift speed or direction quickly and unpredictably. Similarly, ADHD

The Difference that Medication Can Make

- "He is less forgetful, friendlier, less prone to withdrawing into angry silence, and concentrates better at work."
- "I can talk to him again and feel like someone's listening."
- "It's helped her to focus on one thing at a time instead of 10."
- "He says he tastes flavors he's never tasted and, in our garden, sees distinct flowers instead of color blurs. It's like he's stepped into an entirely new world. He's very excited about this!"
- "He is less prone to picking a fight to get energized. I no longer dart out of the house each morning to avoid being yelled at."
- "She can concentrate better, get things done, enjoy life more, and react more calmly to our children who have ADHD."
- "He's zipping through paperwork in record time."
- "She is happier and less frustrated, and I am happy for that."
- "We can discuss sensitive subjects without him stomping away and wallowing in anger or screaming, 'I'm sorry, I'm sorry!'"
- "Stopped her 'motor speech.' She is organized and keeps lists."
- "He's calmer. His wonderful qualities shine instead of being overshadowed by crises."
- "I might not understand the science but I trust the empirical evidence: When my girlfriend takes the medication, she remembers what she needs to remember, doesn't get distracted every two minutes, and therefore stops berating herself constantly for forgetting and getting distracted."

—FROM THE **ADHD PARTNER SURVEY**

partners' medication miracles can get derailed—for example, when they grow so accustomed to living without symptoms that they decide they're cured and stop medication.

When their ADHD partners find and stick with a successful medication regimen, however, support-group members' anecdotes share one predominant theme: *Connections strengthen.* Connections strengthen in the mind of the ADHD partner between cause and effect, between thought and action, between yesterday and tomorrow, and between income and outgo. As a result, connections strengthen between the two partners and between parents and children.

For Angela, the connection between medication and the changes in her husband couldn't be clearer. "Before my husband started taking medication, he could say something inappropriate to me or the children and not even remember saying it or not realize his harsh tone of voice," she remembers. "Now, with medication, he has much better insight on his behavior and is able to direct his actions more mindfully."

Where do these connections originate? In the brain, with the stronger signals traveling between brain cells—courtesy of medication.

The three chapters in this success strategy for understanding medication's role in ADHD treatment explain three key concepts:

- **The connections between brain and behavior**—how messages travel to, from, and within the brain and why important messages might get lost in translation (Chapter 20).
- **The medication protocols recommended by ADHD experts**— for finding the right treatment plan (Chapter 21).
- **The healthy lifestyle habits that maximize medication's effectiveness**—and minimize side effects (Chapter 22).

IN THEIR OWN WORDS: TWO SUPPORT-GROUP MEMBERS' AND ONE ADHD PARTNER'S STORIES

Sally: Enjoying the Peace, the Past Is the Past

My husband, Doug, has been my best friend, business partner, and dad to our kids for 20 years. He's also just about destroyed all of that. With the recent ADHD diagnosis and treatment, I am beginning to exhale. He is more cautiously optimistic, partially thinking it's too good to be true and won't last. And no wonder, after 45 years of considering himself a screw-up.

It took us too long to get to this point, many years of Doug being anxiety-ridden, depressed, and far too dependent on me. The last 10 years, doctors treated him for anxiety and depression, but any improvement was only faint and fleeting. He's taken antidepressants for years, to no avail.

This whole thing came to a head last fall when we had the opportunity to do some lucrative consulting work. In the end, Doug came through, but it was absolute agony for us all; he procrastinated, diverted his attention to non-priority tasks, and rushed through the "boring parts," making lots of mistakes. The only good thing was that this behavior really highlighted his problems, so we saw yet another psychiatrist.

Now, with the ADHD finally being treated, we're on the right track. Clearly, just having a name for his lifelong feeling of being "weird" and experiencing daily success in routine functioning does a lot to allay his depression. He's good at what he does, and now can do it more reliably. This makes him very happy and more confident.

This morning he was "Instant Messaging" with his brother while he talked to me on the phone. There was a longish silence at his end and when I said, "Are you there?" he said, "Oh, sorry, on these meds I can only do one thing at a time." The thing is, he always *thought* he could multitask, but he invariably missed part of one task or another—hence the careless mistakes that dogged his work and required so much mopping up from me.

Here are other examples of the recent "Big" things:

- He spent one hour on the phone untangling a mess with the bank, calmly and competently. Astonishing!
- We have been reorganizing his office—a truly daunting job—and he keeps plugging away. He can even shift back and forth between that project and a job for a client. Wow!
- His old "work process" involved days of agonizing, staying up all hours, chugging vats of strong coffee, and finally leaping into the work just before deadline. He still needs my help with scheduling, but overall he's working steadily and productively with time now for rest and fun. (This alone is a very big deal. He never allowed himself rest or fun before, because he was either feeling bad about procrastinating or scrambling to catch up.)
- The anxiety has retreated; it seems a lot of his "anxiety disorder" came from worrying about he was going to screw up or forget.
- He is relaxed and cheerful. Socializing with him is more fun.
- I need ask him only twice to come to dinner and remind him once to empty the dishwasher and get the trash out to the curb!

I am so filled with gratitude for the support group and these medications. My husband is still charmingly eccentric, and I love him for it. But now I am able to enjoy those qualities without both of us being undone by the deficits. Did I mention his sleep schedule has finally normalized? He used to be up most of the night and slept like a man drugged during the day. Now, we are actually in bed together at the same time. We like this!

What my husband might have trouble understanding is how hard he was to live with. His obsessions, irritability, erratic need for control, dependency, and general energy-sucking seemed perfectly reasonable to him. He couldn't see how it all affected me—and, actually, still can't see it. But frankly, I don't see any point in beating him over the head with it. He didn't act that way on purpose, and we need to keep moving forward without a lot of guilt side-trips. It is enough for me to have the support of the group and to know that I wasn't imagining the problems or creating them.

I'm just enjoying the peace.

John, Abby's ADHD Partner: It All Makes Sense Now

In Chapter 1, Abby briefly explained the before-and-after diagnosis-and-treatment situation with John's work and their marriage. Here John offers his own perspective:

At age 37, I was diagnosed shortly after my wife figured it out. ADHD came as a surprise but made complete sense of the challenges I've had all my life but had resigned myself to.

Actually, the school psychologist when I was in first grade mentioned ADHD, but my parents didn't want to hear that anything was "wrong" with me. They thought I was gifted, and they did the best they could, given scanty information at that time. Maybe I was gifted, but I also had considerable deficits. Do I now wish I'd known since childhood? Sometimes. Then again, struggle can hone a person's character, and I became quite stoical about not giving up the fight to succeed. My wife, though, might say I became too stoical, developing the habit of rigidly choosing stoicism over pleasure. It's a tough habit to break.

At any rate, awareness of what I've been dealing with all my life has helped, but medication has made the most profound difference. (One time I forgot to pack the medication for our vacation, and let's just say we were both shocked at how quickly things can devolve.) It's taken a while to find the right type and dosage—and to then accept that I had to learn new habits. But it was worth it.

I should add I could not have accomplished this without my wife's help, advocating for me with psychiatrists, some of whose qualities ranged from well-meaning ineptitude to arrogant ignorance, despite claiming expertise. She also had to remind me of things, like how great I felt after exercising, because my oppositional mindset made me rebel against the whole idea of "having to" exercise.

Say Goodbye to Sluggo the Wonder Boy

Before medication, I always found my work highly stimulating, so that was my impetus to achieve and focus. That and money—lots of it. (As a kid, I'd coveted James Bond's lifestyle, complete with all the cool gadgets, and set my mind to achieving it.) I could always come up with great ideas or wow a conference crowd with my presentations. The rest of the time, though, I was too much like Sluggo the Wonder Boy.

The fact of the matter is, no matter how stimulating one's work is, it's not stimulating *all* of the time. And yet, to be successful in your work and in your personal life, you do need to focus most of the time.

At work, I'm now better able to program software because I'm more patient and therefore less likely to make mistakes or take shortcuts that I'll regret later. My judgment has improved in evaluating my ideas to see if they're actually worth pursuing or just an old habit of revving up brain stimulation. I'm also much better at stopping to evaluate progress, determining if I'm on track with my goal rather than charging straight ahead with a flawed idea—and getting angry with anyone who tries to convince me to reconsider.

So yes, work is going better and more enjoyable. But have I suddenly become a cheerful "people person"? Let's not go that far. Let's just say that medication has restrained my desire to throttle people who oppose my "grand designs." I do get along better with more coworkers, not solely the ones I find super smart. In fact, I'm now better able to consider their ideas before I tell them, "That's the stupidest thing I ever heard" or "Where did you go to graduate school again?"

Did I mention my sense of humor has improved?

Less Collateral Damage, Better Targeting

People are people. They can still be annoying to work with, and I'm finally realizing how much unrecognized ADHD in other people I used to deal with in high-tech start-up companies. No wonder so many of them went bust. At least now, though, I recognize and avoid those work situations. I can also hold my tongue and think more about the consequences of what I say and do. Overall, I have a calmer approach to everything, maybe because I'm less vulnerable to every fleeting distraction. As a result, there's less collateral damage and better targeting.

I'm more philosophical now and more generous with other people's foibles and my own. My wife points out that I seem happier, but I'm not sure what that means, other than I no longer feel like ripping the lungs out of most people, or my own. Like many other people with ADHD, I used to live with a daily simmering level of frustration. It didn't take much to tip the balance into ugly territory. I thought happy people were just too stupid to know better.

Equally important, I think I'm better able to empathize with people, especially my wife. I also realize now I would probably not have survived this long without her. I would have died on the sofa overdosing on bags of chips and watching weapons technology shows on HDTV.

Initially, I was unsure if my problems with mood and focus were due to ADHD or my crash-and-burn lifestyle—drinking too many sodas, getting little sleep, playing too many video games just to keep the adrenaline flowing, and going to the gym just to fiddle with all the electronic control panels on the machines (my wife's opinion). But when I finally tried medication, my health actually improved—cholesterol and triglycerides dropped, for example—because I was more energetic and less interested in junk food. So, it seems my "bad habits" were more the *side effects* of my brain challenges rather than the cause. Still, they certainly made things worse.

It's also true that I get more pleasure from things now, perhaps because I notice more details. I taste more flavors, for example, and when we go hiking, an activity I always thought I enjoyed, I enjoy it much more. Instead of hitting the trail like a cannon shot and hyperfocusing on reaching the end, as in the past, I'll pick wild berries along the way, appreciate the bird noises, smell the pine trees, and notice the change in seasons. At the end, I'll feel relaxed, not like I've survived the Bataan Death March.

I used to find all kinds of creative ways of marshalling my nonexistent motivation to do something, and too many times it involved getting aggressive or angry. Anger can be very energizing.

Out of the Fog

Before medication, I was mostly in a mental fog. Nothing in my environment was ever very sharp, the way it is now. Would you have guessed that about me? It depends on the situation in which you were observing. In a meeting, I came to life, perhaps too much so, being rather domineering and condescending to those I considered less intelligent. In nonstimulating situations, though, my eyelids might be literally half-closed and I'd slump far down in the chair.

In fact, I think one of the reasons I appreciate my wife more is that I have better access to memory. That means I can actually remember how long it took her to do our onerous income tax filing, everything that she does to keep the household running, the nice things she does for me, and the amazing array of talents she has. If you don't have good continuous memory, you don't appreciate other people's efforts or their struggles. You know it's not exactly magic tricks they're pulling out of a hat for you, but you don't really comprehend the magnitude of the effort.

For Karen: A Chance Discovery Changes Everything

We're confident my partner has ADHD, but she does not want to take medication, and I will not push her. If she someday decides she wants to try it, I will support her. But I would never accept her telling me what to do with my body, and I won't tell her what to do with hers.

To deal with her challenges, she is trying many things, including two coaches thus far, fish oil, changes in diet, a slew of self-help books, and a ceaseless series of Byzantine organizing systems that fail miserably and only cause her more distress.

Sure, I occasionally have a fantasy about some magic pill that could help her behave differently, in ways that don't cause so much frustration for her and me. But I don't get to decide how she should behave, only what I can and cannot live with. I try to be clear about those boundaries, just as I would in any relationship.

⌣⟶

(Two years later, Karen updates the group.)
I stand by much of what I said before, but since then, a few interesting things have occurred.

My hobby is competitive weightlifting. To make a weight class, lifters often resort to strict diets plus a combo of caffeine and herbs. This will drop fat in a hurry, although it will make you feel like hell, *unless*, apparently, you are my partner. Well, this summer I was trying to make weight for a meet and was taking the combo, and Angie was trying to lose five pounds for a part (she's a professional actress). (Warning: This isn't something you want to "try at home." Where we live, this is legal yet still risky if you have any health issues, and we were working with a health professional.)

When she took the combo, oh my God, it was a freaking revelation to her. Suddenly, after the very first dose, she could think and reason like "normal" people. I almost cried. The fog cleared the minute her dose took effect. When it wore off hours later, she felt the fog descend, and hated it. I have to laugh, because when I took this combo, I could focus maniacally for an hour and then became so jittery that I couldn't concentrate at all. I hate it.

Angie Had Thought the Rx Would Simply Speed Her Confusion

It's important to stress that Angie never thought that she "shouldn't need medication." She simply thought that stimulant medication would simply make her confusion move *faster*. She also could not imagine it helping her atrocious memory, until it actually did.

Soon after this discovery, I thought she'd immediately make an appointment to be evaluated for ADHD. But no. She was willing, and had even gotten the forms from a clinic. Then she dragged her feet for months and then lost the forms. Finally, realizing that the ADHD fog had once again enveloped her, I said, "Make an appointment for an evaluation with an appropriate doctor within 30 days, or I will move out." I did not say a word about medication. She made the appointment.

To people on the "outside," that might sound harsh or controlling, but please understand that most of our ADHD partners just don't do "gray area" or nuance. They lose sense of priorities. And they need black-and-white and deadlines—for anything! Yes, she loves me and knew that her probable ADHD was doing serious damage to our relationship. Nonetheless, she would never have gotten around to it otherwise. She was *willing*, but because of her ADHD she couldn't take action until it was incredibly urgent and important—that is, not losing her relationship over it.

Fortunately, she found a great psychiatrist in private practice. (In this country, the national healthcare system seems to not "believe" in adult ADHD, like it's Tinker Bell or something.) He did a thorough evaluation and, sure enough, diagnosed her with ADHD. She took her first pill, and a mere 30 minutes later, she followed her own threads, used a pleasant tone, seemed more relaxed and less anxious, and continued this for three hours.

Now for the Weird Part

But here's what's weird: She didn't even notice at first! She said she felt a tiny bit calmer, but only after it wore off did she realize how much it had helped. When the confusion and pressure came back full force, she was truly shocked.

Later, she also remarked that about an hour after taking the pill, she did notice that I'd suddenly started being very pleasant to her, not so aggressive and obstinate! *I hadn't changed at all; her perception of me did.*

She has a brilliant mind, but her ADHD has limited her intellectual pursuits all her life. In fact, her entire family has made it a long-running painful joke, and that's affected her self-esteem.

I'm convinced untreated ADHD was affecting her health, too. Prior to taking medication, she hardly ever got to sleep at a sensible hour. She'd hyperfocus at her computer. (If I reminded her that she had an early-morning appointment, she'd accuse me of trying to control her.) In her mind, the computer activity calmed her down, but it actually speeded her up and fed on itself until her body was finally exhausted and she stumbled to bed, sometimes as late as 4 A.M. If she did happen to drop off, it was very light sleep and she often had obsessive dreams about whatever she was "researching." Oh, and loads of restless leg action, too. These kinds of behaviors stopped when she began taking medication.

On her current dosage, there is no question of her "losing the sparkle," which is important when your career is on the stage. And she is delighted with the improvements in her focus. She is also getting increasingly articulate about what it is like to have ADHD. The more I understand, the more empathy I have and the less I go into my own frustration and anger cycle.

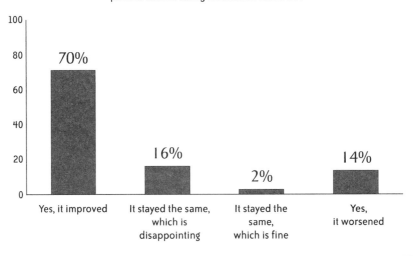

ADHD Partner Survey Snapshot:
Medication and the Relationship

Survey question: "Did the quality of this relationship change after your partner started taking medication for ADHD?"

CHAPTER
TWENTY

Making Connections Between Brain and Behavior

One group member felt guilty for wanting her partner to try medication. But I always saw the pain my wife's impulsivity caused her and I hoped to see that eased. Fortunately, that has happened.

— JOSEPH

Marsha and husband Al aren't pharmaceutical researchers—not even close. Middle-aged and living in a small midwestern town, he's a software engineer, she works in marketing, and most weekends find them tending their organic garden. Nonetheless, they made a rather remarkable neuroscientific discovery one day. It all started when Al's stuffy head cold prompted him to take a decongestant. "The surprising thing was what a sweet, calm, peaceful, fun day we had!" Marsha says.

Al had long refused to take medication for his ADHD, even though his forgetful and irritable behavior severely strained the marriage and held him back at work. Yet by taking the recommended dosage of the decongestant pseudoephedrine, he had ingested a weak chemical cousin of the stimulant medications used for treating ADHD.

Seeking simply to open his nasal passages, Al had opened his mind to ADHD medication's benefits. He had also come eerily close to replicating a landmark study 70 years before, in 1937. That's when physician Charles Bradley accidentally discovered a stimulant's effectiveness in mitigating the symptoms of ADHD.

Decades after this discovery, widespread ignorance still exists in the public *and* medical community about how these medications work. Then again, most people poorly comprehend how our brain affects our behavior. And that ignorance can keep them trapped in cycles of anger, hurt, and confusion. To keep you walking on the path to clarity, this chapter is designed to help you:

- Learn about the accidental discovery that stimulant medications mitigate ADHD symptoms.
- Know why medication for ADHD is thought to improve Executive Function and the ability to "put on the brakes."
- Know that good communications between you and your ADHD partner begin with "good communications" within your partner's own brain and nervous system.
- Grasp, in a very basic way, how our brain cells relay important messages within the brain and between the brain and the outside world.
- Understand the term *chemical imbalance* as it applies to conditions such as ADHD.

1937: Dr. Bradley's "Stimulating" Discovery

Bradley's accidental discovery deserves attention for many reasons. Perhaps most significantly, it helps to counter those familiar (but erroneous) arguments against ADHD medications—in short, that they're a modern scheme by pharmaceutical companies to turn our brains over to the medical-industrial complex, making children and adults compliant drones.

In Bradley's day, children with mental illness or behavior disorders were largely ignored or, worse, warehoused. (It is worth noting that during this era prominent psychologists warned against giving *any* child too much affection, with one advising that a single kiss annually is sufficient.) Bradley, however, had a vision that progress could come only by advancing the field of child psychiatry. And as one of the country's few child psychiatrists in 1937, he worked at a Rhode Island private residential hospital for children with behavioral disorders.

Coincidentally, a distant wealthy relative had founded the hospital, The Emma Pendleton Bradley Home, and named it for his daughter. Emma was an adored only-child who in 1887 fell victim to one of the great influenza epidemics that left thousands of surviving children with severe neurologically based behavior symptoms—and no place to care for them.[25] George Bradley stipulated in his will that the home serve and conduct research to benefit poor children suffering from untreatable brain disorders.

Beginning in the 1920s, the stimulant Benzedrine emerged as the nasal decongestant of its day. First synthesized in 1887 as Amphetamine to relieve the symptoms of asthma, the inspiration for Benzedrine came from *ma huang*, a 5,000-year-old Chinese herbal remedy for asthma containing the active ingredients ephedrine and pseudoephedrine (the medication in Al's cold remedy). Benzedrine didn't work as well for asthma, but the medical community promoted it for raising low blood pressure, treating depression, and stimulating the central nervous system—and it was even sold in an inhaler for relieving swollen nasal passages. Later, World War II soldiers received it to forestall fatigue and improve mood and endurance.

In 1937, Bradley speculated that Benzedrine might ease hospitalized children's headaches following a diagnostic procedure.[26] Unfortunately, the Benzedrine did little to ease the headaches. And while Bradley expected some increased alertness (because this was a known effect of stimulants in adults), a few children became more alert to the point of aggression. Others, however, responded in a most surprisingly positive way. Astonished teachers reported to Bradley that these children showed a striking improvement in their schoolwork *and* their behavior.

Bradley followed this serendipitous discovery with a controlled trial of 30 children. Each child's behavior disorder was severe enough to have warranted hospitalization, he reported, but the patients' intelligence was generally within the normal range.[27] Of the 30, 14 children responded in a "spectacular fashion" in that teachers noted an increased interest in school materials as well as an increased accuracy in performance and drive to accomplish. Moreover, children who had been raucous, aggressive, and domineering became easier-going and congenial. Instead of loudly quarrelling, they discussed their differences more civilly. Instead of darting around pestering others, they settled down to play or read. Bradley wrote:

> To see a single daily dose of Benzedrine produce a greater improvement in school performance than the combined efforts of a capable staff working in a most favorable setting would have been all but

demoralizing to the teachers had not the improvement been so gratifying from a practical viewpoint.

The beneficial effects started the first day Benzedrine was given and halted on the first day it was discontinued. Bradley and his colleagues published their findings in prominent journals, and the media duly reported them. Yet, *25 years passed* before anyone attempted to replicate his study. *Another 25 years* passed before stimulants became widely used for ADHD in children.[28]

To examine all the factors that finally led to the rise of diagnosis and medical treatment of ADHD, first in children and then adults, would require several volumes and much heated debate. For now, the important point is to understand the circumstances behind this beneficial connection:

- The stimulant's effect was discovered accidentally in 1937 by a doctor trying to alleviate children's post-operative pain.
- This doctor worked in a privately funded, compassionately run home.
- The home was founded by parents bereft of neurological medical care who wanted to help others like their daughter.

Medication: The Foundation of Effective Treatment

"The Surgeon General of the United States and the National Institute of Mental Health, as well as leading medical societies such as the American Academy of Pediatrics, American Psychiatric Association, and American Academy of Child and Adolescent Psychiatry, recognize that medication, under the prescription of a treating medical professional and when taken as prescribed, along with other non-medication interventions, provide the most effective foundation for the treatment of ADHD."

—THE NATIONAL RESOURCE CENTER ON ADHD

The Stimulants—Boosting the Braking System

Developed as a milder relative of amphetamines like Benzedrine, Ritalin (methylphenidate) came on the market in 1955. A half-century later, the average person remains mystified by the apparent paradox: How can a *stimulant* help *calm* a restless body or a restless mind?

As best as researchers can determine, certain brain functions associated with ADHD have what you might call "sluggish circuitry." We call this collection of functions Executive Function (EF), because they influence our voluntary (conscious) thought and planning, as discussed in Chapters 2 and 3. It's thought that the stimulants strengthen the brain signals that affect EF.

For example, we are constantly bombarded with stimuli, both from the outside (such as noises or temperature changes) and the inside (such as emotions, thoughts, and even hunger). One critical job of EF is to prioritize or integrate all this stimuli into a cohesive whole—dropping what is *unimportant* and focusing on what is *important*.

Your ADHD partner probably has difficulty handling competing stimuli. That's why, for example, conversation might be a bad idea while he or she is driving the car; focusing on what you're saying can distract from watching the road. There are plenty of other telltale signs that your ADHD partner's brain cells might be picking up more static than signal. Does he or she:

- Hear a tone in your voice that isn't there?
- Hear only half of what you say and fill in the other half with something imaginary?
- Completely miss that obvious look of hurt on your face in reaction to their words or actions?
- Become unnerved at the slightest noise, except when he or she is making it (and then possibly self-medicating with loud TV volume or the noise from a loud motorcycle or car engine)?

In large part, strong EF helps us "put the brakes on" certain behaviors—including being distracted by extraneous stimuli. "What we're doing is trying to turn on the brakes, or the inhibitory systems, and the stimulant medication helps to turn on the brakes," explains Patricia Quinn, a Washington, DC-based developmental pediatrician who has worked for more than 30 years in the field of ADHD and learning disabilities.

When used to treat ADHD, stimulant medication has been shown to increase *salience* [29]—that is, it amplifies priorities and cues in the environment, from a mate's unhappy facial expressions to that overflowing garbage pail to that stack of incoming bills. Priorities become clearer and distractions less alluring.

Good Communication: Why Gray Matter Matters

Katie's husband complained that she communicated poorly. That puzzled her, as her public speaking skills win her national awards. Finally, she said to him, "Let's see, you have a problem communicating with your boss, your family, your friends, and me. It looks like the only constant is *you*."

Talking with her husband, she explains, sometimes resembles that party game where one person whispers a message to the next person and so on until it gets to the last person in line. When the message reaches the end, the first person announces the original message and the last person announces the final message and everyone busts up laughing at the disparity. "But with my husband," she says, "he's that long line of people all by himself!"

Consider this: The ability to communicate effectively (listen well and respond appropriately) relies on the brain's ability to fully take in complicated information from the outside world, interpret it, and formulate a response. It also requires good attention and memory. This comes as a big surprise to couples that have unsuccessfully sought counseling to improve their communication. In fact, their problems might very well stem from poor "communication" within the brain of only one person in the couple.

We've learned a tremendous amount about neuroscience in recent years. Not surprisingly, however, our brains—command center of our intelligence, translator of our sensory world, and director of behavior and movement—are proving vexingly complicated, highly individualistic, and genetically diverse. Furthermore, what happens in each region of the brain and body affects other parts, forming a complex web that makes the world's telephone system seem as simple as strung-together Dixie cups.

So, given the brain's complexity, how is it that stimulant medications boost functioning in key parts of the brain, resulting in such dramatic behavioral changes? To put it simply: The medication "strengthens the signal" as brain cells relay messages to and fro. The more accurately that messages are transmitted, the better our ability to:

- *Communicate with others*—by listening and responding effectively.
- *Communicate internally*—by issuing commands to yourself and reminders to follow through on them.
- *Communicate with the outside world*—through the sensory input and accurate translation of images, noises, touch, tastes, and odors.
  Next, we explore why this is so.

The Brain Explains What the Ear Hears

Many people assume that our sensory functions depend solely on the eyes, ears, nose, tongue, or skin. Yet these senses also highly depend on the *brain*. Once you understand this, you can see how your relationship's communication challenges might lie beyond the power of talk therapy—or even an earwax removal kit. That's because hearing only partially involves sound waves striking the ear.

> Many people assume that our sensory functions depend solely on the eyes, ears, nose, tongue, or skin. Yet these senses also highly depend on the brain.

Yes, our ears catch the sound waves, but it's the *brain's* job to recognize the sounds and process them into words, thoughts, concepts, and context. What carries the pattern of sound waves from the ear to the brain's auditory processing center? A chemical messenger, or *neurotransmitter*. If that neurotransmitter isn't working as it should, much can be lost in translation as the message travels from sensory organs to the brain and back again.

Vision, too, depends on brain processing. In fact, your eyes might be perfectly healthy, but if you suffer damage to your visual cortex (the part of the brain where images are processed), your ability to see might be impaired or even obliterated.

In fact, various studies have examined how ADHD affects visual processing. For example, indications are that ADHD can significantly impair reading comprehension due to problems with sustained attention, processing speed, and working memory.[30] And one study shows that stimulant medications can improve a core component of working memory known to be impaired in ADHD, called visual-spatial memory[31] (the brain function that allows us to recognize and remember letters and symbols), regardless of coexisting reading or language problems.

In fact, many support-group members report that their ADHD partners suddenly start reading books and long articles when they start taking medication. It turns out they didn't need eye surgery nor did they necessarily "dislike" reading or have a learning disability (although learning disabilities often coexist separately with ADHD). Their brains simply weren't fully cooperating with their otherwise competent ability to read.

What about the other senses—of touching and being touched, of tasting and smelling? You guessed it: They all depend on brain connections and communications. Many ADHD partners find their hypersensitivity to touch and textures against the skin diminishes once they start taking stimulant medication, and that can prove quite helpful in the romantic relations department. Even your ADHD partner's internal communications—from one part of the brain to the other—might get mangled or lose signal strength over the long journey from thought to activation. For example, "I must file my taxes this weekend!" might get out-shouted by a more stimulating message, such as "Let's go to the beach!"

Crash Course: How Brain Cells Relay Messages

Neuroscience is complicated stuff, but even a little knowledge can go a long way in understanding your ADHD partner's challenges—and some of your own. So, here's a *vastly* simplified seven-step course on how messages get relayed on the cellular level (keep in mind that it sacrifices scientific accuracy for basic conceptual clarity):

1. Everything we think, do, or feel involves brain connections

To illustrate the complexity of brain-body-environment interaction, let's start with a very simple example, something we're all too familiar with: a mosquito bite.

When a mosquito delivers sensory input in the form of a bite to your skin, the message travels up the spinal cord to the brain. There, through an ornate set of maneuvers it's recognized as "itch," and the brain sends the "scratch" command to the appropriate limb. A flash of a second later you realize that, because you are outside at dusk near a lake in summertime, the culprit was probably a mosquito. Then you decide how to respond—apply repellant, go inside, or put on a shirt—all the while munching on a hamburger and chatting with cousin Harry.

This amazing series of actions and reactions is something we all take for granted.

2. Cells relay messages along neural pathways

How did the itch, scratch, and "Oh, it's a mosquito" messages get communicated? Each of our sensations, movements, thoughts, memories, and feelings results from signals passing through brain cells, called *neurons*. Thus, the pathway that carries messages from source to destination—one neuron at a time—is called a *neural pathway*.

We don't normally think of electricity running through our bodies, but that's exactly how messages move, thanks to electro-chemical reactions from elements such as sodium, calcium, potassium, and chloride. In fact, it is this electrical activity that is measured by an EEG (electroencephalogram) as it examines brain function. (Just one neuron can produce a tenth of a volt of electricity.)

To imagine how a neural pathway works, picture a chain of electrical extension cords laid end-to-end, plug to socket, but not quite physically connected. Each cord represents a neuron, and the small space between one neuron's plug and the next neuron's socket is called the *synaptic gap*. For the message to sustain momentum along the neural pathway to its final destination, it must somehow travel across the synaptic gap and "plug into" the next neuron.

3. Messages travel via neurotransmitters

How does the message make that trip across the synaptic gap? The brain chemicals called neurotransmitters do the job—so called because they transmit the message from one neuron to the next. (Neuro. Transmitter. Get it?)

But where does the message originate? With a stimulus—for example, a thought ("Got to do that paperwork today") or sensory input (that mosquito bite).

Next, the neuron receiving that stimulus translates it into an electrochemical charge. That charge travels from one end of the neuron to the other end, where it triggers release of *neurotransmitters* into the synaptic gap. Those neurotransmitters leap across the gap, plug into the next neuron, and push the message on its way to the final destination.

It might sound simple, but it isn't. For one thing, the "socket" on the receiving side of the synaptic gap is picky; it allows neurotransmitters to plug in only when a specific amount of a specific neurotransmitter shows up. (That's why the term for this socket is *receptor*; it's receptive only to a particular neurotransmitter.)

Here's how people communicate.

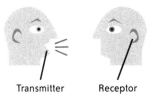

Transmitter   Receptor

Here's how brain cells communicate.

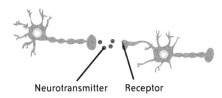

Neurotransmitter   Receptor

Concept courtesy: B.K. Madras. From a National Institute of Drug Abuse publication.

Why is there a gap, anyway? The gap allows the neurons to serve multiple pathways. Consider them tiny hubs in a brain-bogglingly complex communications system. Given that the human brain contains about one hundred billion neurons and messages can zip at up to 240 miles per hour, it seems miraculous that *any* messages make it through our brains intact. So, now you can begin to understand how easily a message can get garbled.

4. When all goes well, messages transmit accurately

When neurotransmitters flow in adequate supply, communications go smoothly and accurately, just like in a well-run office. But when they're disorganized, understaffed, overworked, mismanaged, or plain pokey, message transmission starts resembling a dysfunctional company where gossip runs amok. Each thread contains a germ of truth, but it's coated with inaccuracies and distortions.

5. Meet three important neurotransmitters

At least 50 neurotransmitters have been identified in the human brain, but three are most commonly discussed in terms of ADHD:

- *Dopamine* is associated with motivation, movement, reward systems (including addictive behavior), and proper immune and autonomic nervous system function (the mostly involuntary activities related to the cardiovascular system, respiration, and digestion, as well as perspiration, salivation, pupil dilation, and erection).
- *Norepinephrine* (also called noradrenalin) is the primary neurotransmitter required for alertness, motivation, and concentration. Our brains need it to form new memories and transfer memories to long-term storage. It also influences metabolic rate.
- *Serotonin* promotes "good mood" and normal sleep and plays a key role in regulating memory, learning, blood pressure, appetite, and body temperature.

Dopamine and norepinephrine are also believed to play an important role in our ability to focus and pay attention to tasks.[32] As such, these two neurotransmitters seem most closely associated with ADHD. But researchers are increasingly seeing that serotonin plays a bigger role than previously thought, especially with coexisting conditions such as depression and anxiety, and other neurotransmitters are likely involved as well.

It's important to remember that all these brain chemicals are intensely and intricately interdependent and linked with lifestyle factors such as exercise and nutrition, too.

6. Two key factors can weaken the transmission signal

You've learned that the receptor requires a critical mass of neurotransmitters before it will accept and relay the message. Two factors lessen the chance of achieving that critical mass:

- The neurons don't produce enough neurotransmitters.
- The neurotransmitters don't get a chance *to* do their job.

Why don't they get a chance? Here's one reason. Each neuron has a mechanism that sucks up neurotransmitters back to their "home" neuron after they've relayed their message so they can be recycled. But some of these "vacuum cleaners" are over-eager; they suck up neurotransmitters *before* they can collect in critical mass at the receptor.

In a sense, slowing the vacuum cleaner can address either of the two problems above (which might occur in combination).

Another word for this recycling process is *reuptake*. You've probably heard the term *reuptake* associated with a class of antidepressants called SSRIs, for *Selective Serotonin Reuptake Inhibitors* (these include the brand names Prozac, Celexa, and Paxil).

Depression is generally associated with a lack of critical mass of serotonin molecules at the receptor. The SSRI medications seem to remedy that situation by inhibiting the reuptake of serotonin, or slowing the vacuum cleaner. That way, the serotonin molecules stay in the gap longer, gaining time to accumulate in sufficient number and transmit the message to the next brain cell.

7. ADHD medications slow the reuptake "vacuum cleaner"

ADHD stimulant medications work similarly to the SSRI medications. Instead of targeting the serotonin vacuum cleaner, however, they target the vacuum cleaners for norepinephrine and dopamine. (In fact, most medications used today to treat psychiatric conditions involve slowing the uptake of one or more neurotransmitters.)

Both major classes of stimulants, methylphenidate (MPH) and the amphetamines (AMP), are thought to slow recycling of norepinephrine and dopamine. Furthermore, the amphetamines are also largely thought to *increase* the release of dopamine and norepinephrine by a different mechanism.[33] Whether this more-complicated action of the AMP medications produces a positive or negative effect depends largely on an individual's neurochemistry. You'll learn more on the differences among stimulant medications in Chapter 21.

Does This Mean ADHD is a Chemical Imbalance?

Some people mistakenly conclude that ADHD is caused by a "brain chemical deficiency" and that the medications work to correct the deficiency. Even some medical professionals offer this explanation, perhaps in order to simplify a complex matter. But that's like saying that because aspirin helps headaches, an aspirin deficiency causes headaches.

Yes, ADHD seems related to a chemical imbalance—in the sense that symptoms originate in the brain and are usually alleviated by targeting certain brain chemical pathways. But do all humans have a measurable "normal" or uniform level of these chemicals? Can you be, say, a quart low on dopamine? No. Our unique biochemistries, not to mention our identities, are too complicated for simplistic notions of uniformity.

The fact is, we don't know *precisely* why these medications work. We do have, however, extremely strong hypotheses to explain their actions. And we have overwhelming evidence that they *do* work in mitigating ADHD symptoms.

"We know that the medication works by observation and by measuring behavior," confirms prominent ADHD researcher and psychologist James Swanson, a professor at the University of California, Irvine, School of Medicine and co-author of a literature review that examines the dopamine hypothesis.[34] "We also know by using PET-imaging studies, seeing where the medication goes, that it increases the amount of dopamine at the synapse (the connecting point between two brain cells)," he adds. "And we know that stimulants can create clear improvement in ADHD symptoms *while the medication is in the system.*"

Medication Works Only When It's "Active"

A critical point: Stimulant medications don't "cure" ADHD—the way antibiotics cure an infection. They work more like eyeglasses, in that they work only when they are active in the system. They take effect quickly, but they also wear off after a few hours (from two to twelve hours, depending on the type taken and the individual's biochemistry).

Does Everyone with ADHD Need Medication?

Taking medication remains a personal decision to be made with the help of a well-trained clinician. Before prescribing medication for any particular patient, careful physicians will first explore when and where symptoms prove most challenging and what adaptations the patient has already tried. ADHD education will be emphasized as well as the importance of reexamining poor coping strategies and improving health habits. For some people with ADHD, that is quite sufficient—and life-changing.

Many others, however, find that medication offers the final "piece" that allows them to act more in accordance with their intentions, talents, and abilities. Medication can create dramatic changes—or more subtle ones. Most people, however, report better ability to focus, remain calm under pressure, and more reliably attain their goals. For an idea of where medication ranks as a factor for those ADHD Partner Survey respondents who experienced improvement in their relationship, see the chart below.

ADHD Partner Survey Snapshot: Rating the Helpful Factors

Survey question: "Rate the following factors according to how much each helped to improve your relationship. (Total score should equal 100.)"

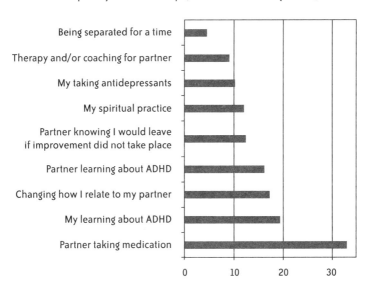

275

Beyond looking at how untreated ADHD affects the patient, the physician should also examine how it is affecting the patient's partner and children. If you find yourself turning to antidepressants or other medication simply to cope with your ADHD partner's behaviors, consider that reason for pause. If your children are suffering from a parent's negligence, authoritarianism, or too many false promises, that's something to consider, too. As one support-group member says: "Sometimes I think half the people on antidepressants wouldn't need them if their partners or others around them were taking stimulants, and then *everybody* would be functioning better."

Perhaps neuroscientific innovations will soon antiquate our notions of ADHD treatment. Some modalities, such as neurofeedback, are already showing promise for certain aspects of ADHD. For today, many people are simply grateful that, as medications go, stimulants' side effects are minimal; they have been extremely well studied over decades of research—studied more than any other medications, in fact—and, when used properly, they act quickly and are thought to clear the system completely.

Reflecting the experience of many support-group members, Mindy is happy that her husband saw the value in trying medication for his ADHD symptoms. Of course he had *survived* without it thus far in life, but at age 46 his coping skills were growing thin and his nerves frayed. He was ready for a change. Taking medication expanded his capacity for pleasure in life and eliminated unnecessary obstacles, irritation, and pain for him and his family. If he had refused, the analogy Mindy offers is this:

> Suppose my husband had lost a leg. His choices would be many. He could use a wheel chair, he could use crutches, or he could get a prosthetic leg. But suppose he refuses any of these devices and when we need to walk somewhere, perhaps with our children, he chooses to hop there on his one leg. As a result, I must carry both of our backpacks. Plus, we must all slow to his pace, bandage his many scrapes from falling, listen to him as he cusses or blames us for walking too fast, prop him up as he hops, and all the while be expected to provide steady, cheerful encouragement.
>
> Would that be fair to him, our children, or me? He has the choice to either limp along, effectively making us join him in his disability, or he can walk upright beside us and we can all enjoy our journey.

CHAPTER
TWENTY-ONE

Rx: Treatment Results That Last

Many of us spent years on the medication roller coaster. Please learn from our missteps. Find a competent physician who will work patiently with you to find the right medication(s) at the right dosage. This is the best "investment" you'll ever make.

— ISABEL

It took Alex two grueling years to convince his wife to seek an evaluation and then treatment for her diagnosis of ADHD. "Now, who knows how long it will take me to convince her to ditch this psychiatrist, who refuses for no logical reason to prescribe stimulants, and find one who actually understands ADHD," he complains. "My wife is skeptical that I or this support group could know something her psychiatrist doesn't. But trust me, it's alarming how little this guy knows." Looking back, Alex wishes they'd been far more careful in selecting a physician.

In Jeanette's case, the irony is that she never found her husband's ADHD a problem—until *after* he started medical treatment for it. "I used to go to bed at night thinking I'm the luckiest wife in the world," she recalls. "Yes, Mike is lousy at paperwork and he doesn't remember to take out the garbage (or what day it's collected!), but he is fun, very good-hearted, and rarely gets angry, and loves being with me and the children."

All that changed soon after Mike learned that he might have ADHD and decided to do something about it. He had recognized in himself the traits he didn't like in his father, including poor follow-through on promises, and wanted to do a better job with his own family. "His attitude was, 'If treatment can help me to be a better person, why not?'" Jeanette recalls.

Unfortunately, under the first physician's care, Mike's personality changed completely after starting medication. "Medication seemed to be a miracle worker at first, but then it ended up making him angry all the time," Jeanette explains. "I went from this perfect marriage to hating my life and being ready to leave him. The worst part was that he didn't realize that things were getting worse, especially the anger, until we were in *major* trouble. As far as he was concerned, his focus was better so that was great. But in reality, his focus was *unrelenting*."

Jeanette found the support-group's feedback critical to realizing what was happening. He was probably either on the wrong type of stimulant medication or at too high a dosage. She also learned how to find a more qualified physician and, more important, convince Frank that he was turning into a father far *worse* than his own.

Stories like this are way too common for the support-group's comfort. As much as we might want to place our faith in our physician's ability to navigate the increasingly complex world of medicine for us, one troubling fact remains: Many physicians, including psychiatrists, are poorly trained to treat Adult ADHD. Some know that and respect their limitations, but some don't. As long as you understand this going in, and as long as you take steps to be a smart healthcare consumer, the chances are good that you will avoid common pitfalls and come out a success story.

"My message to those embarking on this journey," Jeanette says, "is don't be afraid of medication; it can bring great changes. Just be aware."

Indeed, lest you be scared off entirely from pursuing medication treatment, know that, for many, it is a straightforward issue. In fact, ADHD Partner Survey respondents report that when their partner started taking medication, symptoms improved significantly within:

- Hours (15 percent)
- Days (39 percent)
- Weeks (19 percent)

As Jeanette learned, however, the initial "promise" of medications to smooth out the ADHD roller coaster can soon peter out. Support-group members have agonized over this phenomenon for years. Now, the medical community seems to be catching on. "The diagnosis and medical management of ADHD is only the beginning of a course of treatment that should last a lifetime but rarely does," declared psychiatrist William Dodson in a 2006 article for Medscape.[35]

This chapter will support you and your ADHD partner in creating your own success story by helping you to:

- Avoid common pitfalls that lead to low treatment adherence.
- Understand that treatment education and goal setting form the foundation of successful medication treatment.
- Know that each person has a unique biochemistry, which eliminates the possibility of any single medication or standard dose being the best choice for everyone.
- Recognize that it requires a careful, methodical process to find the best fit in a medication regimen.
- Know that ADHD commonly coexists with other conditions, which must be considered in any treatment plan.

The good news is that physicians are increasingly becoming more educated, and these guidelines should help you shop for and recognize competent care when you encounter it.

Why Medication "Miracles" Too Often Vanish

Experts acknowledge that most chronic medical conditions present treatment challenges, with generally about half of patients failing to follow doctors' orders. Still, the situation with ADHD is poor in comparison, some ADHD experts contend, including the high numbers of patients taking medication erratically (that is, not according to a daily regimen) or discontinuing medication entirely. A few large studies point to several factors contributing to this dismal picture:[36]

- Patients did not comprehend the purpose in their taking the medication nor did they understand that treatment could prevent severe consequences.
- Patients had the impression that taking medication for a few weeks would cure ADHD.
- Patients believed that their physician did not recommend continued medication use or felt it useful only in a work environment.
- Patients who were taking short-acting medications seemed to comply more poorly than those on long-acting medications.

Who is responsible for such failures to comply with treatment programs? Actually, there is good reason for noncompliance on both sides. "Many physicians who provide ADHD treatment are family doctors who are not very experienced at using psychiatric drugs, and there are still quite a few psychiatrists who aren't very experienced, either," says Samuel Barondes, professor of neurobiology and psychiatry at UCSF and author of *Better Than Prozac: Creating the Next Generation of Psychiatric Drugs.*

There's also the issue of insurance coverage that fails to support adequate treatment of ADHD. "This kind of treatment is a very individual thing that requires careful monitoring and repeated follow-ups," he says. "You need a lot of time, you have to go slow, get corroboration, do a lot of trial and error, and you need a good relationship with the patient in order to endure the bad trials and the disappointment."

Good treatment also requires cooperation, and frequently patients who come to psychiatrists are not that type. "They can be hard to deal with, often distracted, impatient, or oppositional, and they don't always do what the physician tells them to do," Barondes adds. "The good news is that these medications actually do help a lot of people."

The road to good treatment needn't be fraught with hairpin twists and swerves—or what some support-group members refer to as "Meds Roulette." But if you want a pleasant journey to a desirable destination, you need a trusty roadmap.

Carl—Forcing Square Pegs into Round Holes

Some ADHD partners (or outsiders) might say to us, "You are trying to force a square peg into a round hole! Why can't you just accept us the way we are? Why should we take medication to change us into something we're not?"

The problem is that we are then forced to say, "OK, but if that's just the way you are, then I can't be responsible for taking care of you any more." Our ADHD partners mostly are not going to like it, but you can just say, "Sorry, that's just the way I am."

Good Treatment Plan = Education and Goal-Setting

As with many physical diseases, no official medical protocols exist in the United States for treating *Adult* ADHD. Experts have developed helpful guidelines, however, and made them freely available. (See "Resources" in the back of this book.)

To learn about the steps that you should expect from a clinician expert in treating ADHD, we turn to a prominent ADHD specialist, psychiatrist Margaret Weiss, codeveloper of national guidelines for the Canadian national health system and director of the Provincial ADHD Program at

Vancouver's Children's and Women's Health Centre of British Columbia. She is the principal investigator in a number of ADHD research studies and the author or coauthor of more than 30 publications.

1. Link core symptoms with life challenges

"First and foremost, the patient should know how and why medication can help," Weiss says. The physician "connects the dots" between ADHD symptoms and the patient's past experiences and developmental history. They then discuss the various areas of life in which ADHD might be affecting the patient currently, such as:

- Emotional reactivity; mood changes, temper outbursts
- Risk seeking: inability to tolerate low stimulation
- Inability to initiate or sustain effort in "boring" tasks
- Lack of motivation and low tolerance of frustration
- Poor social skills or lack of social judgment
- Irregular sleep, nutrition, exercise, and other bad health habits

2. Identify treatment targets

When Barbara's husband started taking medication, his driving improved tremendously. But he had never thought his driving was a problem in the first place, so he didn't see the point of continuing to take medication. "Yes, he was happy I no longer griped about his driving, but he didn't associate that with taking medication," Barbara explains. "He just thought I'd finally come to my senses in recognizing what a great driver he is!" Why then did he finally accept that the medication *was* working for him? His boss commended him for making fewer mistakes on the job.

To capture and keep the patient's attention, the physician should focus first on issues the patient sees as problematic. Maybe your ADHD partner's main complaint is procrastination or impulsive eating, but he or she has never noticed problems with attention. In that case, don't expect wild enthusiasm for the treatment target of "improving attention issues"—even if that is *your* primary concern for your partner.

From there, Weiss suggests moving to areas where the person has no idea they're having problems. That information usually comes from a partner or other trusted third party. (See Chapter 12, "Solving ADHD's Double Whammy.") Then, Weiss says, "the doctor can explain how ADHD is affecting the person in ways they don't even realize." For example, your ADHD partner's chief complaint may be procrastinating at work, but your chief complaint is that he or she is not sharing in domestic chores. Or, your ADHD partner might feel he or she is doing great at work, but a recent performance review indicates otherwise.

Focusing on target symptoms offers another advantage: It teaches the patient what to look for. Your ADHD partner, after all, has always experienced the world with untreated symptoms and might not know what is possible or what to look for until his or her attention is drawn to it.

3. Establish a means to monitor treatment targets

Once medication is begun, physicians should measure symptoms against a baseline each month so they can gauge symptom improvement—or worsening. Weiss recommends using rating scales[37] that measure a broad range of symptoms and functioning. This is particularly helpful for patients with coexisting conditions (such as anxiety or depression). Neurotransmitters work in a delicate balance. A little too much of one in relation to another, and symptoms can morph in mystifying ways.

Thus, an important part of treatment is having a tangible method of observing change. This not only helps the physician guide treatment but also helps the person with ADHD "stay the course"—even after the novelty starts to fade regarding the changes brought by medication. It also makes the target concrete by keeping it in focus, reminding the patient and the physician about what they're working toward and where they've been.

Unfortunately, few physicians monitor adult medications closely. "It's critically important, and it's not rocket science, but the utter paucity of clinicians doing it is shocking," confirms psychologist Stephen Hinshaw, a leading ADHD researcher and professor of psychology at the University of California, Berkeley. "You can't notice small improvements or side effects without a monitoring sheet." Yale University psychologist and ADHD expert Thomas E. Brown agrees: "It's amazing how commonly these medications are given with no monitoring."

If the treating physician does not perform this function—and you cannot find another physician who does—you and your ADHD partner can create and fill out your own monitoring sheet and offer it to the physician. Simply take a sheet of paper and make a grid for the week. In the left column, list problematic behaviors. Note each day if the behavior is better or worse and by what degree. Be sure to note the name of the medication, the dosage, and the time of day or night it is taken.

"The goal is noticing patterns and improvements in a measurable and observable way," Hinshaw adds. Avoid general behaviors, such as "being mean," and instead be as specific as possible, such as "interrupting others" or "spending impulsively."

4. Address any concerns or fears about medication

Weiss emphasizes the importance of exploring a patient's apprehensions such as, "It won't be my personality anymore; it will be the pill." These are reasonable concerns for anyone taking medication that affects one's brain. Patients who worry about adverse events should be advised that these are temporary and, in fact, should be fully reported; this data will help the physician fine-tune treatment.

Then, too, a significant number of adults with ADHD have oppositional defiance (to put it simply, they want to do the opposite of whatever is suggested they do). "These people can be very sensitive to being ordered around," Weiss cautions, "and it's really important for physicians to emphasize they are providing opportunities and information."

5. Discuss the timeline of expectations

"Patients with ADHD tend to understand only two units of time: right away or never," Weiss says. Some symptoms may improve in days or even hours. But it is important to wait to judge the full effect of the medication because it can take some time for all the data to accrue.

As challenging situations present themselves, the patient can gauge how their responses differ from the past. "It can also take time for the patient to notice the differences in how people are reacting to him or her or to, for example, evaluate changes in work styles such as efficiency," Weiss points out. She offers these general guidelines:

- Symptoms tend to get better within weeks.
- Functioning gets better within months.
- (And perhaps most important) careful observation may identify changes in development taking place over *years*. For example, the individual who never had a friend now makes and keeps them. Another who could not keep a job has now kept one for a year.

These gradual changes make it even more imperative that there be some form of historical record-keeping.

Last, it's important to remember that big changes are part of life. A parent dies. A job is lost. A baby arrives. Your ADHD partner gets the flu or allergy season hits; both events can affect brain function. If you're not tracking symptoms over time, those variables might obscure clarity in gauging medication's effectiveness.

6. Choose the medication and dosage; orient to the changes

The choice of medication involves many factors: duration of action, coexisting conditions, symptom targets, patient preference, family history, and risk of abuse. (You'll learn more about these factors later in this chapter.) "We have no way to know in advance which medication will work best for a given patient, and there is a significant chance one will work better than another," Weiss explains. "The guideline is to start low, go slowly, and keep increasing until you can determine an optimal risk-benefit ratio."

The physician should continue checking symptoms against rating scales (questionnaires developed specifically to gauge the severity of ADHD symptoms) and against reports from the patient and the partner. Weiss also talks with patients to help them orient to the changes they are experiencing. For example, if your ADHD partner has always been impulsive, volatile, or easily bored, he or she might misperceive loss of this type of "spontaneity" as an undesirable side effect. Then again, people who report a "zombie" effect might need a lower dose.

7. Provide information on taking medications as prescribed

A sheet of instructions should accompany the prescription, clearly stating when and how much of the medication should be taken, including office procedures for follow-up appointments and refills. Many physicians understand their ADHD patients' logistical challenges and call to remind when a refill is soon due. (Stimulant medications typically require a new prescription with each refill.)

Your Role: Know the Facts; Keep the Faith

Support-group members who report positive outcomes typically have taken time to learn about proper ADHD treatment and developed confidence in recognizing it. By and large, they advise newcomers to:

- Work with your ADHD partner in selecting a physician.
- Remember that medication should make things better, not worse.
- Don't be shy about reporting to the physician any untoward side effects, even when your ADHD partner fails to notice.
- Realize that some clinicians view treatment in abstract terms (that is, they aren't living with the patient who has been placed on an overdose of medication—but *you are*).
- Perhaps most critically, maintain faith that, for most adults with ADHD, the proper medication can help, and they persevere in finding it.

Don't be afraid to ask your physician about his or her ADHD treatment guidelines or even to offer a printout of information you consider pertinent. "Many of my patients say they've been doing research online, such as at WebMD, and they've done an excellent job," Weiss confirms. Doctors increasingly seem to welcome patients who take an active role in their care. If you provide a copy of guidelines, she suggests tactfully saying something like, "We've been studying these clinical practice forms because we want to work with you to achieve a good outcome."

Ultimately, you are the mental health-care consumers, Weiss cautions. You must look after your own welfare.

Finding the Right Fit with "Eyeglasses for the Brain"

When you visit your eye doctor for a pair of new eyeglasses or contact lenses, you expect expert help in finding the best lens strength for *your* eyes, not an "average" pair of eyes or what *seemed* to work for a previous patient that day. You would be shocked if your eye doctor simply eyeballed you, asked a few questions, handed you a pair of glasses off the shelf, and waved you away with a flippant "Check back in a month."

The fact is, eye doctors can measure your vision to determine which lenses are most likely to help you see better. Unfortunately, no analogous tests exist to help doctors pinpoint proper ADHD medication treatment. Even highly skilled clinicians cannot accurately predict which medication, at which dose, will work best for a specific patient; a complex interplay of genetics, neurochemistry, and life habits dictates the outcome.

Still, the trial-and-error processes involved with finding the right lens and finding the right medication share significant parallels. That's why it's equally unrealistic to expect that your ADHD partner will "see" as clearly as possible with the first medication, at the first dosage, or even with the first prescribing physician.

"The process requires time and good patient-doctor communication," says psychiatrist Annick Vincent, an ADHD specialist at the Robert-Giffard Hospital in Quebec, Canada, and author of *My Brain STILL Needs Glasses: ADHD in Adults*. "Because ADHD is a chronic, lifelong condition, it pays to take the time to find the right dose and the right medication."

Without zeroing in on a method to find the right medication at the right dose, the patient risks poor outcomes such as these:

- Forever remaining frustrated by unnecessary impairments and continuing to live far below his or her talents and intelligence
- Needlessly tolerating unpleasant side effects

- Suffering side effects from more medications piled on to treat the initial unnecessary side effects
- Quitting the entire effort in frustration

Let's say your partner has "simple" ADHD. That is rarely the case; depression and/or anxiety commonly hitch a ride as ADHD's "traveling companions." (See "When ADHD Has 'Traveling Companions'" on page 292.) But let's assume for this exercise that your partner has ADHD alone.

Again, stimulants are considered the first-line treatment for ADHD—meaning, the first medication class to consider. But many options exist even within this one class, and options are expanding every day. (Even if no stimulant works well for your ADHD partner, plenty of second- and third-line medications are available.) In fact, such abundance might initially feel overwhelming. Just remember, though, that more options mean that people with ADHD now enjoy an unprecedented chance to find the treatment that works best for their individual biochemistry—with a minimum of side effects.

When choosing a stimulant, there are three key factors to consider: class of stimulant, type of delivery system, and dosage.

1. Class of stimulant

Two main classes of stimulants are available:
- *Methylphenidate* (MPH). Brand names in North America include Concerta, Daytrana (a skin patch), Metadate, Methylin, Ritalin, Focalin (a slight variation on MPH), and Biphentin (in Canada).
- *Amphetamine* (AMP). Brand names include Adderall (mixed amphetamine derivatives), Vyvanse (lisdexamfetamine), and Dexedrine (dextroamphetamine).

The MPH class works best for many people, yet has either no effect at all or a negative effect on others, and the same is true for AMP. For about half of ADHD patients, MPH and AMP work equally well. (See "Stimulating Choices" on pages 290-91.) "There is no clinical aspect that may predict who will respond better to which medication," Vincent explains. She discusses the pros and cons of all available medications with her patients and lets them choose which they want to try first. "About seven patients out of ten will be helped with their first choice, and nine out of ten when every product has been tried," she says.

Physician and ADHD specialist Patricia Quinn advises people with ADHD to try both classes of stimulants (MPH and AMP) before moving on to a nonstimulant type of medication. "And you might even talk about switching to another formulation/preparation within the same class before switching stimulant classes."

That brings us to our next category of options: the many variations by which the stimulants are delivered in the body.

2. Type of delivery system

Some people find that a short-acting pill (with an effect that lasts about two to four hours) causes sharp spikes and dips as its action abruptly takes effect and then stops, creating a neurochemical roller coaster. Childhood experience with this has even caused some adults with ADHD to swear off medication forevermore, unaware that today's options typically eliminate those problems.

Another drawback: ADHD patients must *remember* to take their medications several times a day—typically an obstacle in itself, given the nature of why they're taking these medications in the first place.

In recent years, pharmaceutical researchers have focused on three variables—how much, how fast, and for how long—to establish more effective ways to "deliver" the AMP or MPH into the bloodstream. These new extended-release formulations offer not just longer coverage, but also smoother, more reliable delivery. Consider two variants of MPH delivery:

- *Extended-release Example A* mimics a twice-daily dose of a short-acting pill. It releases the first dose upon swallowing and the second dose about four hours later.
- *Extended-release Example B* has a coating that provides the initial dose upon swallowing. The remaining MPH releases slowly but continuously all day at an *increasing rate*.

Each contains the same medication, but one system might work well for a given person and another significantly worse. More examples abound. "You also have different percentages of short- and long-acting within the formulation," Quinn offers. "For example, the percentage ratio might be 20/80 [20 percent of the medication acts immediately; 80 percent, over time], 30/70, or 50/50, and with that comes differing dosage delivery."

An experienced physician will employ helpful strategies to pinpoint the right formulation (or a combination of two) that fits your ADHD partner's lifestyle and periods of "peak demand."

3. Dosage (amount and frequency)

If you've ever had your vision tested, you know that your eye doctor follows a methodical process of "successive approximations." You are asked to view print characters on a chart, one eye at a time, through many strengths of lenses, going slowly up and down until the right strength becomes obvious. Too strong a lens might give you a nauseating headache; too weak a lens might create eyestrain and a different type of headache. Medication dosing is similarly methodical, following pointers such as these:

• *Mind the medication maxim "Start low and titrate slow"*

That is, begin with a low dose and step it up in small increments, gradually, over time. Some people find that the right dose falls in a narrow range. A few milligrams up or down might make a dramatic difference.

Unfortunately, some physicians rely on one "standard" starting dosage, ignoring the fact that no "standard" exists; some people will need a much lower- or higher-than-average dose. Then they compound the error by instructing their patients to double it—and sometimes double it again—too soon. You should also know that height and weight do not determine dosing. A large man might require a dose smaller than a child's.

• *Increase slowly until side effects outweigh benefits*

Do you ask your eye doctor for the weakest lens possible or one that will sharpen your vision the most? "Some patients are referred to our ADHD clinic as so-called treatment failures, but when we either try higher doses or a different product, they improve remarkably," Vincent notes. "In teaching other doctors how to treat ADHD, I strongly emphasize working hard to adjust the meds, finding the 'best eyeglasses' for the brain."

Vincent, Quinn, and virtually all other ADHD medical experts advise slowly boosting the dose until side effects outweigh benefits.

• *Aim for coverage that lasts through the day and evening*

Earlier opinion held that adults needed medication only during work hours. Now most experts stress the importance of long-acting medications, formulations that act *whenever they are needed,* including driving, paying bills, and during family time. "Just as eyeglasses work only when worn, the medication works only when in effect," Vincent emphasizes.

• *Monitor carefully to gauge how long a dose lasts*

It's important to note *when* the medication is taken and *when* problems begin to reappear. Doing so will yield clues to whether problems stem from a rebound when the medication wears off or loses its effect. And, as Quinn cautions, "Just because an extended-release formulation is said to last from 10 to 12 hours, that doesn't mean that some individuals won't metabolize faster or slower. It's important to observe when symptoms seem to be returning during the day. Some people might need to take a second short-acting or extended-release pill later in the day."

Other Points

• *Consider a medical exam first*

Side effects of stimulants are generally not serious. They include trouble sleeping, headaches, anxiety, loss of appetite, and weight loss, according to the National Resource Center on ADHD. Typically, the body adjusts. With some people, stimulants can raise blood pressure; but with others, stimulants actually *lower* blood pressure (presumably because they lessen anxiety and stress). Consequently, a full medical exam should be performed before medication begins.

Joanna: It's Not Just for Work Anymore!

For years, my husband and his doctor said he needed medication only for focusing at work, and I accepted that. But believe me, it wasn't easy.

I thought I was being generous (what a chump I am sometimes!) because he said that the unmedicated him was the "real" him. I wanted him to feel accepted for who he is. But the fact is, my guy is so much calmer, happier, sharper, and good natured when the medication is in effect. After talking with others in the group, it finally hit me: Why should his employer get the good stuff and his family get the chaos? I never thought I had the right to ask him to bring that part of him home.

As usual, only a crisis would get his attention. When I started seriously looking at "my options," he agreed to use the medication on weekends. Hello! He finished projects that have been pending for years and felt quite proud of himself. If he made mistakes, he didn't freak out. He cracked jokes and played with the kids! We were silly and laughed like we used to. He stayed off his computer for hours. Is everything now all hunky-dory? No, but it's a whole lot better. Where medication for ADHD is involved, the rest of life is important, too.

• *Know that medication should not make things worse*

Sometimes the side effects from the wrong medication or dosage are mistakenly seen as character flaws, an "unmasked" coexisting disorder, or the result of stressful events. "Know that the medication shouldn't be making things worse," Quinn warns, "and that, for example, increased focus needn't come at the cost of increased anger."

• *Learn about the ADHD-sleep connection*

ADHD is often associated with sleep disturbances, so sometimes it's necessary to add a medication for sleep or at least improve sleep practices. Interestingly, many people with ADHD find that taking a stimulant helps them get *better* sleep (after all, going to sleep requires *focus*), but others find that the stimulants exacerbate sleep problems. The physician should experiment with formulations taken at various times of the day.

Note: If your ADHD partner seeks a consultation at a sleep clinic, know that many sleep specialists remain unaware of ADHD-related sleep issues, and many even misattribute valid cases of ADHD to insufficient sleep.

* *Know that women with ADHD require special expertise*

Special issues include time-of-month dosing as well as other hormonal concerns and pregnancy. For more information, contact the Web site of the National Center for Girls and Women with ADHD (see Resources).

Stimulating Choices

Which class of stimulant medication is best: amphetamine (AMP) or methyl-phenidate (MPH)? That's easy. The one that works best for the individual who is taking it.

Most new support-group members (and sadly, even some prescribing physicians) don't understand that the two stimulant classes rely on very different chemical actions. Moreover, this difference means that one might work much better—or worse—for a given individual.

A little history: MPH was developed 50 years ago as a milder alternative to AMP. Presumably, that's because it works more simply: MPH primarily blocks the reuptake of dopamine. AMP does that, too, but also accelerates the release of dopamine and increases a metabolite of norepinephrine in the brain, among other effects, according to psychiatrist Charles Parker. He is a Virginia-based psychopharmacologist who writes a popular Web log on neuroscience (CorePsychBlog.com).

With either class, it's easy to know when the dose is too low: It's not working. When the dose is too high, however, you'll often see a very different result in AMP and MPH. "Too high a dose of MPH typically results in the feeling of being 'stoned,'" Parker explains. (Support-group members call it the *zombie effect*.) By contrast, AMP at too high a dose more likely results in anger, irritability, and tension. "The trouble is, many patients don't even recognize these as problematic because they are so focused due to the increased concentration the medication allows them," he adds.

• *Address fears about stimulant abuse*

Frankly, the biggest problem reported in the support group is the ADHD partner forgetting to take the medication altogether, not abusing it. Abuse does happen, though, especially with the shorter-acting medications and most particularly with the AMP class; for that reason, some extended-release stimulants are formulated to thwart abuse.

For more information on the link between ADHD and addiction, read *When Too Much Isn't Enough: Ending the Destructive Cycle of ADHD and Addictive Behavior,* by Wendy Richardson, a Soquel, California-based psychotherapist.

Indeed, many support-group members report that exact phenomenon: An ADHD partner taking AMP in the short- or medium-acting forms enjoys the superhuman productivity it imparts. Some also like the "buzz" it can create; for the highly unobservant, it's a clear sign that the medication is working. (Remember that people with ADHD are more prone to processing information by visceral feelings, not objective data.)

Consequently, adults on too high a dose of AMP often tend to push themselves too hard. Group members note that the overstimulation typically starts catching up with their partners after about two months. That's when medication miracles might make a U-turn into nightmares. But even if no such crash occurs, the daily "jolts" as the AMP medication kicks in and "drops" as it wears off can be more jarring than with MPH, many report. (While MPH generally provides a smoother release, it is still not problem-free.)

For these reasons, some veteran support-group members advocate asking physicians to consider initiating treatment with an MPH medication, reserving AMP for more resistant cases.

Recent innovations in medication delivery have lessened problematic side effects linked to both classes of medication, Parker points out. One of the side effects is agitation. "Whether it happens with MPH or AMP, agitation can be caused by more than the actual pharmaceutical action, it can also be caused by the delivery system," he says. "The short-acting medications are typically more agitating. It's troubling because managed care pushes physicians to use these cheaper medications, but downstream are such side effects."

When ADHD Has "Traveling Companions"

About two-thirds to three-quarters of adults with ADHD will have at least one other psychiatric disorder during their lifetime. These include antisocial personality disorder, anxiety disorders, depressive disorders, bipolar disorder, and substance use disorders (SUD).

No controlled research exists on medication therapy in adults with ADHD and coexisting conditions. The treatment decisions of the medical professional and the individual will be guided by their previous therapeutic and clinical experience, extrapolations from others' clinical experiences, and an empirical approach to the individual's clinical response. Significant coexisting conditions are usually treated first, especially if they cause more impairment.

It is important to consider how the medication for a coexisting disorder will affect the ADHD. For example, treating depression with bupropion (Wellbutrin) may also help ADHD. (It provides a "moderate" response in some adults with ADHD, but the effect is not considered as large as that of stimulants and may take weeks to develop.)

On the other hand, some medications for major depression and bipolar disorder may actually *worsen* ADHD symptoms. In the middle: the SSRIs (such as Prozac, Zoloft, Celexa, Lexapro), which by themselves do not appear to effectively treat ADHD symptoms but do appear to be successful in the treatment of individuals who have coexisting depression and are taking stimulants at the same time.

It is also important to note that medications for ADHD may affect coexisting disorders. For example, stimulants may worsen an untreated anxiety or bipolar disorder.

The risk of stimulant abuse is also greater in adults with an SUD who are actively using. Successful treatment of ADHD, however, tends to decrease the chances of a person with ADHD eventually developing an SUD.

ADHD may commonly coexist with one or more of these disorders:

Disruptive behavior disorders
About 40 percent of people with ADHD have Oppositional Defiant Disorder (ODD), which involves a pattern of arguing, loss of temper, refusing to follow rules, blaming others, deliberately annoying others, and being angry, resentful, and vindictive. Conduct disorder (CD) is also common, occurring

in 20–25 percent of adults with ADHD, and is associated with efforts to break rules without getting caught. It is often described as delinquency.

Research has shown that ADHD and CD students treated with stimulant medicines are not only more attentive, but also less antisocial and aggressive. Also, medication combinations, such as a stimulant with an antidepressant, appear to be very effective.

Mood disorders (depression, mania/bipolar disorder)

Both sad, depressive moods and persistent elevated or irritable moods occur with ADHD more than would be expected by chance.

Depression. Studies suggest that 47 percent of adults with ADHD also have depression. Typically, ADHD occurs first and depression occurs later. They also may share a common genetic link. Researchers have found that stimulants can be combined safely with antidepressants such as Prozac. Newer antidepressants such as Wellbutrin and Effexor may also benefit those individuals with both ADHD and depression.

Bipolar Disorder. Up to 20 percent of adults with ADHD may also manifest bipolar disorder, involving periods of abnormally elevated mood alternating with episodes of clinical depression. Mood must be stabilized before treatment for ADHD is likely to be successful. Patients are first treated with mood stabilizers such as lithium, Depakote, Lamictal, Seroquel, Abilify, or Tegretol. Because these agents usually do not improve the ADHD symptoms, stimulants or antidepressants are often added for that purpose.

Anxiety disorders

As many as 25–40 percent of adults with ADHD will also have an anxiety disorder. These adults often worry excessively, may feel edgy, stressed-out, tired, tense, and have trouble getting restful sleep. These patients also appear less responsive to conventional ADHD treatments. At least one study has shown that children with ADHD and anxiety are more sensitive to negative side effects of stimulant medications. Accordingly, alternative medication regimens may be necessary, including tricyclic antidepressants (such as Norpramin and Tofranil), benzodiazepines (such as Klonopin), and more recently, BuSpar.

Source: Adapted with permission from the National Resource Center on ADHD, "What We Know" information sheets, available at the center's Web site (Help4ADHD.org) or by calling 1-800-233-4050.

CHAPTER TWENTY-TWO

Maximizing Lifestyle Choices, Minimizing Rx Side Effects

Our partners confuse what they want with what they need, in terms of self-medicating with spending, eating, and risk-taking. It feels good in the short term, but creates trouble in the long term. Except they don't usually think about the long term.

— CARL

M eredith strongly suspects that her husband would have been able to enjoy the benefits of stimulant medication if he had known years earlier that he had ADHD. However, he wasn't diagnosed until age 58, and for decades he had employed too many self-medicating bad habits—smoking, eating too much, drinking beer, and getting hurt in reckless sports activities—all in an effort just to feel *right*, to calm the noise in his brain.

"Now, he's not so healthy, and neither, by the way, are our finances," Meredith points out. "The doctor says his heart condition means he can't take the stimulant medication, and the other medications he's tried have done very little. It's pretty ironic, given that if he'd taken the medication years ago, his heart might be healthy today." Even so, simply being able to see and name the invisible enemy, ADHD, helps them cope. Moreover, it's provided helpful cues for dietary strategies such as shunning simple carbohydrates and following a "Zone"-type diet. "Still, I get very jealous hearing others' success stories with medication," she says.

In fact, many people diagnosed later in life *can* take stimulant medications safely. The point of Meredith's story is to illustrate that, for some people, *not* taking medication for ADHD comes with its own risks. It's just one of many ironies of public misperceptions: Being more fearful of stimulant medications than of the smorgasbord of health-damaging habits common to many people with untreated ADHD.

Just as avoiding medication altogether isn't always the healthiest strategy, neither is aiming for the lowest dose or taking it only sporadically. "Those who try to get by on as little medication as possible are undermining their ADHD treatment," says psychiatrist Daniel Amen, author of *Making a Good Brain Great: The Amen Clinic Program for Achieving and Sustaining Optimal Mental Performance*. "At the same time, you don't want to take more than you have to, and that involves maintaining a healthy lifestyle."

That's right. As much as your ADHD partner might like to believe it, no medication can counteract a steady onslaught of junk food, caffeine, adrenaline surges, video games, or all-nighters. Just as poor health habits like these send neurotransmitters scrambling, healthy habits can increase medication's effectiveness.

The catch: Lifestyle changes often remain elusive *until* the adult with ADHD is onboard with medication. Having more initiative and energy for exercise is common. Restful sleep should become more attainable, and tempting substances should hold less allure. "Good habits also provide a greater sense of control in life," Amen says.

He offers these guidelines, noting that they're also helpful for people with ADHD who don't take medication but can follow through on implementing them.

Get exercise
Regular exercise tops every brain expert's list of "must do's." The goal: Intense aerobic exercise for 20–30 minutes five to seven times a week. (A physician should always first approve such lifestyle changes.)

Watch citric acid
This chemical, found in citrus juices, tomato juice, and many preservatives (most snacks wrapped in foil or plastic), can deactivate some medications, especially stimulants. In such case, avoid consuming it an

hour or two before or after taking medications. Also be aware that gastrointestinal alkalinizing agents such as sodium bicarbonate can increase absorption of some stimulants and should be avoided. (Ask your pharmacist about specific medications.)

Manage stress

Chronic stress impairs cognition and diminishes treatment effectiveness. Stress-management techniques are useful, including diaphragmatic breathing (deep breaths in and out). Significantly stressful times might call for medication adjustment.

Get enough sleep

Insufficient sleep can worsen ADHD symptoms. Some adults with ADHD have trouble falling or staying asleep or getting restorative sleep. Others simply become involved with other activities, postpone bedtime, and then sleep too late. For all, good sleep hygiene is important (that includes developing sleep-promoting rituals, such as keeping the bedroom quiet and comfortable, and turning one's face to the sun for 15 minutes first thing each morning).

Eat a balanced diet

Many people with ADHD do better on higher protein and lower carbohydrate diets. Minimize simple carbohydrates (sugar and white flour, rice, or pasta) and eat more complex carbohydrates, such as vegetables and fruits (oranges, pears, grapefruit, apples, and kiwi, but not grapes, dates, or bananas). Increase Omega 3 fatty acids in the diet and through supplements, and take a good multivitamin and mineral supplement daily.

Avoid all caffeine or nicotine

Both substances constrict blood flow to the brain. A cup of coffee or a cigarette might feel stimulating initially but in the end can intensify ADHD symptoms. They also diminish the availability of medication to the brain and can cause heart palpitations that might be misattributed to the medication.

Establish a good relationship with your physician

Choose a physician who is kind, respectful, and a good communicator, one who is experienced in treating ADHD *and* the whole person, not just one or two neurotransmitters. "This might take some detective work because many adult psychiatrists have no clue about ADHD," Amen cautions. "Child psychiatrists who treat adults are sometimes the most knowledgeable because often half of their practice is ADHD."

Watch over-the-counter medications and supplements

These substances can interfere with treatment. For example, St. John's Wort might increase serotonin levels, thereby effectively decreasing dopamine levels. This might help some people but worsen symptoms for others. Clear all such substances with your physician.

Be cautious about generic medications

The Federal Drug Administration permits a variation of approximately 20 percent (up or down) in the active ingredient's bioavailability in generic medications. Optimal medication dosage often falls within a narrow range, so decide if the cost saving is worth the risk. For many people, it's not.

Avoid being penny-wise, pound-foolish

Trying to stay within an insurance plan that includes no ADHD specialists can prove a false economy. Many support-group members have learned the hard way: It's better to pay out of pocket for good initial treatment and then, once a good regimen is reached, see an insurance-plan doctor for medication management.

CHAPTER TWENTY-THREE

Catch Your Breath and Take Five

After years of living with all the frustration and personal hurt arising from my husband's untreated ADHD, I'd become an angry, bitter person. Once the diagnosis came, I knew I had to let go of resentment or we'd never work through this. Of course, my husband had to step up to the plate and start doing things differently, too. Fortunately, he has.

– MARTHA

When musicians "take five," they take a break. Are you and your ADHD partner ready to take a break—from the disappointment, disorganization, and disconnection? If so, "take five" assumes a whole new meaning and offers a fresh approach.

Now that you've learned so much about ADHD, it's time to step back, ponder your particular situation, and make some solid plans for improving your relationship and your home life.

For guidance in streamlining both the big-picture issues and the nitty-gritty practical strategies, we turned to psychologist Arthur Robin, a clinical psychologist in private practice as well as a professor of psychiatry and behavioral neurosciences at Wayne State University School of Medicine. A national lecturer on how ADHD affects couples and families, he is also the author of several books, including (with coauthor Russell Barkley) *Your Defiant Teen: 10 Steps to Resolve Conflict and Rebuild Your Relationship*.

In this final chapter, Robin explains how you and your ADHD partner can "take five" in three key areas and, once again, start making beautiful music together once you understand these critical areas:

- Five factors that determine how well couples and families with ADHD members are able to maintain positive interactions

- Five guidelines for creating positive results
- Five relational "hot spots" (from communication to clutter)
  and how to cool them

First, a story to illustrate the situation that entraps many couples before they learn about ADHD, including why it needn't mean conflict and confusion.

Andrew and Renee: "Before"

Andrew had promised Renee he'd be home by 7 o'clock that evening. As usual, she'd pick up their two children after school, help with homework, and feed them, but then she needed to leave for an important meeting.

Knowing that Andrew often lost track of time and commitments, Renee had called him at 6 o'clock to remind him to be home in one hour. After hanging up, he told himself he had time for "just one more thing." The boss had been breathing down his neck to return that paperwork, so he dove into the pile teetering on his desk. Next thing he knew, it was past 7 o'clock! Racing home, he almost ran a stop sign. "Close call," he congratulated himself. "One more ticket and Renee will never let me hear the end of it. Everybody but her knows these cops are just out to meet quota."

Meanwhile, Renee paced, checking her watch and calling Andrew's cell phone, assuring the kids that Daddy would be home soon. Trying to remain optimistic, she told herself that he was either on the phone or had let his battery run out again. As the minutes ticked by, she grew angry with him and then herself, for trusting him again and for marrying someone so self-centered in the first place. Andrew never seemed to care about disappointing her or the children, and he always found a way to turn around their disappointment and make himself the victim.

Knowing she had to remain composed for the meeting and not wanting to upset the kids, she took a deep breath. The constant stress was giving her a chronic stomachache, and she feared that her increasing distractibility (from always worrying about what *he* was forgetting to do) was degrading her job performance. They couldn't afford to lose the healthcare benefits her job brought them, especially for their son Richard's ADHD treatment.

Expecting an earful, Andrew breezed in the door, already on the offensive. Renee stopped him cold. "Don't bother reeling off your lame excuses and reasons why this is *my* fault." He knew she was serious when she said, "Either you go to Richard's doctor this week and get that ADHD evaluation or I want a divorce. I'm done being a married-but-still-single parent on top of cleaning up your messes."

Andrew cursed her as she walked out. He then retreated to playing video games, waiting for the adrenaline to kick in and regretting the day he got married. He had declined a Happy Hour outing with coworkers, and was Renee grateful? No, and then she has the gall to demand that *he* see a doctor for a kid's disorder! Like *that's* going to happen. She had no idea about the kind of pressure on him at work. Now, with son Richard refusing to go to sleep—and demanding to play the video game, too— that was all he needed!

How had Andrew gotten into this mess—and how would he get out of it? Driving to her meeting, Renee had the exact same thought.

⌒⟶

Andrew and Renee's story illustrates just a few of the ways in which undiagnosed ADHD can challenge a partnership. Each knew they must have wed and had children for a reason, but these days, reason seemed lost in the fog.

"The core characteristics of ADHD predispose the individual to be forgetful, disorganized, and distracted," explains psychologist Arthur Robin. Still, some adults with undiagnosed ADHD might cope relatively well in life until the added responsibilities of a home, a more demanding job, and a child or two overwhelm the already inefficient brain functions.

"By failing to meet responsibilities, communicating poorly, and overreacting emotionally, the ADHD partner elicits negative reactions and what are called blameful attributions from the partner," Robin continues. In other words, you might interpret your partner's miscommunications, emotional flare-ups, and empty promises as proof that your partner doesn't care for you—and react with hurtful or angry accusations. "This all puts distance between the couple and eventually leaves the relationship in shambles," he cautions. The fact that usually neither partner knows why this is happening (namely, untreated ADHD) only compounds the deterioration.

It helps to remember the "Executive Function" model of how ADHD creates challenges in key brain functions, as described in Chapter 3. "The executive functions of the brain cue us to act or not act at the right time," Robin says. "If our executive functions are not operating efficiently, this will affect our actions and, as a result, our interactions with our partners."

Five Factors Affecting Successful Outcome

Robin points to five variables that determine how well couples and families with ADHD members are able to manage conflict and maintain positive interactions. The more problematic these factors, the more severe their impact on partnership. "If the main problem lies in skill deficits, that's easier to resolve because you can teach new skills," he says. "The other areas are more challenging. The good news? Everything that is good for a person with ADHD is good for anyone else." In other words, most of us can bear some improvement in each of these important areas. Maybe even *you*.

1. Skills deficits

These include communication, problem-solving, and behavior-management skills. Negative communication—such as criticism, put-downs, blaming, defending, and interrupting—spurs excessive anger and conflict. Poor problem-solving skills impede conflict resolution.

Deficient skills include failure to:

- Discuss or define the problems
- Conceive of some alternative solutions
- Project the consequences of those solutions
- Agree upon mutually acceptable solutions
- Plan the details of how you will implement the solutions

2. Cognitive distortions

That's the technical term for "jumping to conclusions." It usually happens when we're missing key facts in a given situation but barrel ahead anyway with thoughts and emotional reactions.

Chapter 18 covered the basics of cognitive-behavioral therapy (CBT), specifically the event-thought-feeling-behavior chain of events. Your ADHD partner, typically in the dark about how his or her symptoms have affected life experiences, might have developed a lifetime of cognitive distortions, such as all-or-nothing thinking, mind-reading, and catastrophizing (focusing on the worst-possible outcome). You might bring to the table a few distorted thoughts of your own, such as "My partner is lazy, selfish, uncaring, and (fill in the blank)."

Robin offers an example of how these cognitive distortions can affect couples. Imagine that your ADHD partner has overspent again, thanks to a poor sense of consequences and a high degree of impulsivity. Consider the possible reactions:

You:
Thought: "My partner does not care enough about me to stop doing this."
Feeling: Anger and frustration.
Behavior: Criticize the partner and pull away.

Your ADHD partner:
Thought: "My partner is so rigid and controlling."
Feeling: Anger and frustration.
Behavior: Give a defensive retort to criticism and pull away.

Then again, cognitive distortions can exist apart from those related to ADHD, such as when partners harbor unrealistic expectations that "marriage should be a certain way" or "a partner shows love by doing X." Distortions can spring from family background, too.

3. Family of origin—biology and learning

The formative experiences and unresolved issues we had in our families of origin color our interaction style in intimate relationships. These experiences can influence our choice of a partner and lead us to react to our partners like we reacted to our parents. Toss in family genetics and you have a complicated stew of biology and learning.

Arthur Robin explains: "Let's say you grew up arguing with your parents because untreated ADHD meant you were too distractible and hyperactive to do as you were told. Your biology led you to have trouble cooperating, but then your negative learning history led to all those arguments. So, years later, when your partner points to the same issue, you react in the long-established problematic pattern."

Example: Adults with ADHD who could never do enough to please their parents (and therefore now crave approval) may conclude that they can never do enough to please their partners, thus creating conflict and escalating hostilities.

Example: The adult with ADHD who failed in school and never received help may resist an ADHD evaluation, deny that her own child has ADHD, and refuse to cooperate with treatment. Robin commonly sees that in his practice: "It's a hard thing for some people to face up to, and it needs to be approached gently."

In some cases, he notes, the family of origin's history proves the most challenging. "It's an endless repetitive cycle of biology influencing relating styles that becomes reinforced over generations."

4. Degree of impairment

The more severe the ADHD symptoms and the greater the number of family members with ADHD, the more convoluted the challenges become. Such a situation intensifies and compounds into increased family and marital dysfunction.

5. Coexisting conditions

The presence of additional disorders (such as depression; anxiety; substance abuse; and bipolar, conduct, personality, and oppositional-defiant disorders) complicates the situation. As described in Chapter 21, each requires specific treatments. "It is critical that a competent psychiatrist be consulted who can see each disorder for what it is and treat it appropriately," he says.

Five Guidelines for Positive Results

To tackle the challenges posed by the five factors above and develop new ways of interacting, Robin offers five steps:

1. Optimize medication (repeat: optimize medication)

It's hard to overemphasize the importance of optimal medication treatment. "For a minority of people, medication will be like a light switch going on," he explains. "For others, it will be more subtle." The couple should collaborate with their physician to derive maximum benefit from any prescribed ADHD medications.

It is realistic to expect stimulant medication to enhance performance of tasks that require planning, organization, time-management, sustained attention, working memory, and impulse control. And don't forget frustration tolerance. "Most people don't realize that one way impulsivity manifests is in a lack of control over emotion, and that includes anger," Robin points out.

ADHD partners should *ensure* they are covered by medication during common times of interaction (typically, evenings and weekends), and that their treating physicians have addressed the full range of symptoms. Above all, they should discuss important topics *only* when medication is in effect.

2. Adjust your attitudes

Both parties need to accept that the ADHD partner, no matter how ideal their treatment, will blunder now and then. As these incidents lessen over time, both partners can learn to take them in stride and even occasionally laugh as they work together to repair the damage—instead of making the situation worse by escalating the criticism and defensiveness. Robin uses the term "ADHD moments" to separate the person from the disorder and offers these tips on attitude-adjustment.

Your ADHD partner:
- Acknowledges how ADHD has affected the partnership.
- Accepts responsibility for poorly self-regulated actions.
- Agrees to stop denying, minimizing, and avoiding the issues.
- Learns how to respond nondefensively to negative feedback about ADHD behavior.

You:
- Transform blame into empathy.
- Correctly attribute ADHD behavior to a neurological slip-up, not to malicious intent or lack of caring.
- Understand that it might be very hard for your ADHD partner to start accepting responsibility for actions until he or she knows why they happen (psychoeducation) and receives tools for changing those behaviors (medication and other strategies).
- Realize that your partner may have withstood a lifetime of criticism before meeting you and may therefore be hair-trigger sensitive to your negative judgments. Even as you hold your partner accountable, strive for patience and kindness.
- Learn the difference between "enabling" or "codependent" behavior and accommodate your partner's differences in a way that enhances you both.

Some people do these things naturally, Robin notes, but others need instruction.

3. Learn new skills; practice new habits

Take advantage of this opportunity for both of you to develop new strategies that stand to benefit you in all areas of life:

- Learn effective communication and conflict-resolution techniques.
- Practice empathy, compassion, and forgiveness.
- Make your physical and social environment ADHD-friendly. De-clutter. Streamline. Label. Organize.
- Ask for external help as needed from doctors, therapists, coaches, and professional organizers. As much as you can comfortably afford to, hire out the more contentious chores.

- Anticipate problems and plan to prevent their occurrence.
- Always have a Plan B. Remain flexible while keeping sight of what's important.
- Make liberal use of humor.

4. Cultivate romance

What good are all these plans and strategies if they don't add a little romance to your lives? Even as you work to establish new ways of communicating and getting things done, *remember to have some fun.*

Accept that, at least in the early stages of restructuring your relationship, your ADHD partner might need to program alarms and other unromantic electronic devices that remind him or her to let you know you're cared for, by leaving love notes, bringing home flowers, and giving massages, for example.

Hint to the ADHD Partner: Avoid showy displays—the living room filled with the flowers that always make your partner sneeze, for example, or the hallway lined with so many flaming candles it triggers the smoke alarm. It's not about you congratulating yourself for being super romantic; it's about your partner feeling loved and appreciated. And remember: It's hard to greet romantic gestures with kisses and more if the path to the bed is blocked by clothes, shoes, or spare rototiller parts.

For more ideas on cultivating romance, Robin recommends therapist Jonathan Halverstadt's book, *ADD and Romance.*

5. Focus on resolving the top ADHD partnership challenges

Robin and colleagues conducted a survey several years ago to identify the top trouble spots in marriages where ADHD is involved.[38] They came up with 10 top challenges posed by ADHD symptoms, listed in order of severity from highest to lowest:

1. Doesn't remember being told things
2. Says things without thinking
3. Zones out in conversations
4. Has trouble dealing with frustration
5. Has trouble getting started on a task
6. Underestimates time needed to complete task
7. Leaves a mess
8. Doesn't finish household projects
9. Doesn't respond when spoken to
10. Doesn't plan ahead

Cooling the Five Hot Spots

When Robin examined the underlying issues of these ten trouble spots above, he found they fell roughly into five areas, the "hot spots" that might need a little dousing in your home: communication, organization, time management, memory, and impulsivity.

Of course, ADHD issues rarely fit tidily into little boxes. Instead, they have a way of spilling out and rubbing shoulders with each other. For example, organization affects time management and vice versa in multitudinous ways. To acknowledge this hybridizing effect, the following strategies target five revised hot spots:

1. Communication
2. Organization and Time Management—keeping track of time and remembering important tasks and obligations
3. Organization and Time Management—*completing* tasks
4. Organization—eliminating clutter
5. Impulsivity—"curbing the blurting" and cooling irritability

For each problematic area, Robin breaks out the goals for both of you singly and as a couple:[39]

1. Hot Spot: Communication

You:

- Capture your ADHD partner's attention before saying something important. Use a gesture or loving touch as you make eye contact.
- Don't discuss important matters "on the fly"—while your partner is involved in another activity or as you're going out the door.
- For some topics, e-mail works best. Your partner has time to focus, reread, and mull over a response.

Your ADHD Partner:

- Recognize what good listening means for your partner: that you value his or her opinions and care about your partner.
- Listen first. Respond second. Exert the extra mental effort to really listen. Set aside what you were just doing, what you will do when your partner finishes, your response, or unrelated topics. If you need more time to shape a response, ask for it.
- Use relaxation techniques to clear your mind first.

Both Partners:

- Eliminate distractions (TV, computer, kids) to make the environment conducive to communication and pick a good time for a serious conversation.

- Agree to speak in short sentences and develop new communication techniques that help ensure attention.

2. Hot Spot: Organization /Time Management (Forgetting!)

Your ADHD Partner: Time Management

- Resist the urge "to do just one more thing before I leave the house/go to bed/come to dinner/shut down the computer."
- Call your partner if you're going to be more than 10 minutes late.
- Use alarms, automated e-mails, or whatever it takes to remind you to wind down your workday on time.
- Work with a clock in front of you. Train yourself to glance at it frequently and track your progress toward task completion.

Your ADHD Partner: Memory Prompts

- Leave notes and reminders for yourself on your voice mail or digital recorder.
- Send yourself e-mails or ask your partner to send you e-mails noting tasks, events, or appointments.
- Use sticky notes at work, home, and in the car.
- Always carry a planner or personal digital assistant (PDA) and use it faithfully.
- For especially important occasions, agree that your partner will call you as a reminder—for example, before leaving the office.
- Set up memory prompts immediately on being asked to do or remember something. No procrastinating! Just make it a habit.
- Always carry a pen and paper, notepad, or digital recorder.
- Make consistent use of these memory prompts a lifetime habit, even when it seems boring, inconvenient, or unnecessary. Examples: Alarms on wristwatches, clocks, PDAs, computers, and kitchen timers. Once you see how they simplify life and make it more enjoyable, the habit will come more easily.
- Do not react defensively and let a disagreement escalate to a major conflict when your partner expresses annoyance about your forgetting something. Acknowledge your mistake, outline a remedy to avoid future mistakes, and thank your partner for the helpful feedback. If your partner gave feedback very critically, nicely ask your partner to try a more loving way in the future. (Chances are your partner had been showing *you* patience for some time before your diagnosis.)

As a Couple:
- Work together to make and update "to do" lists.
- Plan a regular time, day or evening, for both of you to review priorities for the next day.
- Set up a "central command" whiteboard and calendar. Keep it uncluttered and restrict messages to a minimum, so they'll be noticed and acted on. Set up an agreement about how it will work. For example, your ADHD partner might agree to check for important messages concerning the day's activities or plans each morning after breakfast.
- Weekend plans: Toward the end of the week, talk about what kind of weekend it will be—fun, chores, or a mix. That way, you each have time to adjust expectations and goals.

3. Hot Spot: Organization/Time Management (Not Finishing!)
Your ADHD Partner:
- "Business before pleasure": Do the unpleasant chore first.
  You know the one, the one you would always avoid.
- Be realistic: Promise less to your partner so you can deliver more when you complete the chore.
- Work on only one major household project at a time.
- Break the task into small chunks and schedule one at a time.
  If you need help doing this, ask your partner.
- Estimate time to completion: Determine the average amount of time by which you typically *under*estimate. Add this time to your estimate, and schedule it.
- Stop the task at the end of the allocated time and finish at another time. This prevents you from hyperfocusing on one task and neglecting others. It teaches you to prioritize.
- Plan on completion: Schedule "make up" times every day. Use them to finish any tasks, and if there are none, do a fun activity.
- Think ahead: Log the actual time it takes to do recurring tasks and check the log before planning a time to do the task the next time it arises (cut the grass, empty the dishwasher, and such).
- Ask your partner to use hugs and other affectionate acts to reward you for each chunk of the task you complete. And instead of nagging when the agreed time to begin a task arrives, agree that your partner will touch you affectionately as a cue to start.

You:

- Offer to collaborate with your partner on reminder systems.
- Hold your partner accountable for mutual agreements to complete tasks, but be matter-of-fact rather than critical.

As a Couple:

- Prioritize a list of household projects; come to an agreement on which projects are necessary and which are distractions.
- Divide responsibility between the two of you.
- Establish times when you will each work on your own tasks, but touch base regularly to keep each other on target.

4. Hot Spot: Organization (Clutter!)

Your ADHD Partner:

- Assign clear-cut places for all of your personal belongings.
- Schedule regular "pick up" times to deal with household clutter.
- Train yourself to *avoid avoidance* when it comes to clutter and putting things away.
- Deal with paper when you first encounter it.
- Ruthlessly throw things away.
- Focus on only one room or portion of a room at a time.

As a Couple:

- Work as a team on organizing parts of the house.
- If necessary, hire a coach or professional organizer to help you clear clutter and set up an ADHD-friendly organizing system.
- Develop a routine for retrieving and processing the mail.

5. Hot Spot: Impulsivity (Including irritability!)

As a Couple:

- Discuss areas of frustration and solve problems creatively.
- To minimize resentment, allot chores according to each person's preferences and talents as much as possible. Neither, however, should have all the "fun" jobs or all the "drudge" jobs.

Your ADHD Partner: Curbing the Blurting

- Be aware of your tendency to blurt things on impulse; repeat to yourself to "watch it," "be careful," and "don't say something I will regret."

- Devise "self-censoring rules." For example, "I will never talk about our finances at parties," and "I will not criticize my partner in front of others." Write that on an index card; carry it with you.
- Engage others in conversation about themselves and their interests. Say little about yourself until you have learned about them.
- Arrange a nonverbal warning between your partner and yourself if you start to say things that should not be mentioned.
- Try to be aware of how others are responding to you. When you notice signs of boredom or fatigue, cut conversation short.
- When you say something your partner finds hurtful, don't invalidate his or her feelings. Listen and try to learn why your words were hurtful, and then apologize if appropriate. Don't become defensive and inflame the situation needlessly.

Your ADHD Partner: Reducing Irritability
- Exercise regularly. Learn relaxation, meditation, yoga, or other techniques, and incorporate them into your daily life.
- Excuse yourself temporarily from the frustrating situation, but do *not* avoid it. Eventually, you have to deal with it.
- Help your partner learn what words to use to help you calm down during an argument.

Andrew and Renee: "After"

Remember the couple at the beginning of this chapter? Renee believed Andrew's undiagnosed adult ADHD was ruining their lives. She said she would leave him if he did not go for an evaluation. Initially, he ignored Renee's ultimatum. "A man had to draw the line somewhere," he figured. Consequently, the couple separated.

At first, Andrew reveled in having no "boss" to answer to. But given time and space to realize how much he missed Renee and the kids—and how haphazardly he managed his daily affairs—Andrew finally admitted to himself the similarities between his son's diagnosed ADHD behavior and his grown-up version of it. He took an interactive test online and, sure enough, he seemed a likely candidate for the diagnosis. He then visited an online forum where other adults with ADHD shared their life experiences, and that made him feel less alone and less "at fault" for—and angry about—a disorder that no one before Renee had ever mentioned.

Meanwhile, Renee joined a "partners of" support group and learned that Andrew's behaviors are common among adults with ADHD, and that change is possible. Given a chance to regroup in a calm house and vent long-simmering frustrations to people who "get it," she slowly regained her footing. She even remembered why she'd fallen in love with Andrew. Her resolve, though, remained strong. She would not return to living life the way she had been before the separation.

Three months later, Andrew pursued an evaluation. When it was determined that he did have ADHD, he began treatment. Knowing that adults with ADHD aren't typically the most accurate self-reporters, Andrew's psychologist asked Renee to complete a questionnaire, too. Andrew was skeptical and even felt insulted, but Renee was relieved that someone wanted the "full picture." She was happy to be involved in Andrew's treatment as long as it meant real change was possible. The psychologist stipulated that the goal was to help Andrew be more autonomous and cooperative, not simply to train Renee to compensate for his deficits *or* to convince Andrew to accept Renee's "rule."

On the Path Toward Change

Andrew saw a physician who explained the benefits of stimulant medication for his particular challenges, and he agreed to try it. He began on a low dosage and slowly increased it until he reached an optimal level. The medication helped Andrew stick to his priorities, finish tasks, really listen to Renee and the children, and restrain himself when the boys' behavior punched his buttons. At work, he began filing reports on time and no longer felt forced to bluff forgotten details when clients called for updates.

Andrew's temper had cooled, but the physician found room for significant improvement and added an antidepressant to the mix. Not only did that brighten Andrew's mood significantly and almost eliminate his irritability, the medication's round-the-clock action provided a much-needed cushion for the periods between the stimulant's effectiveness cycle. The doctor worked with him to find the right antidepressant in a dosage that did not curb libido. In fact, the medication did retard sexual climax a bit, but both Andrew and Renee welcomed that particular side effect.

If reconciliation was going to work, Renee realized, she had to be less accusatory and more understanding of what they were up against. Sure, she was justified in not wanting the past to repeat itself, but as long as improvement started taking place, Renee realized Andrew deserved some breathing room. Then, she set about finding that tricky middle ground between resentfully "enabling" him and not helping him at all.

For two months, Andrew pursued individual cognitive-behavioral therapy geared for ADHD. Then the psychologist saw Andrew and Renee together, to help them establish new patterns of interaction and coparenting. Andrew attended an adult support/discussion group monthly, and he's thinking about hiring an ADHD coach to help him tackle time-management and organizational challenges.

Two Steps Forward and One Step Back Will Do, for Now

Looking back at the years of acrimony, Andrew and Renee sometimes doubted they could ever repair the damage. Each time they hit a setback on their newfound path, they would spiral down into despair. As time went on, however, and they stayed mindful of successes large and small, they developed more compassion for each other. For now, they accept the "two steps forward and one step back" model, and Renee has *almost* stopped waiting for the other shoe to drop. In fact, she's come to view the dropping shoe as more of a slipper than a combat boot.

As the couple agreed to do in therapy, Renee gives Andrew a gentle tap on the shoulder as a signal if he's not listening to her. It took him a while to stop reacting defensively, but he knows how much it means to Renee. For her part, she has stopped reacting when he expresses momentary frustration, which only added fuel to the fire, and that gives him time to adjust to the new patterns.

Realizing that the entire family had gotten caught up in a stimulation-seeking, overscheduled whirlwind, they resolved to pare down activities. By agreeing to halt frivolous purchases, Andrew helped to squeeze a monthly cleaning service into the budget; that alone has eliminated a huge source of contention. Now, instead of gritting their teeth through chores on Saturday, Andrew and Renee find that a family hike or other physical activity goes a long way toward restoring calm.

All is not perfect—nor is that realistic for anyone—but now Andrew and Renee are on a steady path toward peaceable companionship and a happy family life.

Appendix A

Adult ADHD Evaluation and Diagnosis

T here is no single test to evaluate for ADHD. No computer test. No fill-in-the-blank test. No blood test or genetic test.

"You also cannot measure a person's pain or suffering in life by clinical tests," notes psychologist Thomas E. Brown, assistant clinical professor of psychiatry at the Yale University School of Medicine and associate director of the Yale Clinic for Attention and Related Disorders.

Instead, the diagnostic process requires familiarity with ADHD symptoms in adults, informed data collection, and an ability to listen closely and ask perceptive questions. (A physical exam should also be done to rule out thyroid disorders and other conditions that can affect brain function or limit medication choices.)

It's important to remember that ADHD symptoms essentially represent an extreme on a normal continuum of behavior that varies in the population, much like IQ, weight, or height. That's why its diagnosis is not a cut-and-dried matter. To ascertain if a person is "over the line" on this continuum, the evaluating professional must gauge the severity of the symptoms and impairment.

In years past, diagnosing ADHD was more clear-cut, but that actually meant that millions of people fell through the cracks. "ADHD used to be considered a disruptive order of childhood, and its diagnosis was based on observing overt behavior," Brown explains. Today we know that many people, especially adults, have no obvious physical hyperactivity, and we better understand the subtle nature of ADHD symptoms. "We know that impairments related to Executive Function are largely cognitive, covert, and not easily observed," he adds. "They are also complex and interactive, and not easily measured."

Furthermore, the longer the patient goes with untreated ADHD, the higher the chances of having a coexisting condition such as anxiety or depression. "Too often, the ADHD is treated and the coexisting condition is ignored, or vice-versa," he says. "The Diagnostic and Statistical Manual, used by professionals to diagnose psychiatric conditions, separately lists more than 200 disorders, but these are not all different trees bearing different fruit." In fact, these disorders may be linked biochemically as risk factors (that is, having one disorder increases the chances that you'll have another).

For all these reasons, it's wise to make sure you understand the diagnostic process, in general terms, *before* selecting a professional to conduct an evaluation.

- **Who conducts the evaluation?**

Several types of professionals can evaluate for ADHD, including physicians, psychologists, and therapists. It is important to identify a professional who has appropriate state licensing or certification for treating ADHD and who can distinguish ADHD from other physical or psychological disorders (a *differential diagnosis*). If your family physician cannot make a confident referral, contact the closest university teaching hospital. If there is a local chapter of CHADD (see the Resources page at the end of this book), attend and talk to members about their experiences with local professionals. (Always ask the professional about the percentage of patients seen with ADHD; you're looking for a significant number.)

- **The process, in a nutshell**

The evaluating professional gathers data from sources that include behavior rating scales (including the Brown ADD Scales), symptom checklists, and a detailed life history, including any head injuries (even "minor" ones). The clinician also compares client symptoms to the diagnostic criteria in the *Diagnostic and Statistical Manual of Mental Disorders* (*DSM*) listed on the following pages.

Family members or significant others typically are asked to provide information on the patient's history and current challenges. That's because ADHD symptoms often limit or distort recall and self-observation.

Brown stresses the importance of asking about the adult client's abilities in these areas that require executive functioning:

- Holding a job and working productively
- Managing household and finances
- Managing work while nurturing relationships
- Parenting and sustaining partnerships
- Sequencing tasks and completing chores
- Driving in traffic

He also recommends inquiring about health issues, including sleep and appetite, as well as substance use.

- **The trouble with the official diagnostic criteria for ADHD**

The current official criteria are empirically based and rigorously tested, but they were developed with children in mind, *not* adults. Therefore, leading ADHD experts consider them rather problematic in diagnosing adults. Furthermore, the guidelines don't reflect recent thinking about when the signs of ADHD first appear. The current requirement is that impairing symptoms be apparent before age seven. Yet, as Brown points out, some signs are not noticeable until middle school or junior high, college, and even later adulthood. Then, too, parents can provide so much support that impairments are obscured, or a highly intelligent child can compensate for many years before "hitting the wall" of his or her unaddressed symptoms.

- **In the works: New guidelines specifically for Adult ADHD**

The following pages include the Adult ADHD criteria proposed for the next DSM edition, planned for 2011.[40] Psychologist and ADHD researcher Russell Barkley and colleagues designed these criteria to reflect adult issues that are distinct from those in children.

- **Special diagnostic issues for women with ADHD**

ADHD is often missed in women because the symptoms can manifest differently between the genders. The Women's ADHD Self-Assessment Symptoms Inventory (SASI) was developed by psychologist Kathleen Nadeau and physician Patricia Quinn for use as part of a structured interview in conjunction with other diagnostic tools. Besides the traditional ADHD symptoms, it measures difficulties in time management, organization, parenting, life-maintenance activities, hormonal issues, and problem eating patterns. It is available for purchase at the publisher's Web site (ADDvance.com).

- **For more information**

To learn more about diagnostic guidelines, contact the U.S. National Resource Center on ADHD or visit the Web site of the Canadian ADHD Resource Alliance (CADDRA). (See Resources page at the end of this book.)

Current DSM-IV Criteria for ADHD

The year 2000 *Diagnostic and Statistical Manual for Mental Disorders* (DSM-IV-TR) provides the official criteria for diagnosing ADHD, offered here for informational purposes only and modified to make them more accessible to the public. Only trained healthcare providers can diagnose or treat ADHD.

The term *developmental level* refers to the normal milestones associated with a certain age. To qualify for the diagnosis, each of the five points (in Roman numerals) must be met.

These guidelines, established and rigorously tested for diagnosing ADHD in children, might be of more limited value in evaluating adults. For more information, review the previous pages explaining the diagnostic process.

I. Either A or B
  A. Six or more of the following symptoms of inattention have been present for at least six months to a point that is disruptive and inappropriate for developmental level:
    1. Often does not give close attention to details or makes careless mistakes in schoolwork, work, or other activities
    2. Often has trouble keeping attention on tasks or play activities
    3. Often does not seem to listen when spoken to directly
    4. Often does not follow instructions and fails to finish schoolwork, chores, or duties in the workplace (not due to oppositional behavior or failure to understand instructions)
    5. Often has trouble organizing activities
    6. Often avoids, dislikes, or doesn't want to do things that take a lot of mental effort for a long period of time (such as schoolwork or homework)
    7. Often loses things needed for tasks and activities (for example, toys, school assignments, pencils, books, or tools)
    8. Is often easily distracted
    9. Is often forgetful in daily activities
  B. Six or more of the following symptoms of *hyperactivity-impulsivity* have been present for at least six months to an extent that is disruptive and inappropriate for developmental level:
    Hyperactivity:
    1. Often fidgets with hands or feet or squirms in seat
    2. Often gets up from seat when remaining in seat is expected

3. Often runs about or climbs when and where it is not appropriate (adolescents or adults may feel very restless)
4. Often has trouble playing or enjoying leisure activities quietly
5. Is often "on the go" or often acts as if "driven by a motor"
6. Often talks excessively

Impulsivity:
1. Often blurts out answers before questions have been finished
2. Often has trouble waiting one's turn
3. Often interrupts or intrudes on others (for example, butts into conversations or games)

II. Some symptoms that cause impairment were present before age seven years.

III. Some impairment from the symptoms is present in two or more settings (for example, at school/work and at home).

IV. There must be clear evidence of significant impairment in social, school, or work functioning.

V. The symptoms do not happen only during the course of a Pervasive Developmental Disorder, Schizophrenia, or other Psychotic Disorder. The symptoms are not better accounted for by another mental disorder (for example, Mood Disorder, Anxiety Disorder, Dissociative Disorder, or a Personality Disorder).

Source: American Psychiatric Association: *Diagnostic and Statistical Manual of Mental Disorders, Fourth Edition, Text Revision.* Washington, DC, American Psychiatric Association, 2000, by permission.

Proposed Criteria for Adult ADHD in DSM-V

Here are the Adult ADHD criteria proposed for the next edition of the *Diagnostic and Statistical Manual*, planned for 2011.[41] ADHD expert Russell Barkley and colleagues designed these criteria to reflect adult issues that are distinct from those in children, a widely acknowledged limitation of the current official criteria. Research supporting this set of criteria can be found in *ADHD in Adults: What the Science Says*, by Barkley, Kevin Murphy, and Mariellen Fischer.

A. Six (or more) of the following symptoms have persisted for at least six months to a degree that is maladaptive and inconsistent with developmental level:
  1. Is often easily distracted by extraneous stimuli
  2. Often makes decisions impulsively
  3. Often has difficulty stopping activities or behavior when he/she should do so
  4. Often starts a project or task without reading or listening to directions carefully
  5. Often shows poor follow-through on promises or commitments made to others
  6. Often has trouble doing things in their proper order or sequence
  7. Often more likely to drive a motor vehicle much faster than others (excessive speeding)
  8. Often has difficulty sustaining attention in tasks or leisure activities
  9. Often has difficulty organizing tasks and activities
B. Some symptoms that caused impairment were present before age 16 years.
C. Some impairment from the symptoms is present in two or more settings (for example, work, educational activities, home life, social functioning, community activities, etc.).
D. There must be clear evidence of clinically significant impairment in social, academic, domestic (cohabiting, financial, driving, child-rearing, etc.), or occupational functioning.
E. The symptoms do not occur exclusively during the course of a pervasive developmental disorder, schizophrenia, or other psychotic disorder and are not better accounted for by another mental disorder (for example, Mood Disorder, Anxiety Disorder, Dissociative Disorder, or a Personality Disorder).

Source: Russell A. Barkley, Ph.D., 2006, by permission.

Appendix B

"But I Heard That..."
More Background
for the Unconvinced

To the outside world, this just seems the usual Venus-Mars stuff. But it is the degree of the behaviors that people don't understand. Besides, our gay and lesbian support-group members experience the same problems, so how can it be a Venus-Mars issue?

—BETH

"Never in a million years would I have suspected ADHD!" Jennifer explains to the group. "I thought ADHD was a hyperactive little boy's disorder. My husband is 38, six-foot-five, and fairly *listless* when he's not engaged in something that really captures his interest."

Sure, she knew something was out of kilter, especially with his unpredictable temper. Yet, because he always maintained his cool outside the home, she was the one who looked unstable. "I wasn't *unstable*," she says. "I was *de-stabilized*—by his making plans, changing plans, forgetting plans, and expecting me to read his mind about all of it and never be upset that I wasn't consulted. Now I am stunned to learn how much ADHD has affected everything, and how common it is."

Throughout history, whenever we haven't clearly understood a phenomenon, myths have substituted and passed for knowledge. As more of us learn about ADHD, the common misconceptions we explore in this appendix may disappear entirely.

This appendix will help you to:

- Understand that ADHD affects children *and* adults.
- Push aside mistaken notions that ADHD is an excuse for irresponsibility, a "typical human behavior," a by-product of modern life, or a pharmaceutical company invention.
- Know that ADHD is not, in fact, a "controversial" diagnosis and that all significant scientific and medical bodies agree that ADHD is a valid medical condition.
- Realize that, left unaddressed, some ADHD symptoms can yield serious consequences.

"...ADHD Is for Children"

Until the 1990s, most medical professionals viewed ADHD as a diagnosis only for children, specifically physically hyperactive children. (A few in the healthcare industry—thankfully, very few—still mistakenly believe that.) One explanation: They thought that children outgrow ADHD because physical hyperactivity, long considered an ADHD hallmark, tends to lessen with age.

This misperception started changing in the 1970s when a few pediatric physicians experienced in treating ADHD connected the dots—observing "little apples" falling suspiciously close to the tree. That is, their young patients' parents often shared many of the same behaviors, albeit in adult form. For example, they might self-medicate not with candy or boisterous activity but with alcohol or cigarettes.

"In treating children with ADHD, I started asking parents if they used to have problems like this as children, and the spouse would say, 'What do you mean, *used to* have?'" says psychiatrist Paul Wender, who has been called the "Dean of ADHD." Wender is a lecturer in psychiatry at Harvard Medical School. He began studying ADHD four decades ago, establishing himself as a pioneer in its diagnosis and treatment, both in children and adults.

Here's another important point: Most of today's adults who actually have ADHD were never diagnosed as children. In fact, 88 percent of ADHD Partner Survey respondents say their partners were first evaluated and diagnosed as adults, *during this relationship*.

Given modern awareness and diagnostic methods, if your partner were a youngster today, his or her symptoms would stand a better chance of being recognized. Even today, however, many bright children challenged by ADHD fly under the radar screen for years because their intelligence lets them compensate, they have strong parental support, they are in highly structured schools, or no one is paying attention to the problems and connecting the dots. It's only later in life—perhaps college, that first job, that first serious relationship, or that first baby—that they "hit the wall."

In fact, according to ADHD authority Russell Barkley, ADHD is "far more apparent and even more impairing in adults than in children because adults have more domains of responsibility." That is, adults are expected to hold a job, run a household, manage money, look after their health, and, in some cases, provide daily structure for children.

". . .ADHD's Just an Excuse for Irresponsibility"

Psychologist and ADHD expert J. Russell Ramsay has heard that line so many times he's named it one of his top three myths about ADHD (the other two follow shortly).

As the associate director at the University of Pennsylvania's Adult ADHD Treatment and Research Program, he's noticed that clients often expend much-higher-than-average time and effort trying to meet their responsibilities—typically "twice the effort for half the result." Instead of seeking an easy way out, he argues, "They want to gain a measure of predictable cause-and-effect in their lives."

Harold Meyer, founder of The A.D.D. Resource Center in New York City and an ADHD coach, agrees. "People with ADHD usually know what needs to be done," he says. "Their difficulty, and continual frustration for both themselves and others, is in doing what they know or, at times, thinking before they act. Instead of Ready-Aim-Fire, it's Ready-Fire-Aim." Or, as one of Meyer's clients put it, "By the time I think about what it is I should have done, I've already done the first thing I thought about."

Yes, it's true that *some* ADHD partners use the diagnosis as an excuse. Frankly, though, that mostly seems to happen when they don't realize that treatment can largely eliminate the need for excuses of any sort. They've simply learned that their ADHD symptoms are not, as long thought, character flaws that they could change "if they really wanted to." And that, no doubt, must come as a relief.

"...The Symptoms Are Basic Human Behaviors"

Taken singly, ADHD symptoms do resemble typical human behaviors—because they are. "ADHD is a matter of severity, an exaggeration of normal human behaviors," explains physician, author, and ADHD expert Patricia Quinn. Furthermore, you can have a little ADHD or a lot or be somewhere in the middle.

Debunking his second big myth about ADHD (that everyone has it), Ramsay puts it this way: "Saying that everyone who has some trouble with organization and procrastination has ADHD stands akin to claiming that because everyone periodically feels sad or nervous, that everyone has depression or anxiety disorders."

In fact, careful research that measured people with ADHD against a control group revealed that control group members might display only one or two symptoms among the current list of 18 possible symptoms,[42] demonstrating that "everyone" does *not* have ADHD.

"...Modern Life Makes Us All Act 'ADHD'ish'"

It can indeed seem that way. Living in the accelerated 21st century, it's easy to get so overwhelmed and stressed that we occasionally forget details, communicate poorly, snap at loved ones, and get sidetracked from what we're *supposed* to be doing. For people with ADHD, however, such challenges are not transitory or situational but persistent and pervasive.

"Yes, the world really is different now compared to when most of us grew up, because there is so much more to juggle," concedes Quinn. Does that mean our fast-paced life *causes* ADHD? No, she says. Too much stress can impair anyone's brain function, but it doesn't *cause* ADHD.

Here's the bottom line, Quinn says, "When you remove stressors, people with ADHD still have ADHD. In other words, it's not purely stress that inhibits their functioning. It's the lack of skills required to meet challenges." Moreover, our fast-paced world can make someone with ADHD function worse than they might have in earlier times. In fact, some experts say, that is another reason ADHD is being more widely diagnosed: because modern life is demanding more of us than ever before.

Certainly, we're learning that good brain function is vulnerable to the constant stimulation streaming in from cell phones, TV, e-mail, cell phones, and our increasingly noise-filled environment. Some of us habituate to the stimulation as if it were a drug, growing more easily bored and at loose ends when lacking our fix. People with ADHD, however, seem to possess an *exaggerated* tendency to seek stimulation and then suffer more from overstimulation's impairing cognitive effects.

Finally, consider these historical tidbits:
- Widespread ADHD awareness mushroomed in the 20th century, beginning about the time that British physician George Still lectured to the Royal College of Physicians and wrote about components of the

behavior (which he observed ran in families) in a 1902 issue of the prestigious medical journal *Lancet*.[43]

- Before that, the German physician Heinrich Hoffman wrote nursery rhymes in the early 1860s about "Fidgety Phil" and "Little Johnny Head-In-Air," stories that in many experts' minds draw close parallels to ADHD.

- Moreover, ADHD's recorded history might span at least 2,500 years. That's when the Greek physician-scientist Hippocrates apparently observed a condition sounding suspiciously like ADHD. He described patients who had "quickened responses to sensory experience, but also less tenaciousness because the soul moves on quickly to the next impression."[44] No mention of cell phones and video games as causative factors.

"…It's a Ruse to Make Pharmaceutical Firms Rich"

Conspiracy theorists take note: The discovery that neurostimulant medications can mitigate ADHD symptoms happened *accidentally*, in 1937, and it took 50 years for the discovery to make its way widely into clinical practice. (Chapter 20 explains that chance discovery.)

We've known for centuries, perhaps eons, that mild stimulants promote focus and alertness for many people, yet they cause other people to become agitated. Consider the widely consumed stimulants tobacco, coffee, tea, and even sugar. You could say that individuals with ADHD, on one extreme of typical human behaviors, might need extreme amounts of stimulation to feel "right." After all, for most of humankind's history, the mere act of survival and finding enough food to eat involved plenty of stimulation. For some subset of the population, perhaps modern efficiencies and luxuries make it challenging to get sufficient amounts of stimulation *safely, prudently, healthfully, or consistently*.

Why did it take so long for stimulants to be used routinely to treat ADHD? Theories abound, including the fact that early medications had more adverse side effects. Another theory involves professional territorial rivalry.

UCSF psychiatry professor Samuel Barondes, recent chair of the Board of Scientific Counselors of the National Institute of Mental Health, explains the "rivalry" view. During the long decades that psychoanalysis held sway, many clinicians considered this type of "talk therapy" the first-line treatment for depression and schizophrenia as well as ADHD, relegating medications to second-line treatments, if they thought of them at all. "When psychiatric drugs were first introduced," he recalls, "they were *not* warmly received by psychoanalysts, and there's still some tension."

"...ADHD Is a Controversial Diagnosis"

Prowl around on the Internet, and you'll see thousands of Web sites decrying ADHD as a hoax and accusing the psychiatric community of teaming up with the pharmaceutical industry to drum up business. Oh, and while you're visiting these sites, you're typically encouraged to buy a book or some overpriced, questionable brain remedies. Scare tactics sell, it seems.

If you or your loved one has ADHD, however, you know it is a very real disorder. One support-group member jokes that she conducted her own double-blind controlled study, the gold standard of medical research. "The double-blind part," she explains, "was where I closed both my eyes and realized my husband's hypertalkativeness can be just as exhausting for me to listen to whether my eyes are open or closed."

As for serious science, researchers and clinicians became fed up a few years ago with the widespread myths, misconceptions, and outlandish ideas about ADHD. They feared that inaccurate information portraying ADHD as a fraud or a trivial condition would prevent thousands from seeking necessary treatment. In 2002, led by psychologist Russell Barkley, they drafted The International Consensus Statement on ADHD.[45]

The statement clearly and succinctly documents scientific findings regarding the validity and adverse impact of untreated ADHD on the lives of the many it affects. Its 85 signatories include noted physicians, psychologists, and scientists worldwide. An excerpt:

> Occasional coverage of the disorder casts the story in the form of a sporting event with evenly matched competitors. The views of a handful of non-expert doctors that ADHD does not exist are contrasted against mainstream scientific views that it does, as if both views had equal merit. Such attempts at balance give the public the impression that there is substantial scientific disagreement over whether ADHD is a real medical condition. In fact, there is no such disagreement....

To be clear, ADHD is a valid disorder, with a strong physical, brain-centered basis. Even a decade ago, the American Medical Association formed a commission that concluded: "ADHD is one of the best researched disorders in medicine, and the overall data on its validity are far more compelling than for most mental disorders and many other medical conditions."[46] It is accepted as a noncontroversial, valid disorder by these professional organizations, among others:

- U. S. Surgeon General
- American Medical Association
- American Psychiatric Association
- American Academy of Child and Adolescent Psychiatry
- American Psychological Association
- Canadian Psychiatric Association

In 1993, 31 countries had adopted the use of ADHD medication, according to one well-regarded study, and by 2003, 55 nations officially recognized both ADHD as a valid disorder and medication as a treatment for it.[47]

"...ADHD Is a Minor Difference, Not a Big Deal"

ADHD might sound petty to anyone who hasn't lived with it, but it certainly *can* be a big deal. In fact, research points to poor life outcomes for many adults with untreated ADHD.

"The results indicate that the effects of ADHD are severe and create significant impairment in many important aspects of life," says Ramsay, debunking his final "top-three" myth about ADHD (that it is a minor concern). In fact, *many top experts consider ADHD among the most impairing disorders in psychiatry*, worse than depression and anxiety.

Barkley cites numerous studies that point to poor outcomes for people with *untreated* ADHD in these three areas, among others:

1. Education: Less likely to finish school

They are less likely to finish high school or college and more likely to be undereducated relative to their intellectual ability and their family's educational background.

2. Occupation: Job loss, underemployment

"They are seven times more likely to be fired from the job, and will not rise up the economic or employment ladder as quickly as other people without the disorder from the same neighborhood of the same IQ and the same educational level," Barkley says. Moreover, they are more likely to change jobs frequently, either from boredom, difficulty meeting deadlines, or interpersonal problems with coworkers, supervisors, or customers.

3. Interpersonal relationships: discord and divorce

They're likely to burn through friendships and dating relationships faster than average and be more prone to marital discord and divorce. As a population, adults with ADHD show these patterns:

- Experience much higher incidences of separations and divorce (almost double) compared to a representative sample of the U.S. population.[48]
- Tend to marry more frequently, even compared to other adults who sought an ADHD evaluation but proved not to have it.[49]
- Tend to be more dissatisfied than control groups in their relationships, even more so than their mates.[50] And they often have a harder time parenting effectively and consistently.[51]

In Summary

You might have heard ADHD called a *spectrum disorder*, meaning the disorder exhibits varying degrees of severity. It's true that some people have mild cases of ADHD. Too often, though, the public and physicians alike dismiss anything less than the most severe cases of ADHD. Consequently, millions of people never learn why they are continuously dogged by certain problems that feel out of their control—and learn how to gain control. We might compare it to how some of us need eyeglasses to keep from walking into walls, but others need eyeglasses only to see finer details. Still, some might argue, isn't it equally important to see finer details, such as the word *stop* on that big red sign or *payment due* on that bill? And how about the looks of disappointment or hurt on the faces of loved ones who are feeling "unseen"?

By the way, never assume that because millions of people suffer from a condition, society will act quickly to treat it. Consider the discovery that eating citrus fruit prevented scurvy in British sailors. It took more than 100 years for officials to *start implementing* those measures. What's worse, scurvy's symptoms were known, obvious (pallor and abundant spots), and fatal.

Have times changed? Not enough, experts warn. Clinical evidence can take 20 years or more to trickle down to the standard of care—that is, what you'll find in the average physician's office. That goes for everything from hypertension to ADHD.

It also took years for our society to accept the widespread occurrence of depression and anxiety, conditions commonly linked to the brain chemical serotonin. Now, society is slowly accepting that, in similar fashion, ADHD is linked to brain chemicals such as dopamine and norepinephrine.

The choice is yours: to benefit from modern scientific discovery or to languish in old superstitions and misinformation.

Appendix C

In Their Own Words:
Three Views from Decades on the ADHD Roller Coaster

What happens when problematic ADHD behavior patterns go unrecognized and unaddressed for decades? These three first-person stories—from support-group members Mike, Elaine, and Maria—provide a window to understanding. Thousands more stories overlap in themes (the constellation of ADHD symptoms) yet show distinct differences (individual personalities and circumstances). When the partners of adults with ADHD become familiar with such stories, they usually report feeling more breathing room, more support for their perceptions, and eventually a renewed vigor to take steps to improve their situations. They also know they aren't alone. And, for many, that is the first step towards reclaiming their lives.

Mike: Seeing a Ray of Hope After Years of Confusion

I had no idea about adult ADHD or that my wife could have it until just a few days ago. For two decades, I've thought it was something wrong with us—but more specifically me. I had written long letters to myself trying to make sense of what was happening.

I'm 44, a company manager and father of two teenagers. I met Betsy when we were both 21. We moved in together two years later and were married at 25. In the early days, Betsy was fun to be with, intelligent, humorous, and adventurous, with an underlying low confidence that made her seem vulnerable and in need of protection. At that naïve age, I found this attractive. Yes, even then, she could be unreasonable and hard to understand. Her sometimes-loveable impetuousness could often turn

329

dangerously impulsive. Being inexperienced with romantic relationships, I accepted it as part of the territory and hoped she'd grow out of it.

The Early Years: Trying to Make Sense

For the first three years, Betsy worked a few jobs, never happy with any of them, until our first child arrived. That marked the big turning point in our relationship. While parenting requires patience, maturity, and sacrifice, Betsy was largely intolerant and self-centered. I felt like I was trying to bring up a second child—and a difficult one, too—but couldn't understand it and had no frame of reference for it.

Years later, Betsy remains almost always in a state of anxiety and frustration. She has real difficulty seeing other points of view, can't admit being wrong, and tends to see the worst in others, often getting locked into negative thoughts. She has a very bad habit of putting down loved ones in public, a habit that has hurt our kids and me. And if she believes the children need disciplining—sometimes just because they disagree with her point of view on something—Betsy takes punishment to the extreme. It really gets out of hand.

This all puts our children in a real bind. For example, when she denies saying, promising, or doing something they clearly remember happening, what should they do? Deny her reality or their own? If they don't stand up for themselves to some degree, I fear they'll perennially doubt themselves and their perceptions. And that makes me worry about their self-confidence, not to mention their future romantic relationships.

It helps that I am very fond of my in-laws, who've been good to our family. Betsy's father, I'm pretty sure, has ADHD, too. He's a nice guy, very sociable, but he cannot stay on topic. He's also extremely difficult to teach, never wrong, very opinionated, and a terror to drive with. Betsy says she could never live with him again. You'd think she would see the ways in which she and her father are alike, but she doesn't.

Lost Confidence, Lost Ambition

Over the years, by constantly being on the lookout for the next bit of chaos and trying to keep peace in the family—not to mention having little feeling of intimacy—I lost much of my ambition and belief in my potential. Lately, I've been thinking of all the things I might have done in the last 20 years if not for jumping through hoops trying to appease Betsy. She has always been preoccupied by material things, and I've tried to keep her happy. I like having the security of a nice home and a college fund for our children. But on my own I could live just fine without so much "stuff." Life would be much simpler without her buying binges and clutter.

With Betsy, even simple matters take on a taxing complexity. For example, no matter what or how I say something, she takes it personally and negatively, inferring criticism where there was none. I might casually ask if we got any mail today, and she'll bark that she's been trying to make dinner while fighting with our daughter and answering the phone.

Our sex life withered a while ago. I lost interest because it seemed there was no emotion behind it from Betsy. Sex became simply me working to make her climax, which she demanded, and nothing more. So what's the point? I can never share my feelings with Betsy, because she will either make it about her (in her self-absorption, she never sees me) or will use it against me somehow, often sharing it publicly. Only recently did I realize how depressed I had become over the years and started taking antidepressants, which to my surprise has helped a lot.

Striving for Normalcy

As a coping mechanism, I no longer get my hopes up about her promises. I focus on my work, my hobbies, and having our children grow up to be strong, happy, and responsible people, and I believe they need the stability of a home, community, and two parents to achieve those goals. That is why I have stayed with Betsy, sacrificing the possibility of a more intimate relationship. I feel the loneliness, though having close relationships with my children is a blessing. I do still care for my wife, but it is more of a paternal feeling. As difficult as she can be, she still has a place in my heart and will always be the woman who brought our wonderful children into the world.

After staying home with the children for 12 years, Betsy earned her teacher's credential and worked for two years before the politics and administration headaches overwhelmed her. To the outside world, she generally seems pleasant, but she has no close friends. The friends she does make quickly become *persona non grata* if they do something she doesn't like. Of course, the problem is never her; she thinks she is "exceptional." Our children have been identified as gifted and, in her mind, the genes are solely hers.

I've tried for many years to encourage her to try family or marriage counseling. She wanted no part of it. About a year ago, however, she was experiencing depression and went to the doctor for help. She became noticeably nicer—warmer, less irritable—for the short six months that she took antidepressants. I guess then she thought she was cured because she quit.

I would feel much better if I could just tell her that I think she might have ADHD and that it's having a negative effect on everybody, so let's go do something about it. Unfortunately, that would not get me very far.

I wonder if she ever realizes the irrationality behind some of her actions and words. If she does, and lacks the capacity to admit it, I imagine that would just intensify her inner turmoil. If she could just say, "I don't know why I said or did that," it would make life so much easier for all of us. It's just damn tough to live with her belief that she's never wrong, always right.

Finally, my learning that she might not be able to control many of her actions and attitudes, at least until she agrees to an evaluation, helps me to be more accepting. And, finally, finding understanding within the support group has been a lifesaver; after only two days I saw a new world of possibilities and felt hope. But when you learn about the chance for change, that opens a whole new set of questions. Do I now keep hoping that Betsy will "get better" (which would require her to admit she has a problem), or do I give up? Even if she gets help, will we ever be able to regain what we once had so many years ago?

In the meantime, I take responsibility for the decisions I have made and don't feel victimized. I've put strategies in place to protect the family budget, and I handle all finances. Having strong relationships with my children gives great meaning to my life. Work and hobbies also fill some gaps. Eventually, though, I know that I will have to deal fully with this problem and that the chances of us parting after the children leave for college are high.

Update: Ten Months Later

Guess what? Unbelievably, the tide has turned. A few months ago, Betsy took a course on serving special-needs children in the classroom. When the instructor went through the symptoms of ADHD, Betsy clearly recognized herself. By the end of the class, she learned that ADHD often requires medication. She had thought that ADHD meant she was exceptional or gifted, not something that could pose a problem. That class really shifted something for her. She started researching, and I did my best to keep up her enthusiasm without being pushy.

Six weeks ago, she met with a psychiatrist who specializes in ADHD. The doctor did indeed diagnose ADHD and urged Betsy to try a stimulant and perhaps add an antidepressant later if she still shows signs of depression. Even after only a few weeks, I can't tell you the difference that it has made. She is so much more at ease with herself—and easier to live with. Besides being more patient and less frazzled, she's genuinely more solicitous of the kids and me, making an extra effort to do nice things for us.

I'm still holding my breath, wondering if this will be a "phase" she soon grows bored with. I know from the support group that progress often involves two steps forward, one step back. At least now, I have great reason to hope our marriage will continue to improve.

Elaine Clung for Years to "Plan B"; Now It's Time to Act

I married Stan 33 years ago. We're both 54 now. He staunchly denies that he might have ADHD, despite what everyone around him points to as ample evidence. He is denial personified. The clincher came when he lost his job 15 years ago; his poor judgment had cost his employer several hundred thousand dollars.

Though Stan consequently suffered severe depression shortly after that, requiring hospitalization, he dismisses it by saying, "everyone needs a mental health break now and then." To this day, I don't think he has an accurate take on why he was fired. Our children's nickname for him is Bubble Boy, because he's always been in his own world. But would *you* know this if you met him? No. If you didn't live with him, you'd think he's a "regular guy." The stimulation of being around people must jumpstart his brain. Still, even that lasts for only a short while.

I was completely shut down emotionally for many years. There was just so much going on here—with Stan's shenanigans, a son with ADHD, a daughter with learning disabilities, and aging parents—that I just moved from one thing to the next, day by day, in survival mode. Shutting down was my way of protecting myself and being able to just keep putting one foot in front of the other.

Stan's symptoms weren't obvious during our courtship, especially if you didn't know what to look for, and who did 30 years ago? The problems came to light quickly, however, in the early years of fatherhood. Because his parents were strict, I assumed he'd never had a chance to learn things for himself or to express himself; he'd always kept his mouth shut and did what he was told. (It took years for me to learn that he didn't think for himself because he realizes he does it so badly.) I figured things would change over time and he would take a more active and responsive role. Things did change, all right; they got worse.

Stan's impulsivity, forgetfulness, and spaciness, combined with his inflexible, compulsive routines, and authoritarian manner melded horribly with family life. I shudder when I think back to the years when the children were young, just going hour by hour trying to hold on to my sanity in the midst of three people creating unbelievable chaos. One Saturday at the beauty shop, I listened as the ladies gossiped about a woman who'd abandoned her husband and three children. "What kind of woman could do something like that?" they declared. I thought to myself, I don't know about what kind of woman could do that, but I know what kind of *family* can drive any woman or man to *want* to do that.

Back then, I didn't know what was "wrong" with Stan. But what did it matter? He thought everything was fine. I had to just focus on daily survival for the kids and myself.

Classic Challenges: Driving, Finances, Parenting
Stan's behavior became more intolerable over time, if for no other reason than his poor eating and exercise habits. He refuses to go to the doctor or dentist for checkups; things must get to the critical stage before he'll do anything. His bad judgment, poor planning, rigid rules, and no sense of priorities affect every area of our lives, including money.

In business school, he learned to "pay yourself first." That's great, but apparently he skipped the lecture on paying your bills, too! In his typical all-or-nothing fashion, he puts money into savings instead of paying bills or fixing things around the house. As a result, small repairs turned into costly big ones. And he refuses to see that if you avoid interest charges, you'll have *more* money to spend or put into savings. He just looks at what he has in the bank and concludes he'll have less money if he pays bills in full.

Stan doesn't care if the house falls apart. I don't have extravagant needs, but a comfortable, properly functioning home adds to life's enjoyment, especially since I've spent so much time at home. But Stan has no empathy for what the kids or I need or enjoy. Early on, he set up a monthly household allowance that never increased, despite growth spurts, inflation, and an additional child. One day, he was going to the store and I asked him to get a box of cereal. He came back and asked for $1.50, because groceries came out of my meager budget. I almost threw it at him.

As for his fathering, he never knew how to engage the kids unless it was a structured activity, like a board game. Our son would ask him to participate in an upcoming Boy Scouts activity, for example, and because Stan can't say "no," he'd string him along, having no intention of following through. Or he'd simply forget. The only time he became actively involved was when the kids had a disagreement. Then he would jump in barking orders, having no clue what was going on. The kids would yell back, escalating the chaos. Then, he'd dole out a punishment totally inappropriate and impossible to carry out, like grounding them for a month.

Spending so much time at home, I sought comfort and connection in planning a beautiful garden. Yet, in his impulsivity and full-speed-ahead bad decision-making, Stan always destroyed whatever I planted. It didn't matter if I laid down the law and said, "Nobody touches it." He'd *still* forget or simply ignore me. I tried protecting my lilies from his lawnmower with wire fencing, but Stan pulled out the fencing—twice—and mowed them down. And that's pretty much the way it was with all of my hopes and dreams: As soon as I'd nourish them into taking root and blossoming, Stan managed to mow them down.

Why She Stayed

All these years I've buoyed myself with Plan B: leaving the marriage after the children leave the nest. Although there's been many a day when I've felt like running away just for my sanity, I stayed because my children needed a steadying presence. Financial reasons played a lesser role, but I could not properly raise and advocate for two special-needs children while working a full-time job. Shared custody was out of the question. Any interaction with Stan worsened their behavior.

Still, I won't say that I felt trapped or felt like a victim. In my mind, I was prepared to go if things got too bad. It would be hard, but I could do it. And, you know, it's not that things never got "that bad," but by that time, I was so numb that I just didn't recognize how bad it had gotten.

There's something else, too. I admit to a nagging feeling, deep down, that I would never be happy anywhere until I learned how I got myself *into* this mess. How did I miss the red flags? What's wrong with *me*? I had to learn my lesson from it. Others in the support group ask me why I felt responsible for this, when adult ADHD wasn't even on anyone's radar screen three decades ago, but that's just the way I felt.

I guess I have a philosophical streak, too. In the grand scheme of things, I believe I'm right where I'm supposed to be, learning important lessons. Thinking in metaphysical terms helps me to see a larger path.

Changing Expectations, Accepting Reality

Over the years, I told Stan many times that I would *not* put up with this behavior forever. A few years ago, though, he told me, "I'm just a normal guy with a few quirks. If you don't like it, then you can leave." That was the "a-ha!" moment when I realized he was *never* going to get help.

I figure you can either rail against reality, hoping it will go away, or you accept it and start moving through it. From that point on, I grew less frustrated. I stopped expecting much of Stan or asking questions like, "Why did you do that?" because his answers were seldom logical.

For a long time, I had doubted my own perceptions, because he was masterful at confusing the issue. What's more, when other people are around, Stan can be so cheerful and helpful, but the instant we're alone again he reverts to his sullen, selfish, and oppositional self. That's why I long thought that the problem must be mine. Now, I understand that he desperately cares about what others think of him, and that alone seems stimulating enough to spark him into a good show. It also took some time to collect consistent proof that he wasn't always as knowledgeable as he so confidently said he was. Finally, I started doing what I thought was right, his opinion be damned.

For those who say that education about a partner's disorder is the answer, I protest: I *do* accept that he can't help it, though I also know he rejects treatment. I *do* detach and try not taking things personally. But it all still wears horribly on a person. I empathize with new support-group members whose situations resemble mine of years ago. I know what it's like to be at the bottom of that pit, not seeing daylight. You're so tired and stressed, you can't think straight. You just want the crazy stuff to stop. It's hard to think beyond that.

Finding Support, Lifting the Fog

Once the kids had grown and it was just the two of us at home, Stan was harder to ignore. After finding support through an online group, I realized how depressed I had become. Antidepressants helped immensely. I felt like a fog had lifted.

Then, six months after my youngest son moved out, I suddenly realized that it was finally time to activate Plan B! Newly energized, I spent the next six months cleaning cupboards, getting ready for my move. Plan B derailed, however, when I had a routine medical checkup. Two months later, I underwent surgery for breast cancer. It had spread to a lymph node.

You know, over the years I sometimes wondered if an event of this magnitude would awaken Stan into showing some empathy for me. The day he knew I had an appointment to get my test results, he had all afternoon to phone home and check on me but never did. When he arrived home, I was sitting alone on the front porch. He asked about the appointment as he was opening the door—and then let it shut behind him before I could answer. It was a test, and he failed. So much for caring "deep down."

In many ways, I see how Stan is much like his mother; she's always been self-centered, scattered, and not the slightest bit nurturing. Yet he is also like his rigidly authoritarian father. So, I suspect the non-nurturing environment at home magnified what seems to be Stan's brain-based lack of empathy. Still, he bends over backwards to try to please his parents and show he's as successful as his entrepreneurial brother.

When I started receiving chemotherapy, Stan stayed home for a couple of days to "help" but largely just watched TV. If I asked him to get something for me, his jaw tightened in resentment. Mostly, I just didn't have the energy to explain everything to him, knowing that he'd forget it, resist it, or counter every point. Before the surgery, I knew better than to depend on him for food, so I prepared and froze many dishes.

Drifting in and out of a restless sleep one morning after chemo, I recalled a visit with my father, when he was dying in the hospital. He was sharing many fond memories with me, especially about special times with my mother. Then he said to me, "You don't have a lot of wonderful memories with Stan, do you?" I thought to myself, no, in fact I have a lot of bad memories. Remembering my father's words reminded me that life is too short: I do not want to lie on my deathbed reminiscing about all the bad. I want some good memories, too!

Meanwhile, I focused on finishing chemo. I told myself that, if all turned out well, I would soon get back to Plan B. When I got the news that treatment had been successful, my spirits buoyed. Soon, I'll be calling a lawyer to get the ball rolling.

There's only one remaining hitch: It's possible that when I leave Stan, my children will cut me off. Now in their 20s, they see their dad as sort of a doofus while I've always been Super Mom. They're so accustomed to me taking care of everybody, I'm afraid they'll think I'm shirking my duty if I stop—instead of realizing that I'm taking a well-deserved retirement.

It does scare me. They are the only close family I've got now. Slowly, though, I'm coming to terms with that. In the end, I know it's finally time to do what's best for *me*.

Maria: A Strong Partnership Made Stronger

You know, for our 35 years of marriage, I always felt George was *different* in some ways—the way he thought and expressed himself. He says he felt different from other people, too, but couldn't put his finger on it. He's always had this horrible sense of guilt, as if there had been something wrong with him from childhood, a moral wrongness almost, or at least a feeling of deficiency. He'd say things like, "If only I weren't so slow I'd be done on time."

George was diagnosed with ADHD (predominantly inattentive type) only recently, at age 60. When I hear other support-group members' stories now, however, I count my blessings. We've had a wonderful life in so many ways. Still, it hasn't always been easy. Over the years, I've often thought of that classic comedic line: "Did you ever think about divorce? No, but I thought about murder." We both come from families where marriage is a lifelong commitment, and we were both very devoted to this marriage and madly in love. Still are.

From the beginning, George was always late for everything. It took a few years, however, to see how big a problem it was for him. We met when he was in the Air Force. He seemed responsible enough, having a security clearance and working on an important missile program. Workers were expected to be on time. If you were late, you had to report to a commanding officer and get raked over the coals. Of course I didn't know then about these dire consequences and how that was the *only* reason George was never late for work. Now that I understand ADHD, I see why so many people with it do well in the military, because there is a structure and clear rules, with clear consequences if you violate them.

Sure, he was often late for our dates but always had a good excuse, mostly involving work. I didn't think much of it. It was only after we married that I saw "the rest of the story"—how he threw himself into a tizzy each morning rushing to work. And it was only after he left the Air Force that I saw what trouble he had being on time when there weren't dire consequences hanging over him.

338

The Nagging Years

George finished a second undergraduate degree after we married. I'd watch him procrastinate for weeks and cram the night before, driving himself and me nuts. I'd say, "If you start tonight and do a little each night, you'll be done with it by the deadline." He pooh-poohed the idea and got downright irritable. I thought he was being contrary or stubborn. Wanting to do things "his way." He said I was nagging.

Oh, and our family car trips when the kids were young—we would *always* be hours late leaving! The kids and I sat there in the car, packed and ready to go, and George would start fiddling with the sprinkler system or looking for his camera. Plane trips? Same thing. The night before an early flight, I'd be trying to get to sleep at a decent hour, and he'd be rummaging around the bedroom at midnight polishing shoes.

Yes, there were many times I would get upset and frustrated. We didn't argue a lot, but whenever we did fight, it was always over me nagging him. He would go from being defensive to just the opposite. With hindsight and ADHD knowledge, I see that it mostly happened when I would point out what he'd done and ask why. His back was up against the wall, and lacking a reasonable explanation, he'd fall into the martyr routine. The poor me, "I'm just a jerk" thing. Then I'd be filled with remorse that I'd pushed him over the edge. After a while, however, I would pull myself together and see that yes, I'd pushed him, but it also cleared the air of mounting frustrations. Then there'd be more space for some movement and solutions.

He'd also have trouble with something that occupational therapists now call *motor planning*. That's like when you're holding something in both hands and you need to open a door, you have to reorganize yourself. Same thing with his feet. He could trip over almost anything. You know how they used to say President Gerald Ford couldn't walk and chew gum? That's George. Until recently, we never talked about it—it seemed like too vulnerable a subject, I guess—but he laughs about it now that he knows what it is. He also learns more slowly, and is a sequential learner and thinker, not a multitasker. The kids always used to say, "It's a good thing Dad's not an air traffic controller."

With all of those behaviors and more, I still never thought about ADHD. I just thought this is the way my sweet husband was wired and he couldn't change it. And, of course, when I would nag him, I would be a naggy wife, something I did not want to be. So I gave up.

Contradictory Clues Obscured Clarity

Looking back, there were so many contradictory signals. What could I make of them then, before we knew a thing about ADHD? Here was a man who was very physically slow and often clumsy, but loved running and was a great dancer with good rhythm! He danced the waltz and polka very well, but he didn't care for square dancing. That seemed odd to me because he grew up in the country and all five siblings square-danced, but fair enough. It took me years to understand that his dislike didn't reflect *preference* so much as *inability*; the calls came too fast for him to process. I asked him and he confirmed, "Well, yeah, how could anybody keep up with *that*?" I pointed out how ridiculous his statement was, because obviously lots of people *do* keep up with it. There were lots of things like that, me taking at face value his not liking something when actually he simply couldn't do it.

Even during the last 10 years of teaching third-graders, when I became very aware of how ADHD affected children, I still didn't make the connection between their behavior and George's. It just looks so different in children, especially children with hyperactivity. In fact, George is so *not* hyperactive he's more like a sea slug. Why would I have thought he had ADHD? Only in recent years have they talked about the more "sluggish tempo" type. So the pieces finally fell into place.

At one point in our lives, things were rough. George had a new business that wasn't making it, and we had to sell a house that we loved. I was feeling very anxious. That's when my Crohn's disease first emerged. I've had three surgeries for it in the past 15 years, but I'm doing pretty well now. As for all the other "trouble spots" you hear about with ADHD, we've been lucky there. He's never had a traffic accident. No significant trouble with jobs, although he's been out of work for six months or more several times. He's not an excessive spender, though I'm definitely the better financial manager.

A Devoted Dad, a Happy Life

He's been a wonderful father. Our kids are in their 30s now and very close to him. Like his father, George is a very gentle, quiet man. I grew up around macho Italian men, and he was just the opposite, which I loved. I also liked how he treated his mother—respectful and caring. He was good with disciplining the boys, but more much laid-back than I was. He loved our babies, rocked them, and sang to them. Most men weren't doing that 30 years ago.

One thing that made a difference for us is that we did the 1970s "human potential movement" workshops and seminars—The Omega Seminar, the EST training, and so on. We grew together, examining our values and what really mattered to us. George has a tremendous amount of integrity, and I like to think that I do, too. Most workshops emphasized communication. So, we talked a lot.

All in all, George has had a successful, happy life. Yet he can get down on himself when he thinks of what could have been if he'd known earlier about ADHD. Although he's had the diagnosis for three years now, it's taken a while to accept the idea of medication and then to find the right one. After a false start with one stimulant, he's recently started a different stimulant and is thrilled with how he's feeling. He's more alert, less irritable, more easily able to cope with frustrated expectations, more self-accepting and at ease with himself.

Finally: Validation That It's Not Him or Me—but ADHD

For George and me, the turning point came four years ago, when we were touring Asia. Never in our marriage had we been together 24 hours a day for five weeks, and I felt like his mother the whole time!

He'd get lost or distracted and separated from the group. For example, one day he wandered off to take photos of a Shinto shrine. Time came to catch the bus back to our hotel and he wasn't there. I couldn't leave him but I didn't want to get left behind either. How would we get back? I went running to find him and we ran back just in time. After a few weeks of that type of behavior, I just blew up in anger: "This is going to ruin the whole trip if you do this again. Do I have to tie a leash around you?"

We're both nearing retirement and, frankly, the thought of being with him every day struck fear into my heart. Also, for the first time in our married life, I got validation that our problems didn't stem from me nagging or being "super fast." You see, I'm a pretty energetic and efficient person, so we always thought it was me who made him *look* slow. That's what he always said.

The final bit of reality feedback came from the tour group, which included many of our friends. He'd always be the last one on the bus, juggling his tote bag, his backpack, umbrella, hat, and sunglasses. He carried everything because he had a hard time planning what he'd need. And he'd always be misplacing things. People started making little jokes in his presence. He took it in stride for a while, but then he started getting mad and said it was insulting and how he didn't like these people, our friends.

What *really* galled him, I think, was some people were in their 70s and 80s, and he was having much more difficulty than they were.

We had quite a discussion upon our return. I told him, "All these years you've said how it was just me, that no one could keep up with me, and now you're getting feedback from other people, and it's not just me." It was about then that he told me that he was usually the last one in his class at finishing his state's standardized academic achievement tests—starting right from third grade onward. About that time, I showed him a flyer about an upcoming lecture at our school on the brain's Executive Functions. He looked at it and said, "Sounds like me." We went together. As he listened to the speaker describe ADHD and Executive Functions, his jaw dropped. He stayed afterward to ask questions. That was the first time he was willing to admit something was different and that it might be organic.

When he was finally diagnosed, the psychologist said to him, "You're very fortunate to have a supportive wife. One thing you can do is, when she offers a good idea, take it." Before, he would hear my suggestions as just one more sign that he was weak. Now he knows that we're in this together. I don't mind helping him prioritize. What I minded was cleaning up after him or struggling with him. Now, instead of fighting with me, he says, "Okay, I never thought of that." We're both very excited about the changes that the new neurostimulant is bringing. It seems almost too good to be true. Not perfect, mind you, but so much better. So, we shall see.

Working As a Team in Treatment

I've gone with George to the doctors' appointments, and boy was that a good thing. Some of these doctors have been so incompetent, I was glad I was there to validate that for George. In other cases, George just can't process as fast or remember the exchange with the doctor, and he's embarrassed to ask the doctor to slow down or write down an important bit. So, he wasn't always able to assess for himself whether the doc was good.

Meanwhile, these days I don't get angry about things that used to drive me nuts. I might get disappointed or frustrated, but I remember that he can't help it. It's still mainly the same old thing. We'll be going out the door on the way to some event or appointment, and he'll think of one more thing that he hasn't thought of, and we're already running late because he's taken so long to get ready. My getting flustered only makes it worse. I'm learning to take a deep breath and say, "It's more important to get there in one piece." I've learned that additional stress makes the ADHD brain function slower, not faster.

We've always had a good relationship. We have so much in common and love each other deeply, even when we're upset with each other. Yet, because I don't have to monitor everything so much anymore—previously called "nagging"—we have more equality. What we have now, in other words, is a strong *partnership*.

Resources:
For More Information
on ADHD

CHADD (Children and Adults with Attention-Deficit/Hyperactivity Disorder): CHADD is the leading nonprofit organization serving people with ADHD and their families. More than 200 chapters throughout the U.S. and a strong volunteer network offer support for individuals, parents, teachers, professionals, and others. CHADD also sponsors an annual international conference and, occasionally, regional conferences. *Contact:* CHADD.org or 1-800-233-4050.

The National Resource Center on ADHD (a program of CHADD): Funded through a cooperative agreement with the U.S. Centers for Disease Control, the center offers a series of free information sheets in English and Spanish, as well as other services. *Contact:* Help4ADHD.org, or 1-800-233-4050.

CADDRA (Canadian ADHD Resource Alliance): This is an independent not-for-profit association of physicians who support people with ADHD and their families. Members conduct research, treat patients, and design practice guidelines for ADHD. Canadian national guidelines are freely available to physicians and patients. *Web site:* CADDRA.ca.

ADDA (Attention Deficit Disorder Association): This non-profit group provides information, resources, regional meetings, and networking opportunities to adults with ADHD and the professionals who serve them. *Contact:* ADD.org or 1-856-439-9099.

The National Center for Girls and Women with ADHD (NCGW): Cofounded by two leading ADHD clinicians and authors, physician Patricia Quinn and psychologist Kathleen Nadeau, the center promotes awareness and research on the unique issues involving ADHD in females. *Contact:* NCGIADD.org or 1-888-238-8588.

Record Keeping

As you and your partner begin to learn more about ADHD and perhaps pursue therapy and/or medical treatment, it's useful to keep a written record of professional contacts, notes from visits with care providers, and detailed experiences with medication. The following pages serve as a reminder.

_____

_____

_____

_____

_____

_____

_____

_____

_____

_____

_____

_____

_____

_____

_____

_____

_____

_____

_____

Professional Resources

When you attend local support-group meetings and lectures or join an online support group, ask for detailed recommendations on ADHD mental-healthcare providers as well as allied professionals.

Physicians: _____

_____

_____

_____

Therapists: _____

_____

_____

_____

ADHD Coaches: _____

_____

_____

_____

Professional Organizers: _____

_____

_____

_____

Other Professional Resources: _____

_____

_____

_____

Medication History

It's especially useful to keep a detailed history of medication usage. Finding the right medication at the right dosage typically involves a methodical process of trial and error. Sometimes you will see two or more physicians before finding the best care. Some physicians are better than others in taking careful notes. Therefore, it's important that you keep a reliable personal record.

_____

_____

_____

_____

_____

_____

_____

_____

_____

_____

_____

_____

_____

_____

_____

_____

_____

_____

_____

_____

Medication	Dose	Hour taken	Duration of Effectiveness	Benefit(s)	Side Effect(s)	Date begun/ stopped	Concurrent medication (s)

Notes

Notes

.

Endnotes

1. T. E. Wilens and W. Dodson. "A Clinical Perspective of Attention Deficit/Hyperactivity Disorder into Adulthood," *Journal of Clinical Psychiatry* 65 (10) (2004):1301–13.
2. R. C. Kessler, L. Adler, M. Ames et al., "The World Health Organization Adult ADHD Self-Report Scale (ASRS): A Short Screening Scale for Use in the General Population," *Psychological Medicine* 35 (2) (2005): 245–56.
3. R. C. Kessler, L. Adler, R. A. Barkley et al., "The Prevalence and Correlates of Adult ADHD in the United States: Results from the National Comorbidity Survey Replication," *The American Journal of Psychiatry* 163 (4) (2006): 716–23.
4. P. S. Wang, M. Lane, M. Olfson et al., "Twelve-Month Use of Mental Health Services in the United States: Results from the National Comorbidity Survey Replication," *Archives of General Psychiatry* 62 (2005): 629–40.
5. S. Faraone and J. Biederman, "What Is the Prevalence of Adult ADHD? Results of a Population Screen of 966 Adults," *Journal of Attention Disorders* 9 (20) (2005): 384–91.
6. U.S. Bureau of the Census estimates there were 217.8 million persons age 18 years or older as of July 1, 2003.
7. T. E. Froehlich, B. P. Lanphear, J. N. Epstein et al., "Prevalence, Recognition, and Treatment of Attention-Deficit/Hyperactivity Disorder in a National Sample of US Children," *Archives of Pediatrics and Adolescent Medicine* 161 (9) (2007): 857–64.
8. A. J. Zametkin, T. E. Nordahl, M. Gross et al., "Cerebral Glucose Metabolism in Adults with Hyperactivity of Childhood Onset," *New England Journal of Medicine* 323 (20) (1990): 1361–66.
9. J. B. Prince and T. E. Wilens, "Pharmacotherapy of Adult ADHD," in *Clinician's Guide to Adult ADHD*, S. Goldstein and A. Ellison, eds. (New York: Academic Press, 2002), 165–86.

   T. E. Wilens, T. Spencer, and J. Biederman, "A Review of the Pharmacotherapy of Adults with Attention-Deficit/Hyperactivity Disorder," *Journal of Attention Disorders* 5 (2002): 189–202.

   S. R. Pliszka, "Pharmacologic Treatment of Attention-Deficit/Hyperactivity Disorder: Efficacy, Safety, and Mechanisms of Action," *Neuropsychology Review* 17 (2007): 61–72.
10. R. A. Barkley, K. R. Murphy, and T. Bush, "Time Perception and Reproduction in Young Adults with Attention Deficit Hyperactivity Disorder," *Neuropsychology* 15 (3) (2001): 351–60.
11. WGBH Educational Foundation, Boston, "Misunderstood Minds," Documentary, Web site, and Multimedia Library: www.pbs.org/wgbh/misunderstoodminds/attention.html. The PBS documentary was first broadcast March 27, 2002.
12. J. Biederman and S. Faraone, "The Effects of Attention-Deficit/Hyperactivity Disorder on Employment and Household Income," Medscape General Medicine, Psychiatry and Mental Health (posted Jul 18, 2006), www.medscape.com/viewarticle/536264 [requires registration].
13. L. E. Knouse, C. L. Bagwell, R. A. Barkley et al., "Accuracy of Self-Evaluation in Adults with ADHD: Evidence from a Driving Study," *Journal of Attention Disorders* 8 (4) (2005): 221–34.

14. R. A. Barkley, D. C. Guevremont, A. D. Anastopoulos et al., "Driving-Related Risks and Outcomes of Attention Deficit Hyperactivity Disorder in Adolescents and Young Adults: A 3- to 5-year Follow-Up Survey," *Pediatrics* 92 (2) (1993): 212–18.

   R. A. Barkley, K. R. Murphy, and D. Kwasnik, "Motor-Vehicle Driving Competencies and Risks in Teens and Young Adults with Attention Deficit Hyperactivity Disorder," *Pediatrics* 98 (6) (1996): 1089–95.

   R. A. Barkley, K. R. Murphy, G. I. DuPaul et al., "Driving in Young Adults with Attention Deficit Hyperactivity Disorder: Knowledge, Performance, Adverse Outcomes, and the Role of Executive Functioning," *Journal of the International Neuropsychology Society* 8 (5) (2002): 655–72.

   M. Fischer, R. A. Barkley, L. Smallish et al., "Hyperactive Children as Young Adults: Driving Abilities, Safe Driving Behavior, and Adverse Driving Outcomes," *Accident Analysis and Prevention* 39 (1) (2007): 94–105.

   R. A. Barkley, K. R. Murphy, T. Bush et al., "What Contributes to the Elevated Driving Risks in ADHD Adults?," *The ADHD Report* 11 (1) (2003): 1–5.

15. R. A. Barkley, K. R. Murphy, T. O'Connell et al., "Effects of Two Doses of Alcohol on Simulator Driving Performance in Adults with Attention-Deficit/Hyperactivity Disorder," *Neuropsychology* 20 (1) (2006): 77–87.

16. R. A. Barkley and K. R. Murphy, "Identifying New Symptoms for Diagnosing ADHD in Adulthood," *The ADHD Report* 14 (4) (2006): 7–11.

17. T. L. Richards, J. L. Deffenbacher, L. A. Rosen et al., "Driving Anger and Driving Behavior in Adults with ADHD," *Journal of Attention Disorders* 10 (1) (2006): 54–64.

18. R. A. Barkley and D. J. Cox, "A Review of Driving Risks and Impairments Associated with Attention-Deficit/Hyperactivity Disorder and the Effects of Stimulant Medication on Driving Performance," *Journal of Safety Research* 38 (1) (2007): 113–28.

19. C. K. Whalen, B. Henker, L. D. Jamner et al., "Toward Mapping Daily Challenges of Living with ADHD: Maternal and Child Perspectives Using Electronic Diaries," *Journal of Abnormal Child Psychology* 34 (1) (2006): 115–130.

20. Arthur L. Robin, "Snapshots from an AD/HD Marriage," *Attention* 9 (2), 21-27.

21. K. Minde, L. Eakin, L. Hechtman et al., "The Psychosocial Functioning of Children and Spouses of Adults with ADHD," *Journal of Child Psychology and Psychiatry* 44 (4) (2003): 637–46.

22. Discovery Hospital and the University of Illinois Medical Center: Health Library, "Codependency," www.uimc.discoveryhospital.com/main.php?t=enc&id=3060; last medical review Sept 22 2006.

23. J. R. Ramsay, "Current Status of Cognitive-Behavioral Therapy as a Psychosocial Treatment for Adult Attention-Deficit/Hyperactivity Disorder," *Current Psychiatry Reports* 9 (5) (2007): 427–33.

24. T. Spencer, J. Biederman, and T. Wilens. "Stimulant Treatment of Adult Attention-Deficit/Hyperactivity Disorder," *Psychiatric Clinics of North America* 27 (2) (2004): 361–72.

   J. Prince and T. Wilens, 2002 (see first reference in Note 9).

   J. Prince and T. Wilens, "Medications Used in the Treatment of AD/HD in Women," in *Gender Issues and AD/HD: Part Four—Medical Treatment Issues for Women with AD/HD*, P. Quinn and K. Nadeau, eds., (Washington, DC: Advantage Books, 2002), 144–182.

   T. Wilens, T. Spencer, and J. Biederman, "A Review of the Pharmacotherapy of Adults with Attention-Deficit/Hyperactivity Disorder," *Journal of Attention Disorders* 5 (4) (2002): 189–202.

25. Henry H. Work, "George Lathrop Bradley and the War Over Ritalin," Online Archive of the Cosmos Club, 2001, www.cosmos-club.org/web/journals/2001/work.html.

26. Walter A. Brown, "Images in Psychiatry: Charles Bradley, M.D., 1902–1979," *American Journal of Psychiatry* 155 (7) (1998): 968.

27. C. Bradley, "The Behavior of Children Receiving Benzedrine," *American Journal of Psychiatry* 94 (Nov 1937): 577–85.

28. Walter A. Brown, 1998 (see note 26).

29. N. D. Volkow, G. J. Wang, J. S. Fowler et al., "Evidence That Methylphenidate Enhances the Saliency of a Mathematical Task by Increasing Dopamine in the Human Brain," *American Journal of Psychiatry* 161 (7) (2004): 1173–80.

30. Donald M. Quinlan and Thomas E. Brown, "ADHD Often Impairs Reading With or Without Comorbid Dyslexia," (paper presented at the American Academy of Child and Adolescent Psychiatry, New York, October, 2000).

31. A. C. Bedard, R. Martinussen, A. Ickowicz et al., "Methylphenidate Improves Visual-Spatial Memory in Children with Attention-Deficit/Hyperactivity Disorder," *The Journal of the American Academy of Child and Adolescent Psychiatry*, 43 (3): 260–8.

32. U.S. Department of Health and Human Services, National Institute of Mental Health, "Attention Deficit Hyperactivity Disorder," *NIH Publication 3572* (Bethesda, MD: National Institutes of Health, 2003).

33. Jane R. Taylor and J. David Jentsch, "Stimulant Effects on Striatal and Cortical Dopamine Systems Involved in Reward-Related Behavior and Impulsivity," in *Stimulant Drugs and ADHD: Basic and Clinical Neuroscience: Part II: Basic Neuroscience*, Mary V. Solanto, Amy F. T. Arnsten, and F. Xavier Castellanos, eds. (Oxford, England: Oxford University Press, 2001), 109–10.

34. J.M. Swanson, M. Kinsbourne, J. Nigg et al., "Etiologic Subtypes of Attention-Deficit/Hyperactivity Disorder: Brain Imaging, Molecular Genetic and Environmental Factors and the Dopamine Hypothesis," *Neuropsychology Review* 17 (3) (2007); 39–59.

35. William W. Dodson, "Improving Adherence and Compliance in Adults and Adolescents with ADHD," Medscape Psychiatry and Mental Health, Expert Column, www.medscape.com/viewarticle/533044, posted May 30, 2006 [requires registration].

36. N. M. Capone, T. McDonnell, J. Buse et al., "Persistence with Common Pharmacologic Treatments for ADHD," poster presented at the CHADD 2005 Annual International Conference, October 27, 2005, Dallas, Texas.

    A. Perwien, J. Hall, A. Swensen et al., "Stimulant Treatment Patterns and Compliance in Children and Adults with Newly Treated Attention Deficit/Hyperactivity Disorder," *Journal of Managed Care Pharmacy* 10 (2) (2004): 122–29.

    R. J. Sanchez, M. L. Crismon, J. C. Barner et al., "Assessment of Adherence Measures with Different Stimulants Among Children and Adolescents," *Pharmacotherapy* 25 (7) (2005): 909–17.

37. For example, The Weiss Functional Impairment Rating Scale Self-Report (WFIRS-S) is posted free of charge at the Canadian ADHD Resource Alliance Web site: www.caddra.ca/english/pdfs/Chapter_9_15.pdf.

38. Arthur L. Robin and Eleanor Payson, "The Impact of ADHD on Marriage," *The ADHD Report*, 10 (3) 2002: 9–14.

39. Arthur Robin wishes to note that many of these strategies were first detailed by Michael T. Bell in an article called "Dealing with the Impact of ADHD on Marriage," *Attention*, April 2003; 19–23.

40. American Psychiatric Association, "Diagnostic and Statistical Manual of Mental Disorders Fifth Edition (DSM-V) Prelude Project: Research and Outreach," www.dsm5.org/.

41. See note 40.

42. R. A. Barkley, M. Fischer, L. Smallish et al., "The Persistence of Attention-Deficit/Hyperactivity Disorder into Young Adulthood as a Function of Reporting Source and Definition of Disorder," *Journal of Abnormal Psychology* 111 (2) (2002): 279–89.

43. G. F. Still, "Some Abnormal Psychical Conditions in Children: The Goulstonian Lectures," *Lancet* 1 (1902): 1008–12; 1077–82, 1163–68.

44. Attributed to "The Aphorisms," in Francis Adams, tr., *The Genuine Works of Hippocrates* (New York: William Wood and Company, 1891).

45. Russell A. Barkley, "Excerpt from the International Consensus Statement on ADHD January 2002," www.russellbarkley.org/adhd-consensys.htm. Print version: Russell A. Barkley, Edwin H. Cook, Jr., Adele Diamond et al., "International Consensus Statement on ADHD," *Clinical Child and Family Psychology Review* 5 (2) (2002): 89–111.

46. L. S. Goldman, M. Genel, R. J. Bezman et al., "Diagnosis and Treatment of Attention-Deficit/Hyperactivity Disorder in Children and Adolescents," *JAMA* 279 (14) (1998): 1100–07.

47. R. M. Scheffler, S. P. Hinshaw, S. Modrek et al., "The Global Market for ADHD Medications," *Health Affairs* 26 (2) (2007): 450–57.

48. J. Biederman, S. V. Faraone, T. Spencer, et al., "Patterns of Psychiatric Comorbidity, Cognition, and Psychosocial Functioning in Adults with Attention Deficit Hyperactivity Disorder," *American Journal of Psychiatry* 150 (12) (1993): 1792–98.

    J. Biederman, S. V. Faraone, T. Spencer et al., "Functional Impairments in Adults with Self-Reports of Diagnosed ADHD: A Controlled Study of 1001 Adults in the Community," *Journal of Clinical Psychiatry* 67 (4) (2006): 524–40.

    R. A. Barkley, M. Fischer, L. Smallish et al., "Young Adult Outcome of Hyperactive Children: Adaptive Functioning in Major Life Activities," *Journal of the American Academy of Child and Adolescent Psychiatry* 45 (2) (2006): 192–202.

49. K. Murphy and R. A. Barkley, "Attention-Deficit/Hyperactivity Disorder in Adults: Comorbidities and Adaptive Impairments," *Comprehensive Psychiatry* 37 (6) (1996): 393–401.

50. L. Eakin, K. Minde, L. Hechtman et al., "The Marital and Family Functioning of Adults with ADHD and Their Spouses," *Journal of Attention Disorders* 8 (1) (2004): 1–10.

    See Note 21.

    See Note 38.

51. E. Harvey, J. S. Danforth, T. E. McKee et al., "Parenting of Children with Attention-Deficit/Hyperactivity Disorder (ADHD): The Role of Parental ADHD Symptomatology," *Journal of Attention Disorders* 7 (1) (2003): 31–42.

    C. Murray and C. Johnston, "Parenting in Mothers with and without Attention-Deficit/Hyperactivity Disorder," *Journal of Abnormal Psychology* 115 (1) (2006): 52–61.

    L. Eakin, K. Minde, L. Hechtman et al., 2004 (see first reference in Note 50).

Index

About the Author

Gina Pera is an award-winning print journalist based in the San Francisco Bay area. Her work for *USA Weekend* magazine won the prestigious Best Magazine Edition award from The Association for Women in Communications as well as a Unity Award in Media from Lincoln University of Missouri, recognizing accurate exposure of issues affecting minorities and disabled persons.

For the past eight years, she has researched and written about Adult ADHD while also advocating for better awareness and treatment standards. A popular speaker, she provides education and support for the ADHD community, leading discussion groups in Silicon Valley and a 400-member Internet-based group for the partners of adults with ADHD around the world.

A native of Memphis, she enjoys gardening, exploring Bay Area hiking trails with her husband, and connecting with her favorite online communities.

Order Form

1201 Alarm Press

Is It You, Me, or Adult A.D.D.?
Stopping the Roller Coaster When Someone You Love has Attention Deficit Disorder

How to Order:

Online: *ADHDRollerCoaster.com*
Or send this order form by
- **Email:** orders@1201AlarmPress.com
- **Fax:** (888) 891-6668
- **Postal Mail:** 1201 Alarm Press
  P.O. Box 6581
  San Mateo, CA 94403

> **Special offer available only through the publisher:**
> *Buy the paperback and receive a full electronic version (PDF) of the book FREE.*

Quantity:	_____
Price:	_@ $21.95 each_
Subtotal:	$ _____
Sales Tax (California ONLY): Please add 8% for books shipped to California	$ _____
Shipping: USPS Media Mail, @ 6-8 days	$ _Free in U.S._
Faster Shipping:	$ _____

USPS Priority Mail: $3 for first book, $3 each additional book, 4+ books, FREE
Canada and Mexico: $5 for each book; 4+ books, FREE **International:** $10 for each book.

TOTAL:	$ _____

Billing and Shipping Address:

Name: _____

Address: _____

City:_____ State: _____ Zip: _____

Telephone: _____ Email: _____

Payment: Check enclosed   VISA   MasterCard

Card Number:_____ Exp. Date: _____

Signature: _____

Name on card: _____

Order Form

1201 Alarm Press

Is It You, Me, or Adult A.D.D.?
Stopping the Roller Coaster When Someone You Love has Attention Deficit Disorder

How to Order:

Online: *ADHDRollerCoaster.com*
Or send this order form by
- **Email:** orders@1201AlarmPress.com
- **Fax:** (888) 891-6668
- **Postal Mail:** 1201 Alarm Press
  P.O. Box 6581
  San Mateo, CA 94403

Quantity:		_____
Price:		@ $21.95 each
Subtotal:	$	_____
Sales Tax (California ONLY):	$	_____

Please add 8% for books shipped to California

Shipping:	$	Free in U.S.

USPS Media Mail, @ 6-8 days

Faster Shipping:	$	_____

USPS Priority Mail: $3 for first book, $3 each additional book, 4+ books, FREE
Canada and Mexico: $5 for each book; 4+ books, FREE **International:** $10 for each book.

TOTAL:	$	_____

Billing and Shipping Address:

Name: _____

Address: _____

City: _____ State: _____ Zip: _____

Telephone: _____ Email: _____

Payment: Check enclosed   VISA   MasterCard

Card Number: _____ Exp. Date: _____

Signature: _____

Name on card: _____